Introducing Intercultural Communication

Global Cultures and Contexts

Shuang Liu, Zala Volčič and Cindy Gallois

Los Angeles | London | New Delhi
Singapore | Washington DC

© Shuang Liu, Zala Volčič and Cindy Gallois 2011

First published 2011

SAGE Publications Ltd
1 Oliver's Yard
55 City Road
London EC1Y 1SP

SAGE Publications Inc.
2455 Teller Road
Thousand Oaks, California 91320

SAGE Publications India Pvt Ltd
B 1/I 1 Mohan Cooperative Industrial Area
Mathura Road
New Delhi 110 044

SAGE Publications Asia-Pacific Pte Ltd
33 Pekin Street #02-01
Far East Square
Singapore 048763

Library of Congress Control Number: 2009943439

British Library Cataloguing in Publication data

A catalogue record for this book is available from the British Library

ISBN 978-1-84860-035-5
ISBN 978-1-84860-036-2 (pbk)

Typeset by C&M Digitals (P) Ltd, Chennai, India
Printed and bound in Great Britain by TJ International Ltd, Padstow, Cornwall
Printed on paper from sustainable resources

Mixed Sources
Product group from well-managed forests and other controlled sources
www.fsc.org Cert no. SGS-COC-2482
© 1996 Forest Stewardship Council
FSC

Introducing Intercultural Communication

Contents

Acknowledgements

We would like to thank all those who have helped us as we progressed throughout the journey to complete this book. Without their encouragement and support, this book would not have come to fruition. We have all had the privilege of teaching and doing research in intercultural communication, and these experiences have formed our outlook on this fascinating field.

We thank Professor Guo-Ming Chen at the University of Rhode Island in particular for his encouragement at the early stages of development of this project and for his helpful suggestions to improve the book proposal. We are indebted to our colleagues and students, both at the University of Queensland and at other institutions around the world where we have studied, worked, or spent periods of research leave; all of them helped to inspire this project. We are grateful to the many colleagues who have contributed to this book in various ways, including providing feedback on our intercultural communication classes, sharing their ideas with us, and lending us references and photos from their collections. In particular, we are grateful to Professor Carley Dodd from Abilene Christian University, who granted us permission to include his model of culture, and to UNESCO for granting us permission to include some photos from their photobank. Thanks to Eric Louw for sharing his expertise on South African identity with us to inform the writing of the case study in Chapter 8. Thanks also to Pradip Thomas, Zhang Tong, Jaka Polutnik, Karmen Erjavec, Marijana Vukeljic, Tatjana Welzer, and everyone else who has given us support, time, and encouragement.

We express our sincere gratitude to the School of Journalism and Communication at the University of Queensland for offering financial support to employ a research assistant, Joanne McCrossen, to assist with the development of the entire set of Instructor's Manuals for this book and with copy editing of early drafts. Special thanks go to Professor Michael Bromley, Head of School of Journalism and Communication, and Professor Graeme Turner and the Centre for Critical and Cultural Studies, for offering supportive climates that allowed us to finish this book project within the timeframe.

Thanks also to the Commissioning Editor at SAGE Publications, Mila Steele, assistant editor Alan Maloney, others on the editorial staff, and the anonymous reviewers, who reviewed early and final drafts of the manuscript. Their insightful suggestions have greatly contributed to an improved book. We would like to thank everyone from SAGE whose work has transformed the manuscript into its present form.

Finally, we are deeply indebted to our families for their support, love, encouragement, and patience throughout the writing of this book. Special thanks, therefore, go to Annie Liu, Mark Andrejevic, Helga Tawil, and Jeff Pittam.

Introduction: Communicating in a Culturally Diverse Society

*Human beings are drawn close to one another by their
common nature, but habits and customs keep them apart.*

Confucius, Chinese thinker and social philosopher,
511BC–479BC

Since ancient times, clear geographic or political borders have always
been marked between countries, states, cities, and villages. Natural
boundaries such as rivers, oceans, and mountain ridges, or artificial
borders such as walls, fences, and signs, all function as landmarks to
separate country from country, state from state, region from region,
and people from people. However, the spread of culture has never
been confined to these geographic or political territories. For example,
as early as the fifteenth century, Aesop's *Fables* were translated from
Greek – the language in which they were originally written – into
English, thus making them accessible to entirely new cultural, national,
and geographical audiences. Today, the fables, available in innumerable
languages across the world including Chinese, Japanese, French, Russian,
German, and so forth, have permeated our culture as myths and legends,
providing entertainment and moral truisms for children and adults alike.
Regardless of where we live, the colour of our skin, or what language we
speak, it is likely we have at some time encountered many of the morals
or adages of Aesop's stories, for instance, 'A liar will not be believed,
even when telling the truth' from *The Boy Who Cried Wolf*; 'Slow and
steady wins the race' from *The Tortoise and the Hare*; or 'One person's
meat is another's poison' from *The Ant and the Grasshopper*. While we
might not know if the fables were written by Aesop, exactly when they
were written, or how many languages they have been translated into,
the tales still teach us universal virtues such as honesty, perseverance,
modesty, and mutual respect. In addition to the spread of folk literature
like Aesop's *Fables*, cultural products like tools, technology, clothing,
food, furniture, electric appliances, music, customs, and rituals are
spread beyond geographic or political borders.

Culture is defined as the total way of life of a people (Rogers and Steinfatt, 1999). The word 'culture' is derived from the Latin root *colere*, meaning 'to cultivate'. Our language, customs, expectations, behaviours, habits – our way of thinking, doing, and being – have been and continue to be formed over a long period of cultivation within the specific physical environment and social context in which we were born, with which we have grown up, and in which we presently live. During the process of learning and adapting to the environment, different groups of people have learned distinctive ways to organize their world (Dodd, 1998). A group's unique ways of doing and thinking become their beliefs, values, worldviews, norms, rituals, and their communication styles – ultimately, their cultural tradition.

Cultural traditions vary across different groups. For example, the concept of a wedding has a universal meaning, but specific wedding customs and rituals vary from culture to culture. In southern regions of China, the gifts that the groom's parents give to the bride's family often include two coconuts. In the Chinese language, the word 'coconut' is similar in sound to the words 'grandfather and son'. Thus, the gift of coconuts symbolizes a wish for both the longevity of the family's older generations and the ongoing presence of the younger generations, as an extended family of three or four generations is treasured in the Chinese culture. In India, the cultural tradition is for the bride to enter her in-laws' home for the first time on her right foot and to knock over a container of uncooked rice, so as to bring good luck to the house. At a Sudanese wedding, seven broomsticks are burned and thrown away, to symbolize the couple discarding any bad habits that could pose a threat to their marriage. Japanese couples only become husband and wife after they take their first sip of sake, a rice wine drink, at the wedding. Such are the rich variants of cultural traditions.

Culture defines a group of people, binds them to one another, and gives them a sense of shared identity. It is the means by which a society expresses its structure and function, its views of the physical universe, and what it regards as the proper ways to live and treat each other. Expressions and viewpoints vary from cultural group to group. Particular ways of expressing their views of the world form the cultural traditions of a group of people and are shared and accepted by their members as natural, logical, and legitimate ways of thinking, doing, and being.

Cultural traditions go through a process of development and sedimentation and are passed on from generation to generation. Central to this entire process of development and maintenance is human communication. The word 'communication' is derived from the Latin word 'to make common', as in sharing thoughts, hopes, and knowledge. Every cultural pattern and every act of social behaviour involves communication. Culture and communication are inseparable.

Human communication is a product of continual and ongoing phases of development. In the small villages of our early ancestors, information sharing was largely conducted on a face-to-face basis. The successive historical breakthroughs of print, telephone, broadcasting, television, and the internet have progressively expanded the domain of communication beyond the immediate cultural and geographic borders. Correspondingly, our identities today have expanded from social groups, ethnic communities, cities, states, and nations to incorporate factors that are no longer bound by political, geographical, physical, or cultural determinants. The relative ease of global interaction – international business transactions, political exchanges, education, and travel – has brought strangers from different parts of the globe into face-to-face contact. This increased human interconnectedness requires us to communicate competently with people whose cultures are different from our own, that is, to engage in intercultural communication. However, this ability does not come naturally but needs to be learned. We need to educate and equip ourselves with the capability to communicate effectively and efficiently in our increasingly diverse society.

The Study of Intercultural Communication

The roots of intercultural communication can be traced to the Chicago School, known for its pioneering empirical investigations based on the theories of German sociologist Georg Simmel (1858–1918: Rogers and Steinfatt, 1999). Simmel earned his doctorate at the University of Berlin in 1881, and taught there for twenty-nine years before moving to the University of Strassburg. Simmel chose to analyse concepts related to his personal life experiences. As the son of Jewish parents, the anti-Semitism he experienced in Germany undoubtedly influenced his development of the concept of *der Fremde* or 'stranger', the intellectual descendants of which are key concepts in the fields of both sociology and intercultural communication today. The stranger, as defined by Simmel (1950), is an individual who is a member of a system but not strongly attached to it and also not completely accepted by the other members of the system. Simmel's insights on the role of the stranger are part of his general concern with the relationships between individuals. His examination of reciprocal interactions at the individual level within a larger social context inspired much of the research at the Chicago School (Rogers, 1999) and subsequent research in the field of intercultural communication. The notion of communicating with someone who is different to us – an intercultural 'stranger' – lies at the heart of intercultural communication.

The key scholar in translating and applying Simmel's concept of the stranger was Robert E. Park, a former newspaper reporter who also earned his PhD degree in Germany. In 1900 Park took Simmel's course in sociology at the University of Berlin. In 1915, Park began teaching sociology at the University of Chicago. Inspired by Simmel's notion of the stranger, Park developed the concept of social distance, which he defined as the degree to which an individual perceives a lack of intimacy with individuals who are different in ethnicity, race, religion, occupation, or other variables (Park, 1924). Park's student, Emory S. Bogardus, later developed a scale that measured the social distance people perceived between themselves and members of another group. For example, in the scale, respondents are asked such questions as, 'Would you marry someone who is Chinese?' and 'Would you have Chinese people as regular friends or as speaking acquaintances?' (Bogardus, 1933). The Bogardus Social Distance scale quantified the perceived intimacy or distance of an individual's relationships with various others.

As social distance is largely culturally prescribed, intercultural communication is invariably affected. For instance, Australians often use first names with someone they have just met, and in a university setting it is common for students to address the lecturers by their first name. This can be very puzzling to Korean students who are much more formal in their social relationships and only use first names with very close friends who are usually of the same age or social status as themselves. Students in Korea are always expected to address teachers by their title (e.g. Dr, Ms) and surname. One author of this book met a Korean American who had taught at a university in the United States for about twenty-five years and still felt some discomfort when students addressed her by her first name. When asked why she did not explain her preference to her students she answered that she would only do it indirectly, a preferred Asian communication style. If a student addressed her by first name instead of calling her 'Professor Y', she would respond in an unenthusiastic and subdued manner, in the hope that her students would gradually learn the 'appropriate' way to address her as a professor.

Simmel's concept of the stranger and his subsequent derivative concepts all deal with the interpersonal relationship of the individual, with both other individuals and the system of which the individual is a part. Implied in the concept of the stranger is the idea that the individual does not have a high degree of cohesion with the larger system of which he or she is a part. The concept of the stranger also influenced Park to conceptualize the 'marginal man'. A marginal person is an individual who lives in two different worlds, and is a stranger in both. Park studied the children of European immigrant parents in the United States. These individuals typically rejected the European culture and language of their parents, but did not consider themselves to be true North Americans either. Their freedom from the norms of both systems led to a relatively high crime rate. To Park, the marginal person was a cultural hybrid, an individual on the margin of two cultures that never completely fused. Park's concept was later extended to 'the sojourner', an individual who visits another culture for a period of time but retains his or her original culture. The experience of sojourning or visiting often gives individuals a unique perspective for viewing both the host and home cultures. The sojourner later became a favourite topic of study for intercultural communication scholars, leading to concepts such as the U-curve of adjustment model, culture shock, and reverse culture shock (see Chapter 12).

Although the concepts of stranger, social distance, and marginality are among those at the heart of intercultural communication study, this idea did not come together as a discrete scholarly field until after the Second World War. At that time, the United States had emerged as a leading world power and, with the advent of the United Nations, a number of new programmes, such as the World Health Organization, the United Nations' assistance programmes, and the World Bank, were initiated to provide assistance to developing nations. However well-intended not all these development programmes were successful, largely because of a failure to comprehend the multifaceted and interrelated nature of culture. In Thailand, for example, where obtaining pure water was identified as the highest-priority problem, most of the hand-pump wells drilled in hundreds of villages by American development workers were broken within six months (Niehoff, 1964). An investigation into the problem showed that there was no-one responsible for the maintenance of the pumps. When a well was dug on Buddhist temple grounds, the monks would look after the pump and there-fore only those wells were sustainable. The well-drilling project, conceived and implemented as separate and independent from the temple, had not considered the important role that Buddhist monasteries played in Thai culture and the vital contribution they could have made toward the success of the project. An important lesson learned from such costly and frustrating failures was that cultural issues had to be taken into account along with the economic, political, and technical dimensions (Rogers, 1995).

In addition to the problems experienced by development workers, US dip-lomats also experienced cultural frustrations. They were too often poorly trained, lacking in cultural awareness and intercultural communication insight. They usually lived and worked in a small circle of English-speaking individuals, seldom venturing outside the capital city of their posting. In 1946, the US Congress passed an act to provide training to American diplomats and technical assistance workers in the Foreign Service Institute (FSI). Edward T. Hall, the leading anthropologist and teacher at the FSI, and his anthropologi-cal and linguistics colleagues, initially taught the participants the language and anthropological concepts of the nation to which they were assigned. The language programme was successful, but participants reported to Hall that they needed to communicate *across* cultures and thus wanted to understand intercultural differences, rather than simply gaining an understanding of the single culture in which they were to work. In response to these requests, Hall and his colleagues created a new approach that he called 'intercultural com-munication'. The publication of his famous book, *The Silent Language* (1959), marked the birth of intercultural communication study.

At the FSI, intercultural communication meant only communication between individuals of different national cultures. However, as teaching and research in intercultural communication developed over the decades, the meaning of 'culture' in intercultural communication broadened from Hall's original conception of a national culture to any type of culture or subculture. Intercultural communication came to mean communication between indi-viduals who might differ, for example, in ethnicity, socioeconomic status, age, gender, or lifestyle. This broader definition of the field is reflected in most intercultural communication textbooks today. A key figure in broaden-ing this field was William B. Gudykunst, a professor of communication at California State University. In 1983, Gudykunst published an article in which he applied Simmel's concept of the stranger, arguing that the stranger is perceived as unfamiliar by other members of the system so that a high degree of uncertainty is involved. This perspective was later carried through in a textbook, co-authored with Young Yun Kim from the University of Oklahoma, *Communicating with Strangers: An Approach to Intercultural Communication* (Gudykunst and Kim, 1984), in which communication with a stranger was made the key intellectual device to broaden the meaning of intercultural communication. Cultural differences, according to Gudykunst and Kim, could involve a national culture or other types of culture, such as an organizational culture or the culture of the deaf. Focusing on the uncertainty involved in intercultural communication has led scholars to investigate how individuals reduce uncertainty by means of communication, a key area of intercultural communication study.

Today, the subject of intercultural communication is offered to students in the arts, humanities, communication, public relations, business, psychology, political science, and media studies, among other disciplinary fields in universities across the world. However, existing textbooks on intercultural communication primarily concentrate on the US context and/or use the USA as the criterion reference for comparing other cultures. In addition, due to early scholars' focus on interpersonally oriented communication, many existing textbooks do not really explore the enormous impact of mass media on our identity construction and communication behaviour. Given that countries in Europe, Asia, and Oceania are becoming increasingly multicultural, and given the increasing impact of the mass media on our culture and our lives, a textbook that situates intercultural communication in a broader context will help to bridge the gap left by existing textbooks and will have a wider application beyond the US context. That is the impetus for writing this textbook.

Organization of this Book

This book explores the many interconnections between culture, communication, and identities in European, Asian, and Oceanic countries as well as in North America. We adopt a multicultural approach to address various issues in intercultural communication, treating identities as claims which are made, contested, and negotiated in particular contexts and incorporating the critical influence of the mass media on cultural change, identity construction, and communication. Throughout this book, we emphasize the application of knowledge to resolve practical problems. The text is supplemented by *theory corners*, which present brief summaries of the major theories in intercultural communication or influencing its study. In addition, each chapter concludes with a *case study*, taking up its major points through a detailed real-life example. Exercises from various cultural contexts and discussion questions provide opportunities for you to reflect critically upon each chapter and to construct your own understanding of the concepts. This approach fosters critical thinking and deep learning. Striking a balance between theory and practice, this book enables you to:

- develop an understanding of the basic concepts and principles of communication between people from different social and cultural backgrounds;
- recognize the influence of your own culture on how you view yourself and others;
- obtain insights into the social, cultural, and historical dimensions of cultural and subcultural groups in different parts of the world;
- compare the communication behaviour, verbal and nonverbal, of different cultural groups, and link these behaviours to their cultures;
- become more self-reflective, flexible, and open in intercultural encounters;
- ooloct and perform communication behaviour appropriate to diverse cultural settings.

This book begins by identifying different contributors to diversity in our society and the various challenges we face in an increasingly globalized society. When Canadian media culture analyst Marshall McLuhan coined the expression 'global village' a few decades ago, many thought that emerging communication technologies would restore social relations and bring back village-like intimate interactions. Of course the technology McLuhan wrote about was not nearly as developed as it is today; recent developments like satellite communications and the rise of the internet make his vision seem almost prophetic. We can watch and read about the same things at the same time; we can exchange ideas with people on the other side of the world with the same speed and ease that our ancestors did with members of their own village. Yet the rules and guidelines for this interaction are not the same as those of our ancestors, and we have many issues still to explore. Do we really partake of a unified world because the media bring us closer? Who are the inhabitants and the players in this global village? And what roles can intercultural communication play in meeting these challenges?

Following the introductory concepts covered in Chapter 1, Chapters 2 to 7 introduce a range of theories to address historical questions at the intersection of identity, communication, and culture, as well as a number of key issues about the influence of culture on our communication behaviour. Culture is a construction of reality that is created, shared, and transmitted by members of a group (Bonvillain, 2008). As members of a group our culture is locked within us. To explore and express our internal states of being, therefore, we must use a method of symbolic substitution. Most of the time language is our medium of exchange for sharing internal states of being. Language is a set of symbols shared by a community to communicate meaning and experience. Words within a language are an abstraction of our realities. Growing up, we learn to receive, store, manipulate, and generate symbols. People within a culture share the same process of abstraction. If we include culture as a variable in this process of abstraction, we can see how problems may arise when people from different cultures interact with one another. How does culture influence our perception of ourselves and our perception of others who are culturally different from us? How does culture affect our thinking patterns? And in what ways is culture reflected in our verbal and nonverbal communication?

Understanding how our culture influences our behaviours and our concepts of what is considered 'appropriate' and 'normal' reminds us of the boundaries of the different groups we belong to. Chapters 8 and 9 take you beyond the interpersonally oriented communication context to intergroup communication, to look at groups, subgroups, and group identities, as well as how culture influences the development of our relationships with others. Throughout our life we become members of many different groups on the basis of a range of characteristics shared with other members, such as culture, religion, social activities, ethnicity, gender, occupation, or interest, amongst many others. These shared characteristics serve to categorize us into groups and subgroups and the identities we derive from our group memberships develop, transform, and reshape our attitudes and behaviours. Initiating and maintaining relationships with other people in different groups is an important way to develop our own personal identity, because it is in groups that our individuality and distinctiveness are recognized. From our relationships with others we receive feedback that we use to assess ourselves. But this emphasis on shared group experiences and rewards leads to various questions. How do people from different cultures establish relationships with others? How does culture influence what is considered as important in maintaining human relationships? What are the potential barriers that people experience in developing intercultural friendships or intercultural romantic relations? And how can we overcome those barriers?

Conflict is inevitable in all human social interactions. Chapter 10 focuses on the issue of conflict management in intercultural communication and intercultural relations. Conflicts occur at multiple levels: interpersonal, social, ethnic, national, and international. At a time of an increasing number of violent conflicts around the globe, this chapter looks at the potential role of intercultural communication in understanding and transforming these conflicts. Importantly, the chapter also attempts to offer some advice on managing intercultural conflicts. Special attention is paid to the historical reasons for conflicts, for example, those fuelled by a historical antagonism between ethnic groups, such as between Arabs and Jews or Serbs and Albanian Kosovars. With this in mind, several questions are addressed in this chapter. How is conflict conceptualized and dealt with by members in different cultures? What are the communication styles preferred by people from different cultures to resolve conflicts? In what ways can culture influence conflict strategies? And what could be the potential outcomes associated with each type of conflict strategy?

After Chapter 10, the book returns to the broader context of living in a culturally diverse society. Chapter 11 addresses the impact of the mass media on communication, identity construction, and cultural change in our society. We present ways of thinking about media and identity in different geographical, political, and cultural contexts by offering examples of how the media influence us and shape our identities and belongings. We show how the media have historically played an essential part in the imagination of national communities. The creation of a national culture and identity would have been impossible, for example, without the contribution of print and (in recent times) broadcast media. This chapter also addresses the mutual influence of mass media and technology and their joint impact on cultural change.

Chapter 12 addresses the issues surrounding a major contributor to multicultural society – immigration. We explore how large-scale population movements arise from the accelerating process of global integration. The migration of people is linked to movements of capital and commodities as well as to global cultural interchange, which is facilitated by an improved transport infrastructure and the proliferation of electronic and print media. We pay special attention to how migration is considered part of a transnational revolution and how it is reshaping societies and politics around the globe. The 'globalization of migration' is one of the emerging trends likely to play a major role in the next decade. This chapter explores the acculturation process that both migrants and people from host cultures experience. And it is here we ask what acculturation attitudes should ethnic majorities have towards ethnic minorities, and vice versa? And how should we interpret multiculturalism – as a threat or a benefit?

The concluding chapter (Chapter 13) brings us back to the issues raised in Chapter 1 regarding the challenges of living in a culturally diverse society. It explores the dialectic of homogenization and fragmentation of cultures and the human effects of these processes. Arguments about understanding the global through the local context and how local cultures challenge, negotiate, and adjust to globalization are presented. This chapter raises a series of current issues in the study of communication and culture, hence preparing you for further investigations in the field of intercultural communication. Is globalization a form of Westernization? And how do we develop an intercultural competence to enable us to function effectively in intercultural communication?

The purpose of this textbook is not only to explore issues and provide answers but also to enable you to ask further questions in order that you can learn intercultural knowledge and skills as well as become a critical consumer of information in the wider field of intercultural communication. In reading, learning, debating, questioning, and reflecting, your journey to becoming a competent intercultural communicator starts now!

1

Challenges of Living in a Global Society

*I do not want my house to be walled in on all sides and
my windows to be stifled. I want all the cultures of all
lands to be blown about my house as freely as possible.
But I refuse to be blown off my feet by any.*

*Mohandas K. Gandhi, political and spiritual
leader of India, 1869–1948*

Learning Objectives

At the end of this chapter, you should be able to:

- Identify the different contributors to cultural diversity in our society.
- Describe the challenges we face living in a global village.
- Appreciate unity and harmony amidst diversity.
- Recognize the importance of developing sound knowledge and intercultural communication skills.

Living in a Global Village

Our early ancestors lived in small villages; most of them rarely ventured far from their own communities. They lived and died close to where they were born, and much of their information sharing was done through face-to-face communication with others who were much like themselves. Over the years, advances in transportation, improvements in telecommunication technologies, and increases in international business and political exchanges have brought strangers from different parts of the world into face-to-face contact. Consequently, the old villages were opened up to people who were unlike our ancestors. In 1964, Canadian media culture analyst Marshall McLuhan coined the term 'global village' to describe a world in which communication technology – such as television, radio, and news services – brings news and information to the most remote parts of the planet. Today, McLuhan's vision of a global village is no longer considered an abstract idea but a virtual certainty. We can exchange ideas as easily and quickly with people across the world as our ancestors did within the confines of their villages. We form communities and societies and we encounter people from different cultures in business, at school, in public places, in our neighbourhood, and in cyberspace. We may wear clothes made in China; purchase seafood from Thailand; dine out with friends in an Italian restaurant; work at a computer made in the United States; drive a car manufactured in Japan – and so the list goes on. Each encounter with new food, clothing, lifestyles, art, languages, or medicine teaches us new things outside of our 'village' culture.

'Globalization lies at the heart of modern culture; cultural practices lie at the heart of globalization' (Tomlinson, 1999: 1). This quote raises many questions and challenges. Do we actually partake of a more unified or diversified world because communication technologies bring us closer? What kind of challenges do we face living in a global village? This chapter first identifies different contributors to cultural diversity in our society. Advances in technology, modern transportation systems, the global economy, international business transactions, and mass migration make our 'village' more global. In this global village, people are constantly moving across borders and engaging in international exchanges. This chapter describes the various challenges we face living in such a global village and explains the roles intercultural communication can play in meeting those challenges. By recognizing the importance of developing sound knowledge and intercultural communication skills, we can appreciate the unity and harmony amidst the diversity in our global village.

Contributors to Cultural Diversity

Advanced technology and transportation system

Globalization is the process of increasing interconnectedness between societies, so that events in one part of the world have more and deeper effects on people and societies far away (Baylis and Smith, 2001). Today, we can watch and read about the same events at the same time, regardless of the time and space distance. With emails, fax, the internet, bulletin boards, satellites, and telephones, we can contact people any place and any time. If we want a more personal exchange, Skype or video desktop technology can bring a person on the other side of the globe onto the computer screen right in front of us. Words like 'blogs' (an abridgment of the term 'web-log') and 'podcasting' (an amalgam of 'ipod' and 'broadcasting') have appeared in our dictionaries since the beginning of the twenty-first century. Facebook – an online social network – has expanded beyond US universities and is now a global phenomenon, allowing people from all walks of life to post their profiles online and communicate with other users across the world. Voice over internet protocol (VOIP), one of the fastest growing internet technologies, allows people to talk online as if they were on a landline telephone. Instant messaging and texting messages and images by mobile phone can carry visual messages, if an audio channel is inconvenient. The choices of media to connect with other people any place and any time are multiplying.

Theory Corner

Global village

The notion of a global village and the process of globalization pose more questions than answers. Anura Goonasekera (2001) defines globalization as the widening, deepening, and speeding up of worldwide interconnectedness in all aspects of contemporary social life. This interconnectivity breaks down the boundary between East and West. In Asian countries, for example, the metaphor of a global village has caught the imagination of many people, including political leaders and intellectuals. Goonasekera further argues that 'paradoxically, we find that while technology has given the world the means of getting closer together into a global village, this very same technology has also given rise to unprecedented fears of domination by the technologically powerful nations' (2001: 278). Some Asian leaders feel that globalization creates fears of cultural disappearance, particularly among smaller nations. Consequently, the global village is viewed more as a threat to cultural identities than as an opportunity to create a more consensual culture among people.

Reference

Goonasekera, Anura (2001) 'Transnational communication: establishing effective linkages between North and South', in N. Chitty (ed.), *Mapping Globalization: International Media and a Crisis of Identity*. Penang: Southbank. pp. 270–281.

Further reading on globalization and cultural hegemony

Matin-Barbero, Jesús (1993) *Communication, Culture and Hegemony: From the Media to Mediations*. Newbury Park, CA: SAGE.

Advanced communication technologies not only allow communication beyond geographic borders, they also affect how we form relationships with others (see Chapter 9). In past centuries, social relationships were typically circumscribed by how far one could walk (Martin and Nakayama, 2001). With each technological advance – the train, motor vehicle, telephone, or the internet – social relationships have been transformed and expanded manyfold. There are millions of global users of the internet every day. The average user now spends over 70 per cent of his or her time online, building personal relationships including online friendships, sexual partnerships, and romances (Nua Internet Survey, 2006). Evidence of the legitimacy and social acceptance of these types of relationships can be found, for example, in Warner Brothers' popular (1998) movie *You've Got Mail*, which played on the increasing mainstream acceptance of romantic relationships formed over the internet. In the movie, two letter-writing lovers, Kathleen (Meg Ryan) and Joe (Tom Hanks), know each other only by their internet handles of 'Shopgirl' and 'NY152', completely unaware that their sweetheart is in fact the co-worker towards whom they feel a certain degree of animosity. This idea of internet-based romantic relationships is gaining popularity as mobility within society increases. Unlike the telephone, postage, and physical travel, the cost of e-mail, instant messaging, and chatrooms does not depend on either message length or the distance that a message travels. The internet, therefore, provides many opportunities to maintain and receive support from long-distance romantic partners, as it is inexpensive, convenient, quick, and similar to a conversation. The people we exchange emails with on the internet are now more than ever likely to come from different countries, be of different ethnic or cultural backgrounds, and have different life experiences. Advanced communication technologies make our community more culturally diverse than ever before.

Photo 1.1
We continue to be 'connected' during our work or leisure time.
Copyright © Jaka Polutnik. Used with permission.

Not only do we come in contact with more people in cyberspace, but modern transportation systems also bring us into contact with more people physically. Our society is more mobile than in the past. For example, in the 1930s travel from China to Singapore took several months; travellers started the journey in winter and arrived at their destination in summer. Nowadays, the same distance by airplane would take only a few hours! Such ease of mobility changes the nature of society. Families and individuals often and easily move for economic, career, or lifestyle opportunities. A New Zealander can work in Australia; an Australian can work in the USA; an American can work in Britain; a Briton can work in France; a French person can work in Belgium. Increasing mobility and technology make our global village smaller but more diverse. However, while changes in technology have facilitated the exchange of ideas, they have also magnified the possibility for misunderstandings. If we consider that people with the same cultural background may experience problems communicating with each other, we can appreciate more fully the difficulties that people from different cultures may encounter when trying to communicate. Understanding other cultures is a challenge we face today, living in a global society.

Theory Corner

Perspectives on globalization

In the academic literature (Held and McGrew, 2007), there are three different perspectives on globalization: a globalist perspective, a traditionalist perspective, and a transformationalist perspective.

Globalists view globalization as an inevitable development which cannot be resisted or significantly influenced by human intervention, particularly through traditional political institutions, such as nation-states.

Traditionalists argue that the significance of globalization as a new phase has been exaggerated. They believe that most economic and social activity is regional, rather than global, and they still see a significant role for nation-states.

Transformationalists contend that globalization represents a significant shift, but they question the inevitability of its impacts. They argue that there is still significant scope for national, local, and other agencies.

Reference

Held, David and McGrew, Anthony (eds) (2007) *Globalization Theory: Approaches and Controversies*. Cambridge: Polity.

Further reading on globalization

Baylis, John; Smith, Steve and Owens, Patricia (2008) *The Globalization of World Politics: An Introduction to International Relations* (4th edn). Oxford: Oxford University Press.

Global economy and business transactions

Information and communication technologies (ICTs) can transform the potential reach and influence of our economy and business transactions from a local to a global level. *Global transformation* refers to the worldwide economic and technological changes that influence how people relate to one another (Cooper et al., 2007). For example, people in nearly every part of the world can buy Reebok shoes, Levi jeans, or a Sony camera! Cross-cultural business transactions today are as common as trade between two persons in the same village was centuries ago. The clothes we wear, the food we buy from the local supermarket, the cars we drive, the electric appliances we use at home, and the movies we watch may all be from different countries. Indeed, we are being multiculturalized everyday. Our local market is as culturally diverse as the global market. Cultural diversity brings many opportunities, particularly in the economic realm, and helps to make our society the cosmopolitan, dynamic, and exciting place it is today. However, one of the biggest economic and social challenges facing us is to unlock the barriers to the acceptance of cultural diversity in the economy and society as a whole (Beamer and Varner, 2008).

In response to economic transformations, businesses are continually expanding into world markets as a part of the wider process of globalization. Cultural diversity shapes market demand and economic behaviours. For example, in 1991 India began to open its economy to wider trade, and the United States quickly became its primary trading and investment partner – investing some US$687 million in 1997, almost three times as much as the previous year (Cooper et al., 2007). Similarly, multinational corporations are increasingly moving their operations overseas to take advantage of lower labour costs, a trend that has far-reaching implications (Martin and Nakayama, 2001).

Ethnic diversity within workplaces is continually changing the organizational composition of most parts of the world. For example, with numbers of emigrants joining the European workforce from Africa, Asia, and the Middle East, that workforce continues to increase each year. In the United States, the proportion of non-white (Asian, Black, and Hispanic American) men is growing, and this trend is expected to continue (Oetzel, 2002). In the Middle East, many workers come from India, the Philippines, and Southeast Asia, while in Asian countries like Malaysia the workforce is also becoming more diverse. Even though Malays make up a large proportion of the workforce (65 per cent), the term 'Malaysian' – more often than not – is used to refer to people of different ethnicities including Indians and Chinese in Malaysia. Working in cross-cultural teams allows organizations to make use of scarce resources and thus increase their competitive advantage. As a result of such economic and cultural shifts, people with diverse cultural backgrounds are working side by side in many countries, creating a workplace that is intercultural (Beamer and Varner, 2008).

The flow of migrant workers as a result of economic transformation also leads to an increase in ethnic competition. Migrant workers tend to flow from regions with lower economic opportunities toward those with greater opportunities. In Western European countries, for example, with the opening up of national borders within the European Union, European nation-states have been granting social rights – although formally no real political rights – to migrants (Soysal, 1994). This change has increased the perception of competition on the part of the native population. For example, there is a large North African presence in Europe. Reaching 3.5 million today, North Africans began arriving in Europe as early as the 1940s to help rebuild European economies severely weakened by the war. This migration accelerated in the 1950s and 1960s to meet the high demand for low-skilled workers in factories and mines and to compensate for slow demographic growth in Western Europe. For many years, North African immigrants were considered temporary residents (guest workers) and had no share in the social, political, and cultural life of the host societies.

It was only after the 1974 policies of family reunion that immigrants, their families, traditions, and religions became visible in everyday life. France, for example, is home to the largest number of North African immigrants, due to its long colonial involvement in Algeria, Morocco, and Tunisia, followed by Holland, Belgium, Spain, Italy, and Germany. Different citizenship and immigration laws, as well as the socio-political climate of each host country, have determined to a large extent how North Africans have engaged with the host culture. While acknowledging the benefits that can be obtained from a culturally diverse workforce, studies consistently indicate problems that are often experienced by multicultural workers, such as conflicts in expectations, a lack of communication competence, and attitude problems such as mistrust. Thus understanding the cultural tensions created by economic transformations is a challenge we face in the business context of intercultural communication.

Photo 1.2
Ethnic shops in Chinatown in Brisbane, Australia.
Copyright © Shuang Liu. Used with permission.

Theory Corner

The concept of citizenship

According to Habermas (1989) and Arendt (1958), it is important to understand the concept of 'citizenship' both historically and geographically. During antiquity, states began to differentiate between citizens (natives) and aliens (outsiders or foreigners), who were brought to or resided in the territory under their jurisdiction. The distinction between citizens and non-citizens existed in the city-states of ancient

(Continued)

Greece. A *polis* reserved certain rights, privileges, and duties for its citizens, that is, free individuals (men) born into the polis. This concept of citizenship was very exclusive. Not only slaves but also women and those without property were excluded from the political community and the public until the twentieth century. Throughout history, the participation of people in public affairs has always been restricted and limited.

The Enlightenment (in the eighteenth century) was essential for the development of the modern concept of citizenship. This crucial historical development marked the period of the formation of modern nation-states. However, the model of a single nation-state generates national chauvinism and ethnic conflict in some states. Both Habermas and Arendt advocate the concept of *civic citizenship*, but also point to the realities and current policies of exclusion in many parts of the world, such as the policies directed against incoming migrants.

References

Arendt, Hannah (1958) *The Human Condition*. Chicago: University of Chicago Press.

Habermas, Jurgen (1989) *The Structural Transformation of the Public Sphere*. Cambridge, MA: MIT.

Further reading on prejudice

Cunningham, William A.; Nezlek, John B. and Banaji, Mahzarin R. (2004) 'Implicit and explicit ethnocentrism: revisiting the ideologies of prejudice', *Personality and Social Psychology Bulletin*, 30 (10): 1332–1346.

Mass migration and international exchange

One of the most significant contributors to our multicultural environment is the ever increasing flow of people through migration and international exchange (see Chapter 12). According to the Population Division of the Department of Economics and Social Affairs of the United Nations Secretariat data bank (DESA, 2006), the number of international migrants in the world more than doubled between 1960 and 2005, going from an estimated 75 million in 1960 to almost 191 million in 2005 – an increase of 121 million over forty-five years. A growing concentration of international migrants can be found in developed countries. In 2005, Europe hosted the largest number of international migrants (64 million), followed by Asia (53 million), North America (44 million), Africa (17 million), Latin America and the Caribbean (close to seven million), and Oceania (five million). The United Kingdom, for example, has a sustainable immigrant population: approximately a quarter of its 60 million people were born outside of the UK. Immigrants' countries of origin include China, Italy, Greece, India, Sri Lanka, Vietnam, Malaysia, and South Africa, among many others. Statistics from the Population Division of the United Nations reveal that, relative to the total population, there is a higher percentage of international migrants in Oceania (15 per cent) and North America (13 per cent) than in Europe, where international migrants account for nearly 9 per cent of the total population. By contrast, international migrants account for less than 2 per cent of the population of Africa, Asia, and Latin America and the Caribbean.

A steadily increasing proportion of migrant populations is made up of international students, particularly in developed English-speaking countries such as the USA, Australia, and the UK. To date, the United States has been the world's largest receiving country for international students. In 2005–06, the number of international students enrolled in higher education institutions remained steady at 567,766, according to the Annual Report on International Academic Mobility published by the Institute of International Education (IIE, 2006). This marks the seventh year in a row that the United States has hosted more than half a million foreign students. Asia remains the largest region of origin, accounting for 58 per cent of total US international enrolments. India is the leading country of origin for international students, followed by China, Korea, Japan, Canada, Taiwan, Mexico, Turkey, Germany, and Thailand. International students contribute approximately US$13.5 billion to the US economy through their expenditure on tuition and living expenses. The Department of Commerce describes US higher education as the country's fifth largest service sector export.

A similar trend was found in Oceanic countries such as Australia, where education has recently replaced tourism as the country's largest service export – according to IDP Education, a global company that informs and advises international students on Australian education and assists in enrolment in Australian institutions across all sectors (IDP, 2008). The value of Australia's education exports grew by 21 per cent in 2007 to replace tourism as the top service export and the nation's third largest export overall. Australia's top five source countries and regions for international students are China, India, South Korea, Malaysia, and Hong Kong. Figures released by the Australian Bureau of Statistics in February 2008 valued education exports in 2007 at AU$12.5 billion (approximately US$11.8 billion) compared to AU$11.5 billion (approximately US$10.9 billion) for tourism. Australian government statistics show that there were over 450,000 international students in Australia in 2007. According to commentators, education is now a bigger draw for visitors to Australia than the Great Barrier Reef and all the other tourist attractions combined. The flow of international students, particularly those from non-English- to English-speaking countries, inevitably creates both opportunities and challenges for intercultural communication.

Possessing more permanent residential status than international students are those people who migrate to a host country to make a living. They are significant contributors to the multicultural environment of society today. In Australia, for example, immigration has always been a central part of nation building. Since the end of the Second World War, around 6.5 million migrants have come to Australia. In the immediate post-war period only 10 per cent of Australia's population was born overseas (Marden and Mercer, 1998). Today, nearly 25 per cent of the population was born overseas and approximately 200 languages are spoken in the country. The proportion of people from Asian countries is on the increase. Between 2000 and 2005, the number of East Asians in Australia rose by 17 per cent (from approximately 850,000 to 1 million). In comparison, the total Australian population only grew by approximately 5 per cent (from 19.4 million to 20.3 million) during the same period (ABS, 2005).

Photo 1.3
Signs in market squares are in various languages to cater for multicultural customers.
Copyright © Shuang Liu. Used with permission.

Migrants move to their host countries for a variety of reasons, including access to a better living environment or to give their children a good education in an English-speaking country. Others are intent on exploring business opportunities that are unavailable in their home country, while some migrate to seek refugee or political protection. Regardless of their reasons for migration, migrants worldwide dream of the freedom to be their own boss, to have autonomy in their choice of work, and to achieve prosperity in the host country. Small businesses, such as takeaway shops, convenience stores, trading companies, or video shops, are considered by many migrants as paths to realizing their dreams of freedom and financial security. As a result, walking along a street in Sydney, Auckland, San Francisco, or London, one would not have difficulty in finding an Indian restaurant, a Chinese takeaway shop, a Vietnamese greengrocery store, an Italian deli, a Japanese sushi bar, and so on. For example, in Brisbane market squares the signs are in various languages to cater for the linguistic diversity of customers.

The Necessity and Benefits of Intercultural Communication

Multiculturalism

All over the world, nations are trying to come to terms with the growing diversity of their populations (Beamer and Varner, 2008). Behind the overt, visible symbols of cultural diversity is a complex and often implicit concept of *multiculturalism*. At a descriptive level, multiculturalism can be used to characterize a society with diverse cultures. As an attitude, it can refer to a society's tolerance towards diversity and the acceptance of equal societal participation. In attempting to maximize the benefits of cultural diversity, there has been an accompanying awareness of some potential threats to our cultural uniqueness. Globally, host nationals have expressed concerns over the threat that new ethnic cultures may pose to mainstream cultural values, the political and economic power structure, and the distribution of employment opportunities. Some countries are addressing these concerns by trying to control diversity through tighter entry requirements. Other countries are developing governmental policies concerning the rights of immigrants to preserve their home culture within the host country.

Australia, during the nineteenth century, had no restrictions on anyone entering what was then a set of colonies, provided that they were not convicts serving out their time. Consequently, free settlers moved in from Great Britain, Germany, America, Scandinavia, and Asia. Similarly, the slogan for the post-Second World War immigration programme was *Populate or Perish*! However, since 2007 a citizenship test has been in place to check migrants' knowledge of the English language and comprehension of Australian moral principles and history, as well as national and Aboriginal symbols. The test is available in English only, and migrant applicants for citizenship must pass this before their application for citizenship can be lodged.

This restriction of citizenship opportunities is also evident elsewhere. In some countries, such as the People's Republic of China, dual citizenship is not recognized. In Germany, immigrants are considered *Ausländer* (foreigners) and their naturalization is only possible if they agree to renounce their original citizenship and demonstrate loyalty to their 'adoptive' country. These laws have been slightly relaxed since the Social Democrats gained power in the 1990s. Even so, there is raging controversy regarding the amendment of the citizenship laws and its implications for German national identity (Blank et al., 2001). France has built its nation-state, since the nineteenth century, on the premise that all regional and cultural differences should be eliminated. French citizens have to show loyalty to a powerful, centralized nation-state and adhere to universal political values. Linguistic as well as cultural diversity within France has always been seen as a sign of regression and a hindrance to achieving national unity. Even in the United States – a country that historically has afforded a home to people of diverse cultures – the advantages and disadvantages of acknowledging diversity are hotly debated (Cooper et al., 2007). The maintenance of nationalism and continuity in the mainstream culture has been key issues of concern in all countries that receive migrants.

Migrants, on the other hand, have long been forming associations to maintain their ethnic cultural heritage and promote the survival of their languages within a host country's mainstream institutions. In Australia, for example, the Asian value debate has attracted considerable media attention, particularly in response to increased Asian immigration and the continuing emphasis placed on Australia's role in the Asian region as being closely tied to the policy of multiculturalism (Marden and Mercer, 1998). Central to the debate is the question of whether the preservation of ethnic cultures creates a threat to mainstream society (see Chapter 12). The challenge we face is how to promote intercultural understanding so as to reap the benefits of cultural diversity and reduce intercultural tensions. Key to building the necessary understanding between cultural groups is effective intercultural communication.

Building intercultural understanding

Understanding is the first step towards acceptance. The biggest benefit in accepting cultural differences is that cultural diversity enriches each of us. Throughout history, people around the world have accumulated a rich stock of cultural traditions and customs, but we are often not aware of the cultural rules governing our own behaviour until we encounter behaviours that are different from our own. Local laws and customs vary from country to country; if you are unaware of them and act according to your own learned customs when in a country, you may very well end up in prison! For example, it is illegal in Egypt to take photographs of bridges and canals (including the Suez Canal), as well as military personnel, buildings, and equipment. In India, trespassing on and photographing airports, military establishments, and dams are illegal, with penalties ranging from three to fourteen years' imprisonment. Similarly, maiming or killing a cow in India is an offence which can result in a punishment of up to five years' imprisonment. In Thailand, lengthy prison terms of up to fifteen years can be imposed for insulting the monarchy; this includes destroying banknotes bearing the king's image.

If some of these local laws do not make much sense to you, you may find some local customs even stranger. Behaviours which are considered perfectly appropriate and acceptable in one culture may appear harsh or offensive in another. For example, in Saudi Arabia women are legally required to wear the *abaya* – a long black coat that conceals their body shape – in all public places, while men are to avoid wearing shorts as well as short-sleeved or unbuttoned shirts. Public displays of affection, including kissing and holding hands, are considered offensive. Hotels may refuse accommodation to couples unable to provide proof of marriage, because it is illegal for unmarried couples to live together. In Thailand, simple actions such as showing the soles of your feet or touching the top of a person's head are likely to cause grave offence. Even unknowingly breaching local customs may either get you into trouble or make you unwelcome!

We acquire many of our cultural beliefs, values, and communication norms at an unconscious level. Cultural socialization, in addition, can encourage the development of ethnocentrism. *Ethnocentrism* means seeing our own culture as the central and best one, and seeing other cultures as insignificant or even inferior. As Charon (2007: 156) indicates, 'Groups develop differences from one another, so do formal organizations, communities and societies. Without interaction with outsiders, differences become difficult to understand and difficult not to judge. What is real to us becomes comfortable; what is comfortable becomes right. What we do not understand becomes less than right to us.' Ethnocentrism may lead to prejudice, stereotypes, or discrimination (see Chapter 4). It is a barrier to effective intercultural communication because it prevents us from understanding those who are culturally different from ourselves. In contrast to ethnocentrism is *cultural relativism*, which is the degree to which an individual judges another culture by its context (Rogers and Steinfatt, 1999). Cultural relativists try to evaluate the behaviours of a culture using that culture's assumptions about reality. Although one element of a culture, by itself, may seem strange to non-members, it generally makes sense when being considered in light of other elements of that culture (see Chapter 3). To understand another culture, therefore, we need to communicate with its people and broaden our understanding of their practices and beliefs, thus enhancing our sense of cultural relativism – hence the need for and benefit from intercultural communication.

As members of the global village, we can celebrate the richness of the human imagination along with its diverse products. Key to appreciating cultural differences is acquiring intercultural knowledge and developing intercultural skills. Intercultural knowledge opens doors to the treasure house of human experience. It reveals to us myriad ways of experiencing, sensing, feeling, and knowing. It helps us to start questioning our own stance on issues that we may once have taken for granted. It widens our vision to include an alternative perspective of valuing and relating. By understanding the beliefs, values, and worldviews that influence alternative communication approaches, we can understand the logic that motivates the actions or behaviours of others who are culturally different to ourselves. Cultural differences do not prevent us from communicating with each other; rather, they enrich us through communication. Culturally sensitive communication can increase relational closeness and deepen cultural self-awareness (Ting-Toomey and Chung, 2005). The more that culturally diverse people get to know each other, the more they can appreciate the differences and perceive deep commonalities amongst them. Key to building a stock of intercultural knowledge, therefore, is engaging in intercultural communication. Intercultural communication can help us to build our knowledge of other peoples and their cultures, as well as enhancing and consolidating our knowledge about our own culture. The result is invariably greater intercultural understanding.

Promoting international business exchange

According to the *International Business Trend Report* (*Training and Development*, 1999), three competencies that are essential in the global workplace of the twenty-first century are intercultural communication skills, a problem-solving ability, and global leadership. When money and jobs cross borders, there are challenges and opportunities facing individuals of different backgrounds who live and work together (Cooper et al., 2007). People of different ethnic backgrounds bring their cultural baggage to the workplace. In a multinational organization, for instance, Malay employees may heavily emphasize the values of family togetherness, harmony in relationships, and a respect for seniority; whereas Australian employees may value individuality and personal achievement more highly. A workgroup consisting of members from different cultural backgrounds is more likely to experience difficulties in communication or to experience miscommunication, dysfunctional conflict, and turnover, if the group members are not interculturally competent. This is clearly reflected in research conducted by Taylor Cox and his associates (1991) who studied the effects of ethnic differences in groups and the cooperative and competitive behaviours of group members. Their findings indicate that Asian, Black, and Hispanic employees have a more cooperative orientation to a task than Anglos. Ethnic diversity in the workplace creates challenges for management in today's businesses, but attention to diversity issues has the potential to bolster employee morale, create an inclusive climate in organizations, and spark creative innovation.

Communicating with unfamiliar cultures does not simply mean finding a translator to facilitate discussions in a foreign language (Beamer and Varner, 2008). Communication is about unarticulated meanings and the thinking behind words, not just the words per se (see Chapter 2). To understand the significance of a message from someone, you need to understand that person's perception and the most important values in that person's view of the world. You need to know what to expect when someone engages in a particular behaviour. For example, a critical social factor influencing business behaviours – particularly in collectivistic cultures such as China – is the development and maintenance of cooperative relations with business partners (Chan et al., 2002). *Guanxi*, a special type of relationship which contains trust, favour, dependence, and adaptation, constitutes a highly differentiated and intricate system of formal and informal social subsets which are governed by the unwritten law of reciprocity (Zhou and Hui, 2003). Chinese people view human relationships as long term and consequently place great emphasis on cultivating a good relationship with their business partners prior to any business transaction. While economic factors are important to the Chinese, those factors alone cannot sustain motivation to maintain long-term business relations. In fact, non-economic factors such as acceptance, face-giving, complementary social reciprocity, and trust may play a bigger role in influencing decision making. The emphasis on developing *guanxi* is reflected in business negotiations with Chinese partners, which tend to be much lengthier than those with Westerners. As culture profoundly influences how people think, communicate, and behave, it also affects the kinds of deals they make and the way they make them (Salacuse, 1991). A good understanding of cultural differences is vital for promoting mutually productive and successful international business exchanges.

Facilitating cross-cultural adaptation

Cross-cultural adaptation has to be understood as a manifestation of broader social trends that are not confined to the experience of immigrants, but rather as extending to many other kinds of associations and networks as well as into cultural life as a whole. Globalization is a process by which geographic borders as boundaries between nations and states are eroding. It is the contours of transnational spaces and societies and new systems of identity. Advances in technology and transport systems now provide people with greater freedom to travel beyond national borders, as well as with more choices for belonging. Ultimately the interconnectedness between people and the erosion of geographic borders make our 'village' more global but our world smaller. The arrival of immigrants brings various changes to the host cultural environment. Intercultural encounters provide opportunities for understanding between people, as well as the potential for misunderstanding.

Cross-cultural adaptation is not a process that is unique to immigrants; host nationals also have to experience cultural adjustments when their society is joined by culturally different others (see Chapter 12). The tension between immigrants and host nationals often centres on the extent to which immigrants can maintain their heritage culture in the host country. Research conducted on immigrants' cultural adaptation strategies indicates that they identify integrating into the host culture and, at the same time, maintaining their ethnic cultural heritage as their preferred acculturation strategy (Liu, 2007). A key question is whether or not that host society can provide immigrants with an environment in which they feel welcome to integrate. In countries receiving many immigrants, ethnically different populations can be perceived as a threat to collective identity and to the standard of living of the natives. For host nationals, multiculturalism can be interpreted as a threat to their cultural dominance. For migrant groups, however, multiculturalism offers the possibility of maintaining their own culture and still integrating into the host society. Thus policies of multiculturalism that highlight the importance of recognizing cultural diversity within a common framework, as well as equal opportunities, might lead to inter-ethnic distinctions and threaten social cohesion.

The extent to which host nationals allow members of immigrant groups to maintain their own culture and partake in relationships with the dominant cultural group plays an important role in the construction of a truly multicultural society. Promoting inter-ethnic understanding facilitates a cultural adaptation by both migrants and host nationals; the key to inter-ethnic understanding is intercultural communication. Interacting with immigrants is often difficult for host nationals because of differences in language and cultural values and this adds anxiety to intercultural interactions. To reduce anxiety of this nature, we must equip ourselves with knowledge about other cultures. Intercultural knowledge reduces anxiety and uncertainty, making the communication process more smooth and successful. Intercultural knowledge and intercultural communication skills, however, do not come naturally; they have to be acquired through conscious learning.

Summary

This chapter identified different contributors to cultural diversity in our society, delineated various challenges we face as a result of living in a global village, and highlighted the necessity of acquiring skills in intercultural communication. With continued advances in communication technology, improvements in transportation systems, and rapid changes in the global economy and mass migration, the world is becoming a smaller and more interconnected global village. Geographic borders that used to separate people from people and country from country are receding. We now find ourselves coming into contact with culturally different people in our workplaces, stores, public places, neighbourhoods, and cyberspace. You may work side by side with someone whose work habits and cultural practices are different from yours; you may develop friendships or romantic relationships with people who live on the other side of the globe; you may negotiate a business contract with someone who views the world differently from the way you do. Our culture governs our behaviour; however, our way of doing something may be neither the only way nor the only right way. Different cultural customs and practices need to be interpreted in their own contexts. In order to harness the benefits of cultural diversity in our society, we need to develop sound knowledge and skills in communicating with people from different cultures. The study of intercultural communication equips us with the necessary knowledge and dynamic skills to manage differences efficiently and effectively. Only by competently interacting with others who are culturally different from us can our global village survive.

Case Study:
The Cronulla riots

Alcohol, the Australian flag, and raw racism fuelled a violent demonstration by thousands of young people in Sydney, Australia, singing and waving the national flag as they 'reclaimed' Cronulla, a beachfront suburb of Sydney, in December 2005. The incident was known as the Cronulla riots – a series of confrontations between white Australian youths and Middle Eastern Australian youths. Fuelled by drink, the crowd of white youths became a mob, beating up anyone who looked Middle Eastern. That night and the next, carloads of young men of Middle Eastern descent headed for the beach suburbs to launch similarly random and savage acts of revenge.

In the lead-up to the riots, allegations circulated around the local area that groups of Middle Eastern youths had asked white women on the beach wearing bikinis to 'cover up'; a 23 year old man was stabbed in the back outside a golf club by what police described as a group of males of Mediterranean or Middle Eastern appearance; and three off-duty lifeguards from north Cronulla were assaulted by youths of Middle Eastern origin. It was believed that these alleged incidents, among others, prompted a retaliation by Cronulla locals.

On Sunday, 11 December 2005, approximately 5000 people gathered on Cronulla beach to protest against the reported incidents of assaults and intimidating behaviour, where the alleged perpetrators had been identified in earlier media reports as Middle Eastern youths from the suburbs of Western Sydney. The crowd initially assembled without incident, but violence broke out after a large group chased several men of Middle Eastern appearance into a nearby hotel. As the crowd moved along the beach and foreshore area, one man on the back of a utility vehicle began to shout 'No more Lebs!', a chant picked up by the group around him. A small number of demonstrators were wearing clothing that bore racist slogans such as 'We grew here, you flew here', 'Ethnic Cleansing Unit', 'Aussie pride', 'Save Nulla', 'Lebs go home' and 'No Lebs'. Through the remainder of the day, several more individuals of Middle Eastern appearance were allegedly assaulted, including several people who were not ethnic Arabs – among them Turks, a Jewish boy, and a Greek girl. Police and ambulance workers leading the victims away from the riots were also assaulted by groups of people throwing beer bottles. Several dozen people were treated for minor cuts and bruises, while six individuals were evacuated under police escort for medical care. In some cases, police cars were swamped and stomped on as they tried to move from one violent flare-up to another.

Photo 1.4
On 11 December 2005, crowds gathered at North Cronulla, Sydney, Australia, amid Australian flags and an anti-Lebanese fanfare.
Copyright © Warren Hudson. Used with permission.

The police employed riot equipment, including capsicum spray, in order to subdue several of the attackers. Local police at Cronulla had earlier commented that they were sufficiently prepared to deal with any anticipated violence at the beach, but they appeared to be overwhelmed by the sheer number of people who had arrived. A call for reinforcements was placed to police stations in other suburbs. The following nights saw several retaliatory assaults in the communities near Cronulla and an unprecedented police lock-down of Sydney beaches and surrounding areas. Political spokespeople attributed the state of conflict to years of disagreements and simmering hatred between the two main ethnic groups involved in these incidents: white Australians and Middle Eastern Australians. In the years after the September 11, 2001 attacks in New York City, many had begun to feel a sense of fear created by terrorism and a perceived threat from Islamic fundamentalism. This had heightened public awareness of Arab-Australian communities in Sydney and their ongoing differences with non-Muslim Australians.

ABC's *Four Corners* programme interviewed some of the participants – young Anglo-Australians who had joined the seething mob at Cronulla on 11 December 2005 and Middle Eastern men who had taken part in revenge attacks. The report exposed a strong perception of threat among white Australians in the suburb. The white Australian youths expressed their desire for the government to stop appeasing people who follow Islam, for fear that those people would 'out-breed white Australians'. 'Once they get the numbers,' one of the youths remarked, 'they can vote their members into parliament. And once their members are in parliament, they can pass laws, like they've already tried to get the Islamic law into Australia a few times.' To many Arab Australians, the Cronulla riots represented an attack on their entire community. A comment from one youth who twice joined the revenge convoy was, 'When I watched the TV, it hurt me, it hurt everyone ... they hit our innocent people ... so why not, may as well do the same thing.'

The aftermath of the riots on the economy in the local area was enormous. Many of the small businesses in the nearby beachside suburbs reported a significant downturn in trade following the main incident on 11 December 2005, normally a busy time of the year. On 22 December, the BBC reported that some beachside businesses had indicated a slump in takings of up to 75 per cent since the riots. Authorities in Britain, Canada, and Indonesia issued warnings to their citizens visiting the area to be on guard for possible continuing racial violence. Subsequently, the New South Wales state government announced an AU$250,000 (at the time, approximately US$183,000) campaign to bring tourists back to Sydney beaches, including advertisements featuring well-known sports stars, assuring potential visitors that it was safe to visit the area.

References for case study

Jackson, Liz (2006) 'Riot and Revenge' [online]. Accessed 12 May 2008 at http://www.abc.net.au/4corners/content/2006/s1588360.htm
Kennedy, Les and Murphy, Damien (2005) 'Racist Furore as Mobs Riot' [online]. Accessed 12 May 2008 at http://www.theage.com.au/news/national/racist-furore-as-mobs-riot/2005/12/11/1134235948497.html

Questions for discussion

1 What were the causes of tension between white Australian youths and Lebanese Australian youths? How common do you think these tensions are between immigrant and host communities elsewhere?
2 What characteristics of culture can you identify based on the Cronulla riots?

3 What problems does this case reveal about the co-existence of different cultural groups in a host country?
4 What challenges can you identify from this incident regarding promoting multiculturalism in our society?
5 How could we prevent such incidents from happening again in our society?

Key Terms

communication;
culture;
cultural adaptation;
cultural relativism;
diversity;
ethnocentrism;

globalist;
globalization;
global transformation;
global village;
immigrants;
integration;

intercultural communication;
migration;
multiculturalism;
traditionalist;
transformationalist

Further Reading

Cronulla riots

Babacan, Alperhan and Babacan, Hurriyet (2007) 'New racism and fear: the Cronulla riots and racial violence in Australia', *The Journal of Turkish Weekly* [online]. Available at http://www.turkishweekly.net/articles.php?id=261

Kell, Peter (2005, December 19) 'Cronulla Beach Riots: Making waves for the Asia Pacific Region', *Online Opinion* [online]. Available at http://www.onlineopinion.com.au/view.asp?article=3976

Cultural diversity

Australian Government: Department of Education and Training (2005) 'Australian legislation and international law', *Racism: No Way* [online]. Available at http://www.racismnoway.com.au/library/legislation/

Cunningham, William A., Nezlek, John B. and Banaji, Mahzarin R. (2004) 'Implicit and explicit ethnocentrism: revisiting the ideologies of prejudice', *Personality and Social Psychology Bulletin*, 30 (10): 1332–1346.

Globalization

Baylis, John; Smith, Steve and Owens, Patricia (2008) *The Globalization of World Politics: An Introduction to International Relations* (4th edn). Oxford: Oxford University Press.

Held, David and McGrew, Anthony (eds) (2007) *Globalization Theory: Approaches and Controversies*. Cambridge: Polity.

Matin-Barbero, Jesús (1993) *Communication, Culture and Hegemony: From the Media to Mediations*. Newbury Park, CA: SAGE.

Guanxi

Fan, Ying (2002) 'Questioning Guanxi: definition, classification and implications', *International Business Review*, 11 (5): 543–561.

Intercultural communication

Ho, Robert (1990) 'Multiculturalism in Australia: a survey of attitudes', *Human Relations*, 43 (3): 259–272.

Midooka, Kiyoshi (1990) 'Characteristics of Japanese-style communication', *Media, Culture & Society*, 12: 477–489.

2

Understanding Communication

*There are four ways, and only four ways, in which we have
contact with the world. We are evaluated and classified by those four
contacts: what we do, how we look, what we say, and how we say it.*

Dale Carnegie, American author and trainer, 1888–1955

Learning Objectives

At the end of this chapter, you should be able to:

- Recognize the multifaceted nature of communication.
- Identify the components and characteristics of communication.
- Explain widely known models of communication.
- Compare and contrast different levels of communication.
- Understand the influence of culture on communication.

The Essence of Communication

As the opening quote by Carnegie indicates, we make our contact with the world through 'what we do, how we look, what we say, and how we say it'; each of these actions sends a message to the people around us. Babies arrive in this world crying. Before they learn to use language, crying and smiling are their tools of communication. 'Communication – our ability to share our ideas and feelings – is the basis of all human contact' (Samovar and Porter, 1995: 25). The English word 'communication' is derived from the Latin word *communicare*, meaning 'to make common', as in sharing thoughts, hopes, and knowledge. For example, greeting one another is a basic communication act practised in every culture. We may do this by saying 'hello', or by using touch, eye contact, or gestures to exchange greetings. These methods of interaction reflect the functions and characteristics of communication – that is, we use a shared code to exchange messages. Communication requires that all parties understand a common 'language' or code. There are auditory means of exchanging this code, such as speaking, singing, and tone of voice; there are physical means, such as body language, sign language, touch, eye contact, or writing. Every single act of social behaviour involves communication. People communicate to accomplish tasks, achieve goals, share understanding, exchange information, in order to be heard and even to be appreciated. Whether we live in a large city like New York, a small Peruvian village like Los Molinos, a remote region like Christmas Island, or a metropolitan city like Cape Town, we all participate in communication.

Communication is sharing who we are and what we know. We all share our ideas and feelings with others; however, *how* we share them varies from culture to culture. As our contact with people from other cultures expands, the need for competent intercultural communicators increases. Improving our ability to communicate effectively and efficiently can be facilitated by a knowledge of what communication is. This chapter first explores different definitions of human communication and then examines its components and characteristics. Following this, communication models – linear and interactive – are introduced and their theoretical underpinnings discussed. The chapter concludes by identifying different levels of communication and discussing the influence of culture on communication. Analysis provided in this chapter enables you to improve your communication and to understand and appreciate that of others.

The Multifaceted Nature of Communication

Human communication is as old as human history. Cave paintings in prehistorical Europe chart the beginning of human communication. In Australia, paintings by indigenous people can be found on rocks and caves, illustrating an ancient means of communication. Paintings found on the caves and rock of Uluru – a red sandstone monolith in central Australia – reveal that it has been the focus for religious, cultural, territorial, and economic relations among the Aboriginal people of the Western Desert for many thousands of years. Many other means of conveying messages have been used throughout history, via members of our own species and other animals. For example, pigeons were used by European armies to carry military intelligence during the First World War (Greelis, 2007), while warriors in ancient China used burning fires and smoke to send messages to fellow soldiers in different military camps. Human beings have long been used as couriers of communication. For example, in ancient times human messengers were probably the most reliable and efficient means of sending official

Photo 2.1
Aboriginal rock art paintings in Australia illustrate stories in the everyday lives of the Anangu Aboriginal people who live at Uluru – a red sandstone monolith; it is the world's largest at 9.4 km in diameter. Copyright © Zala Volčič. Used with permission.

information and communiqués, even though it meant weeks or months of long, often dangerous travelling time.

Advances in information technology have brought tremendous changes to communication media and to the role of communicators. From print, the telephone, broadcasts, television, satellites, the internet, Facebook, and blogs (web-logs), human communication has expanded beyond the confines of time, space, geographic region, culture, and nation. Every communicator, whether a source or a receiver, is a node on the 'wired' communication network. As Cooper and her associates (2007) pointed out, when we consider our world from such a compressed perspective, the need for mutual acceptance and understanding becomes apparent.

Defining communication

In creating new configurations of sources, messages, and receivers, new communication technologies reinforce the need to examine our existing definitions of communication (Morris and Ogan, 1996). Finding a single definition of communication is a difficult task, as those that exist range widely. Dance (1970) reviewed some 95 definitions of communication published in the 1950s and 1960s. Since then countless other definitions of communication have been added to the list. He concluded that the definitions differed in so many ways that communication might better be theorized as a 'family' of related concepts rather than as a unitary concept. This reflects the multifaceted nature of communication. Consider the simple act of greeting a friend. From the secretion of chemicals in the brain to the moving of one's lips to produce sound, thousands of components are in operation. When we add on cultural dimensions, it becomes even more complex – people from different cultures express the same concept or idea differently. For example, in Australia or New Zealand a casual hello is acceptable as a form of greeting; in Japan, a bow is expected when greeting one's boss; in Arab culture, friends are commonly greeted with a full embrace and a kiss on the cheek; in Serbia, friends kiss three times on the cheek as a form of greeting; in Malaysia, friends may greet each other by folding two hands in front of the chest.

To overcome problems created by the complexity of the concept of communication, scholars concentrate on the aspects of communication that are most germane to their interests (Samovar and Porter, 1995). For example, neurologists look at what the brain and nervous system do during communication; psychologists examine issues related to perception; linguists inspect people's use of language; philosophers are more interested in whether communication is essential to thought; anthropologists focus on the question of whether communication is universal; and in the electronic world, scientists tend to focus on the transfer of data and information from one location to another. Communication researchers are more interested in how people share understanding and meaning through the use of verbal or nonverbal symbols. Each of these disciplines carves out but one piece within the territory of human communication. As each field of study explores its own area of communication, it is very important to be aware that there is no right or wrong definition, and no single definition is conclusive of *all* aspects of communication. Given that our interest lies in communication between culturally different people, our focus is on those elements that influence sharing understanding and meaning between cultures. Thus, in this chapter, we define *communication* as the process by which people use shared verbal or nonverbal codes, systems, and media to exchange information in a particular cultural context.

Different disciplines are concerned with different aspects of communication, and they all contribute to the study of communication as a whole. This study, therefore, is influenced by a variety of fields. Littlejohn (1982) traced contributions to communication theory from disciplines as diverse as literature, mathematics, engineering, sociology, and psychology. According to Littlejohn, the primary source of ideas about communication 'prior to this century, dating back to ancient times, was rhetoric' (1996a: 117). In the rhetorical theory, which originated with the ancient Greek sophists and has traced a long and varied history to the present, communication has typically been theorized as the practical art of discourse. Problems of communication in the rhetorical tradition are regarded as social exigencies that can be resolved through the artful use of discourse to persuade an audience (Bitzer, 1968).

This way of theorizing communication is useful for explaining why our participation in discourse, especially public discourse, is important and how it occurs. A discourse approach to communication holds the possibility that the practice of communication can be cultivated and improved through education and research. We know that some people are better communicators than others and that the best examples of rhetoric can rise to the level of great art. Skills can be learned and improved through practice. Thus, it is reasonable to think that people can become better communicators by learning and practising communication. Equally important, however, is to recognize that every culture has its own communication rules, and the criteria for judging 'good' communicators vary from culture to culture.

Theory Corner

Rhetorical theory

The *rhetorical tradition* views communication as a practical art of discourse (Rybacki and Rybacki, 1991). Rhetorical theory dates back centuries to ancient Greece when Plato, Aristotle, and the sophists were speech teachers. *Classical rhetorical theory* is based on the philosophy that we are rational beings who can be persuaded by compelling arguments. Rhetorical communication deliberately attempts to influence the audience by using carefully constructed messages of verbal and often visual symbols. Those who create rhetorical communication are called *rhetors*, the messages they create are *rhetorical acts*. Aristotle's *Rhetoric* was the most influential rhetorical text for thousands of years and had a significant influence on theories of communication. The model of rhetoric he proposed focuses on three elements in public speaking: 1) *ethos*, based on the personal character or credibility of the speaker; 2) *pathos*, based on putting the audience into a certain frame of mind; and 3) *logos*, based on the arguments made in the speech. Rhetorical analysis used to be confined to public speech, but is now also being used to interpret mass media products such as works on radio, television, and film.

Reference

Rybacki, Karyn and Rybacki, Domald (1991) *Communication Criticism: Approaches and Genres*. Belmont, CA: Wadsworth.

Further reading on rhetoric and discourse

Chatman, Seymour (1978) *Story and Discourse: Narrative Structure in Fiction and Film*. Ithaca, NY: Cornell University Press.

Components of communication

Although definitions of communication vary from discipline to discipline, scholars tend to agree that there is a set of basic components of human communication. Embedded in all definitions of communication are the factors of people, message, channel, and context. Based on this consensus, we can identify eight components of human communication which usually operate simultaneously. In their most basic form, these components are found in every culture (Samovar and Porter, 1995). They are source, message, channel, receiver, encoding, decoding, noise, and feedback. All these components exist in the specific context in which the communication act occurs. Context permeates all communication processes (Jandt, 2007).

Source

A source is the origin of information. A source is someone who needs and wants to exchange information with others. The need may be conscious, such as asking someone directions (seeking information), expressing feelings about a wedding attended (sharing experiences), or assigning tasks to an employee (accomplishing tasks). The need to communicate may also be non-conscious – for example, frowning when hearing music one does not like or disagreeing with another's opinion. Conscious or non-conscious communication is the sharing of thoughts and feelings, with varying degrees of intention by the source, and it affects the feelings and behaviour of another person or a group of people.

Message

The message is the verbal and/or nonverbal form of ideas, thought, or feelings that one person wishes to communicate to another person or group in some place at some time within a specific context. A message is the composition of verbal codes such as language (see Chapter 6) and/or nonverbal codes including facial expressions, body movements, tone of voice, use of space, time orientation, and so forth (see Chapter 7). Each culture has its own way of forming and expressing messages. In India and Bulgaria 'wiggling' the head from side to side may indicate 'Yes', whereas a Dutch person would shake her head to express the same idea.

Channel

Messages must have a means by which they move from one person to another. This route is known as the channel (or channels, as much communication involves several channels at once). The channel can be sound, sight, words, the telephone, the internet, fax, and so on. The primary channels are sound and sight. We receive messages when we listen to and watch each other. The degree to which an individual prefers one channel over another is often determined by his or her culture. In the United States words are highly valued, while in some Mediterranean cultures touching is a major communication channel. In some Asian cultures, such as those of Japan and China, silence is as significant a carrier of messages as words and sound.

Receiver

The receiver is the intended target of the message. He or she normally shares the same code as the source. After a message has been generated and moved along a channel, it reaches a destination – the receiver. This is a person who takes the message into account and is therefore linked to the message source. Of course in most interpersonal communication, participants are both sources and receivers, whereas mass communication may (but not always) be one way. Unlike programmed computers or machines, human beings do not respond uniformly to all messages and nor do they always compose the same message in exactly the same way (Pearson and Nelson, 1997). Individual characteristics, including those related to race, sex, age, education, culture, values, and attitudes, all affect how people both send and receive messages.

Encoding

The code refers to a shared language used by individuals to categorize their experience and to communicate it to others (Rogers and Steinfatt, 1999). Feelings and ideas cannot be shared directly; they must be converted into words and actions in order to be communicated to others. Encoding is the process by which the source uses shared codes to convert concepts, thought, and feelings into a message. This is distinguishable from the encoding process in that the message can be thought of as separate to the source, while encoding is the source's internal process (Samovar and Porter, 1995). Although symbolic representation is universal, the particular words and actions selected and how these are strung together are culturally based. In encoding we select and arrange verbal and nonverbal symbols according to rules that are known and shared by the group. For example, a member of one culture might see a close friend and decide to smile, encoding her message of greeting according to the 'rules' of her language community. A member of another culture might instead place her hands in front of her chest and bow to her friend, encoding the message of greeting according to a different set of cultural rules.

Photo 2.2
People in Jordan use a nonverbal code to communicate.
Copyright © UNESCO; photographer: Jane Taylor. Used with permission.

Decoding

Decoding is the process by which the receiver, as the target of the message, converts the coded message back into meaning. It is a process of assigning meaning to codes. Decoding permits the person in the receiver's position to attach meaning to the source's behaviour. Participants in an interpersonal communication act are both sources and receivers, depending on the position they take at a particular point of the communication act. Like encoding, the interpretation of message is influenced by culture. The same coded message, therefore, may be decoded differently by different people. For example, Italians may regard animated conversation and loud laughing in public as a sign of happiness whereas a Thai woman might believe such outward display of emotions should be reserved for the privacy of one's home.

Noise

Noise interferes with the receipt of a message. All factors that interfere with information transfer can be referred to as noise. Noise can be physical, such as distracting sounds or sights, but it can also be psychological, such as having a headache or worrying about paying bills. Noise can also be semantic, such as different interpretations of a concept like 'press freedom' or 'democracy'. In human communication, the message sent may not be the message received. For example, participants in an interpersonal communication act may have different interpretations of a concept like individualism. In Western cultures, individualism is a positive concept, referring to people as independent, assertive, and goal-oriented. In Japanese culture, however, individualism is more likely to be associated with selfishness and a lack of concern for the group – a negative feature in a culture that traditionally values collectivism and a group orientation. Therefore, a message sent about this concept from a Westerner to someone from an Asian culture may not be perfectly received because of the culturally influenced semantic noise that affects the encoding and decoding of the message. When source and receiver have (even subtly) different interpretations of the same concept, the effect of communication will inevitably be affected. The more heterophilous (culturally dissimilar) the source and receiver are, the more difficult a clear understanding of each other's communication will be (Rogers and Steinfatt, 1999).

Feedback

Feedback refers to the response of the receiver after receiving the message. Feedback is information generated by the receiver and made available to the source, allowing the source to judge the communication while it is taking place. Feedback can function to adjust the attitudes and behaviours of both the source and the receiver and is yet another component that is modified by culture. For example, while members of US culture would feel comfortable saying, 'I don't agree with what you said' as a means of feedback in a conversation, members of Chinese culture would communicate the same thought by taking a deep breath.

Characteristics of communication

Just as scholars agree upon some basic components of communication, so too is there consensus on some of the key characteristics of communication.

Communication is a dynamic process

A process is anything that is on-going and continuous. Communication is a process; you cannot talk about the exact beginning or the end point of a communication exchange. David Berlo (1960) provided a particularly clear statement about communication as a process:

> If we accept the concept of process, we view events and relationships as dynamic, ongoing, ever-changing, continuous. When we label something as a process, we also mean that it does not have a beginning, an end, a fixed sequence of events. It is not static, at rest. It is moving. The ingredients within a process interact; each affects all of the others. (1960: 24)

Although individual verbal messages have definite beginning and ending points, the *overall* process of communication does not. Meanings are dynamic, continually changing as a function of earlier usages and of changes in perceptions and metaperceptions. For example, imagine you came across a classmate in a shopping centre and started exchanging ideas about an assignment due in a week's time. Your conversation would presume an earlier exchange of information (perhaps during class on the previous day) and the communication process may not necessarily end after you have said 'goodbye' to each other.

You might go home and modify your previous assignment framework as a result of talking with your classmate – a continuation of your communication in the shopping centre.

As a dynamic process, communication is more like a motion picture than a single snapshot. A word or action does not stay 'frozen' when we communicate; it is immediately replaced with another one. Communication is also dynamic because once a word or action is employed, it cannot be retracted. We probably all know the saying 'You cannot step into the same river twice', by the ancient Greek philosopher Heraclitus, who was known for his doctrine of change being central to the universe. People cannot experience exactly the same thing twice with exactly the same feeling. As an example, you may see the same film twice, but you may have some different feelings each time. You cannot recapture or repeat exactly the same communicative experience of seeing the film for the first time. Similarly, we cannot take back what we have communicated. Once you have said and done something, it is irretrievable. Once you have hurt a friend's feelings you can choose to apologize, but you cannot unsay what you said or undo what you did. A process is irreversible and unrepeatable (Cooper et al., 2007)

Communication is interactive

Communication is interactive because it requires the active participation of at least two people exchanging messages. To communicate, one has to address another person or persons. Of course, you can communicate with yourself (intrapersonal communication), but you are still interacting with an imagined self. You must therefore act as if you were two people. Human communication not only calls for response, but also is shaped in its very form and content by the anticipated response. The encoding and decoding of messages are influenced by prior interactions between communicators, and feedback influences the subsequent exchange of messages. During this interactive process, communicators may modify the content or form of their conversation. Their thoughts and feelings may also be adjusted during the interaction process. For example, a person's late arrival at a meeting might be interpreted by other attendees as bad manners and they might react with frowns or silence. However, if they then learned that this person's reason for being late was stopping to help someone injured in a car accident, their reactions would most likely change from negative to positive.

Communication is symbolic

A symbol is an arbitrarily selected and learned stimulus that represents something else. Symbols can be verbal or nonverbal, such as a sound, a mark on paper, a statue, Braille, a movement, or a painting. They are the vehicles by which the thoughts and ideas of one person can be communicated to another. Human beings are able to generate, receive, store, and manipulate symbols (Samovar and Porter, 1995). The relationship between a symbol and its referent is arbitrary. For example, there is nothing 'cowy' about the word 'cow' – the link is arbitrary. But when the written or spoken symbol for 'cow' is used, English speakers understand the referent. Words are not the actual objects or ideas, but we use these symbols to create meaning. Meaning resides in people. Imagine how difficult communication can become if two people from different cultures come together with different symbolic understandings. Not only are languages different, but the same gesture can also have different meanings. Patting a child on the head in US culture largely indicates affection; however, in Thai culture this action may be considered offensive as it is thought to damage the child's spirit, which resides in the head.

Communication is contextual

Communication is dependent on the context in which it occurs. A context is the cultural, physical, relational, and perceptual environment in which communication occurs (Neuliep, 2006). A context is also historical, and cultures that are past-oriented may emphasize this facet of context. We interact with others not in isolation but in a specific setting. Communication always occurs in a context, and the nature of communication depends in large measure on this context (Littlejohn, 1996b). Dress, language, topic selection, and the like are all adapted to contexts. For example, attending a graduation ceremony without wearing a shirt or using a profanity in the classroom is likely to be frowned upon, whereas in other contexts these behaviours are more acceptable. Similarly, how do you feel when someone keeps you waiting for 15 minutes? What do you say when you have to leave a conversation while the other person is still keen on talking? This probably depends on the context. Context influences what we communicate and how we communicate – and once again, these rules are culture bound. In Mexico, for example, children are encouraged to move around the classroom and to interact verbally and physically with their classmates; in China, it is expected that students remain in their seats and not talk to one another during class. Context influences how we communicate with others.

Photo 2.3
One of the Chinese stone lions at the entrance of Chinatown in Brisbane, symbolizing protective power.
Copyright © Shuang Liu. Used with permission.

Theory Corner

Can one not communicate?

In 1990, the *Western Journal of Speech Communication* published Michael Motley's article calling for a re-examination of Watzlawick, Beavin and Jackson's axiom that 'one cannot *not* communicate'. The main theme of Motley's article was that, on the one hand, the axiom 'one cannot not communicate' may be taken to suggest that all behaviour is communicative behaviour. On the other hand, several generally accepted postulates of communication, such as that it is interactive, encoded, and symbolic, clearly suggest that not all behaviour is communication behaviour. Following Motley's article, the journal published a forum on 'Can one not communicate?' featuring a response to Motley. The debate centred on whether communication depended more upon the *receiver*'s interpretation of behaviours or on the *sender*'s orientation to those behaviours.

This is an important debate. Certainly much communication is intentional – we will use verbal or nonverbal codes often as an attempt to modify the behaviour of other people. Thus, communication is not a random or unconscious activity, but rather a consciously planned action. People may thus be very surprised that their messages are misunderstood by members of another culture. However, other scholars propose that the concept of intentionality does not account for all the circumstances where unintentionally conveyed messages are assigned meaning, such as yawning at a meeting.

Reference

Motley, Michael T. (1990) 'On whether one can(not) not communicate: an examination via traditional communication postulates', *Western Journal of Speech Communication*, 54: 1–20.

Further reading on communication

Baraldi, Claudio (2006) 'New forms of intercultural communication in a globalized world', *International Communication Gazette*, 68 (1): 53–69.
Craig, Robert T. (1999) 'Communication theory as a field', *Communication Theory*, 9 (2): 119–161.

Models of Communication

In its broadest sense, a model is a systematic representation of an object or event in an idealized and abstract form. Models are somewhat arbitrary by nature. The act of abstracting eliminates certain details in order to focus on other factors. Communication models are representations of communication processes and characteristics; they illustrate the main components of communication and their relationships to each other. Key to the usefulness of a communication model is the degree to which it conforms to the underlying determinants of communicative behaviour (Mortensen, 1972). Communication models help us to recognize the complexity and regularity of the communication process. Just as models are a simplified expression of theory, they are the basis of communication theory. If theories need modification, so too do models.

The linear model

Early scholars conceptualized communication as transmitting information, concepts, understanding, and thought as if this were along a pipeline. According to this model, the communication process is *linear*. The most influential linear model is Claude Shannon and Warren Weaver's mathematical model of communication, presented in their book *The Mathematical Theory of Communication* (1949). Shannon developed the basic model of communication while conducting cryptographic research at Bell Laboratories during the Second World War. When the field of communication study first emerged in the 1950s and 1960s, Shannon's basic communication model was adapted to the process of human communication. As an engineer for the Bell Telephone Company, Shannon's goal was to formulate a theory to guide the efforts of engineers in finding the most efficient way of transmitting electrical signals from one location to another (Shannon and Weaver, 1949).

The model conceives of a linear and literal transmission of information from one location to another. However, Shannon and Weaver were mainly concerned with the technical problems associated with the selection and arrangement of discrete units of information (Mortensen, 1972), so their model does not apply to the semantic dimensions of language; that is, it does not address issues of meaning in message communication. Later they introduced the now widely used concept of feedback – the information that a communicator gains from others in response to his or her own verbal or nonverbal behaviour. Shannon and Weaver's (1949) linear model is, perhaps, the most widely cited communication model in existence. The mathematical theory of information principles upon which it is based is sometimes given by communication scholars as evidence of their field's scientific status (Craig, 1999).

Today, this model is known as the *transmission model* of communication. According to Shannon and Weaver, communication is a process of sending and receiving messages, or transferring information from one mind to another. The transmission model is useful as it allows us to distinguish between communication sources and receivers, and map the flow of information through systems. It also allows for messages to be conceptualized as 'containers' of meaning and for communication to be understood as an act performed in order to achieve anticipated outcomes.

In Shannon and Weaver's model, the message is like an object in a parcel. The receiver opens a parcel and can receive the message (Fiske, 1982). However,

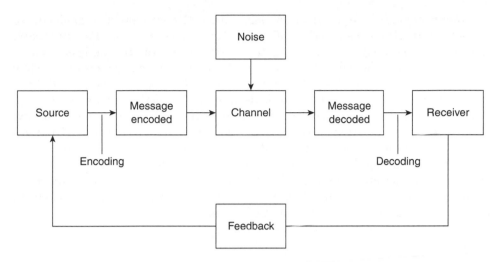

Figure 2.1: The linear model of communication

Source: Adapted from Shannon, Claude and Weaver, Warren (1949) *The Mathematical Theory of Communication*. Urbana: University of Illinois Press. p. 5.

in the actual communication process, speaking and listening are not separate activities and nor do they occur one at a time. Some scholars contend that communication should be viewed as a transactional process whereby the speaker and receiver take turns at being speaker and listener in a linear fashion. Viewing communication as a transactional process means that we can develop a mutually dependent relationship by exchanging symbols (Cooper et al., 2007). In the transactional model of communication, communicators simultaneously send and receive messages rather than acting exclusively as either senders or receivers (Pearson and Nelson, 1997). Nevertheless, communication is still viewed as a linear process in the transactional model.

The transmission model also brings benefits to the study of communication. It makes us alert both to how diverse and relative people's perspectives can be, as well as to the ever-present danger of distortion and misunderstanding in communication. A number of nonmathematical schemas have elaborated on the model (Mortensen, 1972). For example, Harold Lasswell (1948) conceived of analysing the mass media in five stages (the 5W model): 'Who', 'Says What', 'In Which Channel', 'To Whom', and 'With What Effect'. The model raises the issue of the 'effect' of the media. Lasswell's primary interest was in mass communication and propaganda. His 5W model addresses issues related to the communicator (Who), the content of the message (Says What), the means of communication (In Which Channel), the target audience (To Whom), and the media effect on audience perception and/or behaviours (With What Effect). Although the 5W model was intended to direct people to media-effects research, it has also been found to be useful when applied to other forms of communication such as persuasion. In elaborating on the transmission model, George Gerbner (1956) extended the components to include the notions of perception, reactions to a situation, and the message context.

Linear models of communication, particularly the transmission model, have encountered criticism since the 1980s and 1990s. Deetz (1994), Pearce (1989), and Shepherd (1993), among others, have argued that the transmission model is philosophically flawed, full of paradoxes, and ideologically backward. They argue that it should at least be supplemented, if not entirely replaced, by a model that conceptualizes communication as a constitutive process that produces and reproduces shared meaning. Deetz (1994: 568) points out that new disciplines 'arise when existing modes of explanation fail to provide compelling guidance for responses to a central set of new social issues'. Today, the central social issues have to do with who participates in what ways in the social processes that construct personal identities, the social order, and codes of communication. Corresponding with this perspective, therefore, is the need for a model that reflects this element of communication.

The interactive model

Wilbur Schramm (1971) was one of the first to challenge the mathematical model of Shannon and Weaver. He conceived of decoding and encoding as activities maintained simultaneously by sender and receiver; he also made provisions for a two-way interchange of messages. Even mass communication is a two-way process. For example, media organizations may examine audience ratings to gauge the design of their programmes. In this sense, both the audience and the media organization are senders and receivers. The strength of Shramm's model is that it provided the additional notion of a field of experience for the interactants. The model includes context, and postulates that a message may be different in meanings, depending on the specific context. Overall Shramm's model, while it is less linear, still only accounts for bilateral communication between two parties. Complex, multiple levels of communication across several sources are beyond its scope.

Following Shramm, communication scholars such as Everett Rogers and Thomas Steinfatt (1999) put forward a more elaborate interactive model, based on their understanding of communication as a process through which participants create and share meaning in order to reach a mutual understanding. One of the major changes human communication scholars made to Shannon's model was to emphasize the subjectivity of communication. When the source and receiver are individuals instead of machines, their perceptions, paradigms, and past experiences inevitably filter the encoding and decoding process. This subjectivity is one reason why the receiver seldom decodes a message into exactly the same meaning that the source has in mind when encoding the message. Furthermore, the participants exert mutual control over the process rather than serving as either the active source or the passive receiver. This principle of communication applies as much to intercultural communication as it does to other types of human communication exchange. Advocates of the interactive model of communication propose that communication systems operate within the confines of cultural rules and expectations: a message may have different meanings associated with it, depending on the culture in which it is sent and/or received.

In this chapter, we adopt the interactive model proposed by Rogers and Steinfatt (1999) to explain intercultural communication phenomena. This model

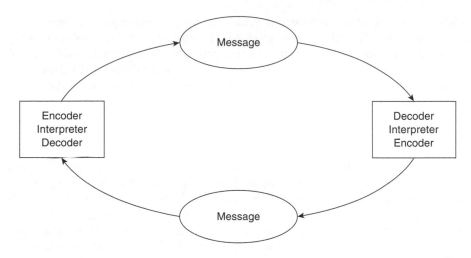

Figure 2.2: Schramm's interactive model of communication

Source: Adapted from Schramm, Wilbur (1971) 'The nature of communication between humans', in W. Schramm and D. F. Roberts (eds), *The Process and Effects of Mass Communication*. Urbana: University of Illinois Press, p. 24.

replaces the terms 'sender' and 'receiver' with 'communicator'; in addition, it incorporates communicator perception into the model. This model represents communication as a process of creating and sharing meaning in order to reach a mutual understanding. The process itself is influenced by communicators' perceptions of the context and of each other. The model also theorizes each communication action as building upon the previous experience of the communicators and as having consequences for future communication. A number of theories in intercultural communication (e.g. communication accommodation theory; see the Theory Corner later in the chapter) share the assumptions of the interactive model. The model reflects well the dynamic nature of the communication process as well as the potential influence of perceived cultural differences on the communication process.

Levels of Communication

Intrapersonal communication

Intrapersonal communication is the process of understanding and sharing meaning within the self (Pearson and Nelson, 1997). This form of communication occurs prior to and during other forms of communication as well. For example, imagine you find a pair of shoes and a coat that you would like to purchase but unfortunately your budget will only allow you to purchase one item, not both. In this case, you may engage in intrapersonal communication; that is, communicating within yourself before making a decision. In fact, intrapersonal communication is not restricted to talking to ourselves. It also

includes such activities as internal problem solving, managing internal conflict, planning for the future, and evaluating ourselves and our relationships
with others. Intrapersonal communication only involves the self, and it must
be clearly understood by the self because it is the basis for all other communication. Although intrapersonal communication is almost continuous, we
seldom focus on our communication with ourselves.

Interpersonal communication

Interpersonal communication is the process of understanding and sharing
meaning between at least two people when relatively mutual opportunities
for speaking and listening exist (Pearson and Nelson, 1997). It deals with
communication between people, usually in face-to-face settings (Littlejohn,
1996b). Like intrapersonal communication, interpersonal communication can
be used to resolve conflicts, solve a problem, share information, improve our
perception of ourselves, or fulfil such social needs as the need to belong or to
be loved. Through our interpersonal communication we are able to establish
relationships with others that include friendships and romantic relationships.
Most intercultural communication is interpersonally oriented.

Misunderstandings or misinterpretation can occur when culturally different interactants bring into the communication process their own cultural
norms governing the communication. Moreover, perceived cultural differences
alone can be a barrier to successful communication outcomes (Dodd, 1998).

Group communication

Group communication refers to purposeful communication in limited-sized
groups in which decision making or problem solving occurs (Pearson and Nelson,
1997). Group communication necessarily involves interpersonal interaction, and
most of the theories of interpersonal communication also apply at the group level
(Littlejohn, 1996b). Small group communication occurs in social organizations
such as clubs, civic groups, and church groups and in business settings such as
workgroups. Groups are an essential facet of organizational characteristics as
they become a contributing factor to the success of organizations. Managers real-
ize that there is a need for employees to work in groups in order to make use of
scarce resources and thus increase their competitive advantage. As a result of the
changes in organizational composition brought about by globalization, one of the
major challenges faced by organizations now is managing diversity in workgroups
(Ayoko, 2007). In a group, the degree of homogeneity or heterogeneity in cultural
background can have an influence on individual communication behaviour.

Organizational communication

Organizational communication occurs in large cooperative networks and
includes virtually all aspects of both interpersonal and group communication.
It encompasses concepts such as the structure and function of organizations,
human relations, communication and the process of organizing, and organizational
culture (Littlejohn, 1996b). Even if you have not given it much thought, you are

surrounded by organizations in your daily life – for example, schools, businesses, governments, healthcare systems, non-profit organizations, and churches. Organizations are understood to come into being through the communicative activities of organizational members (Weick, 1979). Organizational communication is people working together to achieve individual or collective goals (Miller, 1995). The purpose of this type of communication may range from completing a task to creating and maintaining satisfying human relationships. Communication is the key to understanding how organizations work; this sort of understanding can enhance one's ability to engage with all sorts of organizations.

Today, ethnic diversity within the workplace is changing the composition of organizations in most parts of the world, and this trend is likely to continue. Women, non-white men, ethnic minorities, and immigrants continue to join the workforce, instigating demographic changes in organizations that increasingly require people of different cultural backgrounds to work together on a daily basis. Hence, effective intercultural communication skills have become a necessity in organizational settings.

Mass communication

In its traditional sense, mass communication is the process of understanding and sharing meaning with a broad audience through mediated messages. Mass media like radio, television, and newspapers are specifically conceived and designed to reach large audiences. Many aspects of interpersonal, group, and organizational communication are reflected in the process of mass communication. What distinguishes mass communication, however, is the complexity of the process, the rules and conventions involved in understanding the communication product, and the way shared experiences are created for a mass audience.

Mass communication contributes to our economy, influences social conventions, shapes the public agenda, and brings about cultural change. The mass media have become a debating ground for our values and beliefs. New technologies of mass communication are not only changing the structure of existing mass media industries, but also forcing researchers to re-examine their old definitions (Morris and Ogan, 1996). The internet, for example, continually creates new configurations of sources, messages, and receivers. Internet communication takes many forms, from world wide web pages operated by major news organizations or usenet groups discussing hot issues, to email messages among colleagues and friends. The internet is unique in that it allows for almost anyone with access to be a source of information, unlike other media where access is limited to professional sources such as journalists. Sources of messages on the internet can range from one person in email communication to a social group or a group of professional journalists. The messages themselves can be traditional journalistic news stories created by a reporter or an editor, or stories created over a long period of time by one or many non-professional reporters such as bloggers. The receivers of or audience for these messages can also number from one to potentially millions; furthermore, they may move fluidly from a role as audience members to producers of messages. For example, in her role as an audience member, a person might read about a particular incident as it is reported on a news website. Then she may go on to write about it on her personal blog, thus assuming the role of producer. Today, every major television network and cable news service provides information content from servers on the world wide web, and many news services exist only on the internet.

Communication and Culture

Photo 2.4
The internet has become an inseparable part of people's life; here men from Koutiala, Mali, take computer courses.
Copyright © UNESCO; photographer: Serge Daniel. Used with permission.

Culture is a code we learn and share, and learning and sharing require communication (Jandt, 2007). Culture and communication, therefore, mutually influence one another, producing different behavioural patterns in different contexts. Culture influences how we adapt and learn, our perception of reality, language patterns, habits, customs, expectations, norms, and roles – in other words, it shapes what we do, how we look, what we say, and how we say it. Communication and culture are inseparable. One implication of this insight, as Dodd (1998) has noted, is that culture generates symbols, rituals, customs, and formats. In Western cultures, the symbols for success include an individual's acquisition of degrees, promotions, certificates, material objects, and technology. In other cultures, the achievements of the primary group are more important than those of individuals. Cultural misunderstandings occur when we fail to match symbols and a communication system to a culture (Dodd, 1998).

Here is an example. As a cultural practice of modesty, a Chinese technician in a joint venture factory might express some doubt over how to fix a machine breakdown when interacting with his American manager who is supposed to be more knowledgeable than the technician; however, the technician's hesitation might be (mis)interpreted by his American manager as a lack of confidence or ability. Many cultural imprints are subtle and elusive, if not beyond conscious recognition, but we tend to become more aware of the cultural rules governing our behaviour when we interact with culturally different others. Communication involves sharing, like sharing a meal or experience – what is shared and understood in the communication process is meaning. Difficulties may arise when we try to share meaning with people whose communication behaviours are governed by cultural rules that are different from our own.

The intricate link between culture and communication can be illustrated in a number of ways. In the first place, *culture teaches us significant rules, rituals and procedures*, such as our orientation towards time, the perceived degree of power distance, our tolerance of uncertainty, how to dress, when and what to eat, and how to work. The overall process of learning these things is called socialization, which refers to the process by which we develop a sense of proper and improper behaviour and communication within the confines of those cultural rules (Dodd, 1998). Think of one of many thousands of rules your culture or your family may have taught you. As a young child, when you went to dinner at a friend's house, your mother probably told you that before you leave, you should thank the hostess and say the food was very nice and you enjoyed it very much. In this way, you consciously learned the rule of politeness. Politeness however may involve very different rules: in more traditional homes within Slovenia (part of the former Yugoslavia), guests are greeted with bread and salt to show that they are part of the family. What is polite or rude or expected all fall under the rubric of rules, rituals, and procedures taught by our culture. These rules are very important: they are the means by which we determine inclusion and self-worth and they help to define the boundaries between 'us' and 'them'.

Theory Corner

Communication accommodation theory

Communication accommodation theory was developed in the context of intercultural communication in the 1970s (Gallois et al., 2005). The theory is based on three general assumptions: 1) interactions are embedded in a socio-historical context; 2) communication is about both exchanges of referential meaning and the negotiation of personal and social identities; and 3) interactants achieve these functions of communication by accommodating their communicative behaviour, through language, paralanguage, discourse, and non-linguistic moves, to their perception of the other's individual and group characteristics. Accommodation is the process through which interactants regulate their communication. Since its development three decades ago, this theory has stood the test of time and is still generating research up to the present day.

Reference

Gallois, Cindy; Ogay, Tania and Giles, Howard (2005) 'Communication accommodation theory: a look back and a look ahead', in W.B. Gudykunst (ed.), *Theorizing about Intercultural Communication*. Thousand Oaks, CA: SAGE. pp. 121–148.

Further reading on communication and culture

Halualani, Rona T. (2008) 'How do multicultural university students define and make sense of intercultural contact? A qualitative study', *International Journal of Intercultural Relations*, 32: 1–16.

Midooka, Kiyoshi (1990) 'Characteristics of Japanese-style communication', *Media, Culture & Society*, 12: 477–489.

More than simply determining and teaching the 'rules', *culture cultivates and reinforces beliefs and values*. Our core understanding of the world is taught in a cultural context. Consequently, we develop culturally reinforced approaches to thoughts and beliefs about the world. These beliefs and values are reflected in our communication behaviours. For example, Australian culture teaches people the values of a 'fair go' – independence, privacy, competition, 'mateship', and directness. 'Fair enough' – a common Australian expression – reveals the value placed on equality in this specific cultural context. In reflecting these values, the Australian communication style tends to be more direct. For example, it is common for two people to confront each other to 'sort things out' in the instance of interpersonal conflict. In an Asian context, however, a third party might be brought in to act as an intermediary to resolve conflict. This communication style avoids a direct confrontation and losing face and reflects the values of harmony, non-competitiveness, and loyalty to superiors in Asian culture. Both the Asian and Australian approaches are valid within their cultural context and serve to highlight the impact of cultural beliefs and values on communication behaviour.

Furthermore, *culture teaches us how to develop relationships with others*. Any communication event establishes a certain relationship. Initiating and maintaining relationships with others is one of the most necessary and challenging functions of human survival. From our relationships with others we receive feedback that we use to assess ourselves. The relationships formed in a cultural context generate a dynamic of roles and expectations. Where to stand, how far to stand from each other, when to talk to others, when to visit, when to call/not to call people at home, and the level of formality in language are all highly influenced by the nature of the relationship between communicators. According to Yum (1988), East Asian cultures tend to foster a long-term interpersonal relationship characterized by complementary social reciprocity (see Chapter 9). In this type of relationship, people always feel indebted to others. For example, the Chinese saying 'to return a drop of kindness with a fountain of kindness' indicates how important it is for someone to return a favour in a social interaction. On the other hand, North American culture does not treat commitments or obligations as important elements in interpersonal relationship development as do East Asian cultures. Instead, they consider complementary relationships as a threat to freedom or autonomy. Hence, it is common to see Westerners split the bill when having a dinner together with friends.

Our verbal and nonverbal behaviours reflect our cultural imprints. Each culture expects a particular communication style. Features such as loudness, pitch, rate, turn taking, and gestures characterize communication behaviours and vary considerably across cultures. If you buy clothes from a market stall in Hong Kong, you have to be prepared to engage in intensive bargaining – this must be loud and hard. Hence, the stereotypical perception is that Asians are good at haggling over prices. In the United States it would seem unusual to see two male friends kissing in public; in Peru this would be perceived as commonplace. Communication shows us that we are alike and we are different. We are similar in that each of us experiences the same feelings such as anger, joy, sadness, and anxiety. However, *how* we display those feelings is governed by culture. In this respect, our unique cultural experiences and habits keep us apart. Communication is subjective, so symbols do not mean the same thing to every person. Misunderstandings occur because we do not understand each other's cultural rules governing communication behaviour.

Summary

This chapter explored different definitions of human communication and examined its components and characteristics. We explained communication models – linear and interactive – and discussed their theoretical underpinnings. The interactive model is more applicable in the context of intercultural communication. The chapter concluded by identifying different levels of communication and the influence of culture on communication. Finding a single definition for the multifaceted concept of communication is difficult, if not impossible. However, scholars do tend to agree on some basic components of communication and its characteristics. Communication involves people, messages, channels, encoding, decoding, feedback, and noise. People are the sources and receivers (or encoders and decoders) of messages. Communication occurs in a particular context which potentially affects every element of the communication process.

Intercultural communication can occur at different levels, from interpersonal, to group, organizational, and mass communication. Communication is the vehicle by which people initiate, maintain, and terminate their relationships with others. Although you may spend a great deal of your time engaging in communication, you may still find that you do not communicate as successfully as you might wish. Messages are subject to interpretation and, hence, to distorted meanings. Our past experience becomes an inventory consisting of values, sets of expectations, and preconceptions about the consequences of acting one way or another. The receiver's background of experience and learning may differ enough from that of the source to produce significantly different perceptions and evaluations of the topic under discussion. Such differences form a basic barrier to communication. The key to successful intercultural communication is to recognize differences and adjust our communication behaviour according to context and communicators.

Case Study:
Hanging out in the public square

In order to communicate with fellow citizens, we need to have access to different public spaces. The term 'public' comes from the Latin root *publicus*, usually denoting something which belongs to the community. Each culture creates its own public spaces, and public squares, markets, coffee shops, and so on have historically provided the opportunity to share information, convey news, and engage in communication. Hannah Arendt (1958) argues that there is a need for the existence of a common ground where people can relate to each other and physically gather together. What she emphasizes as an explicitly formed space is first of all the *space of communication* – a space in which one can be seen and heard.

An example of a space of communication is that of the Turkish public bath, known as a *hamam*. This is the Middle Eastern version of a steam bath, much like what many Westerners know as a sauna. The *hamam* has an important role in the cultures of the Middle East, serving as a place for gathering, communicating, ritual cleansing, and even as educational and architectural institutions. *Hamams* usually have three rooms: the grand steamy hot room (*caldarium*) for steam-soaking and massage, the warm room (*tepidarium*) for washing with soap and water, and the cool room for resting or napping after the bath with a cup of Turkish coffee or a cup of tea. Men and women use separate sections of a *hamam* and enjoy spending time in these public spaces in order to get to know each other, debate, and relax. In Turkish culture, *hamams* are used for social contact and sometimes for financial and cultural transactions. However, many Western women, upon experiencing *hamams* for the first time, express their shock when they have to walk in their underwear in front of other naked women, as well as bathe for several hours.

Different medieval marketplaces also provide a setting for contact among people, a space devoted equally to commerce and culture, a venue for festivals and fairs and the exchange of books and pamphlets. Over the past two hundred years, market squares have been replaced by commercial streets (Judd, 1995). Today, major cities incorporate spaces of consumption with an emphasis also on spaces of exchange and commerce (Lefebvre, 1991). Shopping malls are the public spaces that we occupy most frequently today – these are the spaces where we meet and encounter each other. As critics point out, we not only shop but also communicate in these spaces (Sennett, 1992).

Another example of an ideal public space for communication is the public square of ancient Greece. Arendt (1958) writes that public spaces depend on public habits, manners, and talents: the ability to welcome strangers and to communicate with others. She argues that this was precisely the case in ancient Greece, that a clear line between public and private realms could be observed in the difference between the *polis* (the sphere where citizens would debate the public affairs, a kind of city-state) and *oikos* (the private sphere of households).

The *agora*, for example, was a big public square as well as a marketplace where the Athenians gathered to walk and chat. It was here that they would discuss and communicate about important public issues; thus, openness, accountability, and accessibility were the conditions for the Athenian urban architecture. Later, the ability to see and hear other people on an equal basis became a new ordering principle: the merchants' quarter was located around the *agora*. It was the place where theatres emerged and where the works of Euripides, Sophocles, and Aeschylus were written and performed. The *agoras* contributed to the development of philosophy – Socrates, Plato, and Aristotle were among the philosophers who would frequently give public lectures – and from this other disciplines emerged, such as rhetoric and history. In public life at this time, there was a great concern with honour and reputation that was expressed in a vital and vibrant public communication in which all citizens were expected to participate. This was the assembly that established the laws of the land.

References for case study

Arendt, Hannah (1958) *The Human Condition*. Chicago: University of Chicago Press.
Judd, Dennis R. (1995) 'The rise of the new walled cities', in H. Liggett and D.C. Perry (eds), *Spatial Practices*. London: SAGE. pp.144–167.
Lefebvre, Henri (1991) *The Production of Space*. London: Blackwell.
Sennett, Richard (1978/1992) *The Fall of Public Man*. New York: Norton.

Questions for discussion

1 What are some of the public spaces that exist in different cultures where people can meet and communicate?
2 What is a *hamam* and how is it being used? Do you have similar facilities in your culture?
3 How would you describe a Greek *polis*?
4 Do you think shopping malls are public spaces? Why?
5 What are the characteristics of the ancient Greek public square? Do we still have such public squares today? How could the ancient Greek public square be compared to the internet forum today?

Key Terms

channel;
classical rhetorical theory;
communication;
communication accommodation theory;
decoding;
encoding;

feedback;
group communication;
interactive model;
interpersonal communication;
intrapersonal communication;

mass communication;
noise;
organizational communication;
receiver;
source;
transmission model

Further Reading

Communication

Baraldi, Claudio (2006) 'New forms of intercultural communication in a globalized world', *International Communication Gazette*, 68 (1): 53–69.
Craig, Robert T. (1999) 'Communication theory as a field', *Communication Theory*, 9 (2): 119–161.

Ephratt, Michal (2008) 'The functions of silence', *Journal of Pragmatics*, 40 (11): 1909–1938.

Gallois, Cindy; Ogay, Tania and Giles, Howard (2005) 'Communication accommodation theory: a look back and a look ahead', in W.B. Gudykunst (ed.), *Theorizing about Intercultural Communication*. Thousand Oaks, CA: SAGE. pp. 121–148.

Motley, Michael T. (1990) 'On whether one can(not) not communicate: an examination via traditional communication postulates', *Western Journal of Speech Communication*, 54: 1–20.

Communication models

Bowman, Joel and Targowski, Andrew (1987) 'Modelling the communication process: the map is not the territory', *Journal of Business Communication*, 24 (4): 21–34.

Gumpert, Gary and Drucker, Marie (1999) 'Models, metaphors, and other scholarly meanderings: renovating models of communication', *New Jersey Journal of Communication*, 7 (1): 9–22.

Communication and culture

Bovillain, Nancy (2008) *Language, Culture and Communication: The Meaning of Messages* (5th edn). Upper Saddle River, NJ: Pearson/Prentice Hall.

Halualani, Rona T. (2008) 'How do multicultural university students define and make sense of intercultural contact? A qualitative study', *International Journal of Intercultural Relations*, 32: 1–16.

Midooka, Kiyoshi (1990) 'Characteristics of Japanese-style communication', *Media, Culture & Society*, 12: 477–489.

Rhetoric and discourse

Chatman, Seymour (1978) *Story and Discourse: Narrative Structure in Fiction and Film*. Ithaca, NY: Cornell University Press.

3

Understanding Culture

Culture is the name for what people are interested in, their thoughts, their models, the books they read and the speeches they hear, their table-talk, gossip, controversies, historical sense and scientific training, the value they appreciate, the quality of life they admire. All communities have a culture. It is the climate of their civilization.

Walter Lippmann, American journalist and sociologist, 1889–1974

Learning Objectives

At the end of this chapter, you should be able to:

• Recognize the multifaceted nature of culture.
• Identify different components and characteristics of culture.
• Define different types of subcultures.
• Appreciate and value cultural diversity.

The Pervasive Nature of Culture

The word 'culture' originated from the Latin word *cultura*, which in turn is from the verb *colere*, denoting 'to till' (as in till the soil or land). In its original meaning, therefore, culture is a process related to the tending of something, such as crops or animals. The word shares its etymology with modern English words such as agriculture, cultivate, and colony. Eventually, the term was extended to incorporate ideas related to the human mind and a state of being 'cultivated'. Generally, the study of culture ranges from aspects that are associated with the arts to the study of the entire system of meanings and the way of life of a society. As Edward T. Hall (1966: x) stated, culture is 'those deep, common, unstated experiences which members of a given culture share, communicate without knowing, and which form the backdrop against which all other events are judged'. Culture fosters a sense of shared identity and solidarity among its group members. Being a member of a cultural group implies that you have been nurtured by its core values and understand what constitutes 'desirable' and 'undesirable' behaviours in that particular system (Ting-Toomey and Chung, 2005). While different people might have different norms for judging behaviours in a particular cultural environment, common to all people is that they see their world through cultural glasses – we all view the world through culturally tinted lenses and we rarely take off these cultural glasses.

Basically, any process or product of human activity can be named as 'culture'. In this general sense, culture consists of a group or community's traditions, customs, norms, beliefs, values, and thought patterns passed down from generation to generation. This includes food, music, language, artifacts, family, organization, politics, stories, the production and distribution of goods, and so on. Culture is not instinctive or innate; culture is learned. As discussed in the previous chapters, communication and culture are inseparable. To study intercultural communication without exploring culture is like studying physics without exploring matter. This chapter discusses the pervasive nature of culture and explores the relationship between culture and communication. Components and characteristics of culture are identified, and various subcultures are examined. The chapter concludes by highlighting the importance of valuing cultural diversity in intercultural communication.

Definitions and Components of Culture

For decades, scholars across the academic spectrum have attempted to define culture. Almost 200 definitions can be located, each attempting to delineate the boundaries and inclusions of the concept by drawing upon such synonymous ideas as community, minorities, social groups, social class, nationalities, geographic units, societies, and so on. This highlights the multifaceted nature of the term.

Defining culture

Scholars in philosophy, anthropology, cultural studies, and communication, among many others, have grappled with and attempted to define culture. For example, the Italian philosopher Antonio Gramsci (2000) conceptualized culture as the creative meaning-making process, constantly being produced and reproduced by multiple groups. He conceived of culture as the means by which people make sense of their social world and represent their active relation to the wider social and material world. Alternatively, American anthropologist Clifford Geertz (1973) defined culture as a web that people themselves have spun. He further proposed that 'culture is the fabric of meanings in terms of which human beings interpret their experience and guide their action' (p.145). There are three aspects to Geertz's 'web' metaphor: firstly, as a web, culture both confines members to their social reality and facilitates their functioning in this reality; secondly, culture is both a product and a process; and thirdly, culture provides contexts for behaviour. Raymond Williams (1989), a British cultural studies scholar, argues that culture is the product of individuals' whole committed personal and social experience; it is the product of a whole people and offers individual meanings. Rogers and Steinfatt (1999: 79) defined culture as 'the total way of life of a people, composed of their learned and shared behaviour patterns, values, norms, and material objects'. While Gramsci, Geertz, Williams, and Rogers and Steinfatt represent only a small number of the scholars who have attempted to define culture, they serve to illustrate the many ways in which culture has been conceptualized across disciplines.

Although definitions of culture vary across different fields, scholars agree that culture is pervasive in human life and governs people's behaviours. Building on this consensus about culture, this chapter defines *culture* as the particular way of life of a group of people, comprising the deposit of knowledge, experience, beliefs, values, traditions, religion, notions of time, roles, spatial relations, worldviews, material objects, and geographic territory. This definition emphasizes the pervasive nature of culture; it also confirms that culture is a process as well as a product of communication. Our attitudes towards work and age, ethical standards, clothing, artistic expressions, rituals and customs, beliefs about health, the concept of time, social and political institutions, religious practices, and even our superstitions, are all reflections of culture. As Dodd (1998: 37) argued, 'Culture is like the luggage we carry', and when we open each pocket of our cultural suitcase, we explore an interrelated set of group identities, beliefs, values, activities, rules and customs, institutions, and communication patterns arising from our daily needs.

Components of culture

Dodd (1998) grouped cultural components into three levels, as shown in the model in Figure 3.1. The inner core of culture is made up of history, identity, beliefs, values, and worldviews; the intermediate layer consists of activities as cultural manifestations, such as roles, rules, rituals, customs, communication patterns, and artistic expressions; the outer layer involves the larger cultural system and includes economic, health, educational, religious, family, and political systems.

The inner core of culture

The inner core of culture consists of the history, identity, beliefs and values, and worldviews of a cultural group (Dodd, 1998). Every culture has a history that is the deposit and carrier of cultural heritage and development. Totems, archives, architecture, ancient languages, and paintings are just some of the ways in which a culture records and expresses its heritage and tradition. The power of origin and heritage demonstrates the continuity of a culture. Culture is passed on from generation to generation, binding its members

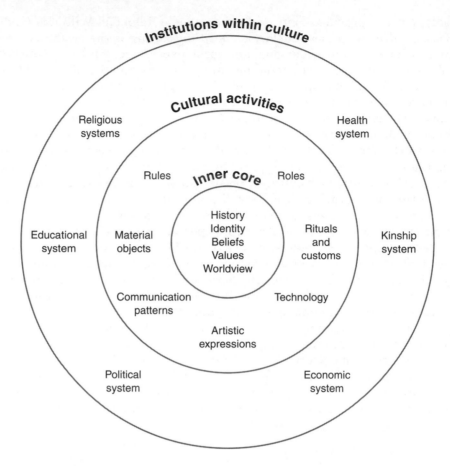

Figure 3.1: A model of culture

Source: Adapted from Dodd, Carley H. (1998) *Dynamics of Intercultural Communication*, (5th edn). Boston, MA: McGraw-Hill. p. 38.

together and providing a sense of *identity*. The multifaceted nature of our identity (or, more appropriately, identities) is experienced and negotiated by many of us in everyday life. Hardly a day passes when we do not come across an identity issue being (re)addressed in a newspaper article, a radio show, a TV programme, or in a conversation with a friend. For example, you probably know the popular saying, 'You are what you eat'. Nowadays, food from many different cultures is available to us, and we can ask how the consumption of 'foreign' food might affect our sense of cultural identity. Daily life and events unfold within an entire spectrum of identities, including our ethnic, national, gender, racial, social, corporate, professional, and sexual identities. Identity gives us a location in the world and reflects the link between us and the society in which we live.

Theory Corner

Conceptualizing identity

The concept of *identity* has been examined extensively from both psychological and sociological perspectives. Erik Erikson (1968), a post-Freudian psychologist working in the USA, states that identity has two forms: identity and difference. The first is identity as a self-differentiation or self-awareness and a sense of personal continuity. The second is the identity that derives from a primary relationship, where identity is connected with a differentiation of the self from the other – this leads to an awareness of one's personal distinctiveness.

Manuel Castells (1997), a well-known sociologist, writes that as communication networks become central to economies and societies, identity becomes an organizing principle of social action in the emerging information society. Castells argues that identities are plural and such a plurality is a source of stress and contradiction in both self-representation and social action. Importantly, identity should be distinguished from what sociologists have traditionally called roles.

References

Castells, Manuel (1997) *The Power of Identity*. Oxford: Blackwell.
Erikson, Erik (1968) 'Identity, Psychological', in *International Encyclopaedia of the Social Sciences*, 7. New York: Macmillan. pp. 46–48.

Further reading on identity

Shore, Chris and Black, Annabel (1994) 'Citizens' Europe and the construction of European identity', in V.A. Goddard, J.R. Llobera and C. Shore (eds), *The Anthropology of Europe: Identity and Boundaries in Conflict*. Oxford and Providence, RI: Berg. pp. 275–298.

It is generally agreed that the term 'identity' refers primarily to a person's subjective experience of her- or himself in relation to the world, and it should, therefore, be differentiated from concepts like 'character' or 'personality'. While one can share character traits with many people, this sharing does not require any active engagement of our being. On the other hand, sharing an identity implies that we actively engage part of our being in order to identify with a certain group. This notion of active engagement indicates that one's identity is formed through *cultural* processes, which are in turn determined by a culture's structures. People belonging to the same cultural group share a common history and cultural identity (see Chapter 8).

Culture is captured for individual human beings as beliefs and values. Each culture has a window through which its members perceive reality and other people. *Beliefs* are an individual's representations of reality viewed through that cultural window. Some beliefs are seen as very likely to be true; others are seen as less probable. People might believe one person is more intelligent than another, or that eating carrots is good for your eyesight. When a belief is held by most members of a culture, it is known as a cultural belief. For example, most Chinese people believe having the number '8' appearing in their phone number symbolizes prosperity, and having the number '6' symbolizes smoothness; thus having both the number '8' and '6' suggests a smooth path to prosperity. Another example of a cultural belief, from Slovenian culture, is where people hang horseshoes over their doors to encourage positive spirits and good luck.

Cultures also have concepts of ultimate significance and of long-term importance, known as *values*, that go beyond statements of truth. Values are what people who share a culture regard as good or bad; they tell the cultural group members how to judge good or bad, right or wrong. Values enshrine within a culture what is worth fighting for, what is worth sacrificing, what should be protected, and what should be given up. Cultural values involve judgments and so values differ across cultures. For example, US American culture teaches people the values of independence, privacy, and competition. Asian culture teaches people the values of harmony, reciprocity, non-competitiveness, loyalty to superiors, and thrift. Hierarchy is valued in Japanese culture while equality is treasured in the USA. Our core understanding of good and evil, right and wrong, true and false, is taught in a cultural context.

Consequently, members of a cultural group share thoughts and beliefs about the world. A culture's belief about nature and the working of the universe is called a *worldview*. Understanding the worldview of a culture can help predict its members' thoughts and behavioural patterns. For example, according to the Christian understanding of human nature, the first humans were created in the image of God. *Genesis* declares that God said, 'Let us make [humans] in our image, in our likeness and let them rule over the fish of the sea and the birds of the air, over the livestock, over all earth, and over all the creatures that move along the ground.' In Japanese Shinto (an ancient Japanese religion), the gods, called *Kami* (deities), take the form of wind, rain, mountains, trees, rivers, and fertility. Nature is sacred: to be in contact with nature is to be close to the gods; hence, natural objects are worshipped as sacred spirits. Believers of Shinto also respect animals as messengers of the gods. From the above examples we can see that a worldview is a belief system about the nature of the universe, its perceived effect on human behaviour, and human place in the universe (Dodd, 1998).

The intermediate layer of culture

The intermediate layer of culture is connected to the inner core, but has more of a capacity to change. This layer consists of activities as manifestations of culture. According to Dodd (1998), cultural activities can be expressed in many ways: technology, material objects, roles, rules, rituals, customs, communication patterns, and artistic expressions. The rituals and customs people observe and the festivals people celebrate reflect the culture. The celebration of Queen's Day in the Netherlands on 30 April every year reinforces the belief that the Dutch Queen is an embodiment of hope and unity in times of war, adversity, and natural disaster. In a different arena, the power of football (soccer) in many countries, starting in Europe and South America, to symbolize a core value of pride in the nation is astonishing – one only need look at the TV viewing parties and celebrations around the Football World Cup to understand this.

Artworks are cultural products. In many paintings by Western artists humans tend to be portrayed as the focal point, whereas in paintings produced by Eastern artists such as those in China, natural scenes or animals are more likely to be the centre of the painting. This reflects the importance and power of nature in the Chinese culture, versus the power of human agency and action in Western European and American culture. In addition to artwork, technology is a very salient feature of a culture, reflected in its transportation, communication, food, clothing, shelter, and tools. What people wear, how they eat and prepare food, the kinds of tools they use for work – all of this reflects the culture of a particular group. As Everett Rogers (1995) states, technology has form (what it is or how it looks), function (what it does and how it works), and meaning (what it represents).

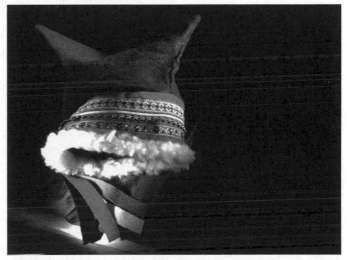

Photo 3.1
The traditional hat of the Sami people – an indigenous group of the Fennoscandian area, more or less disconnected from the European civilization.
Copyright © Jaka Polutnik. Used with permission.

Theory Corner

Popular culture and folk culture

Popular culture refers to products and styles of human expression developed from ordinary people (Lull, 2000). It stands in contrast to what early European scholars referred to as 'high' or elite culture. Popular culture can include such cultural

(Continued)

products as music, talk shows, soap operas, cooking, clothing, consumption, and the many facets of entertainment such as sports and literature. The recognition that a 'pop' culture icon such as Madonna might in fact provide a rich repository of US society's attitudes, values, practices, and beliefs has led to the emergence of popular cultural studies as a discipline.

Folk culture is the localized lifestyle of culture. It is usually handed down through oral tradition. Most anthropologists who study folk cultures see culture as a set of behaviours, patterns of thought, and beliefs. Geertz (1973) writes that a local or a folk culture is comprised of the taken-for-granted and repetitive nature of the everyday culture of which individuals have mastery. Elements of folk culture are often imbued with a sense of place. They carry strong connotations of their original site of creation, even when they are moved to a foreign locale. Handmade patchwork quilts are one example of American folk culture. Folk culture often informs popular culture and even filters into high culture. The minuet dance of European court society, for example, is based on a peasant dance. The consciously self-centred culture of the Amish has been portrayed for comic value in Hollywood films and media reality shows. Similarly, the archetypal costume of the cowboy has been reinvented in gleaming silver by disco dancers.

References

Geertz, Clifford (1973) *The Interpretation of Cultures*. New York: Basic.

Lull, James (2000) *Media, Communication, Culture: A Global Perspective* (2nd edn). New York: Columbia University Press.

Further reading on popular and folk culture

Dyson, Kenneth (1996) 'On being passionate about standards: promoting the voice of aesthetics in broadcasting and multimedia', in K. Dyson and W. Homolka (eds), *Culture First! Promoting Standards in the New Media Age*. New York: Cassell. pp. 129–170.

What we do in a cultural context forms relationships with others; these relationships generate a dynamic of roles and expectations. The behavioural norms associated with these roles and expectations are defined by culture. For example, Ghanaian culture dictates that people address elderly men as 'grandfather', whilst in Japanese culture it is considered respectful for people of a junior status to bow to people of a senior status when greeting them. The overall process of learning these cultural rules is called socialization, which is the lifelong process by which people develop a sense of proper and improper behaviour within their culture.

As well as influencing roles, rules, norms, customs, and rituals, each culture expects particular communication patterns. Communication behaviours such as turn taking, gestures, loudness, directness, and rate are all expected to conform to a culture's expectations. In this, the contrasts between cultures are striking. In China, children are expected to address the friends of their parents as 'aunt' or 'uncle' to show they are seen as a member of the family. In Australia and many other Western countries, children often address adults by their first name to show equality. In Japanese culture, indirectness in conversation is valued as it functions to preserve harmony between the speakers; in North America 'speaking your mind' is preferred in an interpersonal communication act. Intercultural misunderstandings often occur because we do not understand the cultural rules governing the communication behaviour of others.

Not only verbal but also nonverbal communication behaviour is influenced by culture. Our posture, gestures, and concepts of time and space also influence communication. In Western countries people view time with great precision, and punctuality is a cultural expectation. People make an appointment or reservation to see a doctor, go to a hairdresser, or dine in a restaurant. Being late is regarded as bad manners. For example, the Dutch and Germans are very punctual, and being even five minutes late for an appointment is considered inappropriate – if anything, people arrive a minute or two early as a sign of respect. Generally speaking, in Africa, Malaysia, or Latin America, however, people are deliberately a little late, in order not to disturb their hosts' other activities. Meetings may not start until everyone arrives. A doctor may schedule all patients for the 8:00am appointment, and it is the patients' responsibility to work out among themselves whose turn it is to see the doctor. There are core cultural values in both these time orientations – and people with one orientation tend to think that those with the other are lazy or over-punctual. Both culture and communication, thus, are a way of living and a whole social process. The intermediate level of culture reflects our definitions of social and cultural rules as well as our communication patterns.

Theory Corner

Cultural theorists

Biological theories, inspired by the work of Charles Darwin, in most cases construe any human behaviour as physical processes that have developed as an inherent part of human evolution. Biological theories posit humans as merely 'biological species', underplaying the significance of culture. Cultural theorists, on the other hand, understand culture as a powerful force that affects our behaviour and the ways we experience the world. Culture always stands as the opposite of nature. It is not unified or one-dimensional, but fragmented and multi-dimensional. According to Bourdieu (1977), we shape a culture in accordance with its dominant economic

(Continued)

and political system. For example, the collapse of systems such as communism at the end of the 1980s brought incredible transformations to Eastern European cultures, and with that, their way of life. If 'communist culture' propagated solidarity, a one-party political system, state property, and working hard, the new system, called liberal-democratic, fostered a completely different culture – one that mobilized mostly around private property, individualism, consumption, and entertainment.

Reference

Bourdieu, Pierre (1977) *Outline of a Theory and Practice*. Cambridge: Cambridge University Press.

Further reading on culture

Hall, Stuart (1984) 'The culture gap', *Marxism Today*, 28: 18 015–23.
Ladegaard, Hans J. (2007) 'A global corporation', *Journal of Intercultural Communication Research*, 36 (2): 139–163.

The outer layer of culture

The outer layer involves the *institutions of a culture* (Dodd, 1998). Like the intermediate layer, elements of this layer of culture are also tied to the inner core and remain an area for flexibility and change. According to Dodd, institutions are the formalized systems including religion, economy, politics, family, healthcare, and education. Those systems are products of culture.

Religion refers to any system of thought that provides answers to the big question of life, death, and of life beyond death. According to Dodd (1998), religious systems involve beliefs, ceremonies, worship, norms of respect, and spiritual issues. Religion supplies maps for individuals in their journeys towards belief and faith. For example, the 'Abrahamic' faiths (Judaism, Islam, and Christianity) are called monotheistic religions – meaning that each believes in only one God. Hindus tend to be both monotheistic and polytheistic. Buddhism offers the possibility for personal self-realization, and the Buddha is considered a teacher, not a god. In Australia Aborigines value integrated communities, based on beliefs about connections between people and the environment including land and animals. In modern societies, religion is sometimes used to explain events in life, including death, accidents, illness, and even natural disasters. In this sense religion and culture are intertwined. According to the Pew Research Report (2008), in Indonesia, Tanzania, Pakistan, and Nigeria, nine out of ten people acknowledge that religion is very important, and religion is central to the lives of Muslims. Knowledge of religious practices, such as fasting in the month of Ramadan, the annual pilgrimage to the holy places of Mecca, and Friday prayers, can help one to understand a particular culture and avoid cultural mistakes and prejudice. Like culture, however, no religion is superior or inferior to any other.

In addition to religious systems, the economic system of a society reflects its culture. In some remote villages people still use barter trade for business transactions, whereas in more developed regions people are more likely to use cash or a credit card to make a purchase. The development of an economy influences family structure. In cultures where an economic need exists for labour, a marriage model of polygamy (usually one husband with two or more wives) may become institutionalized and acceptable; in other cultures, polygamy is not accepted and only monogamy (one husband with one wife) is legal.

Cultural influences are also reflected in family size. In Western countries, the nuclear family (a unit referring to a father, mother, and siblings) is the major family structure. In other cultures the extended family – which includes the nuclear family and grandparents, uncles and aunts, cousins, and so on – is valued and more likely to be the norm. Although it may vary in expression, the relationship between the economic system, culture, and family system is intrinsic to all cultures.

Political, health, and educational systems are also elements of culture, and they vary across cultures. For example, some countries have a one-party system (communist regimes) whereas others have two or more parties (democratic regimes) governing a country. In some cultures religion and politics are separate, whereas in other cultures they are interrelated – the religious leader may also be a political figure. For example, the Roman Catholic Pope, as leader of his church, holds full legal, executive, and judicial power in its seat, the Vatican City. On the one hand, religion offers the possibility of peace and unites people. On the other hand, religion can play a divisive role when different ethnic groups or nations struggle over resources. In addition, people's beliefs about health and medical care are also shaped by culture. Some societies rely on Western medicine to cure illness; others have more faith in traditional herbal medicine; and still others believe praying is a way to relieve pain and illness. Similarly, a society's educational system also reflects its culture. In some Asian cultures like that of Malaysia, Singapore, or Hong Kong, memorization or rote learning is the preferred pedagogy, whereas in Anglo-Saxon cultures the skills of creative thinking and problem solving are more valued in the classroom. The religion a society practices, the festivals a country observes, the events a

Photo 3.2
The Vatican City in Rome is one of the most sacred places for Christians and attests to a great history.
Copyright © Shuang Liu. Used with permission.

people celebrate, healthcare practice, and the education system can all reveal something about the culture of a group or nation. The outer layer of cultural systems includes numerous aspects of a culture's ultimate survival in ways that are accepted and often sanctioned by law. They are fundamental to the economic, legal, social, and spiritual nature of a culture (Dodd, 1998).

Characteristics of Culture

As we have already seen, culture manifests itself at three levels: inner core, cultural activities, and institutions. We now turn to discuss some important characteristics of culture.

Culture is holistic

Until this point, we have isolated components of culture for ease of description and explanation. In reality, culture functions as an integrated and complex whole. While the various parts of culture are interrelated (Samovar and Porter, 1995), the whole is more than simply the sum of these interconnected parts. As Edward Hall (1977: 13–14) said, 'You touch a culture in one place and everything else is affected.' You might, for example, explore a specific cultural formation, such as the Hindu Annaprasanam, a festive event to celebrate the first birthday of a child. During the Annaprasanam the baby is given a mixture of rice, sugar, and milk, which is generally his or her first solid food after a year's worth of liquid diet. All aspects of the event are interrelated and must be interpreted as a whole – none makes sense on its own.

Another example is the Japanese tea ritual. *Chadō*, or the 'Way of Tea', is a key part of Japanese culture. This tea ritual is a detailed procedure, takes years to learn, and can take up to four hours to perform. In 2002, officials at Japan's National Space Development Agency declared a plan to include a tea room in their section of the International Space Station. Even when confronted with restrictions on time and space, they preferred to include the tea ritual in order to make a symbolic statement about what was most important to them as a culture. The aim of the tea ceremony is to achieve inner peace and harmony, which are valued in Japanese culture. It also aims to open the mind in preparation for meditation (Anderson, 1987). Thus, the tea ritual must be interpreted as an integral part of the whole cultural system.

Culture is learned

Culture is not inborn or biological. The Dutch psychologist and sociologist Geert Hofstede (1991: 32) writes that every person 'carries within him or herself patterns of thinking, feeling, and potential acting which were learned throughout his or her lifetime. Much of these patterns are acquired in early childhood, because at that time a person is most susceptible to learning and assimilating.' We continue to learn culture throughout our lives. For example, we constantly have to learn specific rules and norms governing our behaviours within the communities we live in. A group of people may have potatoes as their staple food, or they may depend on hunting for animals as a source of food. They may grow wheat or breed cattle; they may use science to explain natural phenomena or attribute wind and storms as a result of gods fighting in the heaven – these are all products of cultural learning.

We learn our cultural rules and norms through communication, both at the conscious and unconscious level. A Chinese mother might tell her daughter that once married, she should follow her mother-in-law's ways of doing things around the house, and in doing so, the daughter learns about the expected roles for a married woman. This is cultural learning at a conscious level. Identifying cultural learning at the unconscious level is more difficult, but just as significant nevertheless. While we may be unable to specify a particular experience that taught us about our view of aging, for example, the attitudes we have developed are still the product of our cultural environment. As an example, the French convention of addressing older relatives with the formal pronoun for 'you' – *vous* – whereas younger relatives are called by the informal and intimate *tu*, reinforces the value of respect for older people that is central to this culture, even with all the changes of modern life. Culture is pervasive; it is like the water fish swim in and the air we breathe (Beamer and Varner, 2008). We consciously and unconsciously learn cultural rules as we grow up, from sources like family, friends, teachers, proverbs, adages, and folk-tales. Often we are not able to see their effects on our lives until we encounter different cultural rules or practices.

Culture is dynamic

Culture is subject to change over time; it is not fixed or static. When different cultures are in contact, a cultural change may occur. For example, think of how Russian culture has been changing over the past few years – aspects of its culture noticeably changed after the collapse of communism in 1991. A new cultural and political order, economic recovery, growth, and an increasing openness to Western ideas have led many to see present-day Russia as more 'individualistic' and 'Western'. Credited with facilitating these changes are people like Kseniia Sobchak, who is the daughter of St. Petersburg's first democratically elected mayor. She co-hosts a popular reality TV show, designs fashionable clothes, promotes expensive perfumes, and adorns the covers of glossy magazines, bringing Western cultural products into Russia.

As our cultural environment changes, so does our view of cultural practices. The waltz was considered savage during the 1700s. During the 1800s, the tango was viewed as a primitive dance, too sexual to be socially acceptable – in fact, it was banned in Argentina. Today the tango is very popular all over the world, even in places far removed from its origins, like Finland. Similarly, in the United States rock and roll was decried as too sexual in the 1950s and the 1960s. Nowadays, the waltz, the tango, and the music and dance associated with rock and roll are accepted as part of our social life.

In recognizing the dynamic nature of culture, we also need to be aware that different elements of culture or different layers of culture may not change at the same speed or at the same time. While technology, transportation systems, material objects, and architecture are becoming increasingly similar across different cultures, our beliefs, values, and worldviews – the inner core of culture – can prove more resistant to change. An American may wear the traditional costume of an Indian woman, but their beliefs, values, or world-views may still differ considerably. We could build a city in Africa similar in appearance to New York, but it would still not be New York.

Culture is ethnocentric

The term 'ethnocentrism' refers to the belief that one's own culture is superior to other cultures (see Chapter 4). Anthropologists generally agree that ethno-centrism is found in every culture (Samovar and Porter, 1995). Ethnocentrism builds fences between cultures and thus creates barriers for intercultural communication. How we view a culture invariably affects how we interact with people from that culture. When Captain James Cook arrived in Hawaii in 1778, he described their culture as being savage, animal-like, and hea-then, comparing (unfavourably) the practices of the Hawaiian people to the European culture of which he was a part.

Today we know that no culture is superior to any other, but simply that some cultural practices might appear strange or inappropriate to members of other cultures. Australians think it is cruel that Koreans eat dog meat; Koreans feel it is heartless that Australians and other Anglo-Saxons send their elderly par-ents to nursing homes. Similarly, people in Sweden think Anglo-Saxons are cruel for spanking their children, but many Anglo-Saxons think that corporal punishment is central to bringing up a child properly. Even when cultures are closely related, as the ones in this example are, they can still clash about core values – and when they do, members of each culture feel that they are 'right' and the other culture is 'wrong'. Of course, we do not have to accept or practise what is acceptable in other cultures; in intercultural relations it is recognizing and respecting the differences that is more important. Culture is what is distinctive about the way of life of a people, community, nation, or social group. This implies that no culture is inherently superior to any other and that cultural richness by no means derives from its economic standing.

Subcultures

Within any dominant culture there are micro-cultures, often referred to as *subcultures*. Some scholars call subcultures 'co-cultures'. Subcultures can be categorized by a number of indicators, including gender, ethnicity, profession, social class, organization, and geographic region. In this section, we introduce four types of subcultures defined by ethnicity, social class, organization, and geographic region. Subculture gives its members identity (see Chapter 8). Members of a subculture group can mark their identity through dress code, hairstyle, rituals, and language.

Theory Corner

Ethnography

Classical ethnography refers to a specific research methodology that has been employed to study different cultures and subcultures. According to Gribich (2007: 40), this approach has 'strong links with the anthropological tradition of observation of culture *in situ*'. The purpose of classical ethnography is to describe the whole culture, be it a tribal group or a professional group. Key informants are sought and their voices highlighted. The role of the researcher is that of a 'neutral' reflective observer who documents observational and visual images and asks questions in both informal conversation and formal interviews. This is done in order to identify, confirm and cross-check an understanding of the societal structures, social linkages, and behaviour patterns, beliefs, and values of people within the culture. This will usually involve participation in the setting for several years, learning the language and collecting data. Many ethnographers today spend a shorter time in the field but use a number of data collection techniques to speed up the process of data collection, including focus groups, face-to-face interviewing, participant observation, and document analysis. Data gathered from ethnographic studies often cast light on our understanding of the life and culture of particular communities.

Reference

Gribich, Carol (2007) *Qualitative Data Analysis: An Introduction*. London: SAGE.

Further reading on subcultures

Hebdige, Dick (1979) *Subculture: The Meaning of Style*. London: Routledge.

Ethnic culture

Ethnicity is frequently the basis of a subculture within a larger national culture. *Ethnic groups* are identifiable bodies of people who are of common heritage and cultural tradition passed down through generations. Examples include Chinese Australians, Mexican Americans, Vietnamese Italians, and Greek New Zealanders. Ethnic identity refers to identification with a group with a shared heritage and culture. Some people use the terms 'racial' and 'ethnic' groups interchangeably; others differentiate the two terms by specifying that racial groups emphasize the genetically transmitted traits of physical appearance (Dodd, 1998). Examples of racial groups are Asian, European, Anglo-Celtic, and Aboriginal Australians.

Ethnic groups in the host country are referred to as minority groups. Vietnam, for example, is a multi-ethnic country with over 50 distinct ethnic groups (54 are recognized by the Vietnamese government), each with its own language, lifestyle, and cultural heritage. Many of the local ethnic groups are known in the West as Montagnard or Degar. In Australia there are large Chinese, Greek, Italian, Vietnamese, and Indian communities, to mention just a few within the larger cultural environment. They are all considered as ethnic minority groups, in contrast to the mainstream Anglo-Saxon Australian culture. They observe their ethnic cultural traditions and celebrate their own ethnic cultural festivals.

Photo 3.3
The Indian Dance Festival that celebrates Indian cultures and introduces Indian religions to Belgians.
Copyright © Jaka Polutnik. Used with permission

More than just describing a group's population status in relation to the mainstream group, the term 'minority' is sometimes associated with disadvantage and lower social status. The Sami people in Scandinavia, for example, have long been an economically and socially disadvantaged indigenous minority in the relatively (but not completely) homogeneous cultures of Sweden, Norway, and Finland. Communication between people from an ethnic minority and those from the ethnic majority can be problematic at times due to language and cultural barriers, as well as negative stereotypes (see Chapter 4). For example, it has been reported that recently arrived immigrants in Portugal, mostly from former colonies in Africa and Asia, are residentially segregated in neighbourhoods with poor housing, and they experience cultural barriers and other difficulties.

Theory Corner

Conceptualizing ethnicity

According to Hutchinson and Smith (1996: 6), ethnicity is named after a 'human population with myths of common ancestry, shared historical memories, one or more elements of a common culture, a link with a homeland and a sense of solidarity among at least some of its members'. Special attention is paid to extremes of human experiences, which are always a fertile ground for cultural myths and memories that sustain a large group culture. Similarly, Anthony D. Smith (2007a) views myths and memories as part of a culture, remembered as part of a golden past and the commemoration and celebration of heroic events. Every ethnic group, according to Smith, has a mythologized version of its past in which heroic events (victories/glories and sacrifices/traumas) and heroes (actual historical figures and/ or mythologized characters) occupy a prominent position. These events and characters are often evoked during different occasions and ceremonies to inspire the members of the group, to build social cohesion among them, and to particularize their common identity. For example, the French celebrate their Independence Day to honour the storming of the Bastille, the beginning of the revolution, and the birth of the modern French nation. These celebratory activities have the purpose of enhancing the cultural group's sense of belonging and togetherness.

References

Hutchinson, John and Smith, Anthony D. (1996) *Ethnicity*. Oxford. Oxford University Press.

Smith, Anthony D. (2007a) *Myths and Memories of the Nation*. Oxford: Oxford University Press.

Further reading on ethnicity

Hecht, Michael; Jackson II, Ronald, L.; Lindsley, Sheryl; Strauss, Susan and Johnson, Karen E. (2001) 'A layered approach to ethnicity: language and communication', in P. Robinson and H. Giles (eds), *The New Handbook of Language and Social Psychology*. Chichester, England: Wiley. pp. 429–449.

Subculture defined by social class

Socioeconomic status (SES) can be the basis for a subculture (Brislin, 1988). SES can be derived from a person's income, education, occupation, residential area, and family background. For example, your income can determine where you are most likely to reside, the type of occupation you have and the position you hold, the brand of clothes you wear, the kind of people you tend to associate with, whom you marry, or which school your children attend. The Indian caste system is an example of a hierarchically ordered social class ranking. Class ranking predicts attitudes and communication between different castes within the larger Indian culture. Similarly, previous research in Western countries has found differences between middle-class and working-class parents in regard to the values placed on raising their children (e.g. Gilbert, 2003). Jandt (2007) argues that working-class parents' emphasis on obedience could transfer to their children as obedience to authority, an acceptance of what other people think, and a hesitancy in expressing desires to authority figures outside the home. Research also reveals differences between people of different SES with regard to friendship, prestige, and trust. For instance, prestige and achievement may be more valuable to middle-class members, whereas working-class people may be less trusting of the authority used by more powerful people (Daniel, 1976).

Organizational culture

Cultures also include *organizational cultures*. Each organization has its ways of doing things and its ways of communicating, which together constitute its organizational culture (Pacanowsky and O'Donnell-Trujillo, 1983). Employees hold beliefs, values, and assumptions to organize their behaviour and interpret their experience. Through communication, these beliefs and values develop into organizationally based understanding and shared interpretations of organizational reality. These expectations and meanings then form the framework of organizational culture. The IBM corporation, for example, has a distinctive organizational culture in which male employees are expected to wear dark blue suits, white shirts, and conservative neckties. The dress code reflects a unity and conformity in IBM's management style. On the other hand, innovativeness is an espoused value of the 3M Corporation. Employees who put forward suggestions become heroes for demonstrating the spirit of innovation. In Japanese companies, employee loyalty is highly valued, whereas opportunities for career advancement may be seen as more important in Western organizations. In some organizations, subordinates can address people in management by their first name; in other organizations, employees of lower rank must address senior level managers by their last name and their title. Even subsidiaries of the same company (e.g. IBM) operating in different countries may report value differences (Hofstede, 1980). Members of each organization share a knowledge of appropriate behaviours and use this knowledge to guide their activities at work. Organizational cultures give members a sense of identity.

Regional culture

Geographic region is also a basis for categorizing people into different cultural groups. Regional differences often imply differences in social attitudes, lifestyle, food preferences, and communication. People from rural areas are different from people in urban areas. The Dutch distinguish between two major cultural urban–rural subdivisions in their nation. The most important distinction is between the Randstad (Rim City) and non-Randstad cultures. Randstad culture is distinctly urban, located in the provinces of North Holland, South Holland, and Utrecht. The non-Randstad culture follows the historical divide between the predominantly Protestant north and the Catholic south. Interpersonal relationships may seem tighter in rural communities than those in urban regions, partly due to apartment living and busy lifestyles in urban environments.

    Language or *regional dialect* is also a marker of regional cultures. For example, the Swedish language has been standardized for more than a century, but regional variations in its pronunciation between urban areas and rural ones persist. Similarly, the Japanese language spoken in Okinawa, for example, differs from Japanese spoken in Tokyo, and Mandarin spoken in Beijing is different from Mandarin spoken in Shanghai. Likewise, the American English spoken in Virginia is different from that spoken in Ohio (much less the English spoken in London, Sydney, or Singapore). In addition, climate contributes to regional differences, separating people into different groups. For example, in southern China, where the climate is warm all year round, farmers plant and harvest rice three times a year; in northern China, however, farmers can only plant and harvest rice once a year owing to the long and cold winter. As a result, southerners tend to view northerners as 'lazy', and northerners consider southerners as too money-minded because they seem to devote all their time to making money. Of course, with the development of technology, these attitudes are changing. There are many other jobs (like working in village food-processing factories) that now keep farmers in the northern part of China just as busy throughout the winter as their southern counterparts.

Summary

This chapter explored different definitions of culture, identified the components and characteristics of culture, and introduced four types of subcultures defined by ethnicity, social class, organization, and geographic region. It is difficult to have a concrete definition of culture, because the characteristics used to denote cultural differences are not universally applicable. We define culture as a particular way of life of a group of people, comprising the sum of knowledge, experience, beliefs, values, traditions, religion, concepts of time, roles, spatial relations, worldviews, material objects, and geographic territory. Examples include rites of passage such as birth, marriage, and burial traditions; styles of clothing, language, and literature; religious observations; and artistic expressions such as music, art, and architecture, among others. Identification with a cultural group gives us a sense of identity. Cultural identity is a process; it is never complete, always in flux, contextual, and subject to transformations. Understanding the term 'culture' helps us to value our own cultural identity as well as appreciate that of culturally different others. Although there are many reasons why we identify cultures and cultural groups, one purpose of such an identification is to indicate that groups of people are different from each other. In this way, we recognize differences and value diversity. We can achieve greater knowledge and awareness of the issues of cultural expression, creativity, and art through interdisciplinary thinking about culture.

Case Study:
The Roma people in Eastern Europe

The Roma are a specific cultural and ethnic minority, also known as Gypsies, living in different parts of the world, including Eastern Europe. The Roma people migrated in the Middle Ages from north-west India to Europe. In recent years, we have seen the rise of an increasing level of prejudice and discrimination oriented towards the Roma. Because of their nomadic lifestyle and differences in language and culture, there has been a great deal of mutual distrust and fear between the Roma and the national majorities of the region in which they live, such as that experienced between the Roma and the Slovenes, Hungarians, Romanians, French, Bulgarians, and Serbs. The popular image of the Roma is as thieves and too lazy to work, which has contributed to their widespread marginalization and sometimes persecution.

Throughout the past eight centuries or so Roma communities have been abused, harassed, and chased across Europe. Today, the rise of ethnic conflicts between the Roma and national ethnic majorities is one of the most urgent problems on the agendas of the newly emerging states in Eastern Europe. In the majority of Eastern European states, the Roma are described as one of the most threatened cultural minority groups. From a legal, political, social, and cultural perspective many similarities in the treatment of the Roma throughout the region are noticeable. The 12 to 15 million Roma are often marginalized in Eastern European societies and have no legal protection; their access to education and other social benefits is limited. They are also subject to overt and covert discriminatory discourse in the media, and they are often the target of hate crimes.

Roma culture itself has distinctive beliefs, values, and worldviews, which are manifested in its cultural activities including religion, music, clothing, and communication patterns. Roma people believe in the power of good luck charms, amulets, and talismans, curses, and healing rituals. For example, the Roma concept of *Marimé* is a state of impurity, brought onto a person by the violation of a purity taboo. It also means a sentence of expulsion imposed for the violation of purity rules or any behaviour seen as disruptive to the Roma community. Some Roma consider the part of a woman's body below the waist to be dirty or polluted because it is associated with menstruation. Many women wear long skirts, the bottom of which must not touch any man other than the woman's husband. A pregnant woman is considered unclean and must not give birth in the family home, because it would then become impure. After the birth, anything the new mother touches is later destroyed. This quarantine continues at least until the baptism of the baby.

A Roma typically has three names. The first is known only by the mother; it is given at the time of birth. Its purpose is to confuse evil spirits by keeping the real name of the child from them. The second name is given at the time of baptism; it is the commonly used name within the group. A third, different name may be given when the child is re-baptized in a Christian church. This name is regarded as having little importance except when dealing with non-Roma. In the past, Roma people were typically married between the ages of 9 and 14. This tradition has changed owing to the influence of the surrounding cultures. Pre-marital sex is strictly forbidden and marriages to outsiders are discouraged. The wedding ceremony is usually simple. In some groups, the bride and groom join hands in front of the chief or an elder and promise to be true to each other.

When a person dies, relatives and friends gather around and ask for forgiveness for any bad deeds they may have done to that person. They are concerned that if such grievances are not settled, the dead person might come back as an evil spirit and cause trouble. Clothing, tools, jewellery, and money may be placed in the coffin in order to help the deceased in the next world. Many Roma women, called *drabardi*, practise fortune telling, but fortunes are only read for non-Roma. Other women, called *drabarni*, practise natural healing techniques. Finally, music forms a crucial part of Roma life and makes heavy and distinctive use of trumpets and drums.

Reference for case study

Robinson, Bruce A. (2008) 'The Roma: their history, names, & persecution' [online]. Accessed 10 August 2009 at http://www.religioustolerance.org/roma.htm

Questions for discussion

1 Which beliefs and values of Roma culture seem most different from those of your own culture?
2 What can you learn about the characteristics of culture from this case?
3 Why do you think the Roma still exist as a distinctive cultural group, despite being marginalized or even persecuted?
4 What do you think gender roles are like in Roma culture?
5 How can we promote intercultural understanding between Roma people and the people from majority European cultures?

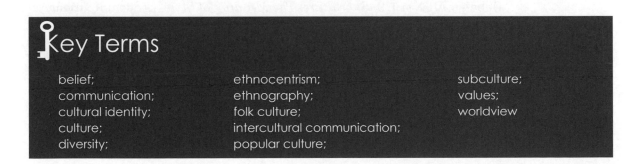

Key Terms

belief;
communication;
cultural identity;
culture;
diversity;

ethnocentrism;
ethnography;
folk culture;
intercultural communication;
popular culture;

subculture;
values;
worldview

Further Reading

Cultural customs and practices

Anderson, Jennifer (1987) 'Japanese tea ritual: religion in practice', *Man: Journal of the Royal Anthropological Society of Great Britain and Ireland*, 22 (3): 475–498.
Department of Foreign Affairs and Trade (2008) 'Travel advice', *Smart Traveller* [online]. Available at http://www.smarttraveller.com.au

Culture and globalization

Anderson, Benedict (1991) *Imagined Communities: Reflections on the Origins and Spread of Nationalism*. London: Verso.

Appadurai, Arjun (1996) *Modernity at Large: Cultural Dimensions of Globalization*. Minneapolis: University of Minnesota Press.

Dyson, Kenneth (1996) 'On being passionate about standards: promoting the voice of aesthetics in broadcasting and multimedia', in K. Dyson and W. Homolka (eds), *Culture First! Promoting Standards in the New Media Age*. New York: Cassell. pp. 129–170.

Ladegaard, Hans J. (2007) 'A global corporation', *Journal of Intercultural Communication Research*, 36 (2): 139–163.

Nederveen Pieterse, Jan (1994) 'Globalisation as hybridisation', *International Sociology*, 9 (2): 161–184.

Cultural identity

Hall, Stuart (1984) 'The culture gap', *Marxism Today*, 28: 18–23.

Shore, Chris and Black, Annabel (1994) 'Citizens' Europe and the construction of European identity', in V.A. Goddard, J.R. Llobera and C. Shore (eds), *The Anthropology of Europe: Identity and Boundaries in Conflict*. Oxford and Providence, RI: Berg. 275–298.

Subcultures

Hebdige, Dick (1979) *Subculture: The Meaning of Style*. London: Routledge.

Hecht, Michael; Jackson II, Ronald, L.; Lindsley, Sheryl; Strauss, Susan and Johnson, Karen E. (2001) 'A layered approach to ethnicity: language and communication', in P. Robinson and H. Giles (eds), *The New Handbook of Language and Social Psychology*. Chichester, England: Wiley. pp. 429–449.

Hofstede, Geert (1991) *Cultures and Organizations: Software of the Mind*. New York: McGraw-Hill.

4

The Influence of Culture on Perception

However, no two people see the external world in exactly the same way. To every separate person, a thing is what he thinks it is – in other words, not a thing, but a think.

Penelope Fitzgerald, British author, 1916–2000

Learning Objectives

At the end of this chapter, you should be able to:

- Define perception and identify three stages of the perception process.
- Delineate the influence of culture on our perception.
- Explain ethnocentrism, stereotypes, prejudice, racism, and how they affect intercultural communication.

The Nature of Human Perception

We receive information about the world around us through our sense of sight, sound, smell, taste, and touch. These stimuli are selected, organized, and interpreted and from them we create a meaningful picture of our world. Much like a computer, the human mind processes information in a sequence of stages akin to data entry or storage and retrieval, with each stage involving a specific operation on incoming information. The first stage of information processing is that of *perception*, which refers to how we see or sense things around us. Human perception is an active process in which we use our sensory organs to identify the existence of all kinds of stimuli and then subject them to evaluation and interpretation. Since the way we behave is influenced by how we perceive the world around us, perception is the very basis of how we communicate with others. The information we select from the data available in our environment is affected by our personal experiences, our psychological states, our values, and our culture among many other factors (Cooper et al., 2007). Based on those perceptions, we make judgments of others and adapt our communication accordingly.

According to psychologist Blaine Goss (1995), the information we manage every day has two origins: external and internal. People, events, and objects are sources of *external* information, while knowledge, past experiences, and feelings make up our *internal* world of information. Successful information processing depends on the merging of external and internal information. In other words, how people enter, store, and retrieve information is a combination of what they are experiencing (external) with what they know and feel (internal). We form images of our world based on this assimilation of internal and external information (Boulding, 1956). Once formed, images become filters that we use to guide our further interpretation of the external world. We bring with us a perceptual frame of reference through which all of our messages are filtered every time we enter into a communicative exchange.

Photo 4.1
Chinese BBQ shop in Chinatown, Brisbane, Australia.
Copyright © Shuang Liu. Used with permission.

Although information processing is a universal phenomenon, it is nevertheless influenced by culture. It follows, therefore, that if culturally different people vary in their interpretation of reality, communication problems may occur. For example, the Chinese consider snakes, turtles, chicken feet, shark fins, and swallows' nests as delicacies, whereas most Westerners baulk at eating these foods.

Similarly, while two Australians engaged in face-to-face communication expect direct eye contact as an indication of engagement and interest in the conversation, in South Korea it is considered polite to cast one's eyes downward during some communication situations (such as when a student is speaking to a teacher). The handshake is considered a common business protocol in many countries, but while a firm handshake is acceptable in the United States a gentle handshake is preferred in the Middle East. Violating expectations of culturally determined behavioural rules potentially impairs further communication. Consequently, it is important for us to understand the nature of perception and how it is influenced by cultural experience. This chapter concentrates on the human perception process. First we identify different stages of this process and then illustrate how perception is connected to our beliefs, values, worldviews, and attitudes. The formation of stereotypes, prejudice, racism, and their relationship to perception is explained, and a discussion on how stereotypes and prejudice can affect intercultural communication concludes the chapter.

Stages of the Perception Process

The perception process consists of three stages: selection, categorization, and interpretation.

The selection stage

The first stage in the process is selection, in which information is received via the senses, then attended to and interpreted by the brain (Jandt, 2007). Selection plays a major part in the larger process of converting environmental stimuli into meaningful experience. We are bombarded with an enormous array of stimuli as part of our everyday lives, but we are limited in the number of stimuli we can meaningfully process. This is where the selection process helps us to discern those stimuli which are immediately or potentially useful to us. For example, if you intend to buy a new car, you are more inclined to pay attention to the 'vehicles for sale' section of your daily newspaper before you make a decision about purchasing a car.

Scholars argue that we do not consciously 'see' an object unless we are paying direct and focused attention to that object, engaging what is known as selective perception. *Selective perception* involves three steps: selective exposure, selective attention, and selective retention (Klopf, 1995). We *selectively expose* ourselves to certain kinds of information from our environment. We *pay attention* to a subset of elements of this information that is immediately relevant to us. Finally, we *selectively retain* for later recall that part of the information that is likely to be used in the future and is consistent with our beliefs, attitudes, and values. For example, if the budget for your new car is $6,000, as you read the 'vehicles for sale' section of the paper you will disregard vehicles priced above your limit and remember the cheaper ones. Likewise, a dieter is more inclined to attend to and remember ingredients and nutritional values on food labels than someone who is not concerned about his or her weight. In a different kind of example, a mortgage holder pays more attention to the activity of interest rates as reported on TV than someone who is not paying off a home loan.

Perception – including selective exposure, attention, and retention – is influenced by culture. As a result, differences in perception can lead to misunderstandings during interactions, especially when those involved are from different cultural backgrounds (Chen and Starosta, 2005). Goss (1995) identified three common perceptual tendencies, all influenced by culture: closure, familiarity, and expectations.

Closure refers to humans' tendency to see things as complete wholes instead of incomplete configurations. Based on a tiny amount of data, people often make inferences about an incomplete figure, thought, idea, or sentence. Figure 4.1 illustrates this point – while the triangle and circle are presented as partial forms, most people tend to see a full triangle and a full circle.

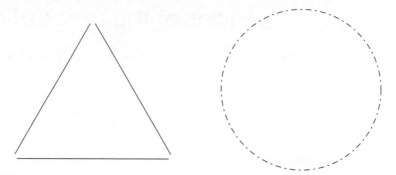

Figure 4.1:   Incomplete triangle and circle

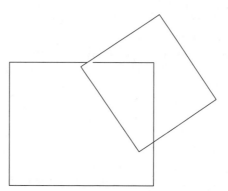

Figure 4.2:   Three irregular shapes or two squares?

Familiarity suggests that people use their existing knowledge to identify what they see. We are more inclined to recognize the familiar rather than the unfamiliar aspects of things. When presented with Figure 4.2, it is likely that people will see two overlapping squares rather than three irregular shapes, the reason being that we are more familiar with the former and tend to look for the familiar rather than the unusual.

Expectation can be illustrated in an old adage that 'We see what we want to see and hear what we want to hear.' This saying is particularly relevant to the process of perception. Perception involves expectations; the more frequently we see something, the more inclined we are to form a 'fixed' image of that thing in our mind which informs our future expectations of it. For example, we expect roses to be red, older people to have white hair, and workers in childcare centres to be female. Over time, these 'fixed' images become habits and make different perceptions difficult. This is demonstrated in Figure 4.3. The saying is well-known, so you might not

Figure 4.3:   Did you notice the grammar error at first sight?

immediately detect the duplication, but instead read it according to your expectation of what it should be.

The notions of closure, familiarity, and expectation illustrate that perception is both a product and a process. As a process, it is a way of forming recognizable objects, thoughts, ideas, and categories of people. As a product, perception represents what we see and experience and is stored in the memory to be retrieved and utilized when we need it.

The categorization stage

As humans we are surrounded by such an enormous amount of information or stimuli from our environment that it is impossible to process this all at once. To function within this environment and select and manage the relevant information from it, we employ mental economy strategies (Neuliep, 2006). *Categorization* is one such strategy, defined as the process of ordering the environment by grouping persons, objects, and events on the basis of their being perceived as sharing similar features or characteristics (Tajfel, 1978). Categories are useful because they help the information processor to reduce uncertainty and increase the accuracy of predictions. Most cognitive psychologists argue that all people, regardless of their culture, engage in categorization. Categories assist us in making attributions about the behaviour of others and help us to recall and recognize information. For example, we categorize people based on skin or hair colour, dress, race, sex, language, occupation, interests, geographic location, or desirable/undesirable qualities. Once people are categorized, other associated collective traits and intentions are also attributed to them (see Theory Corner box below). The fact that membership categories are associated with specific features and activities provides people with a powerful resource for making sense of their social world, allowing them to make discursive connections to the category membership of the actors (Tajfel and Forgas, 1981). Once assigned, therefore, membership of a category comes to imply much more than the original traits on which categorization was based in the first place.

Theory Corner

Attribution theory

Attribution theory was initially developed by Fritz Heider in 1958 and has been modified since that time by Edward Jones, Keith Davis, and Harold Kelley, all of whom are social psychologists. The theory assumes that a person seeking to understand why another person acted in a certain way may attribute one or more causes to the behaviour in question. According to Heider (1958), a person can make two attributions: internal or external. Internal attribution refers to the inference that a person is behaving in a certain way because of something about that person, such as attitude, beliefs, or personality. External attribution instead ascribes situational causes to a person's behaviour. Attributions, whether internal or external, are significantly driven by emotional and motivational factors. While we commonly attribute our own success and others' failures to internal factors, we tend to attribute our own failures and other people's success to external ones. For example, a student who failed a test may blame the instructor for not providing a clear explanation of the material. This externalization of cause diminishes the responsibility of the student. Attribution theory is relevant to the study of human perception. It has been applied in a wide range of areas including psychology, management, criminal law, marketing, education, decision making, and ethics.

Reference

Heider, Fritz (1958) *The Psychology of Interpersonal Relations*. New York: Wiley.

Further reading on attribution theory

Jaspars, Jos and Hewstone, Miles (1982) 'Cross-culture interaction, social attribution, and intergroup relations', in S. Bochner (ed.), *Cultures in Contact*. Elmsford, NY: Pergamon. pp. 127–156.

People categorize for a variety of reasons – to reduce uncertainty, maintain self-esteem, and draw distinctions between ingroups (the groups we belong to) and outgroups (the groups we do not belong to). Research on intergroup relations indicates that once established, categories have a biasing and filtering effect on perceptions, so that the mere categorization of persons into groups is sufficient to foster bias (Tajfel, 1978). According to social psychologist Henri Tajfel, this leads us to the perception that *we* (the ingroup) are who we are because *they* (the outgroup) are *not* what we are. People also tend to label members of competing outgroups with undesirable attributes, while labelling ingroups with desirable qualities. Richard Brislin (1981) claimed that we are all socialized to believe in the superiority of our ingroups. On the positive side, categorization helps to give incoming information a structure and reduces uncertainty in our environment. However, in categorizing people, we can end up overlooking individual elements and overgeneralizing from group membership.

The interpretation stage

Interpretation is the attachment of meaning to data obtained through the sensory organs. It is synonymous with decoding. According to Goss (1995), people filter information physiologically (e.g. hearing, eyesight, touch), sociologically (e.g. demographics, group membership), and psychologically (e.g. attitudes, beliefs, dispositions).

We have already examined how perception combines the internal states of the person with external stimuli from the environment. When interpreting, we tend to rely on familiar contexts and compare new stimuli with them in order to look for clues. The more ambiguous the stimuli, the more room there is for differing interpretations (Pearson and Nelson, 1997). As a result, the same situation can be interpreted differently by different people. For example, eating with one's hands is regarded as normal behaviour in India, but may be interpreted as bad table manners in some Western cultures. Figure 4.4 contains a set of images that a psychologist might ask you to interpret. There are no right or wrong answers, but different people interpret differently depending on their past experiences and their familiarity with the context in which each image is situated.

As we have already seen, perception is the process by which an individual converts physical stimuli from the environment into meaning based on internal experiences. From Figure 4.4 we can learn that while the physical mechanism of perception is much the same in all people – sensory organs such as the eyes, ears, and nose permit us to sense and interpret our environment – assigning meaning is not the same for all people. This is a learned process and therefore subject to cultural influences (Samovar and Porter, 1995).

While perception is an internal process, it is the external forces of culture that primarily determine the meanings we apply to the stimuli that reach us. For example, Anglo-Saxon mothers may interpret assertiveness in their children's speech as positive, whereas Korean mothers who observe the same behaviour in their children might consider them disrespectful and lacking in discipline. Similarly, Americans regard an outspoken person as credible, while Japanese people tend to consider constant talking as a sign of shallowness. In Australia, people tend to respond positively to a direct approach to resolving an interpersonal conflict, yet this same behaviour is frowned upon in most Asian cultures. The issue of interpretation becomes more complex when we factor in further variables such as age, gender, ethnicity, social status, and the relationship between communicators. Misinterpretation of the information perceived has the potential to impede intercultural interactions. The influence of culture on perception and intercultural communication, therefore, cannot be overstated.

What can you see in the pictures below?

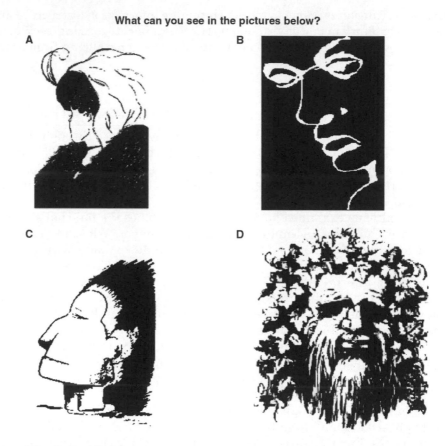

Figure 4.4: Optical illusions

The Influence of Culture on Perception

People behave as they do because of the ways in which they perceive the world. One learns these perceptions and behaviours as part of cultural experience. The influence of culture on human perception has long been studied by social scientists (Segall, 1979), who have explored the notion that perception is partial because we can never completely know everything about the world surrounding us. As Marshall Singer (1987: 9) noted: 'We experience everything in the world not as it is – but only as the world comes to us through our sensory receptors.' The way we respond to the external world is primarily the result of how our cultural filters influence what we see, hear, smell, feel, and taste. Consistent findings from studies in this area suggest that people's ability to select incoming information, categorize, and interpret it differs across cultures. In short, the world looks, sounds, tastes, and feels the way it does because our culture has given us the criteria to apply in order to perceive it. The basic process of perception is the same for all humans, but the content differs because of variations in beliefs, values, and worldviews as well as individual inference habits.

Cultural beliefs, values, and perception

Belief systems are significant to intercultural communication, because they lie at the core of our thoughts and actions. Beliefs are learned and consequently subject to cultural bias. In some cultures, people believe that weather is a product of God's will and will pray for a drought or flood to be alleviated. Other cultures believe that humans should conquer nature and make use of cloud-seeding technology to break long-standing droughts. Beliefs are the basis of our values, which are enduring attitudes about a preference for one belief over another. Values possess a normative dimension, specifying what is good or bad, right or wrong, in a particular context. For example, harmony in inter-personal relationships is treasured in most Chinese workplaces; on the other hand, interpersonal relationships between Australian colleagues are believed to benefit from being upfront and direct. Westerners associate aggressiveness (unless it is very negative) with the values of competition and independence, whereas any aggressiveness is interpreted adversely in an Asian workplace. An understanding of cultural values not only helps us to appreciate the behaviour of other people and know how to treat them with respect, but also helps us to interpret our own behaviour.

Culture and categorization

Studies have found cultural differences in how people categorize objects. Nisbett and Miyamoto (2005) argue that people from Western cultures focus on salient objects and rules when categorizing the environment. By contrast, people in East Asian cultures focus more on relationships and similarities among objects when organizing the environment. For example, a study in which both Chinese and American children were presented with pictures of three objects (e.g. a man, woman, and baby) and then asked to pick two objects out of the three that went together showed that Chinese children tended to group their two objects on the basis of relational-contextual infor-mation (e.g. grouping the woman and the baby together because the mother takes care of the baby). American children, on the other hand, tended to group objects based on shared properties or categories (e.g. grouping a man and woman together because they are both adults).

Most people tend to think in terms of ingroup and outgroup membership when it comes to categorizing people (Neuliep, 2006). In doing so, people also have a tendency to create categories that maximize the advantages of the ingroup. Brislin (1981) argues that people are socialized to believe in the superiority of their own groups. Ingroups are generally associated with desirable qualities such as loyalty, honesty, or trustworthiness, while out-groups are labelled with undesirable qualities such as arrogance, bitterness, or strangeness (Jandt, 2007). Naturally, this has implications for initial intercultural interactions. When meeting someone from another culture for the first time, there may be salient features that can lead us to categorize their entire culture. For example, a British tourist first boarding an MTR (subway) in Hong Kong and hearing a local person chatting loudly on a mobile phone might categorize the entire Hong Kong population as discourteous and inconsiderate of others.

While categorization performs a useful function in reducing the amount of incoming information, it also leads us to ignore individual elements, particularly when categorizing people from outgroups. This tendency to see members of outgroups as 'all alike', without recognizing the individual differences that we appreciate in ingroup members, is called the *outgroup homogeneity effect* (Mullen and Hu, 1989); this is one of the important bases for group-based prejudice and discrimination, which are most extreme when groups dehumanize each other during warfare. On the other hand, categorization can also lead us to minimize differences between members of the ingroup on valued characteristics, but to maximize differences between the ingroup and outgroup on these things. Hence, while allowing the human mind to process information more efficiently, categories are also the basis for prejudgments, which can lead to stereotyping. However, bias of this nature may be reduced by decreasing the distance between ingroups and outgroups. According to Tajfel (1978), when we perceive an outgroup as similar to our group on a valued characteristic, we are more likely to think positively about that group and to engage members in interaction. Perceived similarity reduces uncertainty about intergroup interaction.

Theory Corner

Implicit personality theory

Implicit personality theory describes assumed relationships among personality traits (see Schneider, 1973, for a review of the theory). The theory suggests that we organize our individual perceptions into clusters. Thus, individual personality traits are related to other traits. When we identify an individual trait in someone, we assume the person also possesses other traits in the cluster. There are two traditions associated with implicit personality theory. The first is concerned with the role of general bias in judgments of others. Various researchers have found that people tend to exaggerate the extent of relationships among personality traits. The tendency to presume that someone who has one good trait is likely to have other good traits is called the *halo effect*. In attempting to explain these perceived patterns, researchers have examined the biases implicit in language that lead us to think relationships among traits are stronger than the evidence indicates. The second tradition concentrates on individual differences in person perception. For example, people were found to cluster 'intelligent', 'quiet', and 'friendly' together so that, if we view someone as friendly, we also attribute to them the characteristics of quietness and intelligence. Once we have formed a first impression of someone, we tend to look for cues that are consistent and supportive of this impression and ignore those that are inconsistent.

Reference

Schneider, David J. (1973) 'Implicit personality theory: a review', *Psychological Bulletin*, 79 (5): 294–309.

Further reading on perception and attribution

Maddux, William W. and Yuki, Masaki (2006) 'The "Ripple effect": cultural differences in perceptions of the consequences of events', *Personality and Social Psychology Bulletin*, 32: 669–683.

Culture and interpretation

Culture affects the variables that people use to interpret what they perceive. A study in which students from different cultures were asked to write down their perceptions of different colours found surprising and significant differences in the responses, based on culture (Chen and Starosta, 2005). For example, red for Chinese people represents splendour and wealth and is a wedding colour. In Western cultures white is a wedding colour because it is perceived as suggesting purity. A car decorated with white ribbons is likely to be a wedding car in Western cultures, but such decoration in Asian cultures may instead suggest a funeral – white is a colour of mourning.

As well as objects, we also attribute meanings to events, based on our past experience (Cooper et al., 2007). All events occur in a social context which has specific meaning to the group of people involved. For example, the onset of the New Year is celebrated across cultures, but in very different ways. Unlike Western New Year (based on the Roman calendar), Chinese New Year is based on the lunar calendar and usually

Photo 4.2
Red envelopes with lucky money are customarily given to children by parents or grandparents on Chinese New Year's eve to wish them a smooth and happy new year.
Copyright © Shuang Liu. Used with permission

falls between the end of January and the beginning of February. The celebration lasts 15 days. Celebrations begin on the New Year's eve. Specific traditional dishes are served at dinner to signify wishes or blessings for the coming year: fish for prosperity, chicken representing good luck, and *jiaozi* (a Chinese dumpling) signifying a family reunion. People also put up good-luck papers outside their front door and feed the Kitchen God sweets before he ascends to heaven to report to the Jade Emperor on the family's activities during the previous year (this is a bit similar to the European custom of leaving sweets for St. Nicholas at Christmas). It is also common to see parents or grandparents give children 'lucky money' in bright red envelopes, signifying their wishes for a smooth and happy New Year.

Culture also affects what information people emphasize when making attributions. Listening more and talking less is viewed as showing respect in Japanese culture; in Australia, the same behaviour may be viewed as signifying a lack of confidence. People also try to explain an observed behaviour by attributing it to either personal or situational causes. When we explain someone's behaviour in terms of personality, motivation, or personal preferences, we are using personal attributes. When we explain someone's behaviour in terms of unusual circumstances, social pressure, or physical forces beyond their control, we are using situational attributes. When we make attributions of people's behaviours on the basis of either personality or situational factors, we are prone to biases. In particular, we engage in a self-serving bias – we tend to attribute a positive behaviour by ingroup members to internal factors and their negative behaviour to situational variables. In contrast, we tend to attribute positive behaviour by outgroup members to situational variables and negative behaviour to personality variables (Jaspars and Hewstone, 1982). For example, a student's failure to pass an exam could be attributed to a lack of intelligence on the part of the student (internal factor) or too much social/family pressure as a cause of under-performance (external factor).

These differences in attribution also manifest themselves culturally and can result in misunderstandings. The Chinese are reluctant to say 'no' in business negotiations, especially to foreign business partners, because this may upset harmony. When asked a question to which the answer is 'no', they might instead reply, 'maybe'. Difficulties of this nature have arisen in negotiations between an Australian university and a Chinese government agency over the establishment of an institute to be affiliated with the university. Part of the problem in reaching an agreement is the frustration that the Australian representatives feel with getting either no answer or a 'maybe' in response to significant or difficult questions. A Westerner is more likely to assume that a response of 'maybe' suggests possibility, whereas to a Chinese 'maybe' is an indirect way of saying 'no'. To improve the accuracy of our attributions so as to be more effective in intercultural communication, we can use techniques such as perception checking, active listening, and feedback. These techniques can help us to ensure that our interpretation of another's words or actions is indeed what was intended.

Perception and Intercultural Communication

Culture plays a key role in influencing what information we select from available external stimuli, how we structure the incoming information, and the meanings we assign to the processed information. As a result, it is possible for our cultural socialization to foster ethnocentrism. Higher levels of ethnocentrism can lead to stereotypes, prejudice, and even racism – all of which are barriers to successful intercultural communication.

Ethnocentrism

Gudykunst (2004) points out that one's cultural orientation acts as a filter for processing incoming and outgoing verbal and nonverbal messages. To this extent, all intercultural communication events are inescapably charged with some degree of ethnocentrism. At its most benign, ethnocentrism has the capacity to foster ingroup survival, solidarity, conformity, loyalty, and cooperation (Jandt, 2007).

Ethnocentrism is a continuum; our position on this continuum determines the distance we create when we communicate with people from other cultures or groups. At the high end of the continuum, there is a larger distance between ingroups and outgroups, along with insensitivity to the other group's feelings and perspective. At the other end of the scale, low ethnocentrism reflects a desire to reduce the communicative distance between ourselves and others and the use of inclusive language (Cooper et al., 2007). A high level of ethnocentrism is dysfunctional in intercultural communication, as it creates communicative distance (Gudykunst and Kim, 1984). Highly ethnocentric people tend to engage in self-centred dialogue in which they use their own cultural standards to judge the experience of communicating with others. Ethnocentrism at this level may lead to prejudice, stereotypes, or discrimination and thus prohibits effective intercultural communication by impairing or preventing understanding. In contrast to ethnocentrism, *cultural relativism* is the degree to which an individual judges another culture by its context (Gudykunst, 2004). Taken in isolation, a single element of a culture may seem strange to a non-member, but generally makes sense when considered in light of the other elements of that culture (see Chapter 3). Take the earlier example about eating food with the fingers being more acceptable in India than in an Anglo-Saxon culture. This single difference may seem strange (to both Indians and Anglo-Saxons). However, when one considers this single cultural element within a broader context – that is, the Indian belief that God gives people hands so that they may give and eat food – then this Indian behaviour makes sense to Anglo-Saxons. Interpreting a person's behaviour through their own cultural frame of reference enhances the chances of effective communication. It follows, therefore, that to understand another culture we need to communicate with its people and broaden our understanding of their practices and beliefs, thus enhancing our sense of cultural relativism.

Stereotypes

Group-based stereotypes are preconceived beliefs about the characteristics of certain groups based on physical attributes or social status. Stereotypes are over-generalizations and thus may be wrongly generalized to some members of the group (Hilton and von Hippel, 1996). The term 'stereotype' derives from the Greek word *stereos* meaning 'solid' or 'firm' and *tupos* meaning 'impression or engraved mark'. Thus, in its original sense, 'stereotype' stands for 'solid impression'. In 1798, at the outset of the industrial age, two European printers invented a new way to reproduce images that would fix permanently. This image-setting process was called stereotyping. Walter Lippmann brought the term into modern usage when he applied it in his book *Public Opinion* (1922), using it to refer to a psychological process of forming intellectual images. The mass media's heavy reliance on stereotypes means that we are probably all familiar with those of the ambitious, outgoing American, the romantic Frenchman, the laid back, beach-loving Australian, or the respectful, technology-loving Japanese, among many others, based on such factors as national, ethnic, social, or gender characteristics. The term 'stereotype' is often used with a negative connotation when referring to an oversimplified assumption of the characteristics associated with a group.

Photo 4.3
Dancers at the UNESCO week of Arab culture. Arab and Muslim communities in many countries have been the target of negative stereotypes since 9/11.
Copyright © UNESCO; photographer: Claude Bablin. Used with permission.

Stereotypes can be used to deny individuals respect or legitimacy based on their group membership. A stereotype can be a conventional and preconceived opinion or image based on the belief that there are attitudes, appearances, or behaviours shared by all members of a certain group. These can emerge from an illusory correlation or false association between two variables. For example, since 9/11, Muslim airline passengers, or anyone of Middle Eastern appearance, are more likely to draw the attention of Western airport security than other people. Similarly, since the onset of widespread media coverage of natural and military disasters in some African countries, a group of dark-skinned children are more likely to be categorized by Europeans as refugees or children from a poverty-stricken African village. Stereotypes are forms of social consensus rather than individual judgments; while we do not construct them ourselves, in using them we contribute to the consensus that perpetuates them.

Stereotypes often form the basis of prejudice and are usually employed to explain real or imaginary differences, such as those due to race, gender, religion, ethnicity, social class, occupation, or sexual orientation. Research has shown that stereotypes can have an impact on both the holder and the subject (Steele and Aronson, 1995). For example, non-English speakers are disadvantaged in English-language social and academic settings because of their accent, and their accent is often believed to signify their incapacity to perform as well as the majority group (Woodrow, 2006). Consequently, ethnic minorities may experience anxiety and performance decrement, and consequently withdraw from communication with people of the host culture (Lesko and Corpus, 2006). Should the person perform poorly in a stereotypical domain (e.g. academic performance), the performance can then be concluded as typical, reinforcing the negative stereotype attached to the particular group (Steele et al., 2002). Interestingly, Clark and Kashima (2007) have demonstrated the important role played by narratives in encouraging us to maintain our stereotypes about other groups – we tell and remember stories that emphasize stereotype consistent traits and behaviour.

Theory Corner

Self-fulfilling prophecy

A self-fulfilling prophecy is a statement that becomes true by directly or indirectly altering actions. In Robert Merton's book *Social Theory and Social Structure* (1968), he stated that a self-fulfilling prophecy is a false definition of the situation evoking a new behaviour which makes the original false conception 'come true'. In other words, a false prophecy may sufficiently influence people's behaviours so that their reactions ultimately fulfil it. For example, if a lecturer believes all American students are active participants in the classroom, she might treat them as such by giving them more opportunities to speak in class. Thus, the lecturer self-fulfils her prophecy by encouraging the students to behave in accordance with it.

Reference

Merton, Robert K. (1968) *Social Theory and Social Structure*. New York: Free.

Further reading on perception and behaviour

Miller, Christopher (1996) 'Building illusions: culture determines what we see', *Business Communication Quarterly*, 59 (1): 87–90.

Prejudice

Prejudice is a negative attitude toward individuals resulting from stereotypes (Cooper et al., 2007). Prejudice constitutes generalized evaluations about a person, object, or action that are the result of individual experience, interpersonal communication, or media influence. Prejudiced people distort evidence to fit their prejudice or simply ignore evidence that is inconsistent with their viewpoint (Allport, 1954). Brislin (1981) suggests that prejudice serves several functions, the first of which is utilitarian; our prejudices may be rewarded economically or socially. For example, prejudice against minority groups might put people from the mainstream culture in a more favourable position when competing in the job market. The second function is ego-defensive; prejudice allows us to avoid admitting certain things about ourselves. For example, if you are unsuccessful in some pursuit, you could blame those who were successful and, in doing so, avoid examining the reasons for your own failure and protect your self-esteem. Prejudice also has a value-expressive function, in that it allows people to highlight the aspects of life they value, such as an affiliation with a particular social group. Prejudice also performs a knowledge function. This fourth function allows us to organize and structure our world in ways that make sense to us and are relatively convenient. Thus, it is a learned tendency to respond to a given group of people in a certain way. When we are prejudiced against a group, this can be manifested in biased actions such as discrimination.

Brislin (1981) further categorized prejudice according to the intensity of action or response: verbal abuse, physical avoidance, discrimination, physical attack, and massacre. The first of these five forms of prejudice, verbal abuse, is often accompanied by labelling. For example, verbal abuse motivated by racial prejudice includes a host of racist labels such as 'Chink', 'Pom', 'Nigger', or 'Kaffir'. The second form of prejudice, physical avoidance, occurs when a group of people are disliked and shunned because of their religious beliefs, language systems, and customs. Prejudice of this nature might lead someone to avoid making friends, going out, or working with certain people on the basis of their perceived differences. Discrimination, the third form of prejudice, refers to the denial of opportunities to outgroup members. Discrimination can exist in employment, housing, political rights, educational opportunities, and elsewhere. It is usually based on gender, social class, religion, skin colour, or other physical characteristics. The 'White Australia' policy, an immigration guideline which was not repealed until the 1980s, was one example of this form of prejudice. It legitimized discrimination towards potential immigrants who were not of a 'desirable' ethnic background – initially anyone who was not of Western European origin.

As the degree of discrimination intensifies, physical punishment of the targeted group becomes likely. The widely reported Cronulla riots in Sydney in 2005 (see Chapter 1) were an example of the fourth form of prejudice, physical attack, in which racial discrimination against people of Lebanese or Middle Eastern origin manifested itself as physical violence. The worst form of prejudice is massacre. The burning of women as witches in the American colonies, Hitler's attempted genocide of the Jewish people in Germany and, more recently, the conflict and ethnic cleansing in Bosnia and Rwanda are some examples of this extreme form of prejudice.

Stereotypes and prejudice are developed through socialization. As we grow, we learn stereotypes from our parents, friends, schools, churches, and our own experience. Moreover, the mass media can also play an important role in fostering stereotypes of social groups by constructing the 'image in our heads'. Because stereotypes and prejudice are based on our beliefs and attitude systems, they affect the way we communicate in intercultural encounters. They can inhibit communication, create negative feelings, and cause conflict. To avoid this problem, we need to develop intercultural empathy, projecting ourselves into the position of the other person's position in intercultural communication.

Racism

Racism refers to the belief that some racial groups are superior and that other racial groups are necessarily inferior. It is grounded in a belief in the supremacy of some races over others and that this superiority is biologically based. It therefore devalues and renders certain racial or ethnic groups inferior based on their biological features. As such, racist people believe that race differences cannot be influenced by culture or education and that biological superiority translates into cultural, intellectual, moral, and social superiority. Racism is usually the product of ignorance, fear, and hatred. It is a worldwide phenomenon and often reflects and is perpetuated by deeply rooted historical, social, cultural, and power inequalities in society. The misconceptions it engenders are often founded on the fear of difference, including differences in customs, values, religion, physical appearance, and ways of living and viewing the world. Racism, stereotyping, prejudice, and discrimination are often linked. When a racial group is labelled as inferior, stereotypes about it tend to be negative. Because of this, people become prejudiced against that racial group and discriminate against it.

Racism takes different forms in different contexts and so has been defined in many different ways. Its ultimate effects, however, are universal: it disempowers people by devaluing their identity, destroys community cohesion, and creates divisions in society as well as making it difficult if not impossible for certain groups of people to have political, economic, and social power. It is, therefore, the opposite of the democratic principles of equality and the right of all people to be treated fairly.

Racist attitudes may be manifested in a number of ways, including expressions of racial prejudice and stereotypical assumptions about other cultures, as well as more extreme forms of prejudice such as xenophobia. Racist behaviour can include ridicule, abuse, property damage, harassment, and physical assault. Its underlying beliefs are reinforced by prevailing social attitudes towards people who are seen as different. In many countries, racism is inextricably linked to a colonial and/or immigrant history. In Australia, the indigenous inhabitants were dispossessed of their land and discriminated against by European settlers. Over time, the migration of peoples from all parts of the world led to an increased cultural and linguistic diversity of the Australian population, but there has nevertheless been prejudice and discrimination against people of non-English speaking backgrounds or non-European appearance over much of Australia's history. South Africa, New Zealand, and some Asian countries have similar histories of colonization and the dispossession of indigenous groups; in some countries, this has led to a backlash by such groups and a subsequent discrimination against long-established immigrant groups. In the United States, on the other hand, racism grew in large part from the history of importing slaves from Africa. In most cases, racism is associated with a chauvinist view of who the 'real' members of a culture are. Like all forms of prejudice, it leads to conflicts and difficulties in intercultural communication.

Summary

This chapter concentrated on human perception, which is the basis of communication. It explained how the perception process involves different stages and is influenced by culture. The physical mechanism of perception is much the same in all people: our sensory organs (eyes, ears, nose, etc.) permit us to perceive stimuli in our environment. The sensations received are subsequently routed through the nervous system to the brain, where they are interpreted. Perception is the process of organizing these sensations into recognizable wholes – the first step in assigning meaning. It is both a process and a product. Previous experience produces expectations that continue to act upon further received stimuli.

Regardless of culture, humans process information in a similar way. However, the outcome of interpretation and the process of assigning meaning are not the same for all people. Interpretation is a learned process and thus subject to psychological, physiological, and cultural influences. While the propensity to categorize and stereotype is common to all humans, it is our cultural socialization that influences the way in which this process is fulfilled. To overcome the barriers to intercultural communication created by stereotypes, prejudice, and racism, we need to practise cultural relativism and keep an open mind when interacting with people from different cultures. Our particular ways of doing and seeing are neither the only ways nor the only right ways. All cultures deserve recognition and respect and it is only by bearing this in mind that we can become more effective intercultural communicators.

Case Study:
How are Eastern Europeans perceived by the West?

Since the collapse of communism in 1989 in Eastern European countries (such as Bulgaria, Romania, Serbia, Russia, Poland, the Czech Republic, Slovenia, etc.), there have been heated debates in the public spheres about issues such as how Eastern Europeans are perceived by the West. After the fall of the Roman Empire, the Western European regions became more economically and politically powerful, whereas much of Eastern Europe was subordinated to the rule of imperial powers and relegated to inferior social positions. As is often the case, the dominant population developed explanations in the form of stereotypes to explain and justify the power imbalance and the subjugation of Eastern Europeans. Eastern Europe tends to be associated with being backward, lazy, poor, or inferior. Findings from one survey revealed that respondents from Western Europe associated their Eastern side with attributes like greyness, coldness, alcohol, poverty, unhappiness, melancholy, sadness, crime, corruption, and chaos (Hall, 1991).

On the other hand, Eastern European countries see Western Europeans as heartless, efficiency-driven, and soulless. In Slovenia, a popular saying illustrates their assumptions about the West: 'In heaven, the police are British; the cooks are French; the engineers are German; the administrators are Swiss; and the lovers are Italian.' However, 'In hell, the police are German; the cooks are British; the engineers are Italian; the administrators are French; and the lovers are Swiss.' This popular saying also reveals our commonly held stereotypes: Britons are perceived as logical and systematic; the French people are seen as having a delicious cuisine; the Germans are often portrayed as efficient and hardworking; the Swiss are seen as well organized; and the Italians are believed to be warm and emotional.

Maria Todorova (1997), a Bulgarian scholar, has argued that Western Europeans have historically created the image of both Eastern Europe and the regions of the Balkans including countries such as Serbia, Bulgaria, Romania, Albania, Montenegro, and so forth as the land of violence, primitiveness, bloodshed, and lawlessness. Todorova believed that such negative stereotypes of Eastern Europeans, specifically of people from the Balkans (e.g. Bosnia, Serbia, Bulgaria, Romania, Albania, etc.), were influenced by the media, popular culture, and especially literature. Those cultural products contribute to creating an image of the Balkans as mystical but also dangerous and traditional. Most mainstream cultural texts tend to rely on stereotypes and clichés in their representations of 'us' (the civilized West) and 'them' (the uncivilized East). For example, the famous novel *Dracula*, written by the English/Irish writer Bram Stoker in 1897, displays British perceptions and stereotypes of Eastern Europeans, depicting them as uncivilized and barbaric – and a potential threat to the civilized British culture.

Since the fall of the Berlin Wall and the collapse of the Soviet Union, 28 countries have emerged out of the eight former communist countries in Central and Eastern Europe (CEE). Different research projects in the last couple of years indeed show that Eastern Europeans are still predominantly perceived by their Western counterparts via stereotypes, such as laziness, backwardness, and violence. Despite the expansion of the European Union toward eastern regions to include countries such as Poland, Slovenia, Bulgaria, and Romania, Western European perceptions of the new member states to the Eastern Europe still tend to be monolithic and unchanged (Volčič, 2008).

Nevertheless, the newly emerged countries have been engaging in a range of public campaigns during the past eighteen years in order to change such negative perceptions or stereotypes that the West holds about them into positive ones. They want the West to perceive them as countries possessing democracy, political stability, and a strong market economy. Many Eastern European countries are now attempting to project themselves as cultural, artistic, affordable, modern, sunny, and welcoming places. For example, public campaigns today employ attractive slogans: in Serbia, *Serbia is the Guardian of Time*; in Macedonia, *Come to Macedonia and Your Heart Will Remain Here*; in Slovenia, *On the Sunny Side of the Alps*; in Croatia, *The Mediterranean as it Once Was*; in Montenegro, *The Pearl of the Mediterranean*; in Bosnia, *The Old Europe*.

Governments are also utilizing mass media channels to change negative stereotypes about Eastern European countries. In 2004 the Romanian government backed what was the country's first long-term campaign to change the image of Romania in the West. A comprehensive project, called *Romania: Simply Surprising*, was developed to present Romania as a modern, multicultural, democratic country. TV channels were utilized to advertise the four major Romanian 'assets': Bucharest, Transylvania, the churches of Bukovina and Maramures, and the Black Sea coast. Similarly, in Bulgaria, the mass media played a role in influencing perceptions of Eastern Europe. For example, in 2007, a 45-second commercial with the slogan, *Open Doors to Open Hearts,* appeared on CNN as part of the 'changing perception' campaign to promote Bulgaria as an attractive tourism destination. It is hoped that public campaigns and media products can change negative perceptions and reduce negative stereotypes about Eastern Europe.

References for case study

Hall, Derek (ed.) (1991) *Tourism and Economic Development in Eastern Europe and the Soviet Union*. London: Belhaven.

Todorova, Maria (1997) *Imagining the Balkans*. New York: Oxford University Press.

Volčič, Zala (2008) 'Former Yugoslavia on the World Wide Web: commercialization and branding of nation-states', *International Communication Gazette*, 70 (5): 395–413.

Questions for discussion

1 What are some of the negative stereotypes about Eastern Europeans?
2 What are the major sources of those negative stereotypes? What roles do the mass media play in creating and reinforcing stereotypes?
3 What do you think are the potential consequences of negative stereotypes against certain groups of people?

4 Eastern Europeans are often grouped together as all being the same – of one culture. Could you use implicit consistency theory to explain this phenomenon?
5 What kind of strategies would you suggest to overcome prejudice and stereotypes against Eastern European countries?

Key Terms

attribution theory;	interpretation;	selective attention;
categorization;	outgroup homogeneity	selective exposure;
cultural relativism;	effect;	self-fulfilling prophecy;
ethnocentrism;	prejudice;	stereotype
halo effect;	racism;	
impression consistency;	selection;	

Further Reading

Perception and culture

Bond, Michael H. and Forgas, Joseph P. (1984) 'Linking person perception to behavior intention across cultures: the role of cultural collectivism', *Journal of Cross-Cultural Psychology,* 15 (3): 337–352.

Jaspars, Jos and Hewstone, Miles (1982) 'Cross-culture interaction, social attribution, and intergroup relations', in S. Bochner (ed.), *Cultures in Contact.* Elmsford, NY: Pergamon. pp. 127–156.

Maddux, William W. and Yuki, Masaki (2006) 'The "Ripple effect": cultural differences in perceptions of the consequences of events', *Personality and Social Psychology Bulletin*, 32: 669–683.

Miller, Christopher (1996) 'Building illusions: culture determines what we see', *Business Communication Quarterly*, 59 (1): 87–90.

Miller, Joan G. (1984) 'Culture and the development of everyday social explanation', *Journal of Personal Social Psychology*, 46: 961–978.

Nisbett, Richard E. and Yuri, Miyamoto (2005) 'The influence of culture: holistic *vs.* analytic perception', *Trends in Cognitive Sciences*, 9 (10): 467–473.

Peng, Kaipeng; Ames, Daniel and Knowles, Eric (2001) 'Culture and human inference: perspectives from three traditions', in D. Masumoto (ed.), *Handbook of Culture and Psychology*. New York: Oxford University Press. pp. 243–263.

Stereotyping and racism

Australian Government Department of Immigration and Citizenship (2007) 'Fact Sheet 8: The abolition of the White Australia Policy'. Available online at http://www.immi.gov.au/media/fact-sheets/08abolition.htm

Murphy, Sheila (1998) 'The impact of factual versus fictional media portrayals on cultural stereotypes', *The Annals of the American Academy of Political and Social Science*, 560: 165–178.

Nisbett, Richard E. (2003) *The Geography of Thought: How Asians and Westerners Think Differently and Why*. New York: Free Press.

Peng, Kaiping and Knowles, Eric (2003) 'Culture, ethnicity and the attribution of physical causality', *Personality and Social Psychology Bulletin*, 29: 1272–1284.

5

Cultural Orientations and Behaviours

If we are to achieve a richer culture, rich in contrasting values, we must recognize the whole gamut of human potentialities, and so weave a less arbitrary social fabric, one in which each diverse human gift will find a fitting place.

Margaret Mead, American cultural
anthropologist, 1901–1978

Learning Objectives

At the end of this chapter, you should be able to:

- Identify Hofstede's five dimensions of culture.
- Define Hall's high-context and low-context cultures.
- Compare and contrast cultures on different cultural dimensions.
- Explain value orientations and how they influence communication behaviours.
- Understand the principles governing ethical intercultural communication.

Culture as a Repertoire of Human Behaviours

Culture provides the overall framework for humans to organize their thoughts, emotions, and behaviours in relation to their environment. Our culture guides us in how to think, feel, act, and communicate. At the core of culture are values – defined as an explicit or implicit conception, distinctive of an individual or characteristic of a group – which influence the selection of behaviours (Kluckhohn, 1951). Values are guiding principles for human behaviour, and each culture treasures some values more than others. For example, some cultures value assertiveness while others hold the value of harmony in greater esteem. Our values provide the criteria for us to evaluate our own behaviours and those of others.

The relationship between values and human communication was summarized by Sitaram and Haapanen (1979). First, values are communicated both explicitly and implicitly through symbolic behaviours. Most of our verbal and nonverbal behaviours reflect the values we have learned through the socialization process and have become embedded in our minds. For example, the Japanese proverb 'A single arrow is easily broken, but not ten in a bundle' illustrates the value of collectivism. Nonverbally, the custom of exchanging gifts in China reflects the cultural values of reciprocity (Chen and Starosta, 2005). In addition, the ways people communicate are influenced by the values they hold. Since values function as criteria for us to judge what is appropriate and desirable, they consequently influence the way we interact with others in communication. For example, the Chinese often avoid saying 'no' when someone makes a request that cannot probably be fulfilled. Instead, such a request would elicit a response such as 'We need to think it over' or 'It is a bit difficult', in order to preserve harmony. These examples demonstrate that our culture is a repertoire of our behaviours, as well as the criteria for evaluating behaviours.

This chapter concentrates on the influence exerted by cultural orientations on our behaviours. First, we describe the five best-known cultural dimensions, identified by Hofstede and his associates. Next, we introduce Hall's high-context and low-context dimensions of culture and compare different cultures on them. The value orientations developed by Kluckhohn and Strodbeck are introduced, followed by an exploration of how these influence communication across cultures. This chapter concludes with a discussion of the principles governing ethical intercultural communication.

Dimensions of Culture

Scholars of intercultural relations have proposed several approaches to categorizing and studying culture. This section focuses on two models that have been very influential in intercultural communication studies: Hofstede's cultural dimensions, including the Confucian work dynamism dimension developed by Hofstede and Bond, and Hall's high-context and low-context cultural dimensions.

Hofstede's cultural dimensions

Hofstede (1980: 125) defined culture as 'the collective programming of the mind which distinguishes the members of one human group from another'. Culture plays a significant role in individual decision making, as it is an antecedent of psychological processes (Triandis, 2000): it affects one's thinking, doing, and being. Hofstede (1980) compared work-related attitudes in IMB across more than 53 different cultures and found four consistent cultural dimensions influencing the behaviours of 160,000 managers and employees. He suggested that these cultural dimensions had a significant impact on behaviour in all cultures: individualism–collectivism, masculinity–femininity, power distance, and uncertainty avoidance. Later, a fifth dimension of long-term orientation (also known as Confucian work dynamism) was added to the model by Hofstede and Bond (1988).

Since the publication of Hofstede's book *Cultural Consequences* in 1980, the concept of dimensions of national cultures has been applied in various disciplines, including intercultural training, cross-cultural psychology, management, organizational psychology, sociology, and communication. Hofstede's work is not without criticism, though. For example, McSweeney (2002) commented that nations may not be the best units for studying cultures, that a study of the subsidiaries of one company (IBM) cannot provide information about entire national cultures, and that surveys are not suitable ways of measuring culture. Nevertheless, over the past decades, researchers from different disciplines have tested and added more validations to the IBM scores and contributed to the overall picture originally developed by Hofstede (e.g. House et al., 2004; Triandis, 1995). Up until this date, Hofstede's model has been included in almost all intercultural communication books.

Individualism–Collectivism

This dimension describes the relationship between the individual and the groups to which he or she belongs. In individualistic cultures, the emphasis is placed on individuals' goals over group goals (Triandis et al., 1990). People in an individualistic culture tend to stress the importance of self and personal achievement (Gudykunst, 2004). Social behaviour is guided by personal goals, perhaps at the expense of other types of goals. Individuals are encouraged to pursue and develop their abilities and aptitudes.

By contrast, collectivistic cultures emphasize values that serve and preserve the ingroup by subordinating personal goals to this end. Group membership is more important than individuality, and people are expected to be interdependent and show their conformity to ingroup norms and values. In collectivistic cultures, people do not see themselves as isolated individuals but as interdependent with others (e.g. their ingroup), in which responsibility is shared and accountability is collective. Collectivistic societies are characterized by extended primary groups such as the family, neighbourhood, or occupational group. For example, collectivist values are evident in many traditional Chinese performances, such as the dragon dance, which require the close cooperation of the group rather than exceptional skills by one individual. Cultures are never completely individualist or collectivistic, but can be conceived of as being positioned somewhere along a continuum of individualism versus collectivism. According to Hofstede's (1980) study, countries such as Australia, the United States, Great Britain, Canada, the Netherlands, New Zealand, Italy, Belgium, and Denmark are ranked high on individualism, whereas Columbia, Venezuela, Pakistan, Peru, Taiwan, Thailand, Singapore, Chile, and Hong Kong are ranked towards the lower end of the continuum.

Photo 5.1
Chinese dragon dance in Brisbane to celebrate Chinese New Year.
Copyright © The Chinese Consulate in Brisbane. Used with permission.

A culture's orientation toward individualism or collectivism has important behavioural consequences for its members. Previous research indicates that in collectivistic cultures distinctiveness in the self-concept does not play as important a role as it does in individualistic cultures (Hofstede, 1980). As has been seen in large-scale research programmes like GLOBE (House et al., 2004), Confucian Asia (China, Hong Kong, Japan, Singapore, South Korea, and Taiwan) is characterized by a societal collectivism based on networks, trust, and loyalty to ingroups such as organizations or families. Research has demonstrated that people in collectivistic cultures are more concerned with social acceptance and others' opinions than are people in individualistic cultures (Hui and Triandis, 1986). This is because collectivists are more likely to comply with the wishes of the ingroup than individualists. For example, Lee and Green (1991) showed that reference groups, such as the extended family, neighbours, and friends, have greater influence on purchase decisions for Korean consumers than for American consumers.

It is important to note that individualism or collectivism at the cultural level does not mean that every individual in the culture conforms to the culture's position on this dimension. In a seminal review, Markus and Kitayama (1991) pointed to the vast individual differences within cultures on this dimension. They showed the influence of an individualist (or independent) versus a collectivist (or interdependent) orientation on self-concept, motivation, emotion, and thinking. Their research and other work which has followed it tell us that, in intercultural communication, we need to be aware not only of the cultural values but also of an individual's orientation to them, as both will influence communication in the interaction.

Individualism and collectivism have been associated with direct and indirect styles of communication; that is, the extent to which speakers reveal their intentions through explicit verbal communication. In the direct style, associated with individualism, the wants and needs of the speaker are embodied in the spoken message. For example, saying 'no' to requests made by colleagues is both common and acceptable in the US, the UK, and Australia. In the indirect style, associated with collectivism, the wants and needs of the speaker are not obvious in the spoken message. In China, for instance, requests for help from friends are often made indirectly, so as to avoid embarrassment should the other persons have difficulty in honouring the request. Such an indirect request may be made by describing one's problematic situation and 'inviting' the other person to offer help. The initial offer of help is customarily declined and then later accepted with gratitude upon the second or third offer. Thus, the sincerity of the offer to help can be ensured.

Masculinity–femininity

This dimension describes how a culture's dominant values are assertive or nurturing. In masculine cultures, people strive for a maximal distinction between how men and women are expected to think and behave. Cultures that place a high value on masculine traits stress assertiveness, competition, and material success. Cultures labelled as feminine are those that permit more overlapping social roles for the sexes and place a high value on feminine traits such as quality of life, interpersonal relationships, and concern for the weak. For example, in some cultures it is acceptable for the wife to go out to work while the husband stays home minding the children and taking care of domestic chores. In cultures with more masculine values, however, such a practice would probably be frowned upon. Interestingly, Hofstede (1980) found that women's social role varied less from culture to culture than did men's. According to his study, Japan is top of the list of masculine cultures; Australia, Venezuela, Switzerland, Mexico, Ireland, Great Britain, and Germany also belong to this category. Japanese women are traditionally taught to be obedient and to make household skills and domesticity the centre of their life. A Japanese wife is expected to be an able homemaker and mother. However, these traditions are changing, with women increasingly taking on professions and joining the workforce. Sweden, Norway, the Netherlands, Denmark, Finland, Chile, Portugal, and Thailand represent more feminine cultures.

Power distance

This refers to the extent to which a culture tolerates inequality in power distribution. In cultures with a larger power distance, inequalities among people are both expected and desired. Less powerful people are expected to depend on more powerful people. Children are expected to be obedient toward their parents, instead of being treated more or less as equals, and people are expected to display respect for those with a higher status. For example, in Thailand, where a status hierarchy is observed, people are expected to display respect for monks by greeting and taking leave of them with ritualistic greetings, removing their hats in the presence of a monk, seating monks at a higher level, and using a vocabulary that shows respect. Cultures with a smaller power distance de-emphasize inequalities among people, stressing that there should be interdependence between people of different power levels. In New Zealand, characterized as a low power distance culture, it is common for subordinates to address managers by their first name; in Hong Kong, high in power distance, people of a lower rank in the workplace usually address those of a higher rank with titles to observe hierarchical relationships.

Power distance also refers to the extent to which power, prestige, and wealth are distributed within a culture. Cultures with a high power distance have power and influence concentrated in the hands of a few rather than distributed throughout the population. Those cultures may communicate in a way that reinforces hierarchies in interpersonal relationships. High power distance cultures tend to orient towards authoritarianism, which dictates a hierarchical structure of social relationships. In such cultures the differences between age and status, for example, are maximized. The Philippines, Mexico, Venezuela, India, Singapore, Brazil, Hong Kong, France, and Columbia represent high power distance cultures (Hofstede, 1980). On the other hand, low power distance cultures are characterized by 'horizontal' social relationships. People in these cultures tend to minimize the differences of age, sex, status, and roles. Social interactions are more direct and less formal. Countries such as Australia, Israel, Denmark, New Zealand, Ireland, Sweden, Norway, Finland, and Switzerland score low in power distance. Hofstede (1983) relates an incident in which one of Canada's leading banks invited a Chinese delegation for dinner. When the Chinese found that no welcome toast was proposed at the beginning, they felt uneasy. In Chinese culture, it is customary for the host to show respect by offering a welcome toast at the beginning of the meal. The Canadians' lack of understanding of the hierarchical nature of Chinese society and the associated ways of communicating respect cost them in their business dealings with the visiting delegation.

Theory Corner

Michel Foucault's theory of power

Michel Foucault (2006), a French philosopher, argued that communication rarely takes place between pure 'equals', even though most of our models of understanding communication make this assumption. Social hierarchies are always present, however subtle, in communication interactions. In every culture there is a social hierarchy that privileges some groups over others. These groups hold more power, be it economic, political, or cultural, and they determine to a great extent the communication system.

Foucault's work reveals an interest in questions about where power is 'located' in a culture; who has and who does not have it; how power is distributed; how those in power obtain and keep power; and to what/whose ends power is used. Foucault believed that power is dynamic, flowing through individuals in various contexts and relationships. Importantly, people who are the subjects of power often find ways to resist this power, but this does not mean such resistance is easy.

Power is also institutional in that human institutions embody and sustain power relations. This is true of cultural institutions such as marriage, legal-political institutions, and physical institutions such as prisons, schools, or hospitals. Certain institutional roles (e.g. teachers or the police) can offer occupants more institutional power.

Reference

Foucault, Michel (2006) *History of Madness*. New York: Routledge.

Further reading on power

Loden, Marilyn and Rosener, Judy B. (1991) *Workforce America: Managing Diversity as a Vital Resource*. Homewood, IL: Business One Irwin.

Uncertainty avoidance

This dimension reflects a culture's tolerance of ambiguity and acceptance of risk. Uncertainty avoidance represents the degree to which members of a particular culture avoid or tolerate uncertainty. Some cultures have a high need for information and certainty, whereas other cultures seem to be more comfortable dealing with diversity and ambiguity. In high uncertainty avoidance cultures, people are active and security seeking; cultures weak in uncertainty avoidance are contemplative, less aggressive, unemotional, relaxed, accepting of personal risks, and relatively tolerant. According to Hofstede's scale, Greece, Portugal, Belgium, Japan, Peru, France, Chile, Spain, and Argentina are high in uncertainty avoidance, whereas Denmark, Sweden, Norway, Finland, Ireland, Great Britain, the Netherlands, the Philippines, and the United States all tend to be at the lower end of the scale. These latter cultures are oriented to cope with the stress and anxiety caused by ambiguous situations. They take more initiative, show greater flexibility, and feel more relaxed in interactions. People from high uncertainty avoidance cultures tend to avoid risk taking, whereas those from low uncertainty avoidance cultures are more comfortable with risk and able to cope with the stress and anxiety that it causes (Hofstede, 2001).

High uncertainty avoidance tends to be found in collectivistic cultures. The combined influence of uncertainty avoidance and collectivism can be found in research on consumer behaviour. The decision to purchase imported products, for instance, involves risk taking. The level of perceived risk associated with purchases and the extent of uncertainty tolerance will influence purchasing intentions. For example, risk perception is found to be negatively associated with Asian consumers' willingness to adopt online purchasing (Liang and Huang, 1998). Similarly, Greek consumers have greater concerns for security than British consumers (Jarvenpaa and Tractinsky, 1999). However, the results of other empirical research have been equivocal. Weber and Hsee (1998) contended that people from collectivistic cultures may be more willing to take risks, because in a collectivistic society family and other ingroup members are expected to help a person bear the possible adverse consequences of risky choices. This claim is supported by Yamaguchi (1998), who argued that people tend to perceive less risk when others are exposed to the same risk situation. Nevertheless, the consensus is that people from cultures with different levels of uncertainty avoidance respond differently to risk situations.

Long-term and short-term orientation

This dimension is also called *Confucian work dynamism*. It is concerned with values in social relations. Confucian work dynamism refers to dedicated, motivated, responsible, and educated individuals with a sense of commitment and organizational identity and loyalty. Countries and regions high in Confucian work dynamism are Hong Kong, Singapore, Taiwan, South Korea, and Japan – five economic dragons. Long-term orientation was identified in an international study with Chinese employees and managers (Hofstede and Bond, 1988). It encourages thrift, savings, perseverance toward results, ordering relationships by status, and a willingness to subordinate oneself for a purpose. The long-term orientation was also found to encourage Chinese consumers to place a greater emphasis on the quality of products when making purchasing decisions. For example, quality and utilitarian values were found to be strong predictors of Chinese consumers' intention to purchase Canadian pork sausages (Zhou and Hui, 2003). Short-term orientation, which characterizes Western cultures, is consistent with less saving, spending to keep up with social pressure, and a preference for quick results (Hofstede, 2001).

Hall's high- and low-context cultural dimension

Hall (1976) divided cultures into *low-context* and *high-context*. This dimension refers to the extent to which we gather information from the physical, social, and psychological context of an interaction (high-context) as opposed to the explicit verbal code (low-context). This dimension represents a continuum in which some cultures (e.g. China, England, France, Ghana, Japan, Korea) orient toward the high-context end, whereas others (e.g. Germany, Scandinavia, Switzerland, the United States) are at the low-context end. According to Hall and Hall (1990: 183–184), high- or low-context refers to:

> the fact that when people communicate, they take for granted how much the listener knows about the subject under discussion. In low-context communication, the listener knows very little and must be told practically everything. In high-context communication, the listener is already 'contexted' and does not need to be given much background information.

For people in high-context cultures, much of the meaning is implicit either in the physical setting or in shared beliefs, values, and norms. The context provides much information about the culture's rules, practices, and expectations. Thus, information about the background and procedures is not overtly communicated; instead, listeners are expected to know how to interpret the communication and what to do. Thus, information and cultural rules remain unspoken, as the context is expected to be a cue for behaviour. High-context cultures generally have restricted code systems, in which speakers and listeners rely more on the contextual elements of the communication setting for information than on the actual language – interactants look to the physical, social, relational, and cultural environment for information. By contrast, low-context cultures employ an explicit code to send messages. People rely on an elaborated code system for creating and interpreting meaning, so that little meaning is determined by the context. Information to be shared with others is explicitly coded in the verbal message, procedures are explained, and expectations are discussed.

Kluckhohn and Strodtbeck's Value Orientations

Kluckhohn and Strodtbeck (1961) argued that all human cultures are confronted with universal problems emerging from relationships with others, time, activities, and nature. Value orientations are the means a society uses to solve these universal problems. The concept entails four assumptions. First, all human societies face the same problems; second, they use different means to solve them; third, the means to address universal problems are limited; and fourth, value orientations are behaviourally observable through empirical studies (Condon and Yousef, 1975). Value orientation theory suggests that cultures develop unique positions on five value orientations: the relationship of people with nature (people should be subordinate to/in harmony with/dominant over nature), activity (state of being/inner development/industriousness), time (past/present/future), human nature (people are good/mixed/evil), and social relations (individualistic/collective/hierarchical). Each orientation represents a way of addressing a universal problem.

Theory Corner

Condon and Yousef's model of value orientations

Condon and Yousef (1975) extended Kluckhohn and Strodtbeck's five value orientations to include six spheres of universal problems all humans face. These are the self, the family, society, human nature, nature, and the supernatural, all of which are interdependent of each other. Condon and Yousef derived 25 value orientations encompassed by the six spheres. They claimed that all value orientations exist in every society, but the preferred response to the problem will vary from culture to culture. For example, one value orientation under the sphere of 'supernatural' is 'knowledge of the cosmic order'. In some cultures, people believe this order is comprehensible; in others they believe it is mysterious and unknowable; still others believe that understanding it is a matter of faith and reason.

Reference

Condon, John C. and Yousef, Fathi (1975) *An Introduction to Intercultural Communication*. Indianapolis, IN: Boffs-Merrill.

Further reading on values

Schwartz, Shalom H. and Sagiv, Lilach (1995) 'Identifying culture-specifics in the content and structure of values', *Journal of Cross-Cultural Psychology*, 26 (1): 99–116.

Man–nature orientation

This orientation addresses the question of what the relationship of humans to nature is. A society's conception of the relationship of humans to nature is determined by the worldview of its people. *Worldview* refers to the outlook a culture has about the nature of the universe, the nature of humankind, the relationship between humanity and the universe, and other philosophical issues defining humans' place in the cosmos. Since prehistoric times, humans have made creation stories in order to explain their relationship to nature. This relationship can be a subjugation to nature, living in harmony with nature, or a mastery over nature. Phrases like 'Nature as machine' and its variant 'Nature as storehouse' justify the exploitative relationship between Western civilizations and the environment, where nature is regarded as something that needs to be conquered. For example, in the United States, people make a clear distinction between humans and nature, with humans assuming a dominant role over nature, valuing and protecting it. This viewpoint is evident in the changing of river courses to accommodate city planning (Simmel, 1950).

In Arab culture, humans are part of nature and are supposed to live in harmony with it. This orientation is related to the Islamic view that every-

Photo 5.2
The statue of Buddha symbolizes peace and harmony, valued in Asian cultures.
Copyright © Shuang Liu. Used with permission.

thing in the world, except humans, is administered by God-made laws. The physical world has no choice but to be obedient to God. Humans, however, can choose to obey the law of God; in so doing, they will be in harmony with all other elements of nature. Japanese culture is also characterized by a love of and a respect for nature, believing that humans should live in harmony with nature. They cherish the beauty of nature through *hanami* (cherry blossoms) in spring and *momijigari* (maple leaves changing colour) in autumn, and practise traditional flower arrangements known as *ikebana*. Harmony is a central concept in Japanese culture, influenced by Shintoism along with Buddhist and Confucian traditions. The traditional Japanese garden illustrates this harmonious relationship between humans and nature.

Activity orientation

This orientation addresses the question of what the modality of human activity is. This refers to the use of time for self-expression and play, self-improvement and development, and work. The activity orientation can refer to being,

being-in-becoming, and doing. Protestant cultures, such as that of Britain, perceive paid work as essential: a dominant human activity that occupies a central place in human existence. Human work is understood as a duty that benefits both the individual and society as a whole. Many Americans believe that work should be separated from play and that a feeling of accomplishment is the most important aspect of work. A high value is placed on time and efficiency. In other cultures, earning a living through labour is not only a duty but also a virtue and is thus not separable from other aspects of human existence. In some religious cultures praying is cherished and this is considered to be more important for humans than working.

Time orientation

This orientation answers the question of what the temporal focus of human life is. Cultures differ widely in their conceptions of time. Time orientations can be past, present, or future. Many Western cultures view time in a linear fashion – there is the past, present, and future. This attitude conceives of time as a commodity that can be spent, saved, borrowed, and wasted. When time is considered a tangible object, it becomes something to be managed and used responsibly. For example, most Americans say that they often lack time. This may be partly due to the fact that they are striving for the 'American Dream' – the metaphor for upward mobility, success, luxury, and happiness, all of which consume time. The concept is often regarded as an ideology; Americans feel pressured constantly to do more, earn more, and consume more in order to achieve the ideals of their society. This attitude tends to push people into a constantly hurried state of mind. Time decides when Americans make their appointments, when they do their work, and even how they spend their leisure time. Punctuality is important and being late without a legitimate reason is considered bad manners. Similarly, the Swiss have a reputation for being as punctual and precise as their famous watches. The saying is: *Avant l'heure, c'est pas l'heure, après l'heure, c'est plus l'heure* (Before the hour is not yet the hour, after the hour is no longer the hour). In Switzerland, you are likely to see a clock almost everywhere you go; this is a culture that runs on time and is organized around time.

In other cultures the past, present, and future may not be quite as distinct. Mulder (1996) reports three different conceptions of time in Thai society. The first conception is characterized by continuity. This is the belief in a continuity of life, traditions, and the environment, from ancestors into endless future generations. In this sense time stands still. Past, present, and future are indistinct. The second conception is the 'modern' conception of time – instead of standing still, time in this conception moves ahead toward the future. For example, when a poor Thai farmer migrates to the city for a better life, he or she has to measure time in terms of working hours in a factory instead of in the fields. The third is an animistic conception of time. Communities feel that they are controlled by a strong power beyond their control. Thus, they seek ways to manage this power through various means including worship and animal sacrifices. Thai people worship gods who they believe will help their village in return by sending rain when it is needed.

Photo 5.3
A clock in a public place in Venice uses Roman numerals to show the hours of the day.
Copyright © Zala Volčič. Used with permission.

There are some cultures that do not have a clear sense of time, as revealed in their language. For example, the Hopi language does not have verb tenses, but simply uses two words to express time: one meaning 'sooner' and the other meaning 'later'. Hopi tribes live for the most part in northeast Arizona and are well known for being very peaceful (Malotki, 1983). Another example is the Pirahã, a small Amazonian tribe that has a limited language consisting of relatively few sounds and grammatical constructions and which can be whistled for some purposes (like hunting). Their traditional language appears to have no precise numbers, specific past tense, or written form. There is limited art in this culture and no precise concept of time. Their religion is animistic and they make little reference to history or ancestors. The Pirahã do not (or did not in the past) have a desire to remember where they came from or to tell cultural stories (Everett, 2008). In the old days of Venice, for example, there were clocks on public buildings that showed the position of the sun and moon along with the relative positions of Saturn, Jupiter, Venus, Mercury, and Mars. Today, we can see clocks in public place in Venice that use Roman numerals to show the hours of the day.

Different time orientations can lead people to believe it is possible either to attempt only one task at a time or to multi-task. Hall (1976) categorized time orientations into *polychronic* and *monochronic*. People from a monochronic time orientation view time as linear and tend to do one thing at a time, whereas people from a polychronic time orientation view time as cyclical and attempt to perform multiple tasks simultaneously. For example, Arab markets and stores appear to reflect the culture's polychronic conception of time, resulting in what can appear to be a state of mass confusion as various customers all try to get the attention of a single clerk. Similarly, offices in Arabic cultures may have large reception areas where several groups of people all conduct their affairs at the same time. To someone from a culture with a monochronic time orientation, this arrangement may appear counter-intuitive and confusing. Of course, the division between mono- and polychronic time orientations is not often clearcut. People are capable of both orientations depending on the context.

Human nature orientation

This orientation addresses the question of what the intrinsic character of human nature is. Are we born good or evil, or a mixture of good and evil? Puritan origins in the United States reflect a Christian view that people are born evil but have the potential to become good through self-control and self-discipline. Other contemporary views claim that humans are born with a mixture of good and evil and thus have a choice to be either. Such a belief in rationality is consistent with the belief in the scientific method of inquiry, whereby truth can be discovered through human reasoning. In other cultures, such as the Chinese culture, Confucianism teaches that humans are born free of evil. Buddhism emphasizes the spirituality and goodness of the individual, in what is a more inward-oriented philosophy. The Judaeo-Christian tradition claims that an understanding of the person is bound together with the belief that humans are created in the image of God, suggesting a close relationship between the concept of God and the concept of the person. Humans are seen as sinful, but they can be redeemed during the course of life, since God created humans who are endowed with intelligence and choice. The purpose of human life is to worship God by knowing, loving, and obeying. In Hinduism a person is defined by his or her membership of a caste, so it is difficult to practise the equality of all persons. Differences in human nature orientation are often reflected in a society's criminal laws: some countries believe a suspect is innocent until proven guilty, whereas other countries believe a suspect is guilty until proven innocent.

Relational orientation

The relational orientation addresses the question of what the modality of a person's relationship to others is. It refers to perceptions of the self and the ways in which society is organized. It can be lineal, collateral, and individualistic. In individualistic cultures, people are encouraged to accept responsibility as independent individuals. For example, in such cultures marriage is usually the decision of the individual, and romantic love tends to be the reason for marriage. In collectivistic cultures, such as India, marriage may be considered as too great a decision to be left up to the individuals involved, because marriages present opportunities for familial alliances in a culture where families are very important. In such group-oriented cultures, individuals subordinate their personal needs to their ingroup, particularly their family. If a Chinese youngster passes the national matriculation test and is offered a place in a good university, both parents and other members of the extended family feel they have been given face because honour is the collective property of the family. In the same way, all family

Photo 5.4
Elderly people in Sarajevo, Bosnia, enjoy playing collective games like chess in a public square.

members would feel they had lost face should a single member of the family commit a dishonourable act. Collectivistic cultures tend to be more caring for each other, as there is a strong sense of belonging to some collectivity – a family, neighbourhood, village, class, or organization. In Bosnia, for example, elderly people enjoy playing chess in public squares, which creates an atmosphere of collectivity.

Intercultural Communication Ethics

Ethics is concerned with what is right or wrong, good or bad, and the standards and rules that guide our behaviour. Ethics is different from morals: morals are our personal beliefs, while ethics, according to the Greeks, is the study of what is good for the individual and society. Communication ethics involves how we engage in acts of communication and the consequences of our communication behaviour (Chen and Starosta, 2005). When we engage in an intercultural interaction, we evaluate each other's communication based on our own cultural rules. We make decisions on what is right or wrong, albeit sometimes subconsciously, and apply ethical principles. Scholars in intercultural communication debate whether there are overarching ethical frameworks that we can apply to all cultures, or whether each culture determines its own standard for what is right or wrong. Ethical issues are important in intercultural communication, as the variation in cultural norms may mean a variation in ethical standards.

Approaches to ethics

Debates on approaches to ethics have largely been about two approaches: universalism versus relativism. Proponents of *ethical universalism* believe that there are universal ethical principles that guide behaviour across all societies. Thus, what is wrong in one place will be wrong elsewhere, regardless of time and circumstance (Lowenstein and Merrill, 1990). Universalist approaches are connected with a unilinear model of cultural development which describes all cultures as progressing along a single line of development and converging on a single universal set of values and norms. The Geneva Convention standards on appropriate warfare, and human rights groups who work across geographic and cultural borders, can be considered as illustrative of this universalistic view. The problem with universalism is that universalist approaches attempt to ground ethics variously in religion, nature, history, and reason but largely fail because there is no agreement about what is religiously authoritative, natural, historical, or reasonable (Evanoff, 2004).

Contrary to universalism, proponents of *ethical relativism* believe that ethics is closely related to motive, intuition, and emotion. They believe that while people from different cultures share common needs, interests, or feelings, their ways of acting upon these internal states vary because of cultural differences. Relativists deny the existence of a single universal set of values and norms and instead believe that values and norms are relative to particular individuals or groups (Lowenstein and Merrill, 1990). Relativist approaches are connected with subjectivity in ethics, the preservation of local cultures, and a multilinear model of cultural development which views all cultures as progressing along separate lines of development and diverging with respect to values and norms (Evanoff, 2004). Thus ethical relativists would not judge another's behaviour by their own ethical standards, because they believe that adhering to one's own contextualized truths in intercultural interactions only leads to conflict. Nevertheless relativism, which is widely accepted in the field of intercultural communication, is not without its critics. While acknowledging that various cultures construct ethical systems, cultural relativists fail to address how conflicts between cultures with different values and norms can be resolved. Moreover, there is often a difference between what is done (descriptive ethics) and what should be done (normative ethics).

Evanoff (2004) states that relativism seems progressive but is in fact conservative because it obligates us simply to accept the values and norms of other cultures instead of encouraging us to critically reflect upon them. He proposes a *communicative approach* to intercultural ethics as an alternative to both universalism and relativism. The communicative approach recognizes that humans are socialized into a particular set of cultural norms, but also claims that they are capable of critically reflecting upon and changing them. In addition we are able to critically review the norms of other cultures and make informed decisions about which of these are worthy of adoption or rejection. An ethical dialogue on intercultural communication can take place between specific cultures in specific contexts in relation to specific problems and specific individuals or groups. Thus rather than seeing ethics as fixed, a communicative approach views ethics as dynamic and changing. For example, we no longer find slavery acceptable and we are in the process of creating ethical norms to deal with emerging issues like euthanasia.

Principles of ethical intercultural communication

Bradford Hall (2005) provides a comprehensive overview of intercultural communication ethics. He argues that the controversy between universalism and relativism both enables and constrains creativity and stability in human societies. Therefore, a more appropriate way to examine intercultural ethics is to integrate both universal and relative perspectives (Chen and Starosta, 2005). Just as Hall claims that communication ethics is a combination of constraints and empowerment, one of the golden rules for communication ethics, originally based in religious philosophy, is 'Do unto others as you would have them do unto you.' Similarly, a famous Confucian maxim states, 'Never do to others what you would not like them to do to you.' In this section, we will discuss four ethical principles guiding intercultural communication, based on Chen and Starosta's (2005) work.

Mutuality

Mutuality means we should locate a common space. The key to this principle is human relationships in interacting with others. We need to gain an understanding of the perspective of the other before making any ethical decisions. We also need to build relational empathy with the other party. A spirit of equality, inclusiveness, and a supportive climate is conducive to successful communication outcomes. On the other hand, if either party demands that the interaction be conducted according to his or her own cultural norms, intercultural communication is unlikely to be successful.

Non-judgmentalism

Non-judgmentalism implies a willingness to express ourselves openly and be open minded about others' behaviours. Key to this principle is understanding other people's point of view, power position, and cultural values. As we have said earlier, Indians may eat with their hands because they believe God gives us hands to eat and give food; Muslim women cover their heads with a scarf in public to observe their religious beliefs; Chinese business people often give gifts to their business partners, not to bribe them but to show their desire to establish a good interpersonal relationship, because in China there is an overlap between personal and work relationships. None of these practices may be practised in your culture; the important point here is to recognize and appreciate differences.

Honesty

The principle of honesty requires us to see things as they are rather than as we would like them to be. For example, Elliott (1997) examined the cross-cultural tensions created by the 1995 earthquake in Japan. When the Japanese government was slow to accept the assistance offered by the international community, the US media were quick to criticize what they perceived as ingratitude. However, Elliot uncovered the cultural assumptions that underlay the Japanese response, such as collective self-sufficiency, an emphasis on local-first action, bottom-up decision making, and a lack of emphasis on individual volunteerism. We are socialized into our own cultural rules and norms as we grow up, and hence carry personal biases regarding what is or is not an appropriate way of handling certain situations. In the process of intercultural communication, we must be aware of these biases in order to understand other people's behaviour as it is.

Respect

Respect involves sensitivity to and acknowledgement of other people's needs and wants. Like mutuality, the golden rule with respect is to 'Do unto others as you would have them do unto you.' The platinum rule goes one step further, stating that rather than treating others as you want to be treated, treat them as you think they would want to be treated. For example, religious practices vary widely across cultural and ethnic groups. Muslims fast at a certain time of the year to demonstrate their religious faith; some Buddhists do not eat red meat as an illustration of the religious principle of non-violence; whereas people in Hong Kong offer temple sacrifices of baby pigs in return for a deity's protection. To be an ethical intercultural communicator means to be open to and respect all these practices, even though they may seem to contradict each other. We do not necessarily have to practise what other cultures do, but we need to respect the people who observe those customs and rituals.

Summary

This chapter focused on value orientations and behaviours. Two models of cultural dimensions were introduced. First, we explained Hofstede's four cultural dimensions: individualism versus collectivism, masculinity versus femininity, power distance, and uncertainty avoidance, as well as a fifth dimension developed by Hofstede and Bond – long-term versus short-term orientation. This five-dimensional model has been widely used in cross-cultural research on organizations, individuals, and communities, albeit with some criticism. Second, we discussed Edward T. Hall's high-context and low-context culture model. High-context cultures tend to rely on contextual cues to interpret meaning, whereas low-context cultures rely more on explicit verbal codes as a means of communicating meaning. This chapter also introduced Kluckhohn and Strodtbeck's value orientation theory. Value orientations are the means societies use to solve the universal problems of daily life. Value orientation theory is heuristic, and the five categories cannot encompass all the problems faced by human societies. Condon and Yousef have extended Kluckhohn and Strodtbeck's model, but the variation of cultural values makes it impossible for any one list to be exhaustive. Finally, this chapter discussed three approaches to ethics: universalism, relativism, and a communicative approach. Differences in ethical norms exist across cultures, but there are general principles governing all ethical intercultural communication, including mutuality, non-judgmentalism, honesty, and respect. Successful intercultural communication outcomes depend on communicators' ability to apply those principles to create an understanding and a supportive communication climate.

Case Study:
Dinner at a Japanese home

Dinner at a Japanese home involves the application of many cultural rules. Hofstede's cultural dimensions of collectivism, masculinity, and power distance are all at play, starting from the time of accepting the invitation, to the end of the meal. An understanding of the cultural rules underpinning Japanese customs can ensure that we behave in culturally appropriate and ethical ways when we have the opportunity to dine at a Japanese home.

Acceptance of an invitation to dinner at a Japanese home calls for a gift because reciprocity is important in collectivistic cultures. A bottle of wine or a bouquet of flowers – items that people in the West would commonly bring – are appropriate. Gourmet food items, desk accessories, or tablemats would also be considered appropriate gifts in this situation. A gift is always presented and accepted with both hands. When receiving a gift it is customary to refuse to accept it one or two times with words to the effect that a gift really is not necessary. As a formality, it is then accepted reluctantly but with gratitude. Gifts are not usually opened at this time, but later. This is particularly true if there are several gifts from several different people in the room. The Japanese do not want to put anyone in an embarrassing position with comparisons being made between gifts or to have someone who did not bring a gift feeling embarrassed. Protecting one's 'face' (social image), and particularly that of others, is important in collectivistic cultures. If there is only one person or one group of people from the same family, it is customary to ask them if it is all right to open the gift immediately. The giver always says, 'Yes, please do'. It is not uncommon to hear your Japanese friend thank you again for the gift the next time he or she sees you. In a collectivistic culture, people tend to feel indebted to others.

Japanese culture values time, and punctuality at meetings and appointments is expected. Being late is regarded as bad manners and showing a lack of concern for others (the host's family in this case). A guest is greeted at the door by the host's family, with both parties bowing to each other. The entry area of a house or an apartment is called *genkan*, where shoes are left. You should try to take off your shoes and walk across to the main floor without tracking any dirt into the house. This shows that you care about the host's family (by keeping their home clean). In collectivistic cultures, people tend to show more concern for the well-being and interest of their group (e.g. family, friends, workmates, etc.). Once you are on the main floor of the house, you might be given slippers to wear. You can wear these slippers in every room except for *tatami* mat rooms. *Tatami* mats in Japanese culture are flooring surfaces to be kept as clean as a bed or dining table surface; nothing is worn on the feet in a *tatami* mat room except socks.

In Hofstede's study, Japan ranked high on masculinity; males and females are expected to behave differently on social occasions. While many homes in Japan are now furnished in the Western style, there are still homes where traditional low tables are used during mealtimes and everyone joining the meal sits on the floor. In this case, women are supposed to sit with their knees folded and their legs to one side. Only men are allowed to sit cross-legged. You might want to wait to be seated, as the Japanese often observe a specific seating arrangement. Japan's culture is ranked high on power distance. The host generally would create a climate where a guest would feel respected. The host often reserves a place of honour for guests. Oftentimes, the most important guest is seated furthest away from the entrance. This means that he or she would have the least chance of being disturbed during the meal by other people entering or leaving the room. The host, on the other hand, is supposed to sit nearest to the entrance to the room, assuming the role of serving the guest during the meal.

The collectivistic orientation can be reflected by people's behaviour during the meal. Japanese food is commonly eaten with chopsticks. If food comes from a common platter, there will usually be tongs or a spoon to transfer some onto your plate. If there are no tongs, turn your chopsticks around and serve yourself from the opposite (clean) end. Before eating or drinking, the Japanese always say *Itadakimasu*, a kind of grace before meals that also expresses thanks to the host. Alcohol (e.g. sake) will always be present at a meal. The Japanese believe that the guest should not have to pour his or her own drink into a glass; it is the host's responsibility to keep filling the guest's glass. This collectivistic orientation can also be seen at social gatherings where people tend to fill each other's glasses. The drinking does not start until everyone's glass is filled and the drinking salute of *kampai* (cheers) has been called.

The cultural norms and rules governing behaviour in a Japanese home might sound somewhat complicated but Japanese people do not expect their foreign guests to know all of these. However, knowledge of the cultural dimensions underpinning customs and practices will help you to act in a culturally appropriate way.

Reference for case study

'Customs' [online]. Accessed 24 June 2009 at: http:www.futenma.usmc.mil/new%20joins/customs.htm

Questions for discussion

1 Asians (not only the Japanese) often decline their friends' invitations to dinner when the offer is made for the first time, to show politeness. Is such a practice common in your culture? How should you respond to an invitation?
2 During the meal or at a gathering, the Japanese check their companions' glasses and refill them when needed. What does this reflect about Japanese culture?
3 Do you know some of the 'rules' about using chopsticks in Japanese culture? Are there similar rules governing the use of knives and forks in a Western culture? What are they?
4 What kind of cultural mistakes might a Westerner make when having dinner at a Japanese home?
5 Have you been invited to dinner at a foreigner's home? If yes, what was the thing that struck you as most 'foreign'?

Key Terms

collectivism;
communicative ethical approach;
Confucian work dynamism;
ethics;
ethical relativism;

ethical universalism;
femininity;
high-context culture;
individualism;
low-context culture;
masculinity;

monochronic time;
polychronic time;
power distance;
uncertainty avoidance;
value orientation theory;
worldview

Further Reading

Cultural dimensions

Bochner, Stephen and Hesketh, Beryl (1994) 'Power distance, individualism/ collectivism, and job-related attitudes in a culturally diverse work group', *Journal of Cross-Cultural Psychology*, 25 (2): 233–257.

Lim, Kaih; Leung, Kwok; Sia, Choon Ling and Lee, Matthew K.O. (2004) 'Is e-commerce boundary-less? Effects of individualism-collectivism and uncertainty avoidance on internet shopping', *Journal of International Business Studies*, 35 (6): 545–559.

Culture and behaviours

Chen, S. Xiaohua; Bond, Michael H.; Chan, Bacon; Tang, Donghui and Bachtel, Emma E. (2009) 'Behavioral manifestations of modesty', *Journal of Cross-Cultural Psychology*, 40 (4): 603–626.

Damen, Louise (1995) 'Culture learning: the fifth dimension in the language classroom', *International Journal of Intercultural Relations*, 19 (2): 322–326.

Hofstede, Geert J. (2001) *Culture's Consequences: Comparing Values, Behaviors, Institutions, and Organizations across Nations*. Thousand Oaks, CA: SAGE.

Culture and time orientations

Bluedorn, Allen C.; Felker, Carol K. and Lane, Paul M. (1992) 'How many things do you like to do at once? An introduction to monochronic and polychronic time', *The Executive*, 6 (4): 17–26.

Tsuju, Yohko (2006) 'Railway time and rubber time: the paradox in the Japanese conception of time', *Time & Society*, 15 (2–3): 177–195.

Power and society

Loden, Marilyn and Rosener, Judy B. (1991) *Workforce America: Managing Diversity as a Vital Resource*. Homewood, IL: Business One Irwin.

Value orientations

Kluckhohn, Clyde (1948) *Mirror of Man*. New York: McGraw-Hill.

Schwartz, Shalom H. and Sagiv, Lilach (1995) 'Identifying culture-specifics in the content and structure of values', *Journal of Cross-Cultural Psychology*, 26 (1): 99–116.

Ting-Toomey, Stella and Chung, Leeva C. (2005) *Understanding Intercultural Communication*. Los Angeles, CA: Roxbury.

6

Verbal Communication and Culture

The limits of my language mean the limits of my world.

Ludwig Wittgenstein, Austrian philosopher, 1889–1951

Learning Objectives

At the end of this chapter, you should be able to:

- Recognize the powerful influence of language on intercultural communication.
- Describe the components and characteristics of verbal codes.
- Explain how our language affects our perceptions.
- Identify four communication styles and gender differences in verbal communication.
- Appreciate the influence of culture on verbal communication and identity.

The Power of Language

Individuals bring to the intercultural encounter not only their cultural beliefs and values but also their language. Language is an integral part of human lives and thus has a powerful influence on people's ability to communicate interculturally. The term 'language' may refer not only to spoken and written language but also to 'body language' (see Chapter 7). In this chapter, however, we will focus on verbal codes.

People use language to convey their thoughts, feelings, desires, attitudes, and intentions. We learn about others through what they say and how they say it; we learn about ourselves through how others react to what we say (Bonvillain, 2008). Verbal communication has been studied by scholars from a variety of disciplines, such as anthropology, political theory, and human geography, bringing diverse theories and perspectives into the study of communication and culture. Among those scholars, the most important contributors to intercultural communication are linguists, who address the question of what is unique about human language, as opposed to communication in general. Noam Chomsky, a well-known linguist, wrote in his influential book *Language and Mind* (1968: 14) that 'When we study human language, we approach what some might call the "human essence", the distinctive qualities of mind that are, so far as we know, unique to [humans].' Whether we speak English, French, Swahili, Dutch, German, Japanese, Hindi, Arabic, or any one of the other numerous languages of the world, the important role language plays in communication still holds true. The power of language is vividly illustrated by Ludwig Wittgenstein in the quotation.

The language we speak defines our world and our identity. From childhood, we take for granted that our name describes who we are. A name connects us to our family origins and defines us as individuals. Many refugees or migrants have to change their names when they move into a new language community and this may influence their identity. Moreover, language variations within cultures have an effect on how people communicate and how they categorize themselves. For example, people may use regional dialects to signify their identity as people from a particular region. The language or dialect we speak also influences the way we are perceived by others. The fact that someone speaks another language or speaks our language with an accent influences our social attitudes toward that speaker. Our language attitudes are also influenced by stereotypes and by the situations in which a language is used. When Ireland, Israel, and Slovenia became independent nation-states, each country asserted its own distinct national language (Gaelic, Hebrew, and Slovene, respectively). The languages we speak affect how we act in the world, because different languages/dialects are used in different contexts. For example, immigrants in Canada tend to use English in formal, public settings and their native language in informal, private environments. As some scholars have pointed out, there are many symbolic resources necessary for the cultural production of identity, but language is the most pervasive resource (Fairclough, 2001).

In this chapter, we first explore the nature of verbal codes and the dynamic relationship among language, meaning, and perception. Next, we address the relationship between language and reality through the influential *Sapir-Whorf hypothesis* of linguistic relativity. The chapter then explains how verbal codes, including variations in language and communication styles, can affect communication between people of different cultural backgrounds. The emphasis is on the social aspects of language in a particular cultural context. Finally, we compare gender differences in verbal communication and explore the role of language in constructing identities.

The Components and Characteristics of Verbal Codes

Verbal codes refer to spoken or written language. A verbal code comprises a set of rules governing the use of words in creating a message. We acquire or learn the rules of our native language as we grow up; thus, we can express our thoughts, emotions, desires, and needs easily in our first language. The study of language begins with identifying its components and how they are put together.

The components of human language

When studying human language, linguists focus on different aspects of the language system: sound, structure, and meaning. Lustig and Koester (2010) identified five interrelated components of language: phonology, morphology, syntax, semantics, and pragmatics. Collectively, our knowledge of each aspect of the language system provides us with a holistic understanding of the nature of human language.

Phonology explores how sounds are organized in a language. The smallest sound unit of a language is called a phoneme. The phonological rules of a language determine how sounds are combined to form words. For example, the phonemes [k] and [au] can be arranged to form the word 'cow' in the English language. Mastery of any language requires a speaker to be able to identify and pronounce different sounds accurately. This may prove difficult for second language speakers, particularly those whose native language does not have a similar sound system to the new language. For example, native Russian speakers are likely to speak English with an accent (and vice versa).

Morphology refers to the combination of basic units of meaning – morphemes – to create words. For example, the word 'happy' consists of one morpheme, meaning to feel cheerful. The word 'unhappy' contains two morphemes: happy and the prefix 'un' meaning 'not' or the 'opposite'. Used together they refer to a feeling akin to sadness. Morphemes differ across cultures. In the English language, prefixes or suffixes constitute morphemes as well as individual words, whereas in tonal languages such as Chinese, tones are morphemes and the meaning of units depends on the tone with which the word is pronounced.

Syntax is the study of the grammatical and structural rules of language. We combine words into sentences according to grammatical rules in order to communicate meaning. In English, people use a tense to describe past, present, and future events; in Chinese, adverbs are placed before or after verbs to differentiate past events from future ones. In German, prepositions are often placed at the end of a sentence, whereas in French they are placed before nouns or noun phrases. Every language has a set of grammatical rules that governs the sequencing of words. Mastery of another language means knowing those grammatical rules in addition to building up a stock of vocabulary.

Semantics refers to the study of the meaning of words and the relationship between words and their referents. A command of vocabulary is an essential part of linguistic proficiency in any language. When we learn a second language, we devote much of our time to memorizing words and their meanings, concrete or abstract. However, just memorizing words and their dictionary meanings is often insufficient for successful intercultural communication, because the meaning often resides in the context. Linguists identify two types of meaning: denotative and connotative. *Denotation* refers to the literal meaning of a word or an object. It is basically descriptive. For example, a denotative description of a Big Mac would be that it is a sandwich sold by McDonald's that weighs a certain number of grams and is served with certain sauces. *Connotation* deals with the cultural meanings that become attached to a word or an object. The connotative meaning of a Big Mac may be certain aspects of

American culture – fast food, popular food, standardization, a lack of time, a lack of interest in cooking. Because connotative meanings are emotionally charged, we may make mistakes about the messages we think we are sending to others. For example, in one class, students were asked to bring in some object that reflected them as people. One young woman brought a large seashell. She listed the attributes of the shell as beautiful, delicate, natural, and simple. Other students found different attributes in the shell: empty, brittle, and vacuous.

Language conveys meaning via its components, which are arranged according to rules. For example, morphemes combine with one another to produce meaning of words, and words, in turn, combine to form sentences that yield additional meaning. Talk is achieved through the interdependent components of sounds, words, sentences, and the meaning of a language (Bonvillain, 2008). Linguists have developed descriptive and explanatory tools to analyse the structure of language. The study of language based on the assumption that language is a coherent system of formal units and that the task of linguistic study is to inquire into the nature of this systematic arrangement without reference to historical antecedents is known as structural linguists. The rise of structural linguistics was largely due to the Swiss linguist Ferdinand de Saussure, who compared language to a game of chess. He noted that a chess piece in isolation has no value and that a move by any one piece has repercussions on all the other pieces. Similarly, the meaning of a unit in a language system can be derived by examining those items that occur alongside it and those which can be substituted for it (Saussure, 1983). Structural linguistics dominated twentieth-century linguistics, as opposed to much work in the nineteenth century, when it was common for linguists to trace the history of words. But structural linguistics was also criticized for being too narrow in conception. For example, generative linguistics, headed by Noam Chomsky (see a later section of this chapter), argues that it is necessary to go beyond a description of the location of items to produce a grammar that reflects a native speaker's intuitive knowledge of language.

Theory Corner

Structural linguistics

Structural linguistics views language as a coherent system whereby every item acquires meaning in relation to the other items in the system. Ferdinand de Saussure (1857–1913) claimed that meaning resided within the text (Saussure, 1983). Within each language system, a spoken or written word (the *signifier*) attributes meaning to objects, concepts, and ideas (the *signified* – the mental picture produced by the signifier) in the construction of reality. The relation between signifier and signified is based on convention. For example, the linguistic sign 'dog' (signifier) represents 'a four-legged, barking domestic animal' (signified). We recognize the meaning of the word 'dog' from its difference to other similar-sounding words such as 'hog' and 'cock' which produce different mental pictures. We also use the difference between 'dog' and similar concepts such as 'cat' and 'rabbit' as well as opposing concepts such as 'human' in comprehending meaning.

The structural approach dominated the linguistic fields of the USA in the mid-twentieth century, when the prime concern of American linguists (e.g. Leonard Bloomfield) was to produce a catalogue of the linguistic elements of a language and a statement of the positions in which these could occur. Critiques of Saussure's model argue that abstract concepts like justice, truth, and freedom cannot be tied directly to the outside world, and they mean different things to different people. Hence, it is necessary to understand meaning beyond the text.

Reference

Saussure, Ferdinand de (1983) *Course in General Linguistics,* edited by C. Bally and A. Sechehaye, translated and annotated by Roy Harris. London: Duckworth.

Further reading on structuralism

Unger, Steven (2004) 'Saussure, Barthes and structuralism' in C. Sanders (ed.), *The Cambridge Companion to Saussure.* Cambridge: Cambridge University Press. pp. 157–173.

Pragmatics is concerned with the impact of language on human perception and behaviour. It focuses on how language is used in a social context. A pragmatic analysis of language goes beyond its structural features and concentrates on the social and cultural appropriateness of language use in a particular context. For example, a fairly direct communication style is preferred for resolving interpersonal conflicts in South Africa or Great Britain, but a more indirect approach tends to be favoured in South Korea where the preservation of harmony is strongly valued.

The characteristics of verbal codes

Language is uniquely a human system of communication. Because of their capacity for language, humans have become the most powerful living beings on earth. It is important to stress that communication is symbolic, but not all symbols are linguistic. In linguistics, symbols represent a subcategory of signs, and like signs are not completely arbitrary. The symbol of justice – a pair of scales – could not be replaced by just any symbol, such as a chariot (Saussure, 1983). Symbols, like gestures or cries, may be shared with other animals. There are significant limits on the messages such symbols can communicate (Ritzer, 2004); those messages are mostly formed on the basis of a stimulus

Photo 6.1
A café in Skopje, Macedonia, uses English, Italian, Macedonian, and Albanian to attract customers who speak different languages. Copyright © Zala Volčič. Used with permission.

and are related to the present, without reference to past, future, or imaginary situations. However, the relationship between a linguistic symbol (such as the word 'cow') and its referent (a four-legged animal that gives milk) is completely arbitrary; the same referent is called 'vache' in French. There is no natural relationship between a word and its referent.

Although languages differ, there are some characteristics shared by all of them. Neuliep (2006) identified five common characteristics. First, all languages have some way of naming objects, places, or things. Second, all languages have a way of naming an action. Third, all languages have a way of stating the negative, constructing interrogatives, and differentiating between singular and plural. Fourth, all languages have a systematic set of sounds, combined with a set of rules for the sole purpose of creating meaning and communicating, with no natural or inherent relationship between the sounds and their accompanying alphabet. Fifth, all languages have a set of formal grammatical rules for combining sounds and sequencing words to create meaning. Similarly, Harvey Daniels (1985: 18–36) listed eight general characteristics of human language, encompassing language acquisition and language use:

1 Children learn their native language swiftly, efficiently, and largely without instruction. All children acquire oral language as naturally as they learn to walk.
2 Every language operates by specific rules. Our agreement about the rules of language, however, is only a general one and depends on the cultural context.
3 All languages have three major components: a sound system, a vocabulary, a grammar.
4 Everyone speaks a dialect owing to geographical conditions, but it is important to note that a standard dialect of any language is not inherently superior.
5 Speakers of all languages employ various styles and dialects or jargons.
6 A language is constantly evolving, especially when it encounters other languages. Thus, language transformation is normal and inevitable.
7 A language is intimately related to the societies and individuals who use it. No language is superior to any other.
8 Writing is a derivative of speech. Speech communities can be found everywhere, but not all speech communities have writing.

Language and Perception

All children go through essentially the same process of language acquisition. As Dan Slobin (2000: 110) wrote, 'Children in all nations seem to learn their native languages in much the same way. Despite the diversity of tongues, there are linguistic universals that seem to rest upon the developmental universals of the human mind.' Scholarly debates have centred on the issue of whether language is innately programmed, requiring only minimal environmental stimuli to trigger it, or whether language is actively learned through the general learning mechanisms present while children are growing up. We can divide the language acquisition debate into two contrasting views: nativists versus constructivists (Hoff, 2001).

Noam Chomsky's universal grammar

Noam Chomsky (1975) has claimed that all human languages share a universal grammar that is innate in the human species and culturally invariant. Just as humans are programmed to walk upright, so too are human minds equipped with a set of preprogrammed models that are triggered when exposed to the surrounding language. *Nativists* such as Chomsky argue that language acquisition involves triggering these models, so that only the details of a particular language must be learned (Chomsky, 1980). Chomsky states that language is as much a part of the human brain as the thumb is a part of the human hand. One of the most remarkable features of any language's rule structure is that it allows speakers to generate sentences that have never before been spoken. Chomsky has referred to this aspect of language as generative universal grammar. From a finite set of sounds and rules, speakers of any language can create an infinite number of sentences, many of which have never before been uttered. The commonalities between different languages are so strong that Chomsky and other linguists are convinced that the fundamental syntax for all languages is universal and that particular languages are simply dialects of the universal grammar.

On the other hand *constructivists*, grounded in the work of Piaget, oppose the idea that there is a universal grammar. They argue that language acquisition involves unveiling the patterns of language and thus requires interaction with a structured environment (Piaget, 1977). A famous language acquisition debate between Chomsky and Piaget took place in 1975 at the Abbaye de Royaumont near Paris, nearly two hundred years after the wild boy of Aveyron was found in France. The wild boy of Aveyron lived his entire childhood in the forests and lacked any language before he was found. Piaget saw the wild boy and his mind as an active, constructive agent that slowly inched forward in a perpetual bootstrap operation; Chomsky viewed the boy's mind as a set of essentially preprogrammed units, each equipped with its rules that needed only the most modest environmental trigger to develop. As Hoff (2001) points out, both sides are right, and indeed the line between nativists and constructivists is not clear-cut. Language may be a natural behaviour, but it still has to be carefully nurtured. For this reason alone, in all cultures, language learning is an essential part of formal education.

The Sapir–Whorf hypothesis

Philosophical debates surround the question of the extent to which our perception is shaped by the particular language we speak. *Nominalists* argue that our perception of external reality is shaped not by language but by material reality. Any thought can be expressed in any language and can convey the same meaning (Louw, 2004a). *Relativists* believe that our language determines our ideas, thought patterns, and perceptions of reality (Hoff, 2001). A classic example to illustrate the relativists' view that language shapes our perception of reality is the existence of numerous Eskimo words for 'snow', whereas in English there are fewer words for this concept. The relationship between language and thought is well captured in the Sapir–Whorf hypothesis, which proposes that language and thought are inextricably tied together, so that (in the original and strongest version of the hypothesis) a person's language determines the categories of thought open to that individual. In his book *Language, Thought and Reality* (1956: 239), Whorf states that 'We cut up and organize the spread and flow of events as we do largely because, through our mother tongue, we are parties to an agreement to do so, not because nature itself is segmented in exactly that way for all to see.'

Photo 6.2
Samoan children learning a language in St Mary's Primary School in Apia.
Copyright © UNESCO; photographer: Laura Berdejo. Used with permission.

Edward Sapir (1884–1939), a famous linguist and anthropologist, taught at the University of Chicago and then at Yale University. Sapir published a paper that changed the face of the study of language and culture. He argued that the language of a particular culture directly influences how people think, and that speakers of different languages see different worlds. In 1931, Benjamin Lee Whorf (1897–1941) enrolled in Sapir's course on Native American linguistics at Yale University. In his study of the Hopi language, Whorf learned that in Hopi the past, present, and future tense must be expressed differently from English, as the Hopi language does not have verb tenses. This led Whorf to believe that people who speak different languages are directed to different types of observations of the world. Sapir and Whorf's ideas received great attention and became known as the Sapir–Whorf Hypothesis.

Theory Corner

The Sapir–Whorf hypothesis

Sapir and Whorf claimed that a cultural system is embodied in the language of the people who speak the language. This cultural framework shapes the thoughts of the language's speakers. We think in the words and the meanings of our language, which in turn is an expression of our culture. Sapir and Whorf's ideas have become known as the Sapir–Whorf hypothesis (Whorf, 1956). This hypothesis has two versions: the strong and weak versions. The strong version of the hypothesis, or *linguistic determinism*, argues that the language one speaks determines one's perception of reality. The weak version of the hypothesis, or *linguistic relativity*, makes the claim that our native language exerts an influence over our perception of reality. The differences among languages are thus reflected in the different worldviews of their speakers.

Reference

Whorf, Benjamin L. (1956) *Language, Thought and Reality: Selected Writings*, edited by J.B. Carroll. Cambridge, MA: Technology Press of MIT.

Further reading on language and reality

Giles, Howard and Coupland, Nikolas (1991) *Language: Contexts and Consequences*. Milton Keynes: Open University Press.

Consider some examples of how language categorizes our world. In the Chinese language there are no single words that are equivalent to the English words 'uncle' and 'aunt'. Instead, Chinese has different words for one's father's elder brother, younger brother, mother's elder brother and younger brother – even different words for elder or younger brother-in-laws, and so forth. This diversity of terms may suggest that the interpersonal relationships involved between an individual and his or her extended family are more complex and perhaps more important in China than in English-speaking countries. Arabic has many words for 'camel', whereas English has few. The word 'moon' is masculine in German (*der Mond*), feminine in French (*la lune*), and neither masculine nor feminine in English.

Language categorizes our experiences without our full awareness. Only when an individual learns a second language and moves back and forth between the first and second language does that person become aware of the influence that language has on perception. The Sapir–Whorf hypothesis does not imply that people of one culture cannot think of objects for which another culture has plentiful vocabulary (Neuliep, 2006). Rather, the fact that we do not think of certain concepts or objects in such specificity may mean that such distinctions are less important to our culture. It is worth noting that the same thing applies to the specialized languages of different professions. For example, medical doctors, lawyers, and academics have extensive vocabularies marking their areas of expertise; they learn these terms and the concepts and relationships underlying them as they learn their profession. Thus, the Sapir–Whorf hypothesis shows that language, thought, and culture (including professional and other types of subculture) are closely connected. Language, as a part of culture, affects how we perceive the world and thus influences the meanings that are conveyed by words.

Cultural Variations in Verbal Communication

People from different social or cultural groups may experience similar events; however, there are vast differences in the ways in which they use language to interpret their experiences (Clark et al., 1998). This cultural variation in verbal communication is reflected in language use and translation.

Communication styles and culture

Successful communication depends not only on what is said but also on how the message is communicated. *Communication style* refers to how language is used to communicate meaning. Gudykunst and Ting-Toomey (1988) described four communication styles identified by communication theorists: direct/indirect, elaborate/succinct, personal/contextual, and instrumental/affective. Recognizing the differences in communication styles can help us understand cultural differences underpinning the verbal communication process.

Direct/indirect communication styles

A *direct communication style* is one in which the speaker's needs, wants, desires, and intentions are explicitly communicated. Conversely, an *indirect communication style* is one in which the speaker's true intentions or needs are only implied or hinted at during the conversation. Although both styles are to some extent universally used in communication, research indicates that indirect styles are more likely to be used in collectivist or Asian cultures, such as in Japan, China, South Korea, and Hong Kong, where harmony is considered important for maintaining good interpersonal relationships. Indirect communication styles are also more likely to be used in high-context cultures, where meaning is communicated through context rather than explicitly conveyed in words (see Chapter 5). By comparison, Western cultures generally prefer a direct communication style. As an example, an American student asked his Nigerian friend to give him a lift on an evening when the Nigerian had made a commitment to babysit his niece so that his sister could go to work. However, instead of saying, 'Sorry I cannot do it', he replied by talking about how his sister perhaps could make alternative arrangements or stay home instead of working that night. The American student felt confused as to what his Nigerian friend was trying to say. In American culture, if such a request for a lift is inconvenient, one would simply respond by saying, 'Sorry, I cannot do it.' However, in collectivistic cultures like Nigeria, it is not considered polite to say 'no' to a friend – but it is the responsibility of the person who made the request to figure out that it is not appropriate to ask for the favour. Therefore differences in expectations for appropriate communication styles can lead to misunderstandings between speakers.

Elaborate/succinct communication styles

This dimension is concerned with the quantity of talk a culture values, and reflects a culture's attitudes towards talk and silence (Martin and Nakayama, 2001). The *elaborate style* involves the use of rich, expressive, and embellished language in everyday conversation. For example, rather than simply saying that someone is thin, a comment such as 'She is so thin she can walk between raindrops without getting wet' embellishes and colours the statement. Arab, Middle Eastern, and African-American cultures tend to use metaphorical expressions in everyday conversation. In the *succinct communication style*, simple assertions and even silence are valued. The use of either an elaborate or a succinct style is closely related to Hall's high- and low-context cultures. The elaborate style tends to characterize low-context cultures, in which meaning is conveyed through verbal codes. Conversely, in high-context cultures, where meaning is more often conveyed by contextual cues, silence rather than talk can be used to maintain control in a social situation. For example, a popular saying in Chinese, 'Disaster emanates from careless talk', is illustrative of this point. The Chinese consider wise people as those who talk less but listen more. In Europe, the Finns place a high value on silence and it is not unusual to pass a companiable evening in Helsinki with virtually no words exchanged at all (Carbaugh et al., 2006).

Personal/contextual communication styles

This dimension is concerned with the extent to which the speaker emphasizes the self as opposed to his or her role. Gudykunst and Ting-Toomey (1988) defined a *personal style* as one that amplifies the individual identity of the speaker. This style is often used in individualistic cultures which emphasize individual goals over those of the group. Person-centred communication tends to be informal and is reflected by use of the pronoun 'I'. On the other hand, a *contextual communication style* is oriented by status and role. Formality and power distance are often emphasized. A contextual style is often seen in collectivistic cultures where one's role identity and status are highlighted. For example, instead of using 'you' for all persons, as is the case in English, in Japanese there exists an elaborate system of linguistic forms used to communicate respect to people of different ranks or social status.

Instrumental/affective communication styles

An *instrumental style* is goal-oriented and sender-focused. The speaker uses communication to achieve an outcome. An *affective communication style* is receiver-focused and process-oriented (Gudykunst and Ting-Toomey, 1988). The affective speaker is more concerned with the process of communication than the outcome. For example, in an organization where the boss explicitly tells subordinates what to do and why, communication is instrumental. Instrumental and affective communication styles can also be related to individualism–collectivism and high–low context cultural dimensions. In collectivistic cultures people are more conscious of the other person's reactions and will attempt to sense meaning by situational cues, so that an affective style tends to be preferred. An instrumental style, on the other hand, can often be seen in business and other professional contexts, particularly in Western cultures where verbal explicitness is valued.

Gender differences in communication

Do men and women speak differently? In her seminal work *Language and Woman's Place*, Lakoff (1975) argued that women and men do speak differently, since boys and girls are socialized separately. Deborah Tannen, a discourse analyst, further claimed that men and women express themselves differently because they have different cultures. In her influential 'two-cultures' theory, she states that men usually use verbal communication *to report* about the world (Tannen, 1990). A report is a specific way to communicate in order to maintain independence and status in a hierarchical social order. Women, however, use verbal communication *to create a rapport*, in order to establish a human connection. It is a way of establishing connections and negotiating relationships. Moreover, on the question of who talks more, the usual stereotype is that women are *talkers* and men are *doers* (Mohanty, 2003). On the other hand, academic research has shown that men tend to speak more often in public and they also tend to speak longer in meetings (Tannen, 1994).

Gender differences in verbal communication are a complex and controversial combination of biological differences and socialization. Many linguists argue that language defines gender. Think of words such as 'businessmen', 'chairman', and 'mankind', in which there is a generic male implication. In subtle ways like this, language reinforces social stereotypes (Ardizzoni, 2007). For example, women are often defined by their appearance or relationships; use of the titles 'Miss' and 'Mrs' designates a woman's marital status. On the other hand, men are more commonly defined by activities, accomplishments, or positions.

Theory Corner

Gender-neutral language

Gender-neutral language is a verbal communicative style that adheres to certain rules that were suggested by feminist language reformers in universities during the 1970s. These rules discourage various common usages which are thought of as sexist, such as the generic use of masculine pronouns in referring to persons of either sex. Consequently, a number of new words have been coined, such as 'chairperson' and 'spokesperson', as substitutes for the older, male-oriented words in common use. Feminists hope that by paying attention to gender details in language, the language of the whole society might gradually be reformed, and that people would develop more positive attitudes toward equality between the sexes and other feminist ideas (Gauntlett, 2002). The term 'gender-neutral language' is also called 'inclusive language', 'gender-inclusive language, 'gender generic language', and 'non-discriminatory language'.

Reference

Gauntlett, David (2002) *Media, Gender and Identity*. New York: Routledge.

Further reading on language and gender

Mucchi-Faina, Angelica (2005) 'Visible or influential? Language reforms and gender (in)equality', *Social Science Information*, 44 (1): 189–215.

Pidgins and creoles

Pidgins are formed and used when two communities that do not share a common language come into contact and need to communicate. This is very common, especially in trade or other business activities. Common pidgins based on English, French, Spanish, and Portuguese are used in the East and West Indies, Africa, and the Americas. A pidgin has a reduced grammatical structure and a reduced lexicon (vocabulary), and refers mainly to a small set of contexts – it is about situational use (McWhorter, 2002). For example, a line taken from a comic strip in Papua New Guinea is: '*Fantom, yu pren tru bilong mi. Inap yu ken helpim mi nau?*' Its translation is: 'Phantom, you are a true friend of mine. Are you able to help me now?' Pidgin is not a native language to those using it, but a code system developed for a specific purpose. However, when a pidgin is passed on to future generations who acquire it as a *first* language, it can develop and become a creole.

A *creole* is a new language developed from the prolonged contact of two or more languages. It is a language that expands and regularizes its structural systems, and the next generation learns it as their first language. A creole develops a grammar, morphology, lexicon, phonetics, and phonology: English-based creoles contain words like 'banan' (banana), 'chek' (check), and 'maket' (market). A creole is a full, linguistically complex language in its own right: examples include Hawaiian Creole English and Louisiana Creole French (McWhorter, 2002).

Translation and interpretation

Even when cultures speak the same language, as is the case with Australians and Britons, there can be vocabulary and semantic differences. When cultures that speak different languages come into contact, translation is critical but always imperfect. *Translation* refers to the process of converting a source text, either spoken or written, into a different language. For example, ethnic shops often put up signs in both the host language and their native language to attract ethnic customers. *Interpretation* refers to the process of verbally expressing what is said in another language. Interpretation can be simultaneous, with the interpreter speaking at the same time as the original speaker, or consecutive, with the interpreter speaking only during the breaks provided by the original speaker (Lustig and Koester, 2010). Cultural differences in word usage make translation a difficult task, and two translators rarely agree on the exact translation of any given source text. Translation and interpretation raise issues of authenticity and accuracy as well as the subjective role of the translator or interpreter.

It is very difficult, if not impossible, to translate an entire text word-for-word from one language to another, because different languages may convey views of the world in different ways. Problems of translation arise owing to a lack of equivalence in vocabulary, idiomatic expressions, experience, and concepts (Jandt, 2007). A word-for-word translation can result in awkward (and sometimes hilarious) expressions that puzzle people from both sides. Here are some examples of awkward translations:

- On the menu of a Swiss restaurant, 'Our wines leave you nothing to hope for.'
- In a Copenhagen airline office, 'We take your bags and send them in all directions.'
- Outside a Hong Kong tailor shop, 'Ladies may have a fit upstairs.'
- On the box for a toothbrush at a Tokyo hotel, 'Give you strong mouth and refreshing wind.'

Photo 6.3
Names of popular tourist places in Beijing like Silk Street have been translated into English; however, 'Silk' – the English translation – is a rough sound equivalence of the Chinese name (*Siu Shui*), not a concept equivalence.
Copyright © Shuang Liu. Used with permission.

In addition to lexical equivalence, experiential equivalence can cause problems in translation. If an experience does not exist in a culture, it is difficult to translate words or expressions referring to that experience in that culture's language. For example, the literal translation of an expression in Hong Kong is 'Touch the nail on the door'. It actually means 'No one was home when you went to the house.' The meaning of this expression dates back to those old days in China when, upon leaving their houses, people would hammer a nail in the door instead of locking it. Thus, if a visitor touched the nail when trying to knock on the door, the visitor would know that no one was home. The literal meaning of 'Touch the nail on the door' would not be easily understood by people from another culture in which such a practice had never existed. To translate into another language, the translator has to capture the sense of the original either by adding an explanation to a word-for-word translation or by translating the meaning rather than the exact words. Translation problems like these raise the issue of the role of translator or interpreter.

We tend to consider translators or interpreters as 'intermediaries', simply rendering the source text into the target language (Martin and Nakayama, 2001). The assumption is that anyone who knows two languages can act as a translator. The example of 'Touch the nail on the door' shows that language proficiency alone does not make a good translator. Knowledge of history and culture plays a significant role in how well or accurately a message from one language is rendered into another. Translation involves more than finding a linguistic equivalent; conceptual, idiomatic, and experiential equivalence are also key factors in comprehending messages, particularly in intercultural situations.

Language and Identity

Language binds social or ethnic groups and nations together. Therefore, it defines our identities, as we use language to mark our social, ethnic, and national boundaries.

Language and nationalism

The sense of national unity is concerned with the integrity of the national language, territory, and religion. A contemporary interest in linguistic homogeneity is often traced back to the eighteenth-century German philosopher Johann G. Herder, who claimed that language expresses the inner consciousness of the nation, its ethos, its continuous identity in history, and its moral unity. Nationalists defend their national language against foreign 'pollution' in the belief that moral degeneration would follow. For example, language is seen as one of the most important markers of Serbian national identity, since it is understood as preserving, bearing, and passing down memories over the centuries (Volčič, 2005). Interestingly, majority groups in multi-cultural societies like the United States and Canada can become threatened by other languages, so that significant groups have asserted the dominance of their languages through English-only (in the USA) and French-only (in Quebec) movements (Barker et al., 2001; Edwards, 1998).

Other scholars of language, nationalism, and nation-states argue that, living in a global world and multicultural societies, 'There is no need for all citizens of a nation to be native speakers of a single language, and absolutely no need for a nation's language to be clearly distinct from others' (Barbour, 2002: 14). The fact remains that every nation faces some kind of language dilemma. For example, Louw (2004a) writes extensively about Afrikaans, the first language of 5.9 million people, mostly in South Africa and Namibia. But by the end of the twentieth century, English had replaced Afrikaans as the dominant state language. With the ending of apartheid in 1994, Afrikaners became a

South African minority group, marginalized within a political process geared to 'black empowerment'. Westernized black South Africans have deployed English as a language of state administration and the lingua franca, further marginalizing Afrikaans.

In the case of Eastern European countries, after the collapse of communism the transition from a collectively organized and ideologically based state-socialist system to the capitalist model of liberal society, with a free market economy and democratic political organization, required an avalanche of reforms and the transformation of language. The main reforms were introduced in the spheres of economy, politics, and government. The realm of social relations started to be modified at a high pace and this affected the institutional foundations of societies. The market economy implies competition on the labour market for employment; this produces feelings of insecurity and causes stress in family and intergroup relations. Culture, as a set of significant practices that provide meaning in our daily life, also undergoes changes with the introduction of capitalism as a dominant discourse. Some of these changes are easily observable in language, which is the principal means of representation in a culture. For example, native speakers living in different parts of Eastern Europe have simply appropriated numerous English terms, words, and phrases (e.g. mortgage, down payment, real estate, marketing, and advertising) for daily use.

Language and ethnic identity

Language is a vital aspect of any ethnic group's identity. Often, immigrant groups maintain their cultural heritage and identity by using their native languages in their new cultures and teaching them to their children. Identity based on ethnic language also hinges on the assumption that one's linguistic community is acceptable in a number of ways. The degree of prestige, acceptability, and importance attached to a group's language is known as *ethnolinguistic vitality*. When you are faced with an ethnic or cultural group that is obviously different from your own, this encounter may be brief and unpleasant if you have the feeling that your ethnic or cultural group is being put down. Since language is one of the most clear-cut and immediate ways by which groups are identified, it is quite easy to see how your confidence can suffer if your language is disparaged.

Considerable evidence indicates that speech patterns, dialects, and accents can serve as cues that cause listeners to assign certain attitudes or characteristics to other people. How do you feel in the presence of a conversation you do not understand? Do you feel different if you think the conversation is about you? Dodd (1998) related an anecdote illustrating the relationship between language and identity: a student who came from a rural area of the United States was informed by his mass media professors that his rural accent was inappropriate for broadcasting when he entered a large North American university. This student, as a result, adapted to 'standard' speech to meet the norms favouring standard American patterns of speech. When he went home for Thanksgiving, his mother would not let him in the house because when he knocked and called out, she did not recognize his voice. Her response was that he had to start 'talking right' or he would not be allowed entry. This dilemma is illustrative of how important our language is as an aspect of our identity and group membership.

Summary

This chapter explored the powerful role of verbal codes in intercultural communication. The effect of language on human perceptions was examined by drawing upon the Sapir–Whorf hypothesis, which highlights the close connections between language, thought, and culture. The language we speak influences how we perceive and categorize the world around us. This chapter also introduced four dimensions of communication style identified by Gudykunst and Ting-Toomey (1988): direct/indirect, elaborate/succinct, personal/contextual, and instrumental/affective. These styles of verbal communication are used universally, but how, when, where, and with whom they are used vary from culture to culture. The issues around gender and language, including gender-neutral or inclusive language, were also examined. Finally, the chapter examined the role language plays in defining nationalism and ethnic identities.

Language comprises a set of symbols shared by a community to communicate meanings and experiences. Children learn the rules of their language and are productive and creative in their language acquisition. As we grow up, we learn to receive, store, manipulate, and generate messages and exchange them with others by following the rules and norms governing verbal communication. Language shapes our perception of reality, our attitudes towards others, and others' perceptions of us. In this sense, language is a cultural tool and cannot be fully understood unless it is being placed within its social context. Language is an integral part of our personal and social identities, because the language we speak marks our cultural and social boundaries. If someone speaks as you do, you are more likely to assume that that person is similar to you in other important ways (Lustig and Koester, 2010). Therefore, verbal communication skills form an essential part of intercultural competence. To be an effective intercultural communicator, you need not only to learn another language, but also to learn the social and cultural rules governing the use of that language in specific cultural contexts.

Case Study:
How many languages still exist in the world today?

There are about 6,800 languages spoken in the world today (Everett, 2002): approximately 1,000 in the Americas (15 per cent); 2,400 in Africa (35 per cent); 200 in Europe (3 per cent); 2,000 in Asia (28 per cent); and 1,200 in the Pacific (19 per cent). Not all languages have been 'discovered' by Western linguists (Campbell, 2000). Many languages have disappeared, but so too are new languages being created. This is why many linguists say that the total number of actual languages spoken in the world at a given moment of human history is but a small fragment of the perhaps infinitely large total number of possible human languages (Everett, 2002).

If we look at specific languages and numbers of estimated speakers we can see that the largest number use Chinese (Mandarin), with 1,075,000,000 speakers. English follows with 514,000,000 speakers. The third is Hindustani, with 496,000,000 speakers. The next largest groups are speakers of Spanish (425,000,000) and Russian (275,000,000). The rest of the languages used are Arabic (256,000,000), Bengali (215,000,000), Portuguese (194,000,000), Malay-Indonesian (176,000,000), and French (129,000,000). Most linguists agree that half of the world's languages are endangered and many fear that up to 90 per cent will disappear by the end of this century.

Many languages have not yet been described through written grammars and dictionaries (Campbell, 2000). For example, Hawaiian does not have a written form; knowledge has been passed down from generation to generation orally. Hawaiian is a Polynesian language and a member of the Austronesian language family. It is also closely related to other Polynesian languages including Tahitian, Maori, and Samoan, and is distantly related to Fijian. New-England Christian missionaries arriving in Hawaii in 1820 created their own form of written language. By 1990, there were only about 1,000 native Hawaiian speakers – however, these people have organized themselves politically to encourage the teaching of Hawaiian in schools (Schütz, 1994).

'Safe' languages are languages that have official state support and very large numbers of speakers (e.g. English). 'Threatened' languages are those that have little or no official status and only a small number of speakers, although they may still be taught in schools. For example, less than half a per cent of the Swiss population identifies Romansch as their mother tongue. Despite formal legal protection, the number of speakers of Romansch has been steadily declining for more than seventy years (Dürmüller, 2001). Many linguists predict that it will eventually become one of the hundreds of languages to disappear in the coming century.

If we ask what is lost with the death of a language, the answer is a whole culture. Language is the most efficient means of creating and transmitting a culture and it is thus the cultural community that loses the most when a language dies. When a language disappears, a cultural identity, worldview, and contexts related to that language also disappear. But how and why do languages disappear? Among the many diverse hypotheses about language loss, Crawford (1995) has argued that a language shift may be determined by changes that are internal and external to language communities themselves. For example, economic forces, trade, migration, intermarriage, religious conversion, military conquest, and the mass media all have influences on language change. For languages with no written form, the likelihood of such a loss is considerably greater.

How can a language death be stopped? For a language to survive, it needs to be taught in schools (Everett, 2002). In this way, it can be formally passed on from generation to generation. To prevent a language from disappearing, we also need to ensure it is being used by people. In general, written languages are easier to preserve as compared to spoken words. Speakers of Welsh and Irish have mobilized over the past decades to bring this status to their languages and have been successful to a significant extent; the number of speakers of these languages is increasing.

References for case study

Campbell, George L. (2000) *Compendium of the World's Languages* (2nd edn). London: Routledge.

Crawford, Mary (1995) *Talking Difference: On Gender and Language*. London: SAGE.

Dürmüller, Urs (2001) 'The presence of English at Swiss universities', in U. Ammon (ed.), *The Dominance of English as a Language of Science: Effects on Other Languages and Language Communities*. New York: Mouton de Gruyter. pp. 389–403.

Everett, Daniel (2002) 'From Threatened Languages to Threatened Lives' [online]. Accessed 12 April 2009 at http://yourdictionary.com/elr/everett.html

Schütz, Albert J. (1994) *The Voices of Eden: A History of Hawaiian Language Studies*. Honolulu: University of Hawaii Press.

Questions for discussion

1   Approximately how many languages exist today?
2   What are 'threatened' languages? Do you know of any? Which ones?
3   Why should language loss be an important issue that calls for our attention?
4   Do you know approximately how many people speak your native language? How does it make you feel when you hear a foreigner speak your language?
5   Why do you think it is important for us to keep languages from dying?

Key Terms

communication style;	ethnolinguistic vitality;	pidgin;
connotation;	instrumental/affective style;	pragmatics;
constructivist;	interpretation;	relativists;
creole;	morphology;	semantics;
denotation;	nominalist;	syntax;
direct/indirect style;	personal/contextual style;	translation;
elaborate/succinct style;	phonology;	verbal codes

Further Reading

Communication styles

Carbaugh, Donal; Berry, Michael and Nurimikari-Berry, Marjatta (2006) 'Coding personhood through cultural terms and practices: silence and quietude as a Finnish "natural way of being"', *Journal of Language and Social Psychology,* 25: 203–220.

Gudykunst, William B. and Ting-Toomey, Stella (1988) 'Verbal communication styles', in W.B. Gudykunst and S. Ting-Toomey (eds), *Culture and Interpersonal Communication.* Newbury Park, CA: SAGE. pp. 99–115.

Language and immigrants

Callan, Victor J. and Gallois, Cynthia (1987) 'Anglo-Australians' and immigrants' attitudes towards language and accent: a review of experimental and survey research', *International Immigration Review,* 21 (1): 48–69.

Dixon, John A.; Mahoney, Bernice and Cocks, Roger (2002) 'Accents of guilt? Effects of regional accent, race, and crime type on attributions of guilt', *Journal of Language and Social Psychology,* 21 (2): 162–168.

Language and reality

Carroll, John B. (ed.) (1956) *Language, Thought and Reality: Selected Writings of Benjamin Lee Whorf.* Cambridge, MA: MIT.

Giles, Howard and Coupland, Nikolas (1991) *Language: Contexts and Consequences.* Milton Keynes: Open University Press.

Unger, Steven (2004) 'Saussure, Barthes and structuralism' in C. Sanders (ed.), *The Cambridge Companion to Saussure.* Cambridge: Cambridge University Press. pp. 157–173.

Variations in language use

Mucchi-Faina, Angelica (2005) 'Visible or influential? Language reforms and gender (in)equality', *Social Science Information,* 44 (1): 189–215.

Sebba, Mark (1997) *Contact Languages: Pidgins and Creoles.* London: Macmillan.

Tannen, Deborah (1990) *You Just Don't Understand: Women and Men in Conversation.* New York: William Morrow/Ballantine.

7

Nonverbal Communication and Culture

*Words are a wonderful form of communication, but they
will never replace kisses and punches.*

Ashleigh Brilliant, British author and cartoonist, 1933–

Learning Objectives

At the end of this chapter, you should be able to:

- Define nonverbal communication.
- Understand the importance of nonverbal communication.
- Identify the characteristics and functions of nonverbal communication.
- Delineate different types of nonverbal codes.
- Explain the influence of culture on nonverbal communication.

Universality and Variation of Nonverbal Communication

Broadly speaking, nonverbal communication can be defined as communicating without using words. In this chapter, the term *nonverbal communication* refers to the use of non-spoken symbols to communicate a message. Human communication frequently involves more than the use of a verbal code. Each of us uses nonverbal codes as a means of communicating with others, sometimes consciously and at other times below the level of conscious awareness. Mehrabian (1982) estimated that 93 per cent of meaning is carried through nonverbal communication channels (e.g. voice, body movement, facial expressions) and only 7 per cent of meaning is carried through words. Mehrabian's numbers are not well-supported by data, and other scholars have disputed them. Nevertheless, all agree that a very significant amount of communication is nonverbal.

Many linguists, psychologists, and sociologists believe that human language evolved from a system of nonverbal communication. Humans possess a repertoire of nonlinguistic ways to communicate with one another through the use of their hands, arms, faces, personal space, and so forth. Nonverbal behaviour reveals much about our attitudes, personalities, emotions, and relationships with others (Cooper et al., 2007). For example, there is a plethora of research in psychology studying the cues people give when they are lying – as it turns out this is not easy to judge, but such clues do exist. Effective communication requires that we understand the central role of nonverbal behaviour as part of our communication competence.

The study of nonverbal communication dates back at least to the time of Charles Darwin, who believed that facial expressions such as smiles and frowns are biologically determined. Though body language, as a form of communication, has been recognized since the time of Aristotle, it is the anthropologist Ray Birdwhistell who is recognized as the originator of the scientific study of body language – kinesics. In 1970, Birdwhistell published a book entitled *Kinesics and Context*, in which he argued that nonverbal communication, like spoken language, has its own set of rules. Ekman and Friesen's (1971) early research on facial expressions also illustrated the universality of many emotional expressions. For example, fear is indicated by a furrowed brow, raised eyebrows, wide-open eyes, a partially open mouth, and an upturned upper lip.

Based on subsequent research and observations, scholars have now become convinced that although all humans share basic emotions such as fear, happiness, anger, surprise, disgust, and sadness, the rules governing the display of these emotions vary from culture to culture. We learn display rules through socialization within our cultural context. For example, in Arab and Iranian cultures people express grief openly, whereas people from Indonesia are more subdued in their mourning behaviour. Simple gestures of greeting also differ from culture to culture. Hindus greet one another by placing their palms together in front of their chest while bowing their heads slightly. Japanese people greet each other by bowing their heads to show respect. Australians may tip their head slightly upward to signal 'hello'. An understanding of how nonverbal behaviours communicate messages in our own culture and in that of others can help us to appreciate the influence of culture on communication. As Ramsey (1979: 111) stated:

> According to culturally prescribed codes, we use eye movement and contact to manage conversations and to regulate interactions; we follow rigid rules governing intra- and interpersonal touch, our bodies synchronously join in the rhythm of others in a group, and gestures modulate our speech. We must internalize all this in order to become and remain fully functioning and socially appropriate members of our culture.

This chapter focuses on nonverbal communication and how it influences intercultural communication. We explain the similarities and differences between verbal and nonverbal codes and describe the characteristics and functions of nonverbal codes. Different types of nonverbal codes including body movement (kinesics), vocal qualities (paralanguage), the use of time (chronemics), space (proxemics), artifacts, dress, and smell (olfactics) are identified. Finally, this chapter shows the close link between culture and nonverbal communication. An understanding of how culture can influence behaviour and communication outcomes can improve intercultural communication competence.

Characteristics and Functions of Nonverbal Codes

Comparison of verbal and nonverbal codes and their characteristics

Verbal and nonverbal messages are inextricably intertwined to form the code systems through which members of any culture can convey their attitudes, personalities, beliefs, values, thoughts, feelings, and intentions (Lustig and Koester, 2010). Verbal and nonverbal communication often takes place simultaneously. In the West, we tend to use verbal behaviour to convey the literal or *cognitive content* of a message (what is said), whereas the nonverbal component of the message communicates more of the *affective content* (feelings about what is said). The affective content accounts for much of the meaning we derive from verbal communication and hence can influence how a verbal message is interpreted. While we normally have some control over the words we say, we may inadvertently reveal the true feelings we would prefer to conceal through nonverbal behaviour. Blushing, for example, is very hard to control. Other nonverbal cues may also be involuntary. Thus, if the nonverbal message contradicts the verbal one, we tend to believe the nonverbal message because nonverbal messages are less conscious and often more truthful.

However inseparably verbal and nonverbal codes are linked in a communication event, the difference between the two types of codes is significant. Neuliep (2006) identified three ways in which verbal and nonverbal codes differ. First, the verbal language system is based primarily on symbols whereas the nonverbal system is largely sign-based. A sign, on the other hand, is often a constituent part of what it represents: thunder is a sign of a storm because it is a part of that storm (see Chapter 6).

A second way in which the nonverbal system differs from its verbal counterpart is that its sending capacity is more restricted. For example, it is very difficult, if not impossible, to communicate about the past or future through purely nonverbal codes – likewise, it is hard to communicate nonverbally without seeing or hearing the other person (although devices like emoticons do some of this work). A third difference is that verbal codes have a formal phonetic system and syntax to govern usage, whereas there are few formal rules governing the use of nonverbal code systems. In fact, sign languages and semaphore communication are classified as verbal because they do have such formal rules. Different types of nonverbal behaviour can be categorized, but these categories are much more loosely defined than those for verbal codes.

The meanings of nonverbal behaviour are usually less precise than those of verbal codes and can only be determined within a particular cultural and situational context. This creates a greater potential for misunderstanding both in the same culture and across cultures, but especially in the latter case where communicators may not share the interpretation of either verbal or nonverbal codes.

Theory Corner

Expectancy violation theory

Expectancy violation theory, developed by Judee Burgoon (1978), assumes that humans anticipate certain behaviour from the people with whom they interact. These expectancies may be general – pertaining to all members of a language community – or particularized – pertaining to a specific individual. When expectancies are violated, the violation can exert a significant impact on the communicators' impression of one another and on the outcomes of their interactions. Based on evidence from various experiments, Burgoon concludes that people evaluate communication with others in either a positive or a negative way, depending on their expectation of the interaction and their evaluation of the communicator. A positive evaluation is often directed toward attractive, powerful, or credible others, while a negative evaluation is more likely to be associated with unattractive or less powerful individuals. This theory was initially concerned only with spatial violations, but starting from the mid-1980s it has been applied to other nonverbal behaviour including facial expression, eye contact, touch, and body movement. The theory has also been used to explain emotional, marital, and intercultural communication.

Reference

Burgoon, Judee (1978) 'A communication model of personal space violation: expectation and an initial test', *Human Communication Research*, 4: 129–142.

Further reading on interpreting nonverbal codes

Costanzo, Mark and Archer, Dane (1989) 'Interpreting the expressive behaviour of others: the interpersonal perception task', *Journal of Nonverbal Behaviour*, 13 (3): 225–245.

Elfenbein, Hillary A. and Ambady, Nalini (2003) 'When familiarity breeds accuracy: cultural exposure and facial emotion recognition', *Journal of Personality and Social Psychology*, 85 (2): 276–290.

Functions of nonverbal codes

Knapp and Hall (1997) identified six primary functions for nonverbal communication: to *repeat* a message sent by the verbal code; to *contradict* the verbal message; to *substitute* for a verbal message; to *complement* a verbal message; to *accent* the verbal message; and to *regulate* verbal communication.

Repeat a verbal message

We use nonverbal codes to repeat what has been said on another channel. For example, you may wave your hand while saying goodbye to a friend. Similarly, when someone asks us for directions, it is very likely that we would use our hands to point out these directions while explaining them in words. Verbal and nonverbal communication is usually redundant, which helps us greatly in understanding other people and in sending clearer messages ourselves.

Contradict a verbal message

Nonverbal messages may, however, contradict verbal ones. For example, imagine that your friend is proudly showing you a new dress she has bought. You think the dress is awful and unflattering but do not wish to hurt her feelings. Unfortunately, while telling her you think the dress looks beautiful you may also inadvertently frown. When verbal and nonverbal codes contradict, people tend to believe the nonverbal message because it is considered less controlled and more revealing of our true feelings.

Substitute for a verbal message

Hand gestures in particular can be used to substitute for a verbal message in noisy places or in a situation when a common language is not shared. Police officers use nonverbal codes to direct the traffic flow. In tourist-populated marketplaces, sellers and buyers can use nonverbal symbols to bargain for goods if they do not speak the same language. In radio stations' recording studios, the director must use gestures to indicate to a speaker when to start speaking. In addition, some messages that are difficult to express in words can be communicated nonverbally. For example, you could keep looking at your watch to indicate to your visitor that it is time to go.

Complement a verbal message

A nonverbal message can complement the verbal message; that is, it can add information to the verbal message. For example, a person involved in a car accident may be able to use gestures to describe the accident to the police, while simultaneously conveying the same message in words. A student may jump up and down while saying how happy she is with a final grade. A mother may place a finger to her lips to tell her child to keep quiet in a cinema.

Accent a verbal message

Although accenting and complementing are similar, the former specifically increases or decreases the intensity of a message. For example, a manager may pound his fist firmly on the table to emphasize his feelings while saying 'No' to an unreasonable request for a pay rise from an employee. A child might say 'I love you' while giving you a kiss on the cheek. Alternatively, a colleague may use a neutral tone of voice to *lower* the intensity of positive (or negative) words. In these cases, nonverbal codes accent the emotions conveyed by verbal messages because they add more information to them.

Regulate verbal communication

We can use nonverbal codes to tell others to do or not to do something. A mother may use a stare to stop the naughty behaviour of her children in public places. We may also use voice inflection, head nods, and hand movements to control the flow of conversation or to direct turn taking.

Types of Nonverbal Communication

It is impossible to categorize all the different types of nonverbal behaviour. Not only are they too numerous, but often several types of nonverbal behaviour from seemingly different 'categories' can be used by the same person simultaneously. In this section, however, we examine the seven categories which are argued to be most relevant to intercultural communication: kinesics, proxemics, chronemics, haptics, physical appearance and dress, paralanguage, and olfactics.

Kinesics: body movement

Kinesics refers to gestures, hand and arm movements, leg movements, facial expressions, eye contact, and posture. Ekman and Friesen (1969) developed a system that organized kinesic behaviour into five broad categories: emblems, illustrators, affect displays, regulators, and adaptors.

Emblems are primary hand gestures that have a direct literal verbal translation; these gestures blur the boundary between verbal and nonverbal communication. Within any culture there is usually a high level of agreement about the meaning of a particular emblem. For example, making a circle with one's thumb and index finger while extending the other fingers is emblematic of the word 'OK' in the USA, but it stands for 'money' in Japan and signifies 'zero' in Indonesia. In China people say goodbye with the palm down and wave the hand vertically, whereas Koreans wave goodbye by waving their arm from side to side. In many Western cultures, beckoning people to come with the palm up is common but in some Asian countries people only use such a gesture to beckon dogs.

Illustrators are typically hand and arm movements that function to complement or accent words. Thus, illustrators serve a metacommunicative function; that is to say, they are messages about messages. For example, a person might describe the size of a crocodile she saw while using hand gestures to illustrate its length. Stewart and Bennett (1991) provided an interesting example of cultural differences in using illustrators. An American visitor to Mexico tried to convey the age of his young children to a Mexican by indicating their height. He held up his right hand, the palm open and facing down horizontally at the height of his children from the ground. The Mexican looked puzzled. Later, the American visitor learned that Mexicans would only use that particular hand gesture to indicate the height of a dog or some other animal; human height is indicated with the palm open and held vertical to the ground at the appropriate distance.

Affect displays primarily refer to facial expressions that communicate an emotional state. Through facial expressions we can communicate an attitude, feelings, disgust, happiness, anger or sadness. Some facial expressions are universal (e.g. a smile indicating pleasure and happiness), but the specific meaning attached to a facial expression or other affect display must be linked to its cultural context. For example, a shop assistant may smile at customers to show friendliness and politeness; a mother may smile at her baby to show affection; a student unable to answer a question from the teacher may smile to cover her embarrassment. Besides facial expressions, so too does posture – a person's bodily stance – communicate feelings and emotions. For example, sitting with the soles of one's feet facing another

Photo 7.1
The smile on these Malaysian dancers' faces communicates happiness.
Copyright © Levi Obijiofor. Used with permission.

person communicates disrespect in Thailand and Saudi Arabia, whereas in the United States this posture simply shows that the person feels relaxed.

Regulators include behaviours and actions that govern or manage conversations. We may use eye contact, silence, and head nodding during a conversation to show interest and to indicate turn-taking. If a teacher asks a question and a student does not wish to respond, she can avoid direct eye contact to indicate her unwillingness to speak. However, it is worth noticing that silence during a conversation may not always communicate disinterest. In the Confucian cultural context, silence is regarded as a virtue (also see Carbaugh et al.'s example of Finland in Chapter 6).

Adaptors are kinesic behaviours used to satisfy physiological or psychological needs. For example, scratching an itch satisfies a physiological need while adjusting one's glasses before speaking may satisfy a psychological need to calm down. These behaviours help people to adapt to their environment. The interpretation of any kinesic behaviour depends on its context. For example, sitting with arms and legs tightly crossed could mean a person is feeling cold (e.g. at a train station), defensive (e.g. during an argument), or nervous (e.g. waiting for a job interview).

Proxemics: the use of space

Proxemics refers to the use of space, including territoriality, which stands for the space that an individual claims permanently or temporarily. For example, it is very likely that you still sit in the same seat in a lecture theatre where you sat at the beginning of the semester, even though it is not assigned seating. If someone takes that seat before you, you might feel as if that person had taken 'your spot'. The study of proxemics includes three aspects of space: fixed features, semi-fixed features, and personal space (Hall, 1966). The size of one's office, a fixed feature of space, communicates status and power, while semi-fixed features of space – the movable objects within an office such as furniture and decorations – can communicate the degree of openness of the occupant as well as their status and power. Some people prefer to have their desk facing the door, which tends to make visitors feel welcome. Others prefer to put high bookshelves at the entrance to block the views in and out, which may make people feel a person is less accessible. Personal space refers to the distance within which people feel comfortable when interacting with others. We use space to communicate and the size of that space is not only culturally determined but also influenced by the relationship. People from Latin America or the Middle East often feel comfortable standing close to each other, while people from European countries or North America prefer a relatively greater distance. Lovers stand closer to each other during a conversation than two colleagues would. Cultural norms and the relationship between communicators determine the use of personal space in communication.

Theory Corner

The meaning of spatial relations

Edward Hall (1966) analysed North Americans' use of space and identified four zones of personal space that have meaning in communication. The first is the intimate zone (0–1.5 feet), which is used for intimate communication such as comforting, protecting, and love-making. The second is the personal zone (18 inches–4 feet), which is the distance that people commonly maintain in dyadic encounters. The third is the social zone (4–12 feet), which is the normative distance at social gatherings, in work settings, and during business transactions. The fourth zone comprises the largest distance between persons (12 feet and above). It is generally used in formal communication situations, such as public speaking. Different cultures may have different criteria for a 'comfortable' distance between speakers.

Reference

Hall, Edward T. (1966) *The Hidden Dimension*. Garden City, NJ: Doubleday.

Further reading on proxemics

Burgoo, Judee K. and Jones, Stephen B. (1976) 'Toward a theory of personal space expectations and their violations', *Human Communication Research*, 2 (2): 131–146.

Chronemics: the use of time

Chronemics refers to the use of time. Our concept of time may influence our communication behaviour. A village meeting in an African village does not begin until everyone is ready. A 45-minute wait may not be unusual for a business appointment in Latin America but could be insulting to a North American business person. Hall and Hall (1990) categorized a culture's time orientation into monochronic and polychronic. *Monochronic* time is characteristic of many Western cultures. People with this time orientation view time as linear, much like a progressive path, having a beginning and an end. People from monochronic cultures also believe that this 'path' has discrete compartments; thus people should do only one thing at a time. To a Westerner, time can be bought, saved, spent, wasted, lost, or made up, and observing clock time is important. In contrast, *polychronic* cultures view time as cyclical. People from polychronic cultures prefer operating with several people, ideas, or projects simultaneously. To an Arab, observing clock time is irreligious because only God can determine what will or will not happen. In addition, time can also be viewed from past, present, or future orientations (Cooper et al., 2007). Past-oriented cultures emphasize tradition; present-oriented cultures stress spontaneity and immediacy; future-oriented cultures emphasize the importance of present activities to future outcomes.

Differences in the conception of time can cause frustration in intercultural communication. For example, a US American professor complained about a long staff meeting when he taught at a university in Hong Kong. Unlike his experience of staff meetings in the United States, those he attended in Hong Kong did not seem to follow the agenda items in a linear way. Oftentimes, even upon reaching the seventh item of the agenda, a question raised by someone could still bring the discussion back to the second item on the agenda. Decisions were not made by voting, but rather by a consensus of the people present at the meeting. Thus, each staff meeting commonly lasted for over two hours, which this American professor considered an inefficient use of time. Similarly, people in many Western cultures have to make an appointment to see a doctor. In some Asian cultures, however, this is not done. Patients simply arrive at a time of their own choice and their waiting time depends on the number of other patients in the waiting room on that particular day.

Another example of cultural differences in time conception is use of the calendar. While the Gregorian calendar is used universally, people from different cultures may also use their culture-specific calendars, such as the Chinese lunar calendar and the Buddhist calendar, to record their date of birth or celebrate the New Year.

Haptics: the use of touch

Photo 7.2
Mixed Gregorian and Buddhist calendar dates are shown on the wall of a building in Laos.
Copyright © Joan Burnett. Used with permission.

Haptics refers to the use of touch, the most primitive form of communication. Touch sends myriad messages – protection, support, approval, or encouragement. As usual, when, where, and whom we touch and what meanings we assign to touch differ widely across cultures. The amount of touch also varies with age, sex, situation, and the relationship between the people involved. North American culture generally discourages touching by adults except in moments of intimacy or formal greetings (e.g. hand shaking or hugging). Similar culturally defined patterns of physical contact avoidance are found in most cultures throughout Asia and Northern Europe.

Hall (1966) distinguished between high- and low-contact cultures. High-contact cultures are those that tend to encourage touching and engage in touching more frequently (e.g. Southern and Eastern Europe). British cultures are considered low contact. Even within a low- or high-contact culture, the cultural and social rules governing touch vary. People from Islamic and Hindu cultures typically do not touch with the left hand because to do so is a social insult. The left hand is reserved for toilet functions. Islamic cultures generally do not permit touching between genders, but touching between people of the same gender tends to be acceptable. In many Western cultures, touching between people of the same sex may be interpreted by others as a sign of homosexuality, but in other cultures this practice is normative for everyone.

Physical appearance and dress

Interpersonal communication is often preceded by the communicators' observations of each other's physical appearance. People can wear particular types of clothes to communicate their culture, religion, status, power, personality, self-esteem, and social identity. For example, Muslim women can often be easily recognized by their headscarves which are important symbols of religious faith. More religious or conservative Muslim women usually wear the *jilhah*, meaning 'outer-garment'. This is a long coat-like dress that covers the whole body except for the face and hands. Some Muslim men can be identified by a long white robe and hat.

In most cultures people consciously manipulate their physical appearance in order to communicate their identity. In ancient Chinese culture, women had to bind their feet at a young age because small feet symbolized beauty. Plastic surgery is another example of using physical appearance to communicate messages. According to the American Society for Aesthetic Plastic Surgery, there has been a 222 per cent increase in cosmetic procedures performed in the United States since 1997, with 91 per cent of cosmetic surgery on young women (ASAPS, 2006). As Kathy Davis (1995) noted, in Western societies women are expected to look beautiful because they are considered 'to embody' beauty. Consequently, many women believe they must conform to society's notion of beauty, as it is reinforced as their 'role'.

Perceptions of beauty or physical attractiveness differ from culture to culture. More than three decades of extensive research on female gender portrayal in advertising offers a rich understanding of how beauty is constructed in different cultures (Frith et al., 2005). Frith et al. found that Western women appeared more frequently in clothing advertisements, whereas Asian models were more often used to advertise facial and beauty products. This is consistent with the idea that beauty in the East is related to a pretty face, while the predominant beauty ideal in the West relates to the body as well as the face. Beauty ideals and stereotypes put forth by advertisers can exert a negative pressure on women of different races and there are indications of a continued push in the West towards a white beauty ideal. While white women are pressured to be thin, women of colour may experience not only the societal pressure to be thin but also an impossible expectation to be white.

Paralanguage: quality and characteristics of the voice

Paralanguage refers to the vocal qualities that accompany speech. It can be divided into two broad categories: voice qualities and vocalizations

(Knapp and Hall, 1997). Voice qualities include elements like pitch, volume, tempo, rhythm, tone, pausing, and the resonance of the voice. Vocalization includes laughing, crying, sighing, yelling, moaning, swallowing, and throat clearing. Some scholars also include as paralinguistic vocalizations back-channel utterances such as *um*, *ah*, *ooh*, *shh*, and *uh*, although other scholars categorize these as verbal behaviour – once again, the boundary between verbal and nonverbal behaviour is blurred. Silence is also considered by some (but not all) to fall within the domain of paralanguage. People may use silence to show their respect, agreement or disagreement, apathy, awe, confusion, contemplation, embarrassment, regret, repressed anger, sadness, and a myriad of other things. We interpret a speaker's feelings and emotions based on our perception of the variations in vocal quality. The same words said with different vocal qualities can convey different meanings, as illustrated in the example below:

> Mark, you are going to marry Hillary. (A declarative statement of a fact.)
>
> Mark, you are going to marry *Hillary*? (A question to convey that I thought you were going to marry someone else.)
>
> Mark, you are going to marry Hillary! (An exclamation to express excitement.)
>
> Mark, *you* are going to marry Hillary? (A question to express surprise, e.g. I thought someone else was going to marry her.)
>
> Mark, you *are* going to marry Hillary. (A statement to get confirmation; I thought you just liked her, not loved her.)

Cultural differences are reflected in people's use of paralanguage. Speaking loudly indicates strength and sincerity to Arabs, authority to Germans, but impoliteness to Thais, and a loss of control to the Japanese. The Lebanese proverb 'Lower your voice and strengthen your argument' also emphasizes the value that culture places on controlling one's voice in a conversation. The use of vocal segregates (e.g. *um*, *uh*) may communicate interest, uncertainty, attention, acceptance, or hesitation, and their meanings vary across cultures. In China, people may use *um* or *hai* (for Cantonese speakers) to indicate 'yes' or 'I see' while the other person is speaking. This vocal segregate is used to encourage the other speaker to continue talking, rather than to suggest a change of direction. The appropriateness of vocal qualities is also judged based on gender. For example, laughing loudly is common and acceptable for American women, but it might not be considered as such in Asian cultures. In ancient China, women had to cover their mouth with a handkerchief when they laughed to indicate good manners and politeness.

Olfactics: the use of smell, scent, and odour

Olfactics refers to humans' perception and use of smell, scent, and odour. Compared with other types of nonverbal codes, the study of olfactics has received less academic attention. Research evidence shows that there is a universal preference for some scents that may have biological and evolutionary roots. For example, the fragrances of jasmine, lavender, and roses tend to communicate a soothing and pleasant feeling to people; the perfume industry makes billions of dollars a year by capitalizing on these scent preferences.

Smell can also be used to communicate position, social class, and power. Anthony Synnott (1996) claims that odour is used to categorize people into social groups of different status, power, and social class because the meanings attributed to a specific scent give it a social significance. Synnott argues that perceived foul odours are one of the criteria by which negative identities are attributed to some social or ethnic groups. If a well-dressed man carrying a briefcase and smelling of high-quality aftershave gets into the lift of an office building, others in the lift are more likely to think of him as someone who holds a management position rather than as an ordinary office worker. Nevertheless, people's smell preferences are not universal but vary across cultures. For example, the Dogon people of Mali find the scent of onions very attractive, and young men and women rub fried onions all over their bodies (Neuliep, 2006); the smell of onion from a person's mouth is considered bad breath in many other cultures.

Influence of Culture on Nonverbal Communication

People hold expectations about the appropriateness of others' nonverbal behaviour. These expectations are learned and, thus, vary across cultures. (Interactants from different cultural backgrounds have to learn each other's expectations regarding appropriate nonverbal behaviour) Lustig and Koester (2010) identified three cultural variations in nonverbal communication. First, cultures differ in their specific repertoire of behaviours. Body movements, gestures, posture, vocal qualities, and spatial requirements are specific to a particular culture. For example, shoulder shrugging is commonly used by Westerners when something is not understood, whereas in some Asian cultures this body movement is almost never used; the same feeling is often expressed by shaking one's head. In Australia, people may snap their fingers or raise their hand in a restaurant to get a waiter's attention; in Malaysia people can get a waiter's attention by making a certain sound with their mouth; in Hong Kong, people wave their hand along with the words *mu gai* ('excuse me').

The second cultural variation identified by Lustig and Koester (2010) is that all cultures have display rules which govern when and in what context certain nonverbal expressions are required, permitted, preferred, or prohibited. Display rules govern such things as how far apart people should stand during a conversation, where and whom to touch, when and with whom to use direct eye contact, how loudly one should speak, and how much one should show his or her feelings. For example, Arab men kiss each other on both cheeks in greeting; Chinese men often shake hands; Japanese men bow; and Malaysians put their palms together in front of the chest. A good place to observe this cultural variation in display rules is the arrival terminal of an international airport. Westerners tend to greet their loved ones with hugs and kisses, whereas Asians tend to be more reserved and may hug each other but will generally not kiss each other in public places.

The third cultural variation identified by Lustig and Koeter (2010) is that the meaning attributed to particular nonverbal behaviours differs from culture to culture. In Western countries, it is common to see people smile at strangers or passers-by in their neighbourhood, while this facial expression may be interpreted as rather odd in Singapore or other Asian countries where people do not often initiate a conversation with strangers. On one occasion in China during the peak travel time (before the Chinese New Year), posters were displayed in railway stations advising travellers not to speak to strangers. In Australian universities, it is very common to see students wearing thongs in the classroom; in China, shoes that look like slippers are regarded as improper footwear in the classroom. Interestingly, putting down your lower eyelid with one finger means 'my eye' in English (and French) – that is, 'I don't believe you' – whereas *Chashm* ('my eye') in Farsi means 'I promise'.

Culture and nonverbal behaviour are inseparable. Cultural rules and norms determine what nonverbal behaviour is deemed to be appropriate, where and how to display it, and the meanings attributed to it. Unlike verbal codes, however, there is no formal grammar for nonverbal codes that foreigners can learn to make intercultural communication easier. Members of a particular culture learn the norms for appropriate and inappropriate nonverbal behaviour through the process of socialization. In addition, the application of these rules usually occurs outside of our conscious awareness. We become aware of our culture's rules and norms mainly when we see these being broken. Consequently, when we communicate with people whose repertoire of nonverbal codes differs from our own, misunderstandings are almost certain to occur. Violation of these nonverbal rules or misinterpretations of nonverbal codes can lead to negative attitudes or even conflict. It is important, therefore, for us to be alert to differences in nonverbal codes in intercultural communication, to monitor our own use of nonverbal codes, and to observe those of others.

Summary

This chapter has focused on the importance and characteristics of nonverbal communication. We explained how nonverbal codes are used to *repeat* the message sent by the verbal code; *contradict* the verbal message; *substitute* for the verbal message; *complement* a verbal message; *accent* the verbal message; and *regulate* verbal communication. Seven major types of nonverbal code systems were examined: kinesics, proxemics, chronemics, haptics, physical appearance and dress, paralanguage, and olfactics, and their differences across cultures were discussed. Unlike verbal codes, there is no formal grammar governing the use of nonverbal codes. These rules are learned as part of a culture's socialization process. By looking at different types of nonverbal codes, we can come to a better understanding of the many ways meaning is inferred in different cultures.

We all know the proverb 'Actions speak louder than words.' In essence, this underscores the importance of nonverbal communication. Although there is evidence that some nonverbal codes have universal meanings (e.g. facial expressions of fear or anger), how a behaviour is displayed and the circumstances where it is appropriate vary from culture to culture. In addition, the same nonverbal code may be common and have a clear interpretation in some cultures (e.g. the thumb-up gesture, the 'OK' gesture, head shaking), but it may be meaningless in another culture or even have the opposite meaning. Nonverbal codes send powerful messages, influencing our perception of others and how we are perceived by others. Nonverbal communication skills, therefore, are an important component of intercultural competence.

Case Study:
Yum cha and Chinese culture

Yum cha is an interesting and important part of Chinese culinary culture, particularly for people from Hong Kong and the Guangdong province. In the Cantonese dialect, *yum cha* means 'drink tea'. It refers to the custom of eating *dim sum* (small servings of different Chinese delicacies) while sipping Chinese tea in a teahouse or restaurant. On weekend mornings or lunchtimes, families and friends gather together in a teahouse to drink tea, eat *dim sum*, and chat about things happening around them. In Hong Kong, *yum cha* is also a morning gathering ritual for retired or elderly people to catch up after early morning exercises. In addition to gatherings of family and friends, it is not uncommon for business deals to be sealed in a teahouse instead of in an office. Due to its more relaxed atmosphere, conflicts or disputes between friends or colleagues may also be settled in a teahouse. In fact, *yum cha* has become such an integral part of Chinese culture that a common parting expression between friends is: 'Will catch up with you for *yum cha* when you have time.'

Many culture-bound nonverbal behaviours can be seen at a *yum cha* place. Waiting in line at the entrance for a vacant table, particularly at lunchtime on Saturdays, is normal. Bookings are usually accepted; however, patrons cannot necessarily expect a table to be available upon arrival at the booking time. For example, in a very popular teahouse in Brisbane, Australia, one staff member is placed at the entrance to assign tables to their customers. He keeps two lists: one contains the people who have made a booking; the other contains the names of people who are without an advanced booking but are waiting for a table in the corridor (each person is given a number). When a person who has made a booking arrives, the staff member will make a note and then ask the person to wait. Thus, two 'booking' systems are used for assigning tables. Everyone will eventually have a table, but some may have to wait for a longer time than others. Hardly anyone who arrives at the peak time (e.g. Saturday at 12:30 pm) will be given a table immediately. This system can be confusing and even frustrating to some Westerners who are not used to standing in a queue at the entrance of a restaurant where they have already made a booking.

Photo 7.4
Dim Sum at a Chinese *Yum Cha* place.
Copyright © Shuang Liu. Used with permission.

Tea and *dim sum* are two major components of *yum cha*. Tea is more than a refreshment in China and Hong Kong; it is a way of life. *Dim sum* includes steamed buns filled with pork and assorted dumplings with fillings such as beef, prawn, chicken, and vegetables. *Dim sum* is often served in small portions, normally three or four pieces per dish, and served by waitresses pushing trolleys stacked with bamboo steamers filled with *dim sum* dishes. It is customary for people at each table to share dishes so that they can enjoy a variety of different tastes.

The Chinese teahouse is different from a Western restaurant and there are rituals that are supposed to be followed. First, a Chinese teahouse tends to be noisy. People talk in loud voices and sometimes it is difficult to make oneself heard. Therefore, speaking loudly in a teahouse is not necessarily considered impolite as it would be in a Western restaurant. In a teahouse, waiters walk between tables carrying pots of hot water to refill customers' teapots. But in this noisy environment it is almost impossible to get a waiter's attention to have your teapot refilled by simply raising your voice. The typical way to communicate this message is to lift the lid and put it on top of the pot with the opening half-covered with the lid. This is the polite and customary way to ask for a refill. A sign of good service in a teahouse is when refills occur soon after the lid is lifted open.

In *yum cha* etiquette, it is customary for one person (people at each table take it in turns) to pour tea into other people's cups before filling their own. The nonverbal behaviour to thank the person who has poured tea into your cup is to tap the table with three or two fingers. Finger tapping is also known as finger *kou-tou*; this is a gesture to thank someone in the traditional Chinese style. A story has it that the historical significance of this gesture can be traced back to the Qing Dynasty. When visiting south China on an incognito inspection trip, the emperor went to a teahouse with his companions and guards. To disguise his identity, he joined others at the table in taking turns to pour tea. His companions could not kneel down and *kou-tou* to show gratitude for this great honour because doing so would reveal the identity of the emperor. Instead, they tapped three fingers on the table to represent their bowed heads and their prostrated arms. Times have changed and there is no longer an emperor to whom people should *kou-tou*. However, tapping one's fingers remains the ritual expression of gratitude to someone when being served tea. Nowadays it is more common to see people using two fingers (the index and middle finger) to tap the table instead of three fingers.

Reference for case study

'Hong Kong: Tea & Teahouses' [online]. Accessed 20 April 2009 at http://www.globalgournet.com/destinations/hongkong/hktea.html

Questions for discussion

1 Have you been to a *yum cha* place in your country? What are some of the nonverbal behaviours that you first noticed? What were your reactions to them?
2 Are there any nonverbal behaviours in a Chinese teahouse that you think you understand? Are there any nonverbal behaviours in a Chinese teahouse that are puzzling to you?
3 Is *yum cha* part of your culture? If so, what cultural significance does it have for you? If it is not part of your culture, does your culture have something similar to this?
4 What do you think are some of the potential intercultural misunderstandings in a *yum cha* teahouse?
5 Are there any nonverbal behaviours that people typically use in restaurants in your country? What are they? Could they be misinterpreted in another culture? How?

Key Terms

affective content;	haptics;	
chronemics;	kinesics;	paralanguage;
cognitive content;	monochronic time	polychronic time orientation;
display rules;	orientation;	proxemics
expectancy violation	nonverbal communication;	
theory;	olfactics;	

Further Reading

Culture and nonverbal communication

Archer, Dane (1997) 'Unspoken diversity: cultural differences in gestures', *Qualitative Sociology*, 20 (1): 79–105.

Costanzo, Mark and Archer, Dane (1989) 'Interpreting the expressive behaviour of others: the interpersonal perception task', *Journal of Nonverbal Behaviour*, 13 (3): 225–245.

Elfenbein, Hillary A. and Ambady, Nalini (2003) 'When familiarity breeds accuracy: cultural exposure and facial emotion recognition', *Journal of Personality and Social Psychology*, 85 (2): 276–290.

Molinsky, Andrew L.; Krabbenhoft, Mary A.; Ambady, Nalini and Choi, Susan Y. (2005) 'Cracking the nonverbal code: intercultural competence and gesture recognition across cultures', *Journal of Cross-Cultural Psychology*, 36 (3): 380–395.

Nonverbal communication in general

Ekman, Paul and Friesen, Wallace (1969) 'The repertoire of nonverbal behavior: categories, origins, usage, and coding', *Semiotica*, 1: 49–98.
Hall, Judith A.; Murphy, Nora A. and Schmid, Mast M. (2007) 'Nonverbal self-accuracy in interpersonal interaction', *Personality and Social Psychology Bulletin*, 33 (2): 1675–1685.

Specific nonverbal behaviours and their interpretations in cultural contexts

Burgoo, Judee K. and Jones, Stephen B. (1976) 'Toward a theory of personal space expectations and their violations', *Human Communication Research*, 2 (2): 131–146.
Herzfeld, Michael (2009) 'The cultural politics of gesture: reflections on the embodiment of ethnographic practice', *Ethnography*, 10 (1): 131–152.
Marsh, Abigail A.; Elfenbein, Hillary A. and Ambady, Nalini (2007) 'Separated by a common language: nonverbal accents and cultural stereotypes about Americans and Australians', *Journal of Cross-Cultural Psychology*, 38 (2): 284–301.
Parkinson, Brian (2005) 'Do facial movements express emotions or communicate motives?', *Personality and Social Psychology Review*, 9 (1): 278–311.

8

Categorization, Subgroups, and Identities

You can out-distance that which is running after you, but not what is running inside you.

Rwandan proverb

Learning Objectives

At the end of this chapter, you should be able to:

- Define different types of identities.
- Explain the sources and characteristics of identities.
- Describe theories of identities and identity negotiation.
- Explain the role of identities in intercultural communication.
- Appreciate the formation of identities within the contexts of history, economics, and politics.

The Multifaceted Nature of Identities

Identity is the cornerstone of our times (Castells, 1997) and it gives us a sense of place. As we grow up, we encounter many situations in which we ask ourselves or are asked the question 'Who am I?', which penetrates to the deepest levels of our being. Stuart Hall (1996) defined identity as each individual's particular way of identifying her- or himself within specific cultural contexts. Identity manifests personal or group characteristics and expresses specific memberships. It is generally agreed that the term 'identity' refers primarily to a person's subjective experience of her- or himself in relation to the world, and as such it should be differentiated from concepts like character or personality. One can share character traits with many people, but the sharing of such traits does not require any active personal engagement; however, sharing an identity implies that we actively engage part of our being in order to identify with a certain group. This notion of active engagement indicates that one's identity is formed through cultural processes, which are in turn conditioned by cultural structures. The multifaceted nature of our identities is experienced and negotiated constantly in everyday life.

Broadly speaking, identities can be studied at the individual or collective level. *Individual* (or *personal*) *identity* refers to categorizing an individual as distinct from others, along with the specific relationships the individual has with others. *Collective* (or *social*) *identity* refers to a categorization based on group membership, to make groups rather than individuals distinctive. Identification with and perceived acceptance into a group involves learning systems of symbols as well as values, norms, and rules, all expressing people's group or cultural affiliation. Racial identity, for example, is a type of collective identity. Generally, racial identity involves a human group that character- izes itself and/or is characterized by others as being distinct by some immu- table biological differences. As a defining and controlling characteristic, race has been used not only for social categorization but also for discrimination throughout history. Humans in all cultures desire positive individually based and group-based identities, which are expressed in their communicative inter- actions (Ting-Toomey, 2005a).

We categorize people based on their group membership. Different cat- egories give us social identities and systematically order the world around us. Throughout our lives, we identify with various social groups and hence develop multiple identities. As early as the fifth century BC, Greeks used fac- tors such as blood, language, religion, and way of life to identify what they shared in common with and what distinguished them from Persians and other non-Greeks (Cooper et al., 2007). In addition to culture and religion, identities can be defined by gender, class, race, ethnicity, political orientation, social groups, occupation, and geographic region.

Sometimes we are positioned into categories that we do not want to be a part of. In addition, while some group memberships are voluntary (e.g. religion, occupation), others are involuntary (e.g. sex, age). Because of our multiple group or subgroup memberships, we are always engaged in communicating with people from outgroups (groups we do not belong to). This chapter focuses on categorization, subgroups, and identities. We explain social categorization theories and describe the formation of different types of identities based on gender, ethnicity, culture, and nation. The chapter examines different types of identities through historical and contemporary examples, followed by a discus- sion on the role of identity in intercultural relations. This chapter emphasizes that identity is not given and fixed, but rather, that it is constantly negotiated and reconstructed.

Social Categorization and Identities

As explained in Chapter 4, *categorization* is defined as a process of order- ing the environment through the grouping of persons, objects, and events as being similar or equivalent to one another, based on their shared features or characteristics (Tajfel, 1978). When we selectively perceive stimuli from the external world, we organize and arrange them in meaningful and systematic ways. In everyday life, we try to distinguish individuals, groups, or cultures based on their differences. Such categorization has both advantages and disadvantages; on the one hand, it reduces the complexity of the world and helps us to understand our environment by giving it some structure; on the other hand, categorization – particularly of people – can reinforce stereotypes (Tajfel, 1982). Categorizing people into groups gives us identities at both individual and group level.

Categorization and the formation of identities

Social identity theory claims that identity formation is a product of social categorization (Hogg and Abrams, 1988). Individuals belong to various social categories (e.g. gender, ethnicity, political affiliation) and form identities based on membership of social categories. Through this process, society is internalized by individuals on the basis of social categories. Social identities connect individuals to society through group memberships which influence their beliefs, attitudes, and behaviour in their relationships with members of other social groups.

Personal identity

Personal identity defines an individual in terms of his or her difference to others. The individual creates a self-image and responds to the image created. Others also expect the individual to act in accordance with his her self-image. Aspects of personal identity include physical features, hobbies, interests, family relationships, and social circle, as well as personal aspects of age, sex, nationality, religious affiliation, disability, sexual orientation, and so forth. The specific way in which each of us sees ourselves in relation to those around us and those things that make us unique are all a part of our personal identity. Personal identity consists of the things that pick us out as individuals and make us distinct from others who are similar in some way (e.g. the things that make me distinct from my friends, fellow employees, etc.). Parts of our personal identity, such as sex and genetic characteristics, are given to us at birth. Other parts are created during our childhood and continue to evolve throughout our lives (Denzin and Lincoln, 1998) as we are socialized into society. Personal identity gives individuals a sense of distinctiveness even when they are in a crowd of similar people.

Photo 8.1
Our personal identity picks us out as individuals and makes us distinct from others even when we are in a crowd.
Copyright © Joan Burnett. Used with permission.

Social identity

Social identities are those parts of an individual's self-concept which derive from his or her membership of a group, together with the value and emotional significance attached to such membership (Tajfel, 1978). Social identities pick us out as group members and distinguish our groups (e.g. national groups, sports groups) from other, perhaps competing, groups. Our social identity influences how we live within diverse cultural contexts and relate to a range of social groups and institutions (Jenkins, 1996). Social groups can be marked by family connections, ethnic communities, cultural groups, race, nationality, occupation, or friendship circles.

Individuals construct social categories (like sports clubs, liberals, Jews) and use their beliefs, attitudes, feelings, and behaviours as prototypes to differentiate their own groups from others that are salient in the situation. Hogg and Mullin (1999) argue that individuals are more inclined to align themselves with the norms of their group when they experience a sense of uncertainty. Think of racial identities and what it means to be 'white'. Fanon (1990) writes that white individuals in the West are usually unaware of themselves as belonging to a specific racial group, because being white is taken for granted. On the other hand, people from other racial backgrounds are more aware of their minority group membership, as distinct from the majority. An important consequence of categorizing people based on group membership is drawing the boundary between ingroups and outgroups; some types of groups (e.g. those with a strong collective or group-based orientation) and some contexts (e.g. rivalry or competition for scarce resources) lead to sharper boundaries being drawn than others.

Theory Corner

Stages of identity development

According to Hardiman (2001), there are several stages for social identity development by white people in Western cultures. First, there is an *unexamined identity phase*, characterized by an acceptance of dominant norms and a lack of desire to look into one's identity. Following this is an *acceptance phase*, a stage during which dominant group members internalize the identity imposed by the culture. In the third stage, *redefinition*, a re-interpretation of the dominant culture occurs and may be accompanied by attempts to openly challenge it. The fourth stage is *integration*, whereby white people connect themselves to a dominant culture that reflects an awareness of the special privilege accorded them and an appreciation of the values of minority cultures. Of course, this final stage is frequently not achieved. Identity development may not necessarily follow a linear process, and the length of each stage may vary from person to person.

Reference

Hardiman, Rita (2001) 'Reflections on white identity development theory', in C.L. Wijeyesinghe and Jackson B. Bailey III (eds), *New Perspectives on Racial Identity Development: A Theoretical and Practical Anthology*. New York: New York University Press. pp. 12–34.

Further reading on identity development

Erickson, Erik H. (1980) *Identity and the Life Cycle*. New York: Norton.

Ingroups and Outgroups

For individuals in any culture, there are the groups to which they belong, called membership groups, and groups to which they do not belong, called non-membership groups. Membership groups can be involuntary (like age, race, sex), or they can be voluntary (like political affiliation, religion, occupation). *Ingroups* represent a special class of membership group characterized by an internal cohesiveness among members. An ingroup's norms, aspirations, and values shape the behaviour of its members. When the ingroup is salient, members are concerned about each other's welfare and willing to cooperate without demanding equitable returns. Ingroups are characterized by some shared experiences (sometimes via the mass media) and an anticipated shared future, so that they create a sense of intimacy, solidarity, and trust.

Like membership groups, non-membership groups can be voluntary or involuntary. An *outgroup* is a non-membership group that is salient to the ingroup. An outgroup is seen as distinct from the ingroup or sometimes standing in the way of the accomplishment of the ingroup's goals (Jandt, 2007). Outgroups comprise people whose welfare we are not concerned about, and groups with whom we require at least an equitable return in order to cooperate (Neuliep, 2006). Attributions made about ingroup and outgroup members are typically biased in favour of the ingroup. For example, people have a tendency to ascribe undesirable qualities such as untrustworthiness, arrogance, or dishonesty to outgroups. Ingroup bias occurs along the dimensions by which we compare ingroups and outgroups (e.g. intelligence, language proficiency), even though any real difference may be on another dimension altogether (e.g. national origin). We tend to see outgroups as homogeneous, but to see more variability in ingroups (see Chapter 4).

Different cultures ascribe different meanings to ingroup and outgroup relationships. In individualistic cultures, such as those of the United States and the Netherlands, people are considered independent, and fewer and less sharp distinctions are made between ingroups and outgroups. In more collectivistic cultures like Greece and Nigeria, people are more group-oriented, and individuals are considered interdependent and hence very close to their ingroups.

As survival of both the individual and society is more dependent on the group, sharper distinctions are made between ingroups and outgroups.

Distinctions between salient ingroups and outgroups lead to a sense of belonging, security, and trust. We often treat strangers or outsiders with suspicion, and control them carefully while deciding if we can trust them or not. We tend to be more tolerant of the behaviour of ingroup members than of outsiders, creating a distinction between what is known as '*inside* morals' and '*outside* morals'. The reach of morals is called the scope of justice. Coleman (2000: 118) states, 'Individuals or groups within our moral boundaries are seen as deserving of the same fair, moral treatment as we deserve. Individuals or groups outside these boundaries are seen as undeserving of this same treatment.'

It is important to remember that social identities, and indeed our group memberships, are not fixed. As our membership or the social context changes, we need to reconstruct or renegotiate our social identities. Indian feminist scholar Chandra Talpade Mohanty vividly illustrated this point by drawing upon her own experience (2003: 190):

> Growing up in India, I was Indian; teaching in high school in Nigeria, I was a foreigner (still Indian), albeit a familiar one. As a graduate student in Illinois, I was first a 'Third World' foreign student, and then a person of color. Doing research in London, I was black. As a professor at an American university, I am an Asian woman – although South Asian racial profiles fit uneasily into the 'Asian' category – and, because I choose to identify myself as such, an antiracist feminist of color. In North America I was also a 'resident alien' with an Indian passport – I am now a US citizen whose racialization has shifted dramatically (and negatively) since the attacks on the World Trade Center and the Pentagon on September 11, 2001.

Theory Corner

Identity negotiation theory

Identity negotiation theory, proposed by Stella Ting-Toomey (2005a), emphasizes particular identity domains as influential to our everyday interactions. Individuals acquire and develop their identities through interaction with others, as it is in this way that they acquire the values, beliefs, norms, and styles governing the communication behaviour. There are many possible identities available or ascribed to us, including those of social class, sexual orientation, age, race, ethnicity, and culture. To become effective intercultural communicators, we have to understand both the cultural content and the salient issues of identity domains and how others view themselves in communication.

Identity negotiation theory posits identity as a reflective self-image constructed during the process of intercultural communication. The means of negotiating this identity is described as 'a transactional interaction process whereby individuals in an intercultural situation attempt to assert, define, modify, challenge, and/or support their own and others' desired self-images' (Ting-Toomey, 2005a: 217). Identity negotiation is present through all communication interactions as communicators simultaneously attempt to evoke their own desired identities and challenge or support others' identities. Intercultural communication requires the mindful process of attuning to self-identity issues, as well as being consciously aware of and attuning to the salient identity issues of others.

Reference

Ting-Toomey, Stella (2005a) 'Identity negotiation theory. Crossing cultural boundaries', in W.B. Gudykunst (ed.), *Theorizing about Intercultural Communication*. Thousand Oaks, CA: SAGE. pp. 211–233.

Further reading on identity negotiation

Qin, Desiree B. (2009) 'Being "good" or being "popular": gender and ethnic identity negotiations of Chinese immigrant adolescents', *Journal of Adolescent Research*, 24 (1): 37–66.

Subgroup Memberships and Different Types of Identities

When people say they belong to a specific group or category, their memberships are the basis of their identities. The identities that mark the boundaries between the self and others or those between ingroups and outgroups explain a great deal about why people think and behave as they do. The following section discusses identities based on gender, ethnicity, culture, and nation.

Gender identity

Gender identity is part of a personal as well as a social identity. The term 'gender' entails social roles established for the sexes, while the term 'sex' refers to a biological category, usually determined at birth. Gender is a social interpretation of biological sex and its associated cultural assumptions and expectations. All cultures divide some aspects of human existence into distinct male and female roles, but the content of gender roles – the norms of behaviour, expectations, and the assumptions associated with them – vary across cultures. These characteristics may or may not be closely related to the biological differences between males and females.

Children develop gender-identity constancy by five to six years of age (Lee, 2000). *Gender constancy* is the concept that a child born as a girl will always be female, will adopt female roles, and grow up to be a woman; similarly, a child born as a boy will adopt male roles and grow up to be a man. However, these continuities are not completely clear and must be learned (Dines and Humez, 1995). Piaget (1977) studied the development of gender identity by examining young children's everyday play interactions and found that, by age five, children tend to play with gender-specific toys. For example, girls tend to play more with dolls, while boys play more with *Superman* and *Batman* toys: young boys play together in larger groups, while young girls prefer to play more in pairs and smaller groups. It is also during this period of early childhood that children become aware of stereotypical gender roles. For example, a girl may see her mother cook most of the meals at home and thus learn that cooking is a woman's job; a boy may observe his father carrying out repairs around the house and from this observation start to perceive repairing things as a man's job. Early beliefs about gender roles reflect children's observations of what they see around them, both in their family and elsewhere in the social environment.

However, gender identity is not necessarily limited to male or female. In some societies, another gender identity is possible, culturally defined as a *third gender*. The Native American *berdache* is defined as an individual with two spirits, both masculine and feminine. The *berdache* is believed to have supernatural powers. The *hijra* of India are recognized as a special caste; they are born with male genitals, but do not accept specifically male or female gender roles; instead, they identify themselves as *hijra*. In the Islamic culture of Oman, males who wear clothing that mixes masculine and feminine characteristics and who engage in sexual relations with males are called *khanith* and are also defined as a third gender. The *fa'afafine* of Samoa, the *fakaleiti* of Tonga, and the *mahu* of Hawaii and Tahiti further illustrate that gender identity can be disconnected from gender roles. They are males with a feminized gender identity, being dressed in feminine styles and performing female-designated tasks. Importantly, these third gender roles are defined and accepted not only by the individuals themselves but also by the wider society in which they live. For example, Samoa's social acceptance of *fa'afafine* has evolved from the long tradition of raising some boys as girls. In families with all male children, or in which the only daughter is too young to assist with the women's work, parents often choose one or more of their sons to help the mother. These boys perform women's work and are raised and dressed as girls (see Herdt, 1996).

It is society that defines the gender roles we know as feminine and masculine. For example, masculinity in the West has traditionally denoted strength and rationality, whereas femininity was traditionally associated with physical weakness, emotion, and intuition. People perform their gender identities daily as a matter of routine. However, when we do not identify with the specific norms of our society, when our identity does not fit the dominant culture, or when we do not respond in socially accepted ways to our assigned identity, then we may be disparaged or discriminated against. Resisting an assigned (or *interpellated*; see Theory Corner below) identity can be extremely difficult, since it takes place at a subconscious level. Moreover, the mass media, school, religion, and other social institutions are creators of gender stereotypes which reinforce the gender roles we are supposed to inhabit. For example, males are often shown on television as strong and brave, powerful and dominant, whereas female characters sometimes appear as submissive, emotional, and primarily focused on romantic relationships. These media representations inform and influence our understandings and expectations of gender roles in the real world. As Western norms and stereotypes about gender change, as they have over the past several decades, our identities and social interactions change with them and this process introduces new tensions in the enactment of gender identities. Today in the West, and increasingly in other societies as well, there are intergroup conflicts over the ways in which gender identities and roles should be constructed.

Theory Corner

Interpellation

We like to think that, as individuals, our thoughts, behaviours, and various other social attributes emerge from deep within the core of our being: that we make and create them. At the same time, we recognize that society itself can structure how we think and act; it can shape our hopes and dreams and even our self-understanding. Imagine how different you would be if you had been born in a very different country and culture. You would still be you, but you might think about yourself very differently. Instead of thinking of yourself, say, as German, Indian, or Dutch, you would identify with a different country with different values and priorities – and these values might well become your own. The French philosopher Louis Althusser (1971) described the process whereby a society creates individuals as particular kinds of people as a form of 'interpellation' or 'hailing' (as when someone calls out to you, asking you to respond). For Althusser, cultures interpellate or hail particular types of subjects. When we come to recognize ourselves as the type of subject being called, the interpellation has been successful. That is, we come to identify ourselves with this type of subject and in this respect our sense of identity comes not from within but from the outside – our culture and society that are 'hailing' us.

Reference

Althusser, Louis (1971) 'Ideology and ideological state apparatuses', in *Lenin and Philosophy and Other Essays*. New York: Monthly Review.

Further reading on identity construction

White, Richard (2001) 'Cooees across the Strand: Australian travellers in London and the performance of national identity', *Australian Historical Studies*, 32 (116): 109–127.

Ethnic identity

Ethnicity can be based on national origin, race, or religion (Gordon, 1964). Ethnicity is different from race, but as a concept is often used interchangeably with or in relation to race. However, race is based on biological characteristics while ethnicity is based on cultural characteristics shared by people of a particular race, national origin, religion, or language. *Ethnic identity* refers to a sense of belonging to or an identification with an ethnic group. Individuals associated with a particular ethnic group do not necessarily act in accordance with ethnic norms, depending on their level of ethnic identification. For example, many Australians identify their ethnicity based on the countries from which their ancestors came. Some Vietnamese refugees who came to Australia during the 1970s as adopted orphans may still identify themselves as Vietnamese, although they were brought up in Anglo-Australian culture and may not even have a Vietnamese name. Thus, the content and salience of a person's ethnic identity reveal the significance of his or her ethnicity (Ting-Toomey, 2005a).

Gudykunst (2004: 81) states that 'it is the shared cultural characteristics that influence communication, not the biological characteristics associated with race.' In intercultural communication, therefore, it is our ethnic identification that influences our behaviour when we interact with others who are different from ourselves. For example, in Greek communities family, friends, and relatives form primary identification circles. Greek Australians are known to be group-oriented, as they perceive their universe in terms of the ingroup over the outgroup, with outgroup members often being viewed with suspicion and mistrust (Cooper et al., 2007). This does not necessarily suggest that membership of an ethnic group automatically translates into identification. As Alba (1990: 22) noted, 'Individuals may be ethnic in their "identities" and still consciously reject their ethnic backgrounds.' Skin colour, for example, does not automatically guarantee ethnic identification (Ting-Toomey, 2005a). Tensions can exist between a person's physical attributes or ethnic origin and his/her psychological feeling of belonging to the ethnic group and the values he/she cherishes.

In addition to the value content, ethnic identity is also concerned with the issue of salience. Salience refers to the likelihood that an individual will acknowledge his or her identity in a given context. For example, ethnic identity can be demonstrated by adherence to traditions, customs, language, or way of living. Many scholars today agree that ethnic identity is thus more of a subjective classification than an objective one. It is the extent to which group members feel emotionally bonded by a common set of values, beliefs, traditions, and heritage (Ting-Toomey, 2005a). Second or third generation immigrants, for example, are less likely to feel as close a bond to their ethnic traditions as first generation ones, even though they share the same physical attributes and may even use the ethnic language at home.

Cultural identity

Cultural identity refers to those social identities that are based on cultural membership; they are our identification with and perceived acceptance into a larger cultural group, into which we are socialized and with which we share a system of symbols, values, norms, and traditions. Cultural identity involves the emotional significance we attach to our sense of belonging to a larger culture (Ting-Toomey, 2005a). We are more aware of our cultural identities when we find ourselves in another culture than when we are in our own culture. Our cultural identity comprises elements such as physical appearance, racial traits, skin colour, and language and is formed through socialization. The level of our cultural identification influences our behaviour. For example, Anglo-Australians who strongly identify with Australian culture may value freedom, a 'fair go', and independence more than those Anglo-Australians who only weakly identify with their culture.

Photo 8.2
Gondolas, a traditional Venetian rowboat, are symbolic of Venetian identity.
Copyright © Zala Volčič. Used with permission.

Like ethnic identity, cultural identity also has value and salience content. Value content refers to the criteria that people hold to evaluate appropriate or inappropriate behaviours. For example, in collectivistic cultures such as China, it is considered polite for a smoker to offer cigarettes to those he or she is with at the time, but in the United States, it is less common for a smoker to make such an offer. Also, in China a smoker might start smoking in a public place (where smoking is permitted) without asking for permission from friends he or she is with but who are not smoking at the time; in Australia, such behaviour would be considered inappropriate. Behaviour that is perfectly acceptable in one culture could therefore be considered as selfish and impolite in another.

Cultural identity salience refers to the strength of identification with a larger cultural group. A strong sense of affiliation indicates high cultural identity salience, whereas a weak sense of affiliation reflects low cultural identity salience. Cultural identity salience can be reflected consciously or unconsciously. The more our self-concept is influenced by our larger cultural values, the more likely we are to practise them in communication. Although cultural identity is often defined by one's nation, it is important to note that it is still different from national identity. Cultural identity refers to the sense of belonging to one's larger culture, whereas national identity refers to one's status in a specific nation (Ting-Toomey, 2005a).

National identity

National identity refers to a type of identity that is characterized by one's individual perception of him- or herself as a member of a nation. Smith (2007b: 19) contends that national identity is a politically organized category that is being reproduced and reinvented through different 'symbols, values, memories, myths and traditions that compose the distinctive heritage of a nation, and the identification of individuals with the cultural elements of that heritage'. A national flag hanging outside a government building in every country represents a symbol of national identity because the national flag symbolizes the distinctive character of a nation. Every nation also has a national anthem as a symbol of national identity.

National identity has two main characteristics. First, it is based on a set of common characteristics that hold members of the nation together. These characteristics include a common descent, a shared culture and language, a common historical heritage, and a common legal and economic system (Smith, 1995). National identity creates feelings of national belonging – where you belong is where you feel safe, where you are being recognized and being understood, where you are 'among your own people' – they understand you, as you understand them; and this understanding creates a sense of national identity.

Second, national identity always implies difference – it involves not only an awareness of the ingroup (people from the same nation) but also an awareness of others from whom the nation seeks to differentiate itself. Like other identities, national identity suggests similarity, unity, and difference; it is salient in relation to other nations (Hobsbawm, 1983). In order to distance ourselves from other nations, we create distinctive national markers. France promotes itself as culturally and historically based; the United States prides itself in being free from historical ties.

National identity embraces both political and cultural aspects. The *political* relates to the presence of common political institutions, rights, and duties, while the *cultural* refers to people's sense of belonging to a common cultural heritage (Hutchinson, 1987). A nation's history and myths of origin serve to reinforce the sense of national identity. For example, the Jewish myth is based on the notion of the 'Chosen People' and the story in *Exodus*; the Italians see themselves uniquely descending from the Romans and relate their identity to the history of Roman Catholicism; the Greek identity is founded on the belief that they are the direct descendants of Ancient Greeks; Indians see their roots in the stories of the *Mahābhārata* and *Rāmāyana*; in Japan the myth of origin

Photo 8.3
In front of the Macedonian State Parliament in Skopje stand different statues from an ancient period, representing Macedonian national identity and its ancient roots.
Copyright © Zala Volčič. Used with permission.

starts with the legend of Emperor Jimmu (Seton-Watson, 1977). The historical accuracy of all these myths can easily be challenged. Nevertheless, the power of such myths helps to create a sense of national identity.

Identities and Intercultural Communication

In his famous work 'Negotiating Caribbean identities', Stuart Hall (2001: 123) claimed that 'Identity is a narrative, the stories that cultures tell themselves about who they are and where they came from.' Identities are both externally and internally defined – we are created by ourselves and by others at the same time. Our perception of ourself and others influences how we communicate with those others.

The role of identities in intercultural relations

Our appearance, values, dress, and language all reveal who we are and subsequently influence our relationships with others. For example, theorists of intercultural communication have studied the dominant Western racial category of 'whiteness' in many different ways. They have analysed structural advantage, which is linked to (white) privilege but is not equivalent to it. They have also examined cultural activities that mark white identity. To understand the factors underlying racial identity means to explore new ways of understanding racial identifications as complex social meanings, rather than as objective biological categories. This means that although the existence of visible racial traits is relevant to racial identity, the significance of such traits is always embedded in specific socio-historical relations of power. For example, hair has a power to shape personal and collective identities in the lives of African-American women in the United States, as it represents a particular racial subgroup. Banks (2000) conducted interviews with over 50 black girls and women between 1996 and 1998 to explore the political complexities of African-American hair and beauty culture. Banks argued that hair shaped black women's identities and their feelings about race, gender, class, sexuality, and images of beauty. Since mainstream Western images of beauty do not include tight black curls, the decision by many African-American women to straighten their hair and use pressing combs reflects a devaluation of their natural hair.

Identity conflicts may arise in intercultural situations if one is not treated in the way one expects. Argent (2003) writes that feeling or being made to feel different is a major issue for adopted children, particularly those with different cultural backgrounds from their parents or those with a disability. For an adopted child, the stigma of not living with their birth family, as well as living as a cultural minority, may require a long psychological and cultural adjustment. Many children adopted from minority groups have to conform to the demands of the dominant culture, which means an internalization of dominant norms, assimilation into the dominant culture, and an acceptance of its identity. Similarly, communication between those subgroups defined by socioeconomic class may present problems, because the most basic class distinction is between the powerful and the powerless. If people from social classes with greater power attempt to retain their own positions in a culture, intergroup communication is unlikely to be successful.

Developing intercultural identity

Individuals who acquire an intercultural identity are willing to negotiate these differences. They are able to reach intercultural agreements and they want to integrate diverse cultural elements and achieve an identity extension. In particular, they wish to go beyond an 'unexamined identity', which is the stage of acceptance of dominant norms and a lack of willingness to look into one's identity and reconstruct or negotiate it. One of the widely known approaches to developing this intercultural identity is the *Developmental Model of Intercultural Sensitivity* (*DMIS*), created by Milton Bennett (1986, 1993) as a framework to explain people's reactions to cultural difference. Bennett's argument is that one's experience of cultural difference becomes more complex as one's competence in intercultural relations increases. He observed that individuals confront cultural difference in certain predictable ways as they learn to become more competent intercultural communicators. He organized these observations into six stages of sensitivity to cultural differences, moving from *ethnocentric*, which characterizes the first three stages, to *ethnorelative*, which characterizes the last three stages. Table 8.1 summarizes the characteristics of all six stages.

The DMIS has been used in constructing a competent intercultural identity that aims at understanding other cultures holistically. An open-minded intercultural communicator interacts actively with strangers and never excludes other possibilities beyond the established cultural boundary. Effective intercultural communication requires both an openness to culturally different others and a willingness to negotiate differences. Thus, an intercultural person makes an attempt to abandon cultural stereotypes, prejudices, or ethnocentrism, and to engage in a dialogue with others. As cultural differences presuppose a need for coordination, intercultural identity negotiation should be interpreted as a process of informing, learning, and compromising in order to reach an intercultural consensus. Only when a difference is recognized can we start to reach out toward each other.

Summary

This chapter concentrated on the categorization process and formation of various subgroups, together with different types of identities. We argued that people live with multiple identities and that identities change during the course of our lives. Social categorization leads to the formation of ingroups and outgroups and group memberships based on gender, race, ethnicity, culture,

Table 8.1: Stages of sensitivity to cultural differences

Sensitivity	Stages	Characteristics
Ethnocentric	Denial	One's own culture is experienced as the only real one. Other cultures are avoided by maintaining psychological and/or physical distance. Here, people are generally disinterested in other cultures.
	Defence	One's own culture is experienced as the only good one. The world is organized into 'us' and 'them', where we are superior and they are inferior.
	Minimization	Elements of one's own worldview are experienced as universal. People expect similarities and they may insist on correcting others' behaviour to match their expectations.
	Acceptance	One's own culture is experienced as equal to others. Acceptance does not have to mean agreement – cultural difference may be perceived negatively, but the judgment is not ethnocentric. People are curious about and respectful of cultural difference.
	Adaptation	The experience of another culture replaces perception and behaviour appropriate to that culture. One's own worldview is expanded to include worldview constructs from others. People may intentionally change their behaviour to communicate more effectively in another culture.
Ethnorelative	Integration	One's experience of self includes the movement in and out of different cultural worldviews.

Source of references

Bennett, Milton J. (1986) 'A developmental approach to training for intercultural sensitivity', *International Journal of Intercultural Relations*, 10 (2): 179–195.

Bennett, Milton J. (1993) 'Towards ethnorelativism: a developmental model of intercultural sensitivity', in M. Paige (ed.), *Education for the Intercultural Experience*. Yarmouth, ME: Intercultural Press. pp. 343–354.

and nation. On the one hand, categorization helps us to understand the world by giving it structure; on the other hand, it creates and reinforces stereotypes of people, particularly those from outgroups. Identities can be studied at both individual and collective levels. This chapter discussed the development and characteristics of individual identity, collective identity, personal identity, social identity, gender identity, ethnic identity, cultural identity, and national identity. We also provided social, historical, and political contexts in which different types of identities are situated.

Identity develops through several stages. First, there is the stage of an *unexamined identity*, that of an acceptance of dominant norms and a lack of desire to look into one's identity. There is then an *acceptance stage*, where we can see an internalization of an identity. In the third, the *redefinition stage*, a reinterpretation of the dominant culture takes place and there are attempts to openly challenge the dominant cultural privilege. In the final *integration stage*, one connects belonging to a dominant culture with an awareness of its privilege and an appreciation of the values of minority cultures. The *Developmental Model of Intercultural Sensitivity (DMIS)*, created by Milton Bennett, functions as a framework to explain people's reactions to cultural differences. Intercultural identity can be developed through an openness to culturally different others and a willingness to negotiate differences. Today's world, with such a wide scope of changes affecting our lives on an everyday basis, brings to the surface an uncertainty about our very existence and encourages us to live more reflexive lives. More importantly, such a life necessitates processes of identity construction and identity negotiation, as opposed to the more traditional processes of taking on identity. We are constantly seeking answers to identity questions, such as 'Who am I? Where do I belong? How should I relate to others?' in search of a sense of a place in this ever-changing world.

Case Study:
History of South African identity and apartheid in South Africa

The original inhabitants of southern Africa (from the Cape to Zambezi) were the Khoi-San. Black people originally migrated into the region today known as South Africa from the north in two waves – migrants speaking Nguni moved down the east coast and migrants speaking Sotho moved down through the interior and settled in the inland areas. The Dutch East India Company established a settlement at Cape Town in 1652. The Cape Colony at this time was settled by a mixture of Dutch, French, Germans, and Indonesians (who came to be called the Cape Malays) and from this ethnic mix emerged a new language called Afrikaans, meaning 'African'. The Khoi-San were gradually exterminated or displaced from the region by the black and white settlers. The largest surviving group descended from the Khoi was 'coloureds' – those of a mixed Khoi and Indonesian descent. But some Khoi-San groups remained and survived in the desert regions of Botswana, Namibia, and north-western South Africa.

White settlers moving north and eastwards and black settlers moving south and westwards first encountered each other at the Fish River in the 1770s in what is still known today as the border region. Anglo settlers were first brought into this region in 1820, following the British seizure of the Cape Colony some fourteen years earlier. During the 1820s, Zulu King Shaka began a genocidal war, known as the Difaqane, which generated huge population movements across the whole region. Breakaway groups of Zulus, such as the Matabele, Shangaan, and Ngoni, migrated to the Highveld, Mozambique, Zimbabwe, and Malawi, where they attacked, subjugated, and displaced local people. Sotho people fleeing Zulu and Matabele impis (armies) relocated to western Zambia and Lesotho, leaving the Highveld depopulated. Afrikaners, fleeing British rule in the Cape, migrated to and settled in these Highveld areas during the mid-1830s. After inevitable Highveld battles between the Matabele and Afrikaners, the Matabele fled north and settled in western Zimbabwe, where they subjugated the Shona.

The British later established a colony in Natal in 1843, into which they imported Indian indentured labourers to work on their plantations. After defeating the Afrikaners during the Boer War the British created a unified South African state in 1910. This state was set up to administer the new gold-mining-based economy developed by the British, and to police the cheap black labour system the British developed to run it. Living within this state were some 13 ethnic groups – white Anglos; white Afrikaners; Coloureds (mostly speaking Afrikaans); Indians (mostly speaking English); four Nguni-speaking groups, namely Xhosa, Zulu, Swazi, and Ndebele; three Sotho-speaking groups, namely Sotho, Pedi, and Tswana; plus two other black groups speaking Venda and Tsonga.

The construction of an Afrikaner identity became closely enmeshed with a battle to retain an identity separate from that of Anglos. After the Boer War, an enforced Anglicization programme in schools served to greatly stimulate the growth of Afrikaner nationalism. Afrikaner nationalists came to see Anglicization pressures as a real threat to the survival of all that was Afrikaans and thus sought to make Afrikaans a national language (alongside English) and create separate Afrikaans educational institutions.

From 1910 to 1948, Anglo-South Africans dominated South Africa politically and economically in what has been dubbed a system of 'racial capitalism' – a system that revolved around a gold mining industry that was reliant on cheap black labour imported from across Africa (especially the Transkei, Zululand, Malawi, Mozambique, Botswana, and Lesotho). Racial capitalism created a society based upon the economic integration of different ethnic groups into one unified state, but which simultaneously deployed racial segregation to keep these ethnic groups separate when they were not engaged in labour. Thus, the Anglo-dominated South African state systematized and institutionalized a culture built around white supremacy.

When the Afrikaner-dominated National Party (NP) came to power in 1948, their first actions were to 1) enforce English–Afrikaans bilingualism in the civil service; 2) create separate Afrikaans schools, colleges, and universities (i.e. remove Afrikaners from English-language institutions); and 3) make the teaching of Afrikaans compulsory in English schools. Once the NP had achieved this, they turned their attention to language use by black people. Afrikaner nationalists were unhappy about black people being Anglicized by an education system run by English missionaries. The NP opted to apply the same policy to black people as that being applied to Afrikaners – namely a 'mother language' education for all ethnic groups – as a vehicle to resist Anglicization pressures. Hence they closed the mission schools and created the Bantu education system. The state subsidized the codification of Afrikaans plus South Africa's nine black languages. The NP also created separate media systems in English and Afrikaans and in the nine black languages.

Afrikaner nationalists captured the South African state by winning the 1948 elections. The subsequent system of apartheid was motivated by two fears: 1) Anglicization, or being absorbed into white English-speaking South Africa; and 2) being demographically swamped by black migrants. Afrikaner nationalists opposed an Anglo-ruled South Africa, as they believed Anglo cultural imperialism would destroy their language and culture, and because they also believed this state was assisting Anglo businessmen in importing cheap black labour. The National Party promised to end these perceived (British) threats to Afrikaner interests by implementing its apartheid policy. This involved trying to actively encourage the growth of Zulu nationalism, Xhosa nationalism, and Tswana nationalism in each of these new states. These separate nationalisms were intended to undermine black nationalism. At its heart, apartheid was a migration policy geared to stopping black migration and then reversing the flow by sending black people back to where they had come from. This was a real threat to Anglo businessmen and flew in the face of laissez-faire capitalism. As a result Anglo liberals mounted their opposition to apartheid which continued and increased until it was abandoned and majority rule was adopted in the 1990s.

Reference for case study

Personal communication with Eric Louw in the School of Journalism and Communication at the University of Queensland, Australia. Used with permission.

Questions for discussion

1 Who were the original inhabitants of southern Africa?
2 Why was the Afrikaner identity created and what roles did it play in that particular historical context?
3 What does 'racial capitalism' refer to?
4 What does this case tell us about the role language plays in creating and maintaining ethnic identity?
5 What did Afrikaner nationalists struggle for and why?

Key Terms

categorization;
collective identity;
cultural identity;
ethnic identity;
gender constancy;
gender identity;

identity;
individual identity;
ingroup;
national identity;
outgroup;
personal identity;

social identity;
social identity theory;
subgroups;
third gender

Further Reading

Collective and personal identities

Banks, Stephen P.; Louie, Esther and Einerson, Martha (2000) 'Constructing personal identities in holiday letters', *Journal of Social and Personal Relationships*, 17 (2): 299–327.

Erickson, Erik H. (1980) *Identity and the Life Cycle*. New York: Norton.

Peri, Yoram (1997) 'The Rabin myth and the press: reconstruction of the Israeli collective identity', *European Journal of Communication*, 12 (4): 435–458.

Ethnic identity

Qin, Desiree B. (2009) 'Being "good" or being "popular": gender and ethnic identity negotiations of Chinese immigrant adolescents', *Journal of Adolescent Research*, 24 (1): 37–66.

Phinney, Jean S.; Jacoby, Brian and Silva, Charissa (2007) 'Positive intergroup attitudes: the role of ethnic identity', *International Journal of Behavioral Development*, 31 (5): 478–490.

Gender identity

Mills, Jean (2006) 'Talking about silence: gender and the construction of multilingual identities', *International Journal of Bilingualism*, 10 (1): 1–16.

Stapleton, Karyn and Wilson, John (2004) 'Gender, nationality and identity: a discursive study', *European Journal of Women's Studies*, 11 (1): 45– 60.

National identity

Radcliffe, Sarah A. (1996) 'Imaginative geographies, postcolonialism, and national identities: contemporary discourses of the nation in Ecuador', *Cultural Geographies*, 3 (1): 23–42.

Salazar, Luis Suárez (2009) 'The Cuban Revolution and the new Latin American leadership: a view from its Utopias', *Latin American Perspectives*, 36 (1): 114–127.

White, Richard (2001) 'Cooees across the Strand: Australian travellers in London and the performance of national identity', *Australian Historical Studies*, 32 (116): 109–127.

Intercultural communication and intercultural relations

Barna, LaRay M. (1994) 'Stumbling blocks in intercultural communication', in M.J. Bennett (ed.), *Basic Concepts of Intercultural Communication: Selected Readings*. Yarmouth, MA: Intercultural Press. pp. 173–190.

Moloney, Robyn (2009) 'Forty per cent French: intercultural competence and identity in an Australian language classroom', *Intercultural Education*, 20 (1): 71–81.

9

Developing Relations with Culturally Different Others

It takes a lot of experience of life to see why some relationships last and others do not. But we do not have to wait for a crisis to get an idea of the future of a particular relationship. Our behaviour in little every incident tells us a great deal.

Eknath Easwaran, Indian scholar and author, 1901–1999

Learning Objectives

At the end of this chapter, you should be able to:

- Define the nature and characteristics of human relationships.
- Describe the stages of relationship development.
- Compare and contrast theories on intergroup and intercultural relationships.
- Explain the influence of culture on human relationship development.

The Nature of Human Relationships

Initiating and maintaining personal and social relationships with others is an essential part of human life. We are connected to others in a variety of ways – through social groups, ethnic communities, friendships, family, organizations, online social networks – and we define ourselves and evaluate others through these relationships. William Schutz (1966) claimed that we satisfy three basic needs through our interaction with others: inclusion, affection, and control. *Inclusion* is a sense of belonging or of being involved with others, as well as of including others in our activities. We are members of different groups, categorized by factors such as gender, culture, religion, ethnicity, race, nation, or political affiliation. Maintaining relationships with others in different groups gives us a sense of personal identity, because it is in groups that our individuality is recognized (Mader and Mader, 1990).

Control refers to our ability to influence others, our environment, and ourselves along with our desire to be influenced by others (or not). We can gain control by initiating ideas, supporting others, showing disagreement, resolving conflicts, or giving orders, and we can ask for this control from others through questions and supportive statements. The various roles we play can also satisfy our need for control (Chen and Starosta, 2005). For example, the father in an Indian family often has the power to make decisions regarding the career paths his children are to follow.

Affection refers to showing love to and being loved by others. We all need – to a greater or lesser extent – to share emotions with other people (friends, colleagues, family members). Affection fosters passion, commitment, care, and intimate relationships. In sum, we engage in initiating, maintaining, or terminating relationships with others throughout our lives and we mutually satisfy our social needs through these relationships.

The way we perceive and fulfil social needs is influenced by culture. People from different cultures may meet each other's needs for inclusion, control, and affection differently. For example, in some cultures a man will open the door for a woman to show masculinity and courtesy; in other cultures a woman is expected to walk a few steps behind a man in deference to his masculinity. The influence of culture on developing and fostering relationships with others is the focus of this chapter. We define the nature and characteristics of human relationships and describe the stages of relationship development. Several theories of human relationships, including social exchange theory, the similarity attraction paradigm, and anxiety/uncertainty management theory, are introduced, followed by discussions on the influence of culture in human relationships, drawing on views from different cultures regarding friendship, family, and romantic relations. Finally, this chapter identifies some ways for improving intercultural relationships.

Dimensions of Human Relationships

A *human relationship* can be defined as an interactional process of connecting ourselves with others in the network of social needs (Chen and Starosta, 2005). Some connections occur because of kinship, family, or marriage; other connections exist owing to group membership, such as gender and ethnicity. Still others are made because of shared interests or goals, such as relationships between colleagues, friends, or people in an online social network community. Relationships can be organized along several dimensions.

Dimensions of social relationships

Triandis (1977) suggests four universal dimensions of social relationships: *association–dissociation*, *superordination–subordination*, *intimacy–formality*, and *overt–covert*, as summarized in Table 9.1.

Triandis (1984) argues that, although these four dimensions are universal, the degree to which they are manifested varies across cultures. For example, Chinese families generally are more associative, subordinate, formal, and

Table 9.1: Four dimensions of social relationship

Dimension	Behaviours
Association–dissociation	*Association behaviours* include helping friends, cooperating with colleagues, and supporting others' ideas or actions, whereas *dissociation behaviours* are illustrated in verbal or nonverbal behaviours such as fighting or avoiding the other person.
Superordination–subordination	Examples of *superordinate behaviours* are a supervisor giving orders to workers, while *subordinate behaviours*, in contrast, involve employees obeying orders from above.
Intimacy–formality	*Intimate behaviours* can be seen in a person's self-disclosure, such as revealing personal attitudes and feelings, touching, and expressing emotions. *Formality behaviours* include sending written invitations or other formal communication behaviour.
Overt–covert	*Overt behaviours* are visible to others, like touching, whereas *covert behaviours* are not visible (e.g. evaluating the behaviours of others).

Source: Triandis, Harry C. (1977) *Interpersonal Behavior*. Monterey, CA: Brooks/Cole.

covert than US American families. Triandis also related these four relationship dimensions to cultural dimensions identified by Hofstede (1980) and to Kluckhohn and Strodtbeck's (1961) value orientations (see Chapter 5). For example, associative behaviours are more important in cultures that consider human beings as inherently good, while dissociative behaviours are more important in cultures where human beings are viewed as inherently evil. Superordination–subordination behaviours can be linked to Hofstede's power distance dimension. In high-power distance cultures, subordination and superordination are viewed as natural and acceptable. However, in low-power distance cultures, where equality between people is treasured, superordination and subordination are seen as functions of the differentiated social roles of individuals. In general, individuals in subordinate cultures are deferential to those in power. This is expressed, for example, in the bowing customs observed in Asian nations such as Japan and Thailand; one bows deeply to a superior, who may merely nod in return. By contrast, the Western custom of handshaking only connotes a greeting and signifies equality on the part of those engaged in the handshake.

The intimacy–formality dimension refers to the degree of contact that people in a given culture desire. Edward Hall (1966) called cultures that display a high degree of affiliation 'high-contact' cultures and those that display a low degree of affiliation 'low-contact cultures' (see Chapter 7). In high-contact cultures, people stand closer and use more touching when interacting than in low-contact cultures, where people may feel more comfortable standing farther apart during a conversation.

The overt–covert dimension, as Triandis suggests, relates to the level of tightness or looseness in a culture. Cultures toward the tight end of the continuum are characterized by more role-bonded relationships such as the social hierarchy observed in India. Tight cultures tend to be more collectivistic and high context. On the other hand, cultures at the loose end of the continuum are characterized by fewer role-bonded relationships. Loose cultures tend to be more individualistic and low context. Triandis argues that more overt behaviour is seen in loose cultures and more covert behaviour in tight cultures. One explanation is that contextual cues play a greater role in communication between tightly bonded people than between loosely bonded people.

Dimensions of interpersonal relationships

Lustig and Koester (2010) identified three dimensions of interpersonal relationships: control, affiliation, and activation. *Control* (like Schutz's view of 'control need') involves power: the level of control we have over others, ourselves, and the environment is dependent on the amount of power we have to influence the people and events around us. For example, we have more control over our financial status if we have a good source of income and knowledge of financial planning. In a different form of power, when guests are present in a home, a mother may use eye contact to control her children's behaviour. We also give control to others by the way we address them. For example, we tend to address doctors by their title and last name, whereas we might call our local butcher by his first name.

Similar to Schutz's (1966) needs for inclusion and affection, Lustig and Koester (2010) define *affiliation* as the degree of friendliness, liking, social warmth, or immediacy that is communicated between people. Affiliation between speakers engaged in a conversation can be expressed through eye contact, close physical proximity, touching, smiling, and a friendly tone of voice. People from high-contact cultures, such as those of the Mediterranean region and Latin America, tend to show affection more openly by touching more frequently, standing closer to each other during a conversation, and using more emotional expressions.

Activation in this model refers to the ways people react to the world around them. Some people seem very energetic, excitable, and quick; others value and exude calmness, peacefulness, and a sense of inner control (Lustig and Koester, 2010). What constitutes an acceptable or appropriate level of activation in communication also varies from culture to culture. For example, Germans value order and control. They like to compare themselves to a symphony orchestra because of its emphasis on rules, regularity, and punctuality. Italians use opera as a cultural metaphor to define themselves, because of its emphasis on emotion, drama, and the lyrical use of language. Italians tend to engage in more animated conversations by using expressive hand gestures and vivid facial expressions. By comparison, Chinese people tend to be more reserved. Some Westerners comment that they do not know what the Chinese are thinking in a conversation because they do not reveal their feelings through facial expressions and tend to use neutral words. This is also true for other Asian cultures like those of Malaysia or Thailand. Asian people are taught to avoid extremes in communication; being neutral is considered a virtue. How a particular trait is perceived or displayed in a specific culture, therefore, must be interpreted against the beliefs, values, norms, and social practices of that culture.

Characteristics of human relationships

Human relationships comprise individuals' connection to others. The first characteristic of a human relationship is *interdependence*. For example, a friend may depend on you for acceptance and guidance and you may need support and respect from that friend. We learn about ourselves and others through interpersonal relationships (Pearson and Nelson, 1997). Sometimes our self-concept is strengthened by the confirmation we receive from others, but at other times our self-perception is at variance with others' perception of us. Similarly, interpersonal relationships can assist us in understanding others. Interpersonal relationships allow us to test our stereotypes about others, particularly people from outgroups whose cultural or social norms we are not familiar with.

In another model, Chen and Starosta (2005) identified five characteristics of human relationships. First, human relationships are *dynamic*. They are in a state of development and transformation through communication. Second, human relationships are *hierarchical*. Based on the level of intimacy or closeness, human relationships can be arranged in a hierarchical order ranging from strangers to intimate friends. The required degree of inclusion, control, and affection vary depending on the hierarchical order of the relationship. Third, human relationships are *reciprocal*. Reciprocity occurs when individuals in a relationship network can satisfy each other's social needs. Fourth, human relationships are *unique*; they are rule-governed with different rules for different types. Fifth, human relationships are *interdependent* and *irreplaceable*. Individuals in a human relationship network connect to each other and share emotions with each other. Moreover, human relationships are irreplaceable in that one person's place in the relationship network (e.g. loss of one friend) is not replaceable by another person (e.g. another friend).

People in relationship networks, particularly interpersonal relationships, continually try to maintain balance amid changing circumstances and seemingly opposing needs (Lustig and Koester, 2010). Leslie Baxter (1988) referred to the basic contradictions in human relationships as *dialectics*. She identified three dialectics as important sources of tension in interpersonal relationships; in turn, these have implications for intercultural relations (see Table 9.2).

Theory Corner

Social exchange theory

Social exchange theory aims to explain the development of interpersonal and intercultural relationships. Developed by John Thibaut and Harold Kelley, the basic assumption of this theory is that individuals establish and continue social relations on the basis of their expectations that such relations will be mutually beneficial (Kelley and Thibaut, 1978). When we enter a relationship, we usually evaluate the rewards we are likely to gain and the costs we are willing to pay. If the calculated rewards are greater than the costs, we will continue to develop the relationship. If not, we may leave the existing relationship and seek a new one.

The rewards of human relationships can be expressed in the form of satisfaction, happiness, self-esteem, acceptance, and friendship. The costs may involve money, time, unhappiness, dissatisfaction, losing face, and frustration. Our culture provides an implicit theory about what is considered as important in what type of relationships. For example, studies in East Asia have reported that social forces such as power and status are important in the development of business relations.

Reference

Kelley, Harold H. and Thibaut, John W. (1978) *Interpersonal Relations: A Theory of Interdependence*. New York: Wiley.

Further reading on social exchange theory

Muthusamy, Senthil K. and White, Margaret A. (2005) 'Learning and knowledge transfer in strategic alliances: a social exchange view', *Organization Studies*, 26 (2): 415–441.

Table 9.2: Dialectics in interpersonal relationships

Dialectics	Definition	Cultural implication
Autonomy-Connection	The extent to which individuals want a sense of separation from others (autonomy) or a feeling of attachment to others (connection).	Culture teaches its members the appropriate range of autonomy and connection when communicating with others (e.g. individualistic versus collectivistic cultures).
Novelty-Predictability	The dynamic tensions between people's desire for change (novelty) and stability (predictability) in their interpersonal relationships.	The level of uncertainty avoidance in culture suggests the range of desired novelty and predictability.
Openness-Closeness	The extent to which individuals want to share (openness) or withhold (closeness) personal information.	Collectivistic cultures encourage openness to ingroup members but closeness to outgroup members.

Source: Baxter, Leslie (1988) 'A dialectical perspective on communication strategies in relationship development', in S.W. Duck (ed.), *Handbook of Personal Relationships: Theory, Research, and Interventions*. New York: Wiley. pp. 257-273.

Stages of Human Relationship Development

Berger and Calabrese (1975) argued that relationships develop in three phases. In the *entry* phase, communication is governed by a set of social norms. The communication patterns in this stage are structured and the content focuses mostly on demographic information. Our interactions with strangers or those people we meet for the first time are examples of this entry phase. The second phase is *personal*. Communication content in the personal phase goes beyond the superficial (e.g. the weather or sharing demographic information) and may include information on personal problems, attitudes, and opinions. The relationship between interactants becomes more intimate and the communication styles they use are often more informal and relaxed. The third stage of relationship development is the *exit* phase. In this phase, the relationship begins to deteriorate and the frequency of interaction decreases. Interactants are no longer interested in maintaining the relationship and tend to avoid communicating.

Irwin Altman and Dalmas Taylor (1973) proposed their social penetration theory to explain the development of relationships through the exchange of information. This theory states that, as an interpersonal relationship develops, the interpersonal exchange of information moves from the superficial and impersonal to intimate and personal. The depth of information exchange reflects one of four stages of relationship development: orientation, exploratory affective exchange, affective exchange, and stable exchange. The *orientation* stage is characterized by a superficial information exchange about, say, the weather or demographic information. The *exploratory affective* stage involves an exchange of information on the periphery of our personality, such as who we are and how we evaluate ourselves (e.g. intelligent or hardworking). In the *affective exchange* stage, people feel more comfortable exchanging opinions and attitudes, such as 'I think Jenny is too bossy and arrogant'. At the *stable* exchange stage, an intimate relationship is developed and people can freely express their true feelings. The frequency and amount of interaction also increase as the relationship develops. A key concept in social penetration theory is *self-disclosure*, which refers to the process of revealing personal information that another person would be unlikely to discover through third sources.

Although self-disclosure is used in almost all cultures as a means of developing relationships, cultural norms and values govern the degree to which it is acceptable in interpersonal relationships. For example, US Americans generally feel comfortable sharing family problems or tensions with colleagues. In Chinese culture, self-disclosure about family problems is only expected to take place between close friends or relatives. As Xi described (1994: 155), 'For Americans, self-disclosure is a strategy to make various types of relationships work; for Chinese, it is a gift shared only with the most intimate relatives and friends.' On the other hand, cultural norms govern what content is considered private and what is public (or appropriate for self-disclosure). For example, in

China it is common to ask and to disclose information of one's income and age, even when meeting for the first time; in England, however, people are hesitant to reveal such private information – in this case, norms about self-disclosure are reversed.

Culture and Human Relationship Development

Cultural beliefs, values, and norms regulate relationship development. In this section, we introduce Yum's (1988) relationship model and discuss relationship practices across cultures.

Yum's model of human relationships

The five types of relationships identified by Yum (1988) have been widely applied in intercultural communication research. They are: particularistic versus universalistic, long-term versus short-term, ingroup versus outgroup, formal versus informal, and personal versus public relationships.

Particularistic versus universalistic relationships

The subject of particularistic relationships was raised by John Condon, an intercultural communication scholar, in the 1970s. Condon (1977) noted that in a culture where *particularistic relationships* are desired, people maximize differences in age, sex, and status and encourage a mutuality and interdependency between cultural members. Particularistic societies tend to be more hierarchically structured, and human relationships are established in accordance with the levels of hierarchy accepted by the society. Communication is governed by specific cultural rules concerning who people talk to, what to talk about, and when and how to talk about it in specific social contexts. Yum (1988) found that particularistic relationships are practised more in East Asian countries. For example, in Singapore people tend to develop friendships with others of a similar social status. Similarly, because marriage in collectivistic cultures like China implies an alliance of two families, couples usually come from a similar social class. The Chinese metaphor 'Bamboo door matches bamboo door and wooden door matches wooden door' illustrates this, implying that the matching couple need to come from 'matching doors' (status and family background).

   In contrast, in cultures where *universalistic relationships* are desired, people establish interpersonal relationships based on rules of fairness and equality. Yum (1988) found that universalistic relationships are practised by North Americans. To them, the development of an interpersonal relationship relies on the principle of equality not hierarchy. The rules governing ways of addressing people, for example, illustrate the level of hierarchy in a society. Employees in Australia may address their bosses using first names, whereas such a practice is not common in Malaysia.

Long-term versus short-term relationships

Long-term relationships are preferred in East Asian cultures, where a social reciprocity is viewed as centrally important. People in these cultures always feel indebted to others (Chen and Starosta, 2005). For example, the Chinese always try to return a favour from friends with much more than they received, as expressed in the Chinese adage, 'One should return a drop of kindness received with a fountain of kindness.' This practice is intended to maintain the existing relationship over a long period of time or permanently. When friends go out for a meal, often one person pays the bill for the whole group – the shared understanding is that, as friendship is considered long-lasting, there will be many opportunities in the future for each person to reciprocate in a like manner. The same friendship practices are characteristic of Slavic cultures; friends pay for everyone in a friendship circle and each person paying only for him- or herself seems rude.

Yum (1988) found that short-term and symmetrical reciprocity is more characteristic of North Americans' interpersonal relationships. Commitment to a long-term interpersonal relationship is rarer and not considered so important. In cultures where short-term relationships are commonly practised, people consider freedom and independence as important, and the flexibility to initiate or terminate relationships as an individual choice is treasured. Hence, it is a common practice for North Americans to split the bill when having a meal with friends. The value placed on long- versus short-term relationships is also reflected in communication styles. For example, US Americans are usually very direct when they need to say 'no' to friends. However, the Japanese tend to say 'maybe' or 'that would be somehow hard' instead of a direct 'no'.

Ingroup versus outgroup relationships

The boundary between ingroups and outgroups is much more clearly drawn in East Asian cultures (see Chapter 8). To East Asians, ingroup membership ties suggest similarity, trust, and affinity, ultimately leading to the development of close interpersonal relationships. On the other hand, the boundary between ingroup and outgroup members is less clearly defined for North Americans, British people, and other Western Europeans who establish relationships to fit specific contexts. They feel comfortable being affiliated with a relatively large number of groups, even though relationships based on these affiliations are often brief (Condon and Yousef, 1975).

Formal versus informal relationships

The practice of formal and informal relationships in a society depends on the hierarchical structure of the society. In vertical cultures like those of East Asia, relationship development is more formal than in horizontal cultures like North America. East Asians are more comfortable with initiating a relationship using a third party as a go-between. This can also avoid embarrassment or a loss of face if the other party does not want to enter into a relationship. Germans are also formal when introducing and meeting others and reserve informality for their close friends and family.

The form of address used in social interactions reveals the desired formality. For example, Chinese, Japanese, Slavic, and Arabic language systems contain many pronouns used to indicate the degree of formality and relationship intimacy between interactants (Condon and Yousef, 1975), whereas English is less specific in this area. Directly initiating a relationship characterizes horizontal cultures, where interactions are usually less formal. For example, it is common for Australians at social functions to approach strangers and introduce themselves by saying, 'I'm … ', unlike in Hong Kong, where more commonly a go-between would say, 'Let me introduce my friend to you … '.

Photo 9.1
Chinese and Australians at a gathering. Initiating relationships with others tends to be more formal in Chinese culture.
Copyright © The Chinese Consulate in Brisbane. Used with permission.

Personal versus public relationships

Yum noted that an overlap between personal and public relationships characterizes East Asian cultures. For example, a Chinese business person about to embark on negotiations would start the conversation with small talk, asking questions about the other person's family. Gift-giving is also a common practice in Chinese business culture – it is not a sign of bribery as some Westerners view it, but an attempt to build trust and a good relationship so that smooth and cooperative transactions in the future can be expected. Because of the blurred boundary between personal and public relationships in Asian cultures, people tend not to separate the issue from the person. Thus, if someone criticizes a suggestion made by a manager, the manager may view the criticism as a personal attack. At meetings, therefore, people in Asian organizations are cautious about bringing up negative comments about managers or leaders.

In contrast, an emphasis on privacy, individualism, autonomy, and self-reliance encourages North Americans to keep their public and personal relationships separate. Colleagues are less important as a source of friends for Americans than for Asians. Westerners may argue with or criticize each other at a meeting, but laugh and chat over drinks after that meeting; they can separate the issue from the person. A frequent complaint by Chinese business people about their Western counterparts is that, in business negotiations, Westerners are more 'money-minded' than 'people-oriented'. The reason for this is cultural; Westerners tend to be issue-focused and to start business negotiations by going immediately to the business at hand, without showing an interest or concern in their Chinese counterpart's personal life. Moreover, gift-giving is not a tradition among Western business people. Together, these behaviours may make Chinese business partners feel that they are not respected or have not been 'given face'.

Friendship, romantic relationships, and family

Friendship is one of the most important interpersonal relationships people develop with others, and it usually involves high levels of intimacy, self-disclosure, and involvement. We choose our friends based on shared interests, goals, and liking. Because friendship is voluntary, it usually occurs between people who are similar in important ways.

Theory Corner

Similarity attraction paradigm

The similarity attraction paradigm was proposed by Byrne (1971). The basic premise of this paradigm is that, if we perceive that our attitudes are similar to some people, we are attracted to them because the similarity in attitudes validates our view of the world. However, actual similarities in attitudes and self-concept may not be related to our attraction to them; rather, we are attracted to others based on a *perceived* similarity. Think about the similarities you have with your ethnic group that make you want to form relationships with them and also how a lack of perceived similarity with members of other ethnic groups influences your communication with them. In the initial stages of getting to know strangers, we tend to focus on general attitudes and opinions. As we get to know them, we search for similarities in central concepts such as worldviews or core values. The similarity attraction paradigm and social identity theory have been applied by intercultural scholars like William B. Gudykunst and Young Y. Kim to study identities and intergroup relations.

Reference

Byrne, Donn (1971) *The Attraction Paradigm*. New York: Academic.

Further reading on interpersonal relationship development

Ferrin, Donald; Bligh, Michelle and Kohles, Jeffrey (2007) 'Can I trust you to trust me? A theory of trust, monitoring, and cooperation in interpersonal and intergroup relationships', *Group & Organization Management*, 32 (4): 465–499.

Although friendship is universal across cultures, our interpretation of the term varies from culture to culture. Thais are likely to view a person as a whole and a friend is accepted either completely or not at all. The Chinese have a more conservative definition of friends than Westerners do. Chinese expect friends to be involved in all aspects of each other's lives, to anticipate each other's needs, and to provide advice on various matters when needed. Family members of friends tend to know each other as well. Condon (1985) noted that the language people use to describe their friends can reflect underlying cultural values about the meaning and importance attached to a friendship. For example, among Chinese and Mexicans, a friend is referred to as a brother or a sister, suggesting collectivistic cultural values and a lasting bond. In Australia, friends are referred to as 'mates' but not as brothers and sisters.

Romantic relationships are another important interpersonal relationship that is influenced by culture. There are enormous differences in cultural beliefs, values, norms, and social practices about love, romance, dating, and marriage. Casual dating for romance among Americans is not viewed as a serious commitment that will necessarily lead to marriage (Lustig and Koester, 2010). If lovers choose to get married it is because of their love for each other, not because of any external cultural commitment or obligation. Although family members may be consulted before a final decision is made, the choice to marry is primarily made by the couple themselves. In India, casual dating relationships for romantic expression among unmarried individuals are still not common. A marriage is usually arranged by the parents with the consent of the couple (see the case study below). For example, an Indian speech pathologist who works in Sydney asked his mother in India to find him a wife. His mother compiled a list of 14 women who she believed would be suitable, and the son went back to India for three days and picked one from the list. After consent had been obtained from the girl's parents, a wedding ceremony was held in India. At that point, the couple knew very little about each other; it was not until nine months after the marriage when the wife joined her husband in Sydney that the couple began to get to know each other and develop affection. Similar patterns of familial arrangement can also be found in Muslim cultures, in which marriages are seen as alliances between families. In both Indian and Muslim cultures, romantic love is believed to be something that develops after marriage and not before. In China, a marriage is seen as an important link between families and not just between the couple concerned. Consequently, the selection of a spouse usually requires the approval of an entire extended family.

Family relationships are also characterized by cultural variations. Among members of European cultures, family life is primarily confined to interactions between parents and children. Members of an extended family rarely live together in the same household or take an active part in the daily lives of the nuclear family members. In China, the family is the primary means through which a person's social life is extended. For example, Chinese children's first friendships are usually with the children of their parents' colleagues or friends. In Australian culture, families are often peripheral to the social networks that people establish. Moreover, the roles of family members are more clearly defined in Asian cultures. Gender roles, for example, are well defined in South Asian cultures; men make the major decisions, provide for the family, and are the head of a family. Women are expected to take care of the family and perform household duties, although nowadays more and more women are joining the workforce and working side by side with male colleagues. Owing to the changes in traditions and the effects of globalization, arranged marriage is not as common now, but there is still significant pressure on couples not to divorce, as to do so reflects badly upon the whole family. Similarly, in India, conflict between married couples is an issue for members of the extended family. In a traditional method of mediation, male elders consider the conflict between the couple, decide who is wrong, and agree on how that party should change in order to fix the problem and maintain the marriage.

The power of decision making in families is influenced by cultural values and constraints. In collectivistic cultures, such as those of Japan, Korea, India, and China, families play a pivotal role in making decisions for children, including the choice of university, profession, and even of marital partner. For example, in the movie *Bend it like Beckham*, the Indian girl's parents felt they should decide which career path their children should follow. Thus, they wanted her (Jess) to go to university to study medicine, even though it was her personal desire to become a professional football player. In individualistic cultures, children are taught early on to be independent, to make their own decisions, and to plot their own career paths. The parents' role is to support their children in achieving their goals. In Chinese families, it is not uncommon to see grown-up children, even after they are married, still living in the parental home. Some parents encourage their married sons to live with them so they may take better care of them. In contrast, children in Western cultures are encouraged to move out of the family home when they become adults.

Developing Intercultural Relationships

Today, it is more likely than ever that we live with culturally different others in our own cities and countries. Hence, developing good intercultural and intergroup relations becomes an important part of our life.

Creating an awareness of cultural norms governing relationships

Relationship development is governed by cultural norms and values. People's knowledge of what constitutes appropriate or acceptable behaviours regarding a certain relationship varies across cultures. Moreover, people's interpretation of the same type of relationship also varies across cultures. For example, friendship is universal to all cultures, but who can be called a friend and what a friend means differ depending on the culture. In Australia, the term 'friend' can be used to refer to neighbours or colleagues or even someone a person has just met. The boundaries between ingroup and outgroup in Australia may not be as hard to cross as they are in some collectivistic cultures. For collectivistic cultures like that of Greece, the line between ingroups and outgroups is much sharper. 'Non-Greek' can mean a stranger to a Greek community. Cultural differences are also reflected in what is considered as private or intimate information. In China, it is perfectly appropriate to ask a married acquaintance about his wife; in the United Arab Emirates, this would be considered a major breach of social etiquette. In New Zealand, it is appropriate to talk about national and international politics; in Korea, similar topics would be avoided. In Hong Kong, a discussion about income and religion among colleagues is acceptable; in the United States, such information is only shared with close friends or family members. Thus, when we develop relationships with culturally different others, we need to take into consideration what constitutes the appropriate information to exchange in order to reduce uncertainty at the initial encounter.

Theory Corner

Anxiety/uncertainty management theory

Anxiety/uncertainty management theory was developed by William B. Gudykunst (2004) based on the uncertainty reduction theory proposed by Berger and Calabrese (1975). The theory argues that effective interpersonal and intercultural communication is a function of how individuals manage the anxiety and uncertainty they experience when communicating with others. Uncertainty refers to individuals' ability to predict and/or explain others' feelings, attitudes, and behaviour. The reduction of uncertainty leads to an increase in both the amount of communication and the level of interpersonal attraction. If the amount of uncertainty present in initial interactions is not reduced, further communication between the people is unlikely to occur.

Anxiety is the affective equivalent of uncertainty. It stems from feeling uneasy, tense, and worried about what might happen, and is based on a fear of potentially negative consequences. Because intercultural communication involves people from dissimilar cultures, there is always the possibility of anxiety and uncertainty. To behave both appropriately and effectively in an intercultural encounter, one must make an accurate assessment of a range of information about people, message, context, and cultural norms, so as to reduce uncertainty/anxiety in order to optimize effective communication outcomes.

(Continued)

References

Berger, Charles R. and Calabrese, Richard J. (1975) 'Some explorations in initial interaction and beyond: toward a developmental theory of interpersonal communication', *Human Communication Theory*, 1: 99–112.

Gudykunst, William B. (2004) *Bridging Differences: Effective Intergroup Communication* (4th edn). Thousand Oaks, CA: SAGE.

Further reading on uncertainty reduction in intercultural communication

Miller, Ann and Samp, Jennifer (2007) 'Planning intercultural interaction: extending anxiety/uncertainty management theory', *Communication Research Reports*, 24 (2): 87–95.

Interpreting behaviours in their cultural context

Given the influence of cultural variability on relationship development and the ever increasing diversity in our society, we need to foster our understanding of culturally different others and appreciate the differences in acceptable or appropriate practices in different cultures. Based on previous scholars' work, Chen and Starosta (2005: 133) emphasized the importance of developing 'cultural synergy' or a third culture, whereby people from different cultures negotiate their cultural differences and build a common ground for communication. Such a process requires interactants to adapt to each other's cultural differences. Communication is the key to developing intercultural relationships. Successful intercultural communication requires us to understand the meanings that different cultures attribute to different types of human relationships and also the cultural rules governing interactions between people involved in different types of relationship.

Recognizing cyberspace as a site of intercultural communication

Communication technologies allow us to initiate relationships with other people via the internet. Cyberspace provides an arena for intercultural communication, where people across the world can connect in social networks. Indeed, the growth of social networking sites, such as Facebook and Myspace, is of great interest to scholars of intercultural communication because of the opportunity they provide to maintain and expand such networks independent of spatial constraints. For example, online dating services allow subscribers from different countries to build profiles of themselves and to contact or be contacted by other users with a view of developing romantic relationships. While forms of internet communication make international phone calls relatively inexpensive, they require a relatively high level of engagement. Online social network sites, by contrast, allow for the maintenance of extended networks at a relatively low intensity of engagement; people can add contacts and keep in touch at their convenience. Rather than having to track down new phone numbers and addresses, such sites allow for constant contact, even if contacts have moved or are travelling. Individuals who travel abroad, for example, can collect online social contacts and easily stay in touch with them when they return home. Internet technology helps to de-territorialize extended social networks by transposing them into cyberspace, where geographic distance is collapsed. Online social networking sites, therefore, are also an important site for intercultural communication insofar as the ability to maintain extended social networks raises the issue of cultural norms and practices.

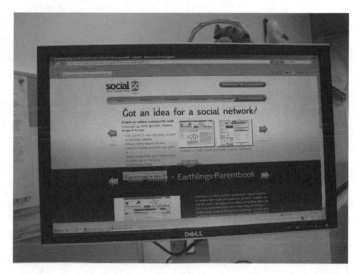

Photo 9.2
Social networking sites have become an important arena for culturally different others to meet and communicate.
Copyright © Shuang Liu. Used with permission.

Although various types of social networking sites serve to increase opportunities for communicating with culturally different others who are perhaps geographically located elsewhere, online social networking also creates the possibility of deception – an issue that has received scholarly research in recent years. In Caspie and Gorsky's (2006) study of chatroom users, for example, over 60 per cent of the respondents reported that deception online was widespread. With the emergence of profile-based social networking sites, including online dating sites, online self-presentation is no longer limited to text-based descriptions; instead, the profile photograph becomes a critical component for relational success (Hancock and Toma, 2009). Hancock and Toma found that female online daters, compared to males, are more likely to use profile photographs as a tool to showcase their physical attractiveness. Online social networking, although not without its problems, facilitates contacts with people that transcend geographic and cultural confines, and thus has become an arena of intercultural communication.

Summary

This chapter defined various types of human relationships and their functions in fulfilling our needs for inclusion, control, and affection. We identified different models of relationship development and discussed how cultures vary in their interpretations of relationships. Developing relationships with culturally different others is a challenge for people living in a multicultural society. People from different cultures may have very different interpretations of various types of relationships and the rules governing appropriate behaviour within these. This chapter introduced social exchange theory, the similarity attraction paradigm, and anxiety/uncertainty management theory – all of which have been widely applied in studying intercultural relations. In addition to a discussion on the influence of culture on various types of interpersonal relationships, including friendships, romantic relationships, and families, this chapter also noted the role of the more recently developed social networking websites in developing intercultural relationships. The chapter concluded with an emphasis on the importance of recognizing differences, a willingness to adapt, and the motivation to build intercultural understanding in developing intercultural relationships.

Case Study:
Love by arrangement in India

India is the world's second most populated country, approaching a total of one billion people. It is a country of extreme diversity, with multiple languages, religions, castes, and classes. Arranged marriages have a long tradition in Indian society. There is no greater event in an Indian family than a wedding and it is not uncommon for middle- or upper-class weddings to have a guest list of over 500 people. Arranging and conducting weddings is a complex process, from the match-making and engagement to the actual wedding (which can last up to five days). Marriage is deemed essential for virtually everyone in India. A Hindu marriage joins two individuals for life, so they can pursue *dharma* (duty), *artha* (possessions), *kama* (physical desires), and *moksa* (spiritual release) together.

For an Indian person, marriage is a great watershed in life, marking the transition to adulthood. Generally, this transition occurs as a result of the efforts of a whole community. Arranging a marriage is a critical responsibility for parents and the extended families of the bride and groom. Marriage alliances entail a redistribution of wealth as well as building and restructuring social relations. Some parents begin marriage arrangements on the birth of a child. In the past, Indians were likely to marry at a young age; in smaller communities such as Rajasthan, children under the age of five could be united in marriage. Legislation which mandates minimum marriage ages has been introduced over the past decades, but such laws have had limited effects on actual marriage practices.

An arranged marriage begins with the parents discussing their expectations with their son/daughter before they embark on the search for a match. The following elements are usually important in a quest for compatibility:

- Values and personal expectations: these should match.
- Age and height: the girl should generally be younger and shorter than the boy.
- Looks: should be acceptable to each partner.
- Religion: this should be the same.
- Mother tongue and caste: preferably the same.
- Diet (vegetarian or not, use of alcohol and cigarettes): this may differ, but only if acceptable to each partner.
- Education: this should be to a similar level.
- Astrological signs and attributes: these should be compatible, if the two families concerned believe in astrology.

India's dominant wedding traditions are difficult to categorize, especially on the basis of religion. Essentially, India is divided into two large regions with regard to Hindu kinship and marriage practices: the north and the south. Additionally, the various ethnic and tribal groups in the central, mountainous north, and eastern regions follow a variety of other practices. Broadly, in the Indo-Aryan-speaking north, a family seeks marriage alliances with people to whom that family is not already linked by blood ties. On the Indo-Gangetic Plain, marriages are contracted outside a village, sometimes even outside a wider collection of villages, but with members of the same caste. Thus, in most parts of north India, a Hindu bride goes to live with strangers in a home she has never visited. In contrast, marriages between cousins (especially cross-cousins; that is, the children of a brother or sister) and even between uncles and nieces (especially a man and his elder sister's daughter) are common in south India. Among Muslims in both the north and the south, marriage between cousins is encouraged.

In many communities throughout India, a *dowry* has traditionally been given by a bride's kin at the time of her marriage. In ancient times, this dowry was considered a woman's wealth – property due to a beloved daughter who had no claim on her natal family's estate – and typically included portable valuables such as jewellery and household goods that a bride could control throughout her life. Over time, the larger portion of a dowry has come to consist of goods and cash payments given directly to the groom's family. Throughout much of India in the late twentieth century, dowry payments escalated, and a groom's parents now sometimes insist on compensation for their son's higher education and even for his future earnings, to which the bride will presumably have access. Some of the dowries demanded

Photo 9.3
In a pre-wedding ceremony of the Indian Christian community,
the bride-to-be is given milk – a symbol of fertility.
Copyright © Pradip Thomas. Used with permission.

today are quite oppressive, amounting to several years' salary in cash as well as items such as motorcycles, air conditioners and expensive cars. Among some lower-status groups, large dowries are currently replacing traditional bride-price payments. The dowry is becoming an increasing burden for the bride's family. Anti-dowry laws do exist but are largely ignored, and a bride's treatment in her marital home is often affected by the value of her dowry.

Pre-wedding ceremonies include both the engagement and the arrival of the groom's party at the bride's residence, often as a formal procession. The specific rituals involved may vary across religious groups. For example, in an Indian Christian community known as the Syrian-Christians, the bride-to-be is given milk – a symbol of fertility. This tradition is probably borrowed from Hinduism. The post-wedding ceremonies involve welcoming the bride to her new home. The wedding rituals themselves vary, based on family traditions.

Reference for case study

A Short Hindu Wedding Ceremony [online]. Accessed 16 July 2009 at http://aprendizdetodo.com/wedding/

Questions for discussion

1 What does a wedding generally signify in Indian culture?
2 How has the concept of a dowry changed over time? What is your view of this practice?
3 Some cultures and religions (e.g. Jewish and Hindu) place a lot of social pressure to marry within the culture, but many individuals nonetheless find love across cultural boundaries. What can you learn from the case study about out-of-culture marriages?
4 What are some of the reasons for choosing not to date interculturally? Are there any reasons (apart from romance itself) for choosing to date interculturally?
5 What beliefs, thoughts, feelings, and attitudes do couples have in common? What differences are there between couples? What conflicts do you think might occur in an intercultural marriage?

Key Terms

affection;
anxiety/uncertainty
   management;
control;
formal versus informal
   relationships;
high-contact cultures;
human relationships;

inclusion;
ingroup versus outgroup
   relationships;
long-term versus short-term
   relationships;
low-contact cultures;
personal versus public
   relationships;

similarity attraction
   paradigm;
social exchange theory;
social penetration theory;
third culture;
universalistic versus
   particularistic relationships

Further Reading

Human relationship development

Ferrin, Donald; Bligh, Michelle and Kohles, Jeffrey (2007) 'Can I trust you to trust me? A theory of trust, monitoring, and cooperation in interpersonal and intergroup relationships', *Group & Organization Management*, 32 (4): 465–499.

Johnson, Amy; Wittenberg, Elaine and Haigh, Michel (2004) 'The process of relationship development and deterioration: turning points in friendships that have terminated', *Communication Quarterly*, 52 (1): 54–67.

Intercultural relationships

Clausen, Lisbeth (2007) 'Corporate communication challenges: a "negotiated" culture perspective', *International Journal of Cross-Cultural Management*, 7 (3): 317–332.

Foeman, Anita K. and Nance, Teresa (2002) 'Building new cultures, reframing old images: success strategies of interracial couples', *Howard Journal of Communication*, 13 (3): 237–249.

Ladegaard, Hans (2007) 'A global corporation', *Journal of Intercultural Communication Research,* 36 (2): 139–163.

Miller, Ann and Samp, Jennifer (2007) 'Planning intercultural interaction: extending anxiety/uncertainty management theory', *Communication Research Reports*, 24 (2): 87–95.

Online relationship and social networking

Chan, Darius and Cheng, Grand (2004) 'A comparison of offline and online friendship qualities at different stages of relationship development', *Journal of Social and Personal Relationships*, 21 (3): 305–320.

Wojcieszak, Magdalena (2009) '"Carrying online participation offline" – mobilization by radical online groups and politically dissimilar offline ties', *Journal of Communication*, 59 (3): 564–586.

Social exchange theory

Muthusamy, Senthil K. and White, Margaret A. (2005) 'Learning and knowledge transfer in strategic alliances: a social exchange view', *Organization Studies*, 26 (2): 415–441.

Third culture

Cockburn, Laura (2002) 'Children and young people living in changing worlds: the process of assessing and understanding the "third culture kid"', *School Psychology International*, 23 (4): 475–485.
Metzger, Gustav (2007) 'The Third Culture', *Theory, Culture & Society*, 24 (1): 137–145.

10

Managing Intercultural Conflicts

If we have no peace, it is because we have forgotten we belong to each other.

Mother Teresa, humanitarian and advocate for the poor and helpless, 1910–1997

Learning Objectives

At the end of this chapter, you should be able to:

- Identify different sources of intercultural conflicts.
- Describe the stages in the conflict process.
- Compare and contrast different conflict styles.
- Recognize the influence of culture on conflict management.
- Develop communication strategies to effectively manage intercultural conflicts.

Pervasiveness of Intercultural Conflicts

The growth in intercultural contact increases the opportunities for understanding, but also the possibilities of misunderstandings between people, groups, communities, organizations, and nations. If misunderstanding or miscommunication goes unmanaged, it can result in conflict. The word 'conflict' has the Latin roots *com* (meaning 'together') and *fligere* (meaning 'to strike'). To 'strike together', the conflict parties have to be linked in an interdependent manner. This chapter adopts Putnam and Poole's (1987: 552) definition which conceptualizes *conflict* as 'the interaction of interdependent people who perceive opposition of goals, aims, and values, and who see the other party as potentially interfering with the realization of these goals'. This definition highlights three elements of conflict: incompatible goals, the interdependence of the parties involved, and communication.

Conflict permeates all social relationships. Just as relationship development occurs at different levels, so too does conflict. At the individual level, conflict occurs between two (or several) persons when they are disagreeing with each other, or competing for something (often scarce resources); such conflict is defined as *interpersonal conflict*. For example, two co-workers competing for the title of 'model worker', available to only one person in the same workshop, with each believing that the other person does not deserve the title, may engage in interpersonal conflict. *Intergroup conflict* occurs when two cultural or social groups perceive disagreements over resources, power, territory, or the like (Gudykunst, 2004). In an organization, conflicts may occur between aggregates of people, for example, between the sales and supplies departments or between management and unions. *Interorganizational conflict* involves disputes between two or more organizations; in this case, the organizations themselves have intergroup disputes. For example, organizations like IBM and Microsoft may engage in interorganizational conflict when they are developing new products or competing for a larger market share. *International conflicts* refer to disputes between nations. In the context of intercultural encounters, *intercultural conflict* involves a perceived or actual incompatibility in goals, interests, resources, values, expectations, processes, or outcomes between two or more people from different cultures (Ting-Toomey, 1994). For example, in a Sino-American joint venture operating in southern China, the Chinese manager prefers an authoritarian leadership style whereas the American manager likes democratic and participatory decision making. Conflict sometimes occurs when the two managers have to cooperate to accomplish a project. As culture influences communication at all levels, intercultural conflict can be interpersonal, intergroup, interorganizational, or international.

Although conflict is pervasive in all societies, our view of conflict and our conflict management styles are culture-bound. Individuals from different cultural groups bring with them diverse and complex value assumptions, expectations, and verbal and nonverbal communication rules and norms that govern the conflict process. Similarly, communities with different cultural patterns and belief systems create their own distinctive norms governing their behaviour. Hence intercultural conflict involves perceptions filtered through our cultural lenses. The pervasiveness of conflicts and the importance of managing them constructively make the study of intercultural conflict of great significance.

This chapter first describes potential sources of intercultural conflict, and identifies different stages in the conflict process. We then discuss the influence of culture on conflict management styles. Conflict styles are made up of communicative behaviours because communication is the means by which conflicts are socially defined and the instrument through which influence is exercised. As culture acts as a guide and predictor of communication behaviour, conflict in intercultural settings must be viewed in terms of culture and communication (Liu and Chen, 1999). Intercultural miscommunication often lies at the heart of intercultural conflict. A lack of cultural awareness and appropriate intercultural responses can result in unrealistic expectations, frustrations, anger, and the failure to establish friendly social relationships (Dodd, 1998). This chapter concludes by suggesting some ways to effectively manage intercultural conflicts.

Potential Sources of Intercultural Conflict

Whether communication is cooperative or competitive depends on what is shared, perceived, and experienced between the communicators – individuals, groups or organizations, and so forth. Cooperative behaviour builds a sense of trust and leads to the sharing of beliefs and attitudes and a desire for both sides to be satisfied in the relationship or interaction (Fisher-Yoshida, 2005). However, when the communication space shrinks or even closes because of perceived or real differences, conflicts may occur. The sources of intercultural conflict are myriad: differences in beliefs and values; incompatible goals; bias and prejudice; ethnic and racial prejudice; historical grievances and hatred; and political, territorial and economic disputes.

Theory Corner

Types of conflicts

Conflicts can be categorized as affective, cognitive, and goal-oriented (Amason, 1996). *Affective conflict* arises from interpersonal tension and is largely emotional in nature. When affective conflict arises, disagreements over personal, individually oriented matters become detrimental to personal and group performance, and emotions seem incompatible. *Cognitive conflict* arises from the perceived disagreements between the two parties about viewpoints, ideas, and opinions. These conflicts are common and usually result from individual incompatibility. Disagreements among individuals are bound to occur, since they bring different ideas, opinions, and perspectives to the table. Cognitive conflict, some argue, is beneficial because it requires individuals to engage. For example, in experiencing cognitive conflict as a result of being part of a team, team members learn from one another's ideas, opinions, and arguments. In *goal conflicts*, people disagree about preferred goals and ends. For example, an externally imposed group goal might be at odds with a key personal goal.

Reference

Amason, Anne C. (1996) 'Distinguishing the effects of functional and dysfunctional conflict on strategic decision-making: resolving a paradox for top management teams', *Academy of Management* Journal, 39: 123–148.

Further reading on conflict styles

Gabrielidis, Cristina; Stephan, Walter; Ybarra, Oscar; Dos Santos Pearson, Virginia M. and Villareal, Lucila (1997) 'Preferred styles of conflict resolution: Mexico and the United States', *Journal of Cross-Cultural Psychology*, 28 (6): 661–677.

Globalization and the rise of racial violence

Many intercultural communication scholars argue that globalization is experienced unevenly around the world (Harvey, 2001). On the one hand, information technology can be used to empower marginalized communities, like those in developing countries, to engage in global knowledge sharing. On the other hand, large populations who do not have the resources to connect to the new types of global systems have been further marginalized by globalization. Thus, while different international networks of production and consumption are expanding, we are still witnessing increasing racial violence and crime against vulnerable groups like migrants, asylum seekers, and refugees in all parts of the world. Indeed, hostilities against ethnic and religious minorities in the world are on the rise everywhere (e.g. conflicts against the Roma people in Europe, Muslims in India, Tutsis in Rwanda, Kurds in Iraq, Bahas in Iran, and so on). According to a report released by the Heidelberg Institute for International Conflict Research (HIICR, 2007), the number of conflicts observed per year rose from 81 in 1945 to approximately 300 in 2006. Most of these conflicts are *low-intensity conflicts*, but do involve the use of military armed forces adopted at least by one party involved in a conflict.

The number of *high-intensity conflicts* involving a series of intense, complex battles between conventional military forces or even the use of nuclear weapons also rose from 7 in 1945 to 41 in 2004. The all-time high was 49 high-intensity conflicts in 1992, shortly after the collapse of the Soviet Union. Today, fewer conflicts are fought through the organized use of large-scale violence, but more and more disputes are waged with the sporadic use of violence, such as ambushes, guerrilla attacks, bombings, and the like (HIICR, 2007). Jitpiromsri's (2006) study of the conflicts in Thailand's deep south and southern border provinces provides an example of violent intercultural conflicts. Jitpiromsri explored the history of these provinces, plagued by political, religious, and cultural conflicts, which were annexed to Thailand in the 1900s. More than 80 per cent of the population in these provinces are Malay Muslims who are now demanding independence. Since the new resurgence of violence in 2004, roughly 3,071 people have been killed and 4,986 injured (Jitpiromsri, 2008). At this time of increasing numbers of violent conflicts on different scales around the globe, we must identify potential sources of intercultural conflict and also understand the potential role of intercultural communication in comprehending and transforming them.

Ingroup/outgroup bias and prejudice

Ingroup and outgroup bias has been one of the major sources of intercultural conflict in all societies throughout history. As earlier chapters explained, all of us categorize people into ingroups and outgroups and develop perceptions of us and *them* in our identifications. Origin and ancestry myths reinforce the sense of unity among ingroup members by suggesting that they share a common history and a way of being that capture the uniqueness of their group or nation. Every nation has a narrative that explains its origin and distinctiveness and, in one way or another, justifies that nation's contemporary state. Many of these myths and stories, although inspiring and largely accepted by the people and supported by the state, are challenged by other groups in society. Indeed, often these stories do not have a strong foundation in historical events. For example, Italians see themselves as uniquely descending from the Romans and relate their identity to the history of Roman Catholicism, while the Greek identity is founded on the belief that they are the direct descendants of the Ancient Greeks: however, the historical accuracy of all these myths can be easily challenged.

The strength of origin and ancestry myths lies instead in that they form points of consensus around which a sense of national unity can be developed and maintained. Such myths are understood as sites of social memory and also used by members of an ethnic or national group to draw boundaries between ingroups and outgroups. The unfavourable attitudes and exclusion of outgroups based on origin and ancestry myths can often lead directly to intercultural conflict (Levi-Strauss, 1962). As one example, Mostar is a city in Bosnia and Herzegovina that is famous for its ancient bridge. This elegant structure was designed by the Ottoman (Turkish) architect Mimar Hayruddin and completed in 1566. In 1993, during the Bosnian war, it was destroyed by the Croatian army as a way of destroying part of Bosnia's Muslim history. Today, the city remains divided between Croats (mainly Catholics) and Bosniaks (mainly Muslims).

Photo 10.1
The historic bridge in Mostar divides Croats (mainly Catholics) and Bosniaks (mainly Muslims).
Copyright © Zala Volčič. Used with permission.

In a society where different groups exist, more often than not there is uneven distribution of power among such groups. Consequently, the group in power will have a greater influence on the ingroup/outgroup dynamic in their society. It is important to note that the processes of inclusion and exclusion result from an interaction, or the lack of it, between social agents (e.g. individuals and groups) and social institutions (e.g. educational institutions, the media, regulatory bodies, government agencies, and law enforcement agencies). If the attributes of these social agents are seen to support the state and nation, the interaction results in social inclusion, and access to resources will be granted. However, if the agents' attributes are not deemed to be relevant and useful to the system, then exclusion and conflict are likely to follow. For example,

Louw (2004b) describes the story of twentieth-century South Africa as one of exclusions, racial conflicts, and apartheid (see Chapter 8). Apartheid – a racial policy which was constructed by the ethnic white minority and which dominated South Africa until 1992, served to maintain the political and economic supremacy of the white ethnic minority. Louw argues that apartheid was premised not only upon the notion of white supremacy but also upon political partition. It was a strategy constructed by a powerful minority in order to hold on to their political power. Such a racial policy, based on ingroup and outgroup bias and prejudice, then resulted in many interethnic and interracial conflicts in South African history.

Historical grievances and interethnic hatred

The cultural relationship between past, present, and future is crucial in understanding intercultural conflict (Martin and Nakayama, 2000). Although everyday intercultural conflicts are often based on cultural ignorance or misunderstanding, some intercultural conflicts are based on hatred and centuries-old antagonisms, often arising from long-standing historical grievances. For example, tensions between Muslims and Orthodox Christians in the Balkan region have been ongoing since the Turks conquered Serbia and the rest of the Balkans in the fourteenth century (Colovic, 2002). The defeat of Christian armies in the famous Battle of Kosovo in 1389 has been perceived as the epitome of Serbian sacrifice, and the theme of the Serbs defending Christian Europe against Islamic expansionism has been appropriated into Serbian history. This was evident in the prism of victimhood through which the military conflicts in Bosnia and Kosovo in the 1990s were often represented – as Serbs defending themselves, the Serbian nation, Yugoslavia, and/or Christianity. Today, the conflicts in Bosnia still persist largely because of these historical grievances (Erjavec and Volčič, 2007).

Intercultural conflicts due to historical hostility, hatred, and grievances are also illustrated by the disputes between the Mexican government and Mexican Indian farmers, known as Zapatistas (the Zapatista National Liberation Army). Few international events over the last decade have captured the global imagination as much as the Zapatista uprising in Chiapas, Mexico, in 1994. The impoverished Indian farmers, led by the rebel leader, Subcomandante Marcos, advocated a rebellion against the Mexican government with minimal violence to change the oppressive economic and political conditions. At that time, the Mexican government was creating an image of the country as socially and economically stable, but the Zapatistas argued that poverty, landlessness, inadequate healthcare, illiteracy, and governmental corruption were ruling Mexico. They fought for land, justice, democratic reforms, and the end of Mexico's one-party state (McCowan, 2003). In this case, the historical antagonism between poor Mexican Indian farmers and the Mexican government led to new forms of hostility and hatred.

Interethnic hatred as a result of cultural ignorance is illustrated clearly by the continuing practices of anti-Semitism. *Anti-Semitism* refers to a negative perception of Jews (Office for Democratic Institutions and Human Rights; ODIHR, 2008). Historically, rhetorical and physical manifestations of anti-Semitism were directed toward Jewish individuals or their property, Jewish community institutions, and their religious facilities. Examples of contemporary anti-Semitism can be found in the media, schools, the workplace, and in the religious sphere. According to the Anti-Semitism Worldwide Report (2007), anti-Semitic manifestations have become an increasingly pervasive phenomenon in European countries.

The Report introduced the term *Islamophobia*, which refers to expressions against anything Muslim (Said, 1994a). Over the last twenty years or so, in various countries such as Afghanistan, Turkey, Algeria, Singapore, the Netherlands, the United Kingdom, Bosnia, and Canada, Islamic female clothing and the interpretation of Islamic law have become the focus not only of political debate and legal battles but also of political aggression. For example, the Netherlands are known throughout the world as one of the most tolerant nations, but the murder of the Dutch filmmaker Theo van Gogh in 2004 by a Muslim immigrant with Moroccan origins, Mohammed Bouyeri, challenged this image (Buruma, 2007). At the time of the murder, van Gogh had collaborated with Ayaan Hirsi Ali in making the film *Submission*, which attempted to demonstrate that the Qur'an considers women to be fundamentally inferior to men. Ayaan Hirsi Ali is a Somali refugee and former Muslim arguing against Islam in the name of women's emancipation. In the days that followed the murder of van Gogh, a number of mosques were daubed with racist symbols and an Islamic school was set ablaze. Although the intensity of the incidents decreased soon afterwards, the sense that ethnic/religious conflicts existed in this multicultural country remained. The Dutch's opposition toward Muslims living in the Netherlands was on the rise. Similarly, in April 2007 a local imam and his pregnant wife in Kostroma, Russia – both dressed in traditional Muslim clothing – were approached, pushed, and beaten in the street by two youths who all the while demanded that they leave the country. Crimes of this kind are sometimes justified by their perpetrators through historical grievances and interethnic hatred.

Theory Corner

Orientalism

Edward Said was a well-known Palestinian scholar and the author of the highly influential book *Orientalism* (1994b). This book offers a classical framework for understanding relationships between the 'West' and the 'Rest' – Muslims in the Middle East. Based on his analysis of the work of painters, historians, linguists, archeologists,

(Continued)

travellers, and colonial bureaucrats, Said demonstrates the links between knowledge and power in the context of the relationship between Western and Muslim societies and argues that European domination is not only about political and economic interests but also about cultural power. He created the term *Orientalism,* which refers to a specific kind of discourse that fosters the difference between the familiar (Europe, the West, 'us', the democratic and civilized) and the strange (the Orient, the East, 'them', the uncivilized and barbaric).

Orientalism, Said contends, rests upon four dogmas. First, the Orient is undeveloped and inferior while the West is rational, developed, humane, and superior. Second, the Orient lives according to rules inscribed in its sacred texts, rather than in response to the changing demands of life. Third, the Orient is eternal, uniform, and incapable of defining itself, thereby justifying the vocabulary used by the West to describe it. Finally, the Orient is either something to be feared (e.g. Islamic terrorism) or to be controlled by pacification, by occupation, or by development.

Reference

Said, Edward (1994b) *Orientalism.* New York: Vintage.

Further reading on Orientalism

Cooper, Melinda (2008) 'Orientalism in the mirror: the sexual politics of anti-Westernism', *Theory, Culture & Society,* 25 (4): 25–49.

Political, territorial, and economic disputes

Intercultural conflict can arise from inequalities, political disputes over territory, economic control over resources, and cultural disputes over language and religion. For example, the violent conflict in Palestine represents a political dispute over territory. Historically, the most fundamental bonding among various Jewish groups was the Zionist dream of building a Jewish state in Palestine – the Promised Land (Hestroni, 2000). Zionists began buying land and settling throughout Palestine in the late nineteenth century and continued until after the establishment of Israel in 1948. Zionists thought of Palestine as desolate, despite the fact that Palestinians were living there. This point is especially important in understanding the continuing conflict between Jews and Arabs over this land, with each side seeing it as their people's homeland. The conflict did not cease with the establishment of Israel in 1948 but has continued until the present day. Meanwhile, the land has become a central component in both Jewish identity and the Israeli national identity.

In addition to territorial claims, international and intercultural conflict can occur as a result of a prohibition against speaking one's own language. The rise in both status and usage of the English language coincided with the gradual disappearance of the Welsh language, supported by state institutions. For example, Welsh children were forced to speak English at school and were punished for speaking Welsh. In recent times, a movement for the resurgence of the Welsh language, accompanied by Welsh nationalism, has reversed this decline to some extent. Today, the number of speakers of Welsh as a first language is rising. The recent devolution of political power in the UK has meant that Welsh now has

Photo 10.2
Both Arabs and Jews claim the old city of Jerusalem as 'theirs'.
Copyright © Helga Tawil-Souri. Used with permission.

a higher status and is supported by state institutions in Wales, which has also helped in its revival. Cultural icons like Bryn Terfel and Katherine Jenkins promote the Welsh identity throughout the world, demonstrating the possibility of a peaceful rather than a violent reclaiming of its cultural status.

Economic issues can also underlie intercultural conflicts. Such conflicts are often expressed through cultural differences by blaming minorities (e.g. immigrants) for economic pressures in a society. The prejudice and stereotypes that lead to such intercultural conflict frequently result from a perceived economic threat and competition. In a study conducted in Australia, Anglo-Australians were found to view the promotion of cultural diversity and equal societal participation as more of a threat than a benefit when compared with ratings on the same items by Asian immigrants (Liu, 2007). In particular, Asian immigrants were viewed by Australians, more than by the immigrants themselves, as a burden to the economy of the host country and a threat to host nationals in a competitive job market.

Political, territorial, and economic disputes begin when a society fails to provide reasonable equality for its various groups of citizens. Toward the end of the last century, scholarly works in the area of intercultural and international conflicts became prominent in addressing the relationship between conflict and concepts such as identity, culture, history, and the nation-state. Many of them addressed these relationships in the aftermath of the immense social changes in the world at the end of the twentieth century. For example, the fall of the Berlin Wall, the collapse of the Soviet Union, the end of apartheid in South Africa, and the civil war in the former Yugoslav region signified the end of an era that was marked by a high tension between nations advocating different concepts of social order and development. Today more than ever before, there are claims for a recognition of ethnic and cultural identities in the rapidly changing international cultural environments fuelled by increasingly complex flows of cultural and economic goods (Erjavec and Volčič, 2007).

Stages in the Conflict Process

Individuals, groups, or nations do not move suddenly from peaceful coexistence to conflict. Rather, as Louis Pondy (1967) indicated, people move through stages as a conflict develops and subsides. According to Pondy, the first phase, *latent conflict*, involves a situation in which conditions are ripe for conflict because of the incompatibilities and interdependence that exist between the two parties. The second phase, *perceived conflict*, occurs when one or more of the parties believe that these incompatibilities exist. It is possible to have latent conflict without perceived conflict. For example, two ethnic groups might have different value orientations, say about our relationship with nature. This difference in worldviews may not be an issue for either group unless there is a need for them to reach a consensus about how to conquer drought, for example: to pray for rain or use cloud-seeding technology. During the third phase, *felt conflict*, the parties will begin to formulate strategies about how to deal with the conflict and to consider various outcomes that would or would not be acceptable. These strategies and goals are then enacted in communication during the *manifest phase*. Finally, the last phase discussed by Pondy is *conflict aftermath*, which emphasizes that conflicts can have both short-term and long-term consequences. Even after a manifest conflict is concluded, the conflict can still change the nature of the interactants' relationship and functioning in the future.

Table 10.1: Stages of the conflict process

Stages	Characteristics
Latent conflict	Conditions are ripe for conflict because incompatible goals and interdependence exist between parties.
Perceived conflict	One or more parties believe incompatible goals and interdependences exist.
Felt conflict	Parties begin to focus on conflict issues and formulate strategies to deal with the conflict.
Manifest conflict	Conflict and conflict strategies are enacted through communication between parties.
Conflict aftermath	Conflict seems 'settled'. However, it can have short-term and long-term effects on the relationship between the conflicting parties.

Source: Pondy, Louis R. (1967) 'Organizational conflict: concepts and models', *Administrative Science Quarterly*, 12: 296–320.

One illustration of the development of a conflict is the dispute between German nudists and Polish puritans on the Baltic Sea island of Usedom (Boussouar and Mailliet, 2008). Straddling the border between Germany and Poland, Usedom is divided into German and Polish parts. For over fifty years nudist beaches have been the norm on the German side, as naked bathing is not considered unusual in Germany (latent conflict). However, the removal of border controls between Germany and Poland as part of the Schengen agreement in January 2008 has enabled Polish people to stroll along the leafy coastal paths to nearby German towns (perceived conflict). Many are shocked by what they see (felt conflict). For the Polish people, sunbathing nude where people go walking is unacceptable. Poland is approximately 80 per cent Catholic, which has influenced their views on nudist bathing; as one Polish national remarked, 'It's horrible, we would never bathe naked, we are Catholic.' While nude bathing can lead to a fine in Poland, for Germans of all ages who enjoy swimming and sunbathing on naturist beaches, the disapproving glances from Polish walkers are incomprehensible and intrusive (manifest conflict). Hence, the island of Usedom has become the site of a culture clash – the centre of a conflict of values. Both Poles and Germans cheered in December 2007, when the barbed-wire border was dismantled as part of the Schengen agreement; the cultural walls, however, have proved more difficult to demolish. As a temporary resolution, the authorities plan to put up signs marking the boundaries of the nudist beach in both German and Polish (conflict aftermath). Clearly, if this conflict is not managed properly, in the long term it may have international repercussions.

Conflict Management Styles and Approaches

Conflict management styles

Conflict management styles are strategies that people adopt to handle conflict. The application of different conflict strategies leads to different outcomes. Blake and Mouton (1964) first classified five conflict management styles: avoiding, competing, accommodating, compromising, and collaborating. *Avoiding* is a physical withdrawal or refusal to discuss the conflict. *Competing* is linked to a use of power to gain one's objectives, even though it means ignoring the needs of an opponent. Competing is highly assertive and does not require cooperation. The outcome of this strategy is that you win and the other person loses. *Accommodating* refers to behaviours that conceal or play down differences by emphasizing common interests. If you chose to apply an accommodating strategy, you would sacrifice your own interests to satisfy those of the other party; that is, you lose and the other party wins. A *compromising* strategy aims to find a midpoint between the opposing parties – both parties involved in a conflict try to work out a solution so that everyone gets something, although no-one may get everything.

Compromising involves both assertiveness and cooperation and is a popular way to resolve conflicts because neither side wins or loses. In a *collaborating* strategy, the conflict agents are encouraged to find a solution where both sides can win. It is considered the ideal way to handle conflict in most situations, but it is not often used because it requires more time, a willingness to negotiate, assertiveness, and cooperation, and not all conflicts have win–win solutions.

Here is an example to illustrate the application of the five conflict strategies in resolving an interpersonal conflict. Imagine that your boss has informed you that your advertising firm has just signed a contract to produce a television commercial for a toy factory. You and one of your colleagues need to work on Saturday in order to get the draft proposal ready for a meeting with your client on Monday. However, neither you nor your colleague wants to work on the weekend because you both have other plans. If you want to maximize your own interest, you could exercise your power as the project team leader to force your colleague to work long hours on Saturday while you stay home fulfilling your personal commitments (a competing strategy). On the other hand, if you wish to sacrifice your own interest in order to show concern for your colleague who has a birthday party scheduled over the weekend, you could go to the office instead of your colleague (an accommodating strategy). Finally, you could talk with your colleague to see whether you could each work for half a day or evening and free up some time over the weekend to accomplish the task, which might (or might not) allow you both to complete your personal plans as well (a compromising or, if you are lucky, collaborating strategy). The application of different conflict styles requires different levels of assertiveness and cooperation from the conflict parties.

Conflict management approaches

Two major approaches are evident in the literature on intercultural conflict. The first one is conflict as normal. This approach views any type of conflict as an opportunity to grow and as a chance to develop and build relationships. Augsburger (1992) suggested that there are four main assumptions underlying this approach: 1) conflict is normal and useful; 2) all issues are subject to change through negotiation; 3) direct confrontation is valuable; and 4) conflict always represents a renegotiation of the contract, a release of tensions, and a renewal of relationships. Advocates of the conflict-as-normal approach believe that working through conflicts provides potential benefits, including acquiring new information about other people or groups and increasing the overall integrity and cohesiveness of the parties involved. Therefore, conflict can be understood as a renegotiation of the contract and should be celebrated. With this in mind, individuals should be encouraged to think of creative solutions to conflict situations. The most desirable response is to recognize and work through conflict in an open and constructive manner.

The second approach is conflict as destructive. This approach views conflict as unproductive, negative, destructive, and dangerous for relationships. Augsburger (1992) also summarized four assumptions for this approach: 1) conflict is a destructive disturbance to peaceful situations; 2) the social system should not be adjusted to the needs of its members, but rather, members of a society need to adapt to the established values; 3) confrontations are destructive and ineffective; and 4) agents involved in a conflict should be disciplined.

Ting-Toomey (1994) suggested that the conflict-as-normal orientation grows from an attempt to protect the individual, while the conflict-as-destructive orientation rises from a higher value attributed to maintaining harmony in relationships and saving other's face. She differentiated two basic concerns in managing conflict: concern for self-face and concern for other-face. These dimensions describe the motivational orientations of individuals or groups.

Theory Corner

Face-negotiation theory

Face-negotiation theory was developed by Stella Ting-Toomey (1988, 2005b) and applies comprehensively to managing intercultural conflicts. Erving Goffman defined 'face' as the favourable social impression that a person wants others to have of him or her. The concept of face is about self-identity and other-identity consideration in a communication event. Face is tied to the emotional significance and estimated calculations that we attach to our own social self-worth and that of others. Face can be threatened, enhanced, given, saved, and negotiated. Face threat may be experienced when we are not treated in the way we think we should be. If the discrepancy is large, individuals engage in 'facework', employing verbal and nonverbal behaviour to restore face loss.

Ting-Toomey identified three face orientations: self-face concern, other-face concern, and mutual-face concern. She claims that face orientation determines how negotiators enact facework, which is also influenced by culture. Self-face is the protective concern for one's own image when face is threatened in a conflict situation; other-face is the concern for the other party's image in the conflict; mutual-face considers both parties' image. While face and facework are universal phenomena, how we negotiate face varies across cultures. For example, individualists are found to be more concerned with protecting self-face in dealing with conflict, whereas collectivists are more concerned with other-face images or saving mutual-face images.

(Continued)

References

Ting-Toomey, Stella (1988) 'Intercultural conflict style: a face-negotiation theory', in Y.Y. Kim and W.B. Gudykunst (eds), *Theories in Intercultural Communication*. Newbury Park, CA: SAGE. pp. 213–235.

Ting-Toomey, Stella (2005b) 'The matrix of face: updated face-negotiation theory', in W.B. Gudykunst (ed.), *Theorizing about Intercultural Communication*. Thousand Oaks, CA: SAGE. pp. 71–92.

Further reading on face-negotiation theory

Oetzel, John G. and Ting-Toomey, Stella (2003) 'Face concerns in interpersonal conflict: a cross-cultural empirical test of the face negotiation theory', *Communication Research*, 30 (6): 599–624.

The Amish, for example, see conflict not as an opportunity for individual growth but as a distress to their community. Legal and personal confrontations tend to be avoided because the use of force is discouraged in the Amish culture. Similarly, in Chinese culture, harmony in social relationships (interpersonal, intergroup, interorganizational, or international) is valued. A Chinese saying, 'Everything prospers in a harmonious family', reflects the belief that conflict should be reduced, if not avoided, as it disturbs harmony. Cultural groups that view conflict as destructive often avoid direct confrontation in a conflict situation and may instead seek to use a third party in order to avoid a direct confrontation and save face. This third-party intervention may be informal, such as when a friend is asked to intervene, or formal, such as when legal or expert assistance is sought. This 'peacemaking' approach to conflict values harmony and the protection of face in a conflict resolution.

Influence of Culture on Conflict Management

Culture defines values and interests, shapes perceptions and our choice of alternatives, and influences conflict outcomes (Pedersen and Jandt, 1996). Overall, the cultural background influences the ways in which people view and resolve conflicts. In any conflict there are different levels of engagement, as well as different aspects that are elevated, thus determining what gets acknowledged and what gets resolved (Fisher-Yoshida, 2005). Therefore, a comprehensive understanding of how culture can influence conflict management strategies helps us to achieve better outcomes.

Cultural dimension and conflict management

Ting-Toomey (1994) identified the individualism–collectivism cultural dimension (see Chapter 5) as one of the key cultural variables in the management of intercultural conflict. In individualistic cultures independence, freedom, privacy, and self-esteem are considered important (Triandis, 1995); thus conflict strategies tend to be goal-oriented, focusing on problem solving, and communication is direct. On the other hand, in collectivistic cultures people are willing to sacrifice some personal interest in order to maintain good relationships with others during conflict and may choose accommodating or avoiding communication styles. Okabe (1983) found that Americans tend to use explicit words like 'certainly', 'absolutely', and 'positively' in interactions, whereas Japanese people prefer to use implicit and less assertive expressions such as 'maybe', 'perhaps', and 'somewhat'. In conflict management, people from individualistic cultures, therefore, tend to state their own position directly, defend their ground, and justify their decisions. People from collectivistic cultures, by contrast, tend to express their views indirectly (e.g. 'Maybe what I said is incorrect, but … '; 'Perhaps we could do it this way … '; 'Let's not consider this for the time being … '). In such situations, it is up to the other party to work out the underlying meaning and intention of the speaker.

Cultural context and mediation

Conflict management strategies are not meaningful unless they are understood in the context of culturally learned expectations and values (Liu and Chen, 2002). Context stimulates, sustains, and supports behaviour. Thus, it is important to interpret behaviour in terms of its intended expectations and values, consistent with its context. Conflict strategies that are not sensitive to each culture's unique context are not likely to succeed. Each cultural context has developed its own constraints and opportunities for constructive conflict management. Merry (1989) described how mediation practices across cultures are dependent upon context, where the process rather than the substance of an agreement becomes the focus. In every culture, there are 'conflict transformers' who can help disputants to think in new ways about the conflict in an atmosphere of mutual respect. For example, an elder or the chief of a village may be brought in to resolve a dispute between two villages or between two villagers. Mediation can also occur between two nations. The promise of a Palestinian nation, for example, was 'born' at the signing of the Oslo Accords on 13 September 1993 (Oslo I) – a pledge of peace between Israel and the Palestinians – as a result of mediation by the international community. Subsequently, between then and the outbreak of the Second Intifada seven years later, state-building and development efforts were significant in the territories. This example illustrates the potential positive outcome of mediation in a conflict situation.

Cultural values and negotiation

Conflict management, to a certain extent, is negotiation in order to reach a solution that satisfies both sides. Lewicki et al. (2003) identified eight cultural variables that affect the effectiveness of negotiations: the way the negotiation is defined; the parties at the negotiating table; the protocol that is followed; the style of communication; the time frame; the perception of risk; whether the negotiation is group or individual; and the way an agreement is shaped and enforced. These factors highlight the intricacies of addressing conflicts when the parties involved frame the conflict according to different cultural values. For example, in individualistic cultures conflicts can be resolved directly through face-to-face negotiations. In more collectivist-oriented cultures, this may not be possible. Rather, a third party may need to perform a type of shuttle diplomacy between the conflicting parties, guiding them toward a resolution. It is worthy of mention that third-party intervention is employed in both individualistic and collectivistic cultures, but the nature and role of the third party is different. In more individualist cultures, the third party is usually a neutral mediator who guides the resolution process without adding in his or her own beliefs. In collectivistic cultures, this mediator is more likely to be a known and trusted person who is expected to recommend the desired course of action.

Effective management of intercultural conflict

Culture influences how conflict is perceived and interpreted; effective intercultural conflict management, therefore, requires intercultural awareness and sensitivity (Chen and Starosta, 2005). In *Managing Cultural Differences*, Harris and Morgan (1987: 257) proposed a five-step method of managing intercultural conflict, based on their study of British and American business people. The five steps are: describe the conflict in a way that is understood in both cultures; analyse the conflict from both cultural perspectives; identify the basis for conflict from the two cultural viewpoints; resolve the conflict through synergistic strategies; and determine if the solution is working interculturally. For example, American culture values hard work, competition, personal achievement, and determination. From an American perspective, British businesspeople can appear to lack an aggressive approach and the ability to engage in competition. From the British perspective, however, American businesspeople can seem impatient and too eager to prove themselves to their superiors. To sacrifice the quality of their life simply to be more efficient may not seem worthwhile to the British. This conflict might best be resolved through the use of synergistic strategies, which refer to 'a dynamic process in which the opposing parties combine their actions and work by adapting and learning different viewpoints through empathy and sensitivity' (Chen and Starosta, 2005). This might involve becoming more aware of the other culture's values and the priorities set on them.

In addition to Harris and Morgan's model, Ting-Toomey (1994) has provided specific suggestions for effective conflict management in individualistic and collectivistic cultures. For people from individualistic cultures operating in a collectivistic cultural context, Ting-Toomey gave seven suggestions to help manage conflict effectively: understand the opponent's face-maintenance assumptions in order to keep a balance between humility and pride and between shame and honour in communication; save the opponent's face by carefully using informal consultation or a go-between to deal with low-grade conflicts before they fall irrevocably into face-losing situations; give face to opponents by not pushing them into a corner with no leeway for recovering face; avoid using too much verbal expression and learn how to manage conflicts by effectively reading implicit and nonverbal messages; be empathetic by listening attentively and respecting the opponent's needs; put aside the explicit and direct communication skills practised in the West and learn to use an indirect communication style; and tolerate the opponent's tendency to avoid facing the conflict by being patient, thereby maintaining a harmonious atmosphere and mutual dignity. These strategies have been widely applied in academic research and practice.

Communication is the means by which conflict is defined, managed, and resolved. Based on the literature, we propose the following communication strategies:

- *Focus on common ground and reduce disagreement.* Intercultural conflict occurs because of an incompatibility between the goals, interests, resources, values, expectations, processes, or outcomes of two or more parties. Our attempts to establish and maintain intercultural relationships sometimes fail because others dislike what we like or vice versa. One way to restore balance in a relationship is to seek commonalities by emphasizing the shared goal of accomplishing a task, or a common desire to restore peace or get a fair share of the resources. An emphasis on common ground fosters positive attitudes which, in turn, can ease tension and reduce negative feelings or stereotypes.

- *Practise relational empathy.* Relational empathy refers to seeing an issue from the perspective of the other party. Relational empathy skills such as active listening can form the starting point for the conflict management process (Dodd, 1998). Listening involves the process of interpreting the attitudes, emotions, and values underpinning spoken messages. To understand our own and others' deeply held cultural values and to engage those values in a culturally appropriate way are important in effective conflict management.

- *Develop a positive communication climate.* Conflict is more likely to be resolved effectively in a positive communication climate, whose characteristics include support, non-judgmentalism, and open-mindedness. During the process of conflict negotiation, both parties should avoid emotional presentations such as angry or insulting remarks. Another way to build a good communication climate is to deal with one issue at a time. Although intercultural conflicts can be the result of historical grievances and long-standing hatred, bringing up too many unresolved issues at any one time may obscure the question in hand or escalate conflict. It is better to devote one's attention and resources to one issue at a time.

Summary

This chapter described several potential sources of intercultural conflict (racial violence; ingroup/outgroup bias; historical grievances and ethnic hatred; political, territorial, and economic disputes). It identified different stages in the conflict process and highlighted the influence of culture at each stage of the conflict process. This chapter also discussed the influence of an individualism–collectivism cultural dimension on conflict styles and described the influence of cultural context on conflict communication and mediation. Conflict styles are actually communication behaviour because communication is the means by which conflicts are socially defined and the instrument through which influence is exercised. Intercultural miscommunication lies at the heart of intercultural conflict. To conclude the chapter, we suggested some strategies for effectively managing intercultural conflict.

Intercultural conflict occurs at multiple levels – interpersonal, intergroup, interorganizational, interethnic, and international. The intensity of intercultural conflict can range from individual acts of disrespect, as well as localized, short-lived riots and group violence, up to large-scale violence. It is important to recognize the importance of cultural context, including the economic, historical, and political contexts in which a conflict is situated, and to develop culturally appropriate strategies for managing conflict effectively. As conflict is pervasive in all social relationships, we need to identify the potential sources of intercultural conflict and understand the potential role of intercultural communication in resolving these conflicts.

Case Study:
Violent conflicts in the former Yugoslavia

The Socialist Federative Republic of Yugoslavia (the former Yugoslavia) was established in the aftermath of the Second World War in 1946. From its inception it was a socialist state, ruled by the Yugoslav Communist Party with Josip Broz Tito at its helm. The country's territory incorporated seven ethnic groups: Albanians, Bosnian Muslims (today known as Bosniaks or Bosnjaks), Croatians, Serbs, Slovenes, Macedonians, and Montenegrins. The country was divided into six republics, broadly aligning with the ethnic composition of the population: Bosnia and Herzegovina, Croatia, Serbia, Slovenia, Macedonia, and Montenegro. Albanians lived in the southern parts of Serbia (Kosovo), while Bosnia and Herzegovina had the greatest level of ethnic mix, including Bosnian Muslims, Orthodox Serbs, and Catholic Croats.

Yugoslavia established the peculiar international position of being in between the Eastern and Western blocks. Although under a socialist political system, citizens of the former Yugoslavia enjoyed more freedom than those of other eastern European countries, as illustrated by being allowed to possess a passport and to travel internationally. The country also had a reasonable degree of economic stability, although the level of individual and civic freedom was limited and its economic growth was slow in comparison to that of Western countries. Nevertheless, the post-war period of 1950–1985 was characterized by social stability, cultural vibrancy, and limited but steady economic progress.

Photo 10.3
Panoramic view of Zagreb, a city in the former Yugoslavia, and now the capital city of Croatia.
Copyright © Zala Volčič. Used with permission.

Before the death of President Tito, the level of tolerance among ethnic groups was quite high and hence the country enjoyed a fairly stable political community and social solidarity (Velikonja, 2003). Although different ethnic identities were visible in the society, a Yugoslav identity slowly started to emerge – by 1981 there were over a million people self-identifying as Yugoslavs. After the death of Tito in 1980, however, the suppressed nationalisms once again emerged into the political sphere. Both major ethnic groups, Serbs and Croats, claimed to have been the victims of a continued persecution by the other, which, they argued, dominated the Yugoslav Federation. In 1986, the Serbian Academy of Science and Art prepared a *Memorandum* – a list of Serbian grievances about their position in the Federation. Much of the document dealt with the 'genocide' of Serbs in Kosovo and articulated the need for Serbs throughout Yugoslavia to mobilize against their perceived persecutors. The Serbian politician Slobodan Milosevic rose to power in 1987 and produced supposedly scientific data supporting the construction of a 'Greater Serbia'. Its vision was that all ethnic Serbs needed to live in the same state.

The bloody Yugoslav dissolution in 1990 was caused by both internal transformations (e.g. Slovene and Croatian independence, the rise of President Milosevic in Serbia) and global geopolitical developments that signified the collapse of communism. In 1991, a seemingly fratricidal civil war began. Emphasizing the importance of Orthodoxy, Islam, and Catholicism alike to nationalisms as a symbol of collective national identity, the Slovene cultural theorist Velikonja (2003) suggested that religious groups became isolated from one another in the former Yugoslav context. Both Serbs and Croats exploited their own past in order to present themselves as victims. However, the political elites in both Serbia and Croatia agreed on one issue: the question of how to divide up the Bosnian territory. In both countries the mainstream positioned Bosnian Muslims as little more than an invented and artificial nation with no historical claim to Bosnian territory. For Croats and Serbs alike, the Muslims were the harbingers of a dangerous Islamic conspiracy, poised to take over the Balkans and Western Europe. Mainstream political discourse there remains dominated by nationalistic myths that constitute a particular version of the Serbian and Croatian past (Susa, 2005).

The wars of the 1990s resulted in an estimated 102,000 deaths and millions of refugees (Skjelsbaek and Smith, 2001), and were defined as the bloodiest conflicts in Europe in the post-Second World War period. These wars were also the first conflict to have been formally judged as genocidal since the Second World War, with many of the key individuals involved subsequently being charged with war crimes. All sides committed war crimes of ethnic cleansing, the establishment of concentration camps or collective centres, and the destruction of physical property that included some 1,400 mosques.

After more than three years of bloody conflict, the Dayton Peace Agreement brought an end to the Bosnian war on 14 December 1995. Although fighting ceased at that time, the conflict still remains far from completely resolved. Today, international control over military forces is still present. The international community negotiates the peace in Bosnia and Herzegovina. The seven former Yugoslav states conduct separate existences, with Kosovo being the last region to declare independence in February 2008.

References for case study

Skjelsbaek, Inger and Smith, Dan (eds) (2001) *Gender, Peace and Conflict*. London: SAGE.
Susa, Gordana (2005) *The Return of Hate Speech*. Oxford/New York: Blackwell.
Velikonja, Mitja (2003) *Religious Separation and Political Intolerance in Bosnia-Herzegovina*. College Station, TX: Texas A&M University Press.

Questions for discussion

1   When and how was Yugoslavia created? How is it different from the former Yugoslavia?
2   What are some of the main reasons for the collapse of the former Yugoslavia? What have been the subsequent impacts on its people?
3   What types of conflicts were mostly played out during the Yugoslav civil wars? Compare these to other wars.
4   Do you think peace agreements can help stop violent conflicts? Do you have any examples to illustrate your points?
5   What measures can we take to prevent such violent conflicts from happening in the future?

Key Terms

accommodating;
affective conflict;
anti-Semitism;
avoiding;
cognitive conflict;
collaborating;
collectivism;
competing;

compromising;
conflict;
face-negotiation
  theory;
goal conflict;
globalization;
high-intensity conflict;
individualism;

intercultural conflict;
intergroup conflict;
international conflict;
interpersonal conflict;
Islamophobia;
low-intensity conflict;
Orientalism

Further Reading

Conflict styles and culture

Gabrielidis, Cristina; Stephan, Walter; Santos Pearson, Virginia M. Dos
and Villareal Lucila (1997) 'Preferred styles of conflict resolution: Mexico
and the United States', *Journal of Cross-Cultural Psychology*, 28 (6):
661–677.

Cultural dimension and conflict management

Chua, Erni and Gudykunst, William B. (1987) 'Conflict resolution style
in low- and high-context cultures', *Communication Research Reports*,
4: 32–37.
Morris, Michael H.; Avila, Raymon A. and Allen, Jeffrey (1985) 'Achievement
American-style: the rewards and costs of individualism', *American
Psychologist*, 40 (12): 1285–1295.
Soeters, Joseph L. (1996) 'Culture and conflict: an application of Hofstede's
theory to the conflict in the former Yugoslavia', *Journal of Peace Psychology*,
2 (3): 233–244.

Face-negotiation theory

Oetzel, John G. and Ting-Toomey, Stella (2003) 'Face concerns in interpersonal
conflict: a cross-cultural empirical test of the face negotiation theory',
Communication Research, 30 (6): 599–624.
Ting-Toomey, Stella; Gao, Ge; Trubinsky, Paula; Yang, Zhizhong; Kim, Hak Soo,
et al.. (1991) 'Culture, face maintenance, and styles of handling interpersonal
conflict: a study in five cultures', *International Journal of Conflict Management*,
2 (4): 275–296.

Interpersonal conflict

Tsai, Jeanne L. and Levenson, Robert W. (1997) 'Cultural influences on emotional responding: Chinese American and European American dating couples during interpersonal conflict', *Journal of Cross-Cultural Psychology*, 28 (3): 600–625.

Intercultural and international conflict

Bercovitch, Jacob and Schneider, Gerald (2000) 'Who mediates? The political economy of international conflict management', *Journal of Peace Research*, 37 (2): 145–165.
Schulz, Markus S. (2006) 'Transnational conflicts: central America, social change, and globalization', *International Sociology*, 21 (2): 425–427.

Orientalism

Cooper, Melinda (2008) 'Orientalism in the mirror: the sexual politics of anti-Westernism', *Theory, Culture & Society*, 25 (4): 25–49.

11

Mass Media, Technology, and Cultural Change

The media's the most powerful entity on earth. They have the power to make the innocent guilty and to make the guilty innocent, and that's power. Because they control the minds of the masses.

Malcolm X, African-American leader, 1925–1965

Learning Objectives

At the end of this chapter, you should be able to:

- Describe the impact of globalization and technology on the mass media.
- Explain how the mass media shape our thinking, doing, identities, and communication.
- Understand the influence of the mass media on cultural change.
- Identify skills in understanding the media and culture.

The World of Mass Media

The mass media are all around us, playing a significant role in producing and representing our cultures. Almost all aspects of our everyday life – from food to clothing, housing, education, entertainment, and transportation – are affected by the mass media. The media not only bring us news, but also function as sources of education, entertainment, and identity construction. McLuhan (1964) stated that as the hammer extends our arm and the wheel extends our legs and feet, the mass media extend our connection to parts of the world where our physical bodies cannot reach. They shape our thinking, doing, and being. For example, we often judge others by the type of media they consume – the newspapers they read, the movies and television programmes they watch, and the internet sites they use.

Questions about the reach and influence of the media also link to wider global issues. For example, what happens when the media cross national and cultural boundaries? What role do the mass media play in our seeing and understanding the world? What happens when a Western television programme is imported into a non-Western context? Becker (2004) studied the effects of mass media on teenage girls in Fiji, who had experienced no previous exposure to media outlets such as television. Before being introduced to television, the girls had had little awareness of the Western 'ideal' of a thin body shape. However, after several months of viewing American television programming and its representations of successful, attractive, and thin women, the Fijian girls began to feel that their body shape was too large to be successful and employable. This example shows that media representations of powerful foreign (in this case Western) ideals of beauty can influence people's perceptions of themselves and others, even in a distant part of the world.

By extending our connections to the rest of the world, the mass media can promote a better understanding, appreciation, and connections between different cultures and facilitate intercultural communication. On the other hand, the media can also achieve the opposite: increasing misunderstanding, fear, and antagonism through a repetition of negative stereotypical representations of people. For instance, the media can perpetuate stereotypes regarding age, gender, sexuality, and religion. This chapter focuses on the role of the mass media in intercultural communication. To do so, we first describe the impact of globalization and technology on the mass media. We then explain how the mass media function to construct our symbolic social reality which, in turn, shapes our communication and identities. The influence of the media on cultural change is also discussed. Based on this analysis, the chapter suggests ways to develop skills in understanding the media and culture.

Globalization, Technology, and the Mass Media

Few would dispute that we live in a much more interconnected world today, and at the core of this interconnectivity is globalization. Globalization is a complex process involving rapid social change that occurs simultaneously across a number of dimensions (economy, politics, communication, physical environment, culture). Each of these transformations interacts with the rest.

Globalizing the mass media

The mass media, even radio and film with their broad reach, were largely local and national until well into the twentieth century. Now increasing connections and interdependencies among institutions and people around the world direct our attention to media globalization as a central phenomenon of the contemporary era. All societies are now part of a global system connected by a range of communication networks. The global media culture has manifested itself through a variety of signifiers, such as the Barbie Doll, McDonald's fast food, Coca-Cola, MTV, *Baywatch*, Youtube, and even beauty contests such as 'Miss World'. The international reach of the media has created exciting new vistas of a global village. Television, satellite dishes, computers, and the internet open up borders around the world. Mass communication has become a vehicle for globally relevant media events. This feature testifies to the overwhelming success of the mass media, which allows people around the world to witness and experience the same event simultaneously: the Olympics, crises, famine, war, conflicts, earthquakes, and presidential elections.

The rise of global media is closely tied to technology. Two media technologies – radio and motion pictures – contributed very significantly to this rise. As early as 1914, 85 per cent of the world's film audiences were watching American movies (Gupta, 1998). More recently, satellite broadcasting and the internet have reduced the geographic distance of mass communication. Star-TV, for example, is one of the most popular regional satellite and cable television operations in the world. Its coverage reaches from the Arab world to South and East Asia. It carries global US and British channels as well as Mandarin and Hindi channels targeting regional audiences. The varieties of language and culture define a new type of geocultural television market that stands between the US-dominated global market and national/regional television markets. In 1995, Star-TV reached 53.7 million households in 53 countries, in English, Mandarin, and Hindi (Gupta, 1998).

However, the media do not operate in a vacuum: they are always tied to political and economic systems. It is impossible to consider identities, communication, democracy, capitalism, nationalism, and the media as separate and autonomous. Their interaction is precisely what shapes the very nature of the social order and our daily lives. For example, Swedish and Scandinavian films in general are globally known for focusing on landscapes, a very slow pace of life, and melancholic feelings. As such, they reflect a specific culture. In northern Nigeria, it is part of its culture to watch films and television programmes in an open public or community sphere. Keyan Tomaselli and William Heuva (2004) reported that in 1996 only 3.5 per cent of African households owned televisions. According to UN statistics, in the mid-1990s there were only 37 million television receivers in Africa out of 1.3 billion worldwide (Fair, 2003). Television ownership in many parts of Africa is still limited to the elite; so it is not surprising to see many people sharing one television set.

McQuail (2005) identified two approaches in studying the mass media: media-centric and society-centric. A *media-centric* approach attributes great autonomy and influence to the media and concentrates on the impact of the media's own sphere of activity (e.g. the study of direct media effects). In contrast, a *society-centric* approach posits the media as a reflection of political and economic forces. For example, the German media reflect the federal political system of that country. Each of the country's 16 regions regulates its own private and public broadcasting and operates public television and radio services through a consortium representing the major sectors and groups, including political parties, churches, unions, and business organizations. Similarly, Turkey's media reflect the larger

Photo 11.1
Television is the most popular medium in Istanbul, Turkey.
Copyright © Zala Volčič. Used with permission.

Turkish society, dealing with issues of secularization (e.g. should anchor-women be veiled?) and the representation of minorities such as the Kurds. The Turkish Radio and Television Corporation (TRT) has four national, one regional, and two international television channels. In Latin America, we find *telenovelas*, since Latin America is one of the world's largest producers of television serial melodramas. Televisa, Venevision, and Globo – the leading networks in Mexico, Venezuela, and Brazil respectively – distribute *telenovelas* all over the world, thereby attracting a broad audience across nations, age, and gender. For much of the world, television remains the medium that most radically shapes social relations.

Theory Corner

Cultural studies

The cultural turn in media studies dates back to the first half of the twentieth century. Cultural-studies scholars are interested in the role culture plays in both preserving and transforming social relations. Whereas the study of art, music, or literature has a history of focusing on formal or aesthetic elements, cultural studies' approach is more interested in the relationship between cultural products (e.g. popular music, movies, radio) and the societies that create and circulate them. Moreover, cultural-studies scholars tend to focus on those popular cultural forms that are not traditionally studied in academic settings, like popular TV shows, rap music, and romance novels (Turner, 2003). Examples of cultural-studies projects are studies of the reaction of audiences in the Middle East and the Netherlands to the TV show *Dallas*, the reasons that women read romance novels, and the way reality TV portrays changes in the way we think about privacy.

Reference

Turner, Graeme (2003) *British Cultural Studies: An Introduction* (3rd edn). London: Routledge.

Further reading on cultural studies

Ang, len (1998) 'Doing cultural studies at the crossroads: local/global negotiations', *European Journal of Cultural Studies*, 1 (1): 13–31.

Political economy of the mass media

Who owns and controls the mass media? What impact does this ownership and control have over media content and on the broader society? Where does the funding for the mass media come from and where do the profits go? Does advertising affect journalists and editorial policy? Is there a separation of the news and advertising departments? Do the mass media rely too much on information provided by government or industry? These are some of the questions raised by media political economy scholars. The term *'political economy'* in media research is often associated with questions about the domination of state or economic power in media spheres. Scholars in the political economy of media investigate processes of privatization, concentration, commercialization, and deregulation (where the market replaces the state). For example, they are interested in the conditions in which individuals can own many media corporations and the consequences this has on democratic practices and media choices. These scholars claim that, globally, media landscapes are heavily dominated by a handful of gigantic media corporations and transnational corporations. The most important of these are Disney, Time Warner, Viacom, and News Corporation. News Corporation's owner, the Australian-born American media mogul Rupert Murdoch, also owns Sky Television, which broadcasts all over the world. Like Murdoch, in Italy Silvio Berlusconi has built a media business empire out of construction and media interests in his native Milan. He is one of Italy's wealthiest men and owns three of the country's seven television channels and several leading newspapers.

Scholars in media political economy have made consistent efforts to investigate both the extent to which our view of the world is shaped by such a concentration of power in certain media corporations and the resulting impact on informed participation in our democratic societies. For example, the Walt Disney Company is now one of the six largest media corporations in mass media in the world, owning media production companies, studios, theme parks, television and radio networks, cable TV systems, magazines, and internet sites. Focusing on an image of magic, joy, and fun, its products are welcomed by parents, teachers, and children alike and are a powerful force in creating children's culture. However, some commentators have raised concerns about the role of Walt Disney movies in constructing children's imaginary worlds (Wasko, 2001).

The issue of gender illustrates these concerns. The female characters in Disney movies often present a particular idealized version of femininity – highly sexualized bodies, coy seductiveness, always needing to be rescued by a male. *Snow White* cleans the dwarves' cottage to please them; Ariel gives up her voice in order to win the prince with her body in *The Little Mermaid*;

Mulan almost single-handedly wins a war only to return home to be romanced; and *Beauty and the Beast*'s Belle endures an abusive Beast in order to redeem him. Of similar concern is the scarcity of genuine and realistic representations of race and ethnicity in Disney animated features. When these do appear, they tend to merely reinforce cultural stereotypes. For example, African-Americans are presented as humans/orang-utans in *The Jungle Book* and are completely absent in *Tarzan*'s Africa; Latinos and African-Americans are represented as street-gang thugs in *The Lion King*, Asians as treacherous Siamese cats in *Lady and the Tramp,* Arabs as barbarians in *Aladdin*, and Native Americans as savages in *Peter Pan* and *Pocahontas*. An important area for research is to study, the way audiences in different cultures perceive these images and the impact this has on their subsequent behaviour.

Theory Corner

The Frankfurt School and critical media theory

The Frankfurt School was formed by scholars working in different disciplines from psychology to history: Max Horkheimer, Theodor W. Adorno, Herbert Marcuse, Leo Löwenthal, and Erich Fromm. Because of the Nazi regime, they had to leave Germany for the USA. While in exile there, members of the Frankfurt School experienced the rise of media culture in film, popular music, radio, and television. They argued that the media are largely commercially produced and controlled by big corporations and thus by commercial imperatives in subservience to the system of consumer capitalism. They believed that the media produce content in order to cultivate, maintain, organize, and utilize the audience as a product.

The term *critical media theory* is often associated with the Frankfurt School. Adorno (2001), a key critical media theorist from the Frankfurt School, developed the term 'culture industry' to call attention to the industrialization and commercialization of culture. Critical media theorists argue that the culture industry (media) aims to perform the dual task of attracting and sustaining the attention of the audience, while ensuring that that audience continues to consume rather than critique the product. Critical media theory aims to critique an oppressive and alienating modern industrial capitalist order, characterized by a growing dominance of instrumental reason on the social, political, and cultural life.

Reference

Adorno, Theodor W. (2001) *The Culture Industry: Selected Essays on Mass Culture* (2nd edn). London/New York: Routledge.

Further reading on critical theory

Kellner, Douglas (1989) *Critical Theory, Marxism, and Modernity*. Cambridge and Baltimore: Polity and Johns Hopkins University Press.

Homogeneity and heterogeneity of media content

There are two ways of conceptualizing the relationship between global and local media. One way posits that the media flow from 'the West to the Rest', resulting in a global homogeneity of products, lifestyles, cultures, identities, tastes, and attitudes. For example, television programming not only offers entertainment but also reflects the sheer power and influence of global corporate culture. It shapes lifestyles and values and replaces lost traditional institutions, communities, clans, family, and authority. The mass marketing of culture now takes place through satellite cables, mobile phones, Walkmans, VCDs, and DVDs. All over the world, people of all ages are exposed to the same music, sporting events, news, soap operas, and lifestyle. Young people in so-called 'Third World' countries are the largest consumers of this global culture. The success in sending global information has perhaps an unintended, negative effect: the same media that inform globally also dominate globally. Some observers see the media as a support system for one culture to dominate another culture – an uneven process called hegemony (Jandt, 2007); the argument is that the mass media can colonize the thinking and values of a specific society.

Global media flows bring about cultural hybridization (Kraidy, 2005). This process and impact of media convergence and globalization can be seen in a number of transnational television channels launched in the past few years. Many of these channels seek to target ethnic groups beyond their national borders. For instance, CBC TV (Greek Cypriot Satellite Television), broadcasts in Greek; Zee TV broadcasts in Hindi across Asia; Med TV targets the Kurdish population in Europe; MBC, Al-Jazeera, TRT, and Al-Arabiyya broadcast in Arabic across the Middle East and North Africa and are watched by Arabs around the world; and TRT-INT targets the Turkish population across Europe. While television channels become the agent for a new global corporate vision, internet technology also contributes to the hybridization of culture by connecting people across the world. The global village in cyberspace is posited by these scholars as a modern Atlantis, where men and women can make choices offered by a free market economy and consumer culture. However, by the same means, the computer age also introduces subtle damage. Like video, film, and global entertainment, the internet has the potential to become a substitute for human interactions, community, and civic life, as adults and children alike spend increasing hours surfing, chatting, and shopping online. We live in a media-saturated world.

Internet technology and alternative media

Internet technology has created another type of 'hybrid' media, called *alternative media* or blogging, to provide space for online users to make their voices heard and to make mass communication interactive. Blogs (web-logs) have assisted different political dissent movements to question and critique authoritarian regimes around the globe. For example, bloggers in Iran were extremely active during the 2009 elections, covering the street protests. In Zimbabwe the democratic opposition has resisted Robert Mugabe's regime and its monopoly of information sources in rural regions by e-mailing daily news bulletins to other rural sites, where they are printed and distributed by children on bicycles. In Russia, the Netherlands, and Argentina, alternative media – such as *The Atlantic* – have surpassed many traditional news organizations by posting round-the-clock updates about global affairs. It is believed that alternative media are increasingly removing journalism from professionals employed by commercial organizations. Instead control is handed over to the audience. This dramatic shift in news production and dissemination provides that audience with platforms that foster a dialogue rather than a monologue. Blogs have excited both public and scholarly interest, with utopian claims that they can transform passive media users into active media producers. The desire to tell one's story to the world, to write about one's personal experiences, or to give one's opinions on world events through a blog site has become a favourite media practice. In many ways, then, the internet has become as much about interacting with others as about accessing information. However, there is some evidence that this optimism is misplaced. The power relations present in an offline world also appear online, and the dialogue, even though freer and more interactive, still resembles the rhetoric to be found in most offline public spheres.

The Mass Media and Symbolic Social Reality

In his book *Public Opinion* (1922), Walter Lippmann described an island where a handful of French, English, and German people lived in harmony just before the First World War. A British mail steamer provided their only link with the outside world. One day, the ship brought news that the English and French had been fighting the Germans for over six weeks. For those six weeks the islanders – technically enemies – had acted as friends, trusting the 'pictures in their heads'. Lippmann's simple but important point is that we must distinguish between reality (the outside world of actual events) and social reality (our mediated knowledge of those events), because we think and behave based not on what truly is but on what is perceived to be. Three decades after Lippmann put forward his idea of these 'pictures in our heads', a genuine investigation began into how the pictures we receive and interpret from the media differ from the world outside; in other words, how the media represent reality. The importance of the mass media as sources for those 'pictures in our heads' leads us to question how closely the media world actually resembles the world outside. The extent to which we see the mass media as distorting the real world depends on how we think the media should act.

The media and the construction of social reality

Following the work of Lippmann, scholars now largely accept that reality is socially and culturally constructed, understood and mediated. The mass media are one of the critical agents in this social construction of reality. Media content may be based on what happens in the physical world, but it singles out and highlights certain elements over others. Reality is necessarily manipulated when events and people are relocated into news or prime-time stories. In doing so, the media can emphasize certain behaviours and stereotype people. One of the most obvious ways in which media content structures a symbolic environment is simply by giving greater attention (more time, space, prominence, etc.) to certain events, people, groups, and places than others. The media can thus be used to manufacture consent, legitimize political positions, or cultivate a particular worldview. This is defined as the 'CNN effect' – the ability of television pictures to influence people so powerfully that important military and political decisions are driven by those pictures rather than by policies (Robinson, 1999). In some instances, a nation may decide to support a decision to go to war with another country where they have never been and about which they have a very limited knowledge except for what they have learned from the mass media. This is not new, as shown by the example of the Spanish–American war at the beginning of the twentieth century being propelled by an unsubstantiated US media report (from the then media mogul William Randolph Hearst) that the battleship *Maine* had been blown up by a Spanish mine in Havana (Robinson, 1996). Today, however, the potential for distortion is magnified by the mass media's greater reach and prominence.

Media mediation is also evident in the pervasiveness of celebrities in the media. Coverage of celebrities now dominates magazines, televisions, and newspapers. Magazines and specialist 'insider' television programmes routinely present detailed information about celebrities' personal lives and everyday routines – romantic involvements, shopping habits, trips, leisure activities, and family issues – rather than their professional lives. In Brazil, for example, even though the fascination with celebrities is a relatively new phenomenon, the growing number of media outputs dedicated to fame, such as reality programmes, talk shows, websites, and magazines, has greatly increased the number of celebrities in the national market (Turner, 1994). Among Brazil's 15 weekly magazines in 2008, ten had mainly a celebrity-oriented content. As such, the media have a fundamental role in the construction of the famous: models, entertainers, athletes, hair stylists, fashion designers, as well as anyone directly related to them, such as spouses, children, and even pets.

The media play a crucial role in constructing reality, particularly one that we have no direct access to. Tuchman (1978) analysed the role of news in the construction of social reality. In her view, news is simultaneously a record and a product of social reality. The final news story contains only part of the actual event covered, but in the eyes of a reader, viewer, or listener it is timely and accurate. Had it not appeared as a news item, it might have had no reality for the audience. At the same time, audiences make their own meaning in order for a story to make sense to them. Thus, the news source is socially constructed as a reliable basis upon which assumptions of truthfulness are made. Dayan and Katz (1992) discussed the role of different media events in

Photo 11.2
Thousands of reporters were at the Beijing 2008 Olympics.
Copyright © Yang Xia. Used with permission.

the creation of reality. *Media events* are large-scale interruptions of everyday life, when all the media attend to one event and ceremonially mark it (e.g. coverage of the Olympic Games). In August 2008, television coverage of the Beijing Olympic Games broke all previous records for Olympics coverage. According to the International Olympic Committee, the Beijing Olympics attracted 21,600 accredited journalists, including 16,000 broadcasters and 5,600 writers and photographers. From 8 August to 24 August 2008, they sent news, pictures, and stories to millions of viewers around the globe. These media events, in Dayan and Katz's (1992: 207, 211) terms, have the quality of 'a civil religion' and 'electronic monuments'.

Research on media effects

Research on media effects is central to understanding the role of the media in constructing social reality and in understanding how audiences make meanings out of different media products. When the mass media emerged in full force at the beginning of the nineteenth century, questions about the impact of the media on public opinion, individual beliefs, and political structures began. Concerns over the potential political and cultural power of the mass media, and the desire to quantify media effects on audience and society, are therefore not only a product of recent globalization but also have historically accompanied the phenomenon of the mass media (Couldry, 2000).

Audience analysis

Audience analysis deals with audience tastes, preferences, habits, and demographics. This type of analysis studies why, say, we like particular radio programmes more than others or why the American television show *Desperate Housewives* is so popular around the world. One of the most commonly applied models for audience research is *uses and gratifications theory,* first formulated in the 1940s. Uses and gratifications theory ask the question: 'What do people do with the mass media?' rather than 'What do the mass media do to people?' Herzog (see Rubin, 1986) studied the gratifications that women listeners received from radio daytime serials, and drew the conclusion that there were three main categories: emotional release, wishful thinking, and advice seeking. Morley (1980) analysed media texts to determine the 'preferred' meaning of the text, and interviewed viewers from different social backgrounds to determine how and why people found the preferred meaning in the text. In a more recent study, Morley (2000) interviewed families about their television viewing to reveal the impact of gender on power over the remote-control, programme choice, viewing style, and the amount of viewing. In his study, men and women offered different accounts of their viewing habits, in terms of their power to choose what and how much they viewed and their viewing styles. Audience studies have been crucial in promoting the idea that audiences are not passive but active agents in media consumption. People make their own choices about what they do when consuming media products.

Audience studies have also been highly influential in studying media effects on immigrants. Immigrants have always been quick to use the mass media in order to reduce the geographic and spatial distances between the host country and their home country. While radio, video recorders, and films once served as the primary tool of maintaining contact with immigrants' culture of origin, it has now become commonplace to find personal websites for immigrant communities (or diasporas), where images of the homeland are presented and important information about it is relayed to family and friends. Ethnic newspapers have also become popular as our world becomes more multicultural. Kolar-Panov's (1997) research on the use of VCRs and video letters among the Croatian and Macedonian communities in Australia showed the role of the media in framing

immigrants' cultures. News of the horrific events occurring in the former Yugoslavia, received by immigrants through these diasporic channels, influenced the nature of their close homeland connections. Naficy (1993) explored the ways in which Iranian refugees in Los Angeles made use of television programmes both to reflect on their existence in a new culture and to nostalgically remember the Iran they left behind. Robins (1996) studied second generation Turks in Italy and found that they modelled themselves on neither the home nor the host culture, since they watched Turkish, German, European, and African television programmes alike. Liu (2006) found that Chinese ethnic media played a significant role in Chinese immigrants' perception of themselves and of mainstream culture in Australia.

Photo 11.3
Chinese ethnic newspapers published weekly in Brisbane are accessible to Chinese communities free of charge.
Copyright © Shuang Liu. Used with permission.

Media effects on perceptions of social reality

At the beginning of the First World War, the image of the media as all powerful gradually evolved in the assertion of their power to persuade citizens to do just about anything. The *magic bullet theory* claims that the mass media have a direct, immediate, and powerful effect on a passive mass audience. Other scholars argue that the media influence masses of people indirectly, through a *two-step flow* of communication. The first stage is the direct transmission of information to a small group of people who stay well-informed (opinion leaders). In the second stage, those opinion leaders interpret and pass on the messages to less directly involved members of society (followers). The two-step flow model later evolved into a *multi-step flow model,* which claims that information that flows in a culture or group actually is filtered through a series of opinion leaders before reaching all other segments of that group or culture.

Theory Corner

Cultivation theory

George Gerbner's cultivation theory postulates a relationship between heavy television viewing and people's worldview. Specifically, he suggests that exposure to vast amounts of violence on the screen conditions viewers to see the world as an unkind and frightening place. For almost two decades, he headed an extensive research programme that monitored the level of violence on television, classified people according to how much TV they watched, and compiled viewers' perceptions of risk and other socio-cultural attitudes. His cultivation explanation of the findings is one of the most cited and debated theories of mass communication (Griffin, 2006).

Like McLuhan, Gerbner regards television as the dominant force in shaping modern society. But unlike McLuhan, who views the medium as the message, Gerbner believes that television's power comes from the symbolic content of the real-life drama frequently broadcast on television. In his view, the TV set is a key member of the household, with virtually unlimited access to every person in the family. It dominates the symbolic environment, telling most of our stories most of the time.

Reference

Griffin, Erin (2006) *A First Look at Communication Theory* (6th edn). Boston, MA: McGraw-Hill.

Further reading on cultivation effects

Skeggs, Bev; Thumim, Nancy and Wood, Helen (2008) '"Oh goodness, I am watching reality TV": how methods make class in audience research', *European Journal of Cultural Studies,* 11 (1): 5–24.

Media effects on agenda-setting

Researchers on *agenda-setting* propose that has the mass media focus our attention on certain aspects of life, and in doing so, set the agenda for us. Agenda-setting scholars claim that while the media definitely do not have the power to tell audiences specifically what to think, they are able to tell audiences what to think about (Newbold, 1995). As Robinson (1999) suggests, the most useful way to conceptualize the CNN effect is to view it as an agenda-setting agency. Muhamed Sacirbey, Bosnian ambassador to the United Nations, once remarked: 'If you look at how humanitarian relief is delivered in Bosnia you see that those areas where the TV cameras are most present are the ones that are the best fed, the ones that receive the most medicines. While on the other hand, many of our people have starved and died of disease and shelling where there are no TV cameras' (Seib, 1997: 90). When images of starvation, anarchy, and human misery appear on television screens, television becomes the de facto 'must-do-something' framework for everyone, including international policy makers.

Theory Corner

Agenda-setting theory

Journalism professors Maxwell McCombs and Donald Shaw proposed agenda-setting theory in the 1970s. They believed that the mass media had the ability to transfer the salience of items on their news agendas to the public agenda (McCombs and Shaw, 1972). The theory has two interconnected points: it affirms the power of the press while still maintaining that ultimately individuals are free to choose. Like the initial Erie County voting studies conducted by Paul Lazarsfeld and his team, the focus of agenda-setting is on election campaigns. The theory argues that there is a cause-and-effect relationship between media content and voters' perceptions. Although they did not use the largely superseded magic bullet conception of media influence, McCombs and Shaw ascribed to broadcast and print journalism the significant power to set the public's political agendas. Over the past decades, numerous empirical studies have been conducted to test the match between the media's agenda and the public's agenda. Some studies support the hypothesis, whereas others find that the media affect the salience of some issues for some people only some of the time.

Reference

McCombs, Maxwell and Shaw, Donald (1972) 'The agenda-setting function of the mass media', *Public Opinion Quarterly*, 36: 176–187.

Further reading on agenda-setting

Cho, Hiromi and Lacy, Stephen (2000) 'International conflict coverage in Japanese local daily newspapers', *Journalism and Mass Communication Quarterly*, 77 (4): 830–845.

Media effects on identity construction

The mass media play an important role in forming our identities. At an individual level, through the media we cultivate values and lifestyles; we are reminded of the sharp contrast between rich and poor; and we are provided with social models for our behaviour. Television, for example, shapes our perceptions and expectations of how life should be lived and which group we should identify with. The rich drive expensive foreign cars, wear designer clothes, and patronize expensive pubs and five-star hotels, a lifestyle that is beyond the imagination of someone living in a village in Indian. The mass media bring images of these people to us and thus function as a powerful tool of education to shape our identities, lifestyles, and values.

Scholars have explored the important role of the mass media in the historical development of national cultures and identities (see Morley and Robins, 1995). Media and cultural production have a key role in reconstituting national, religious, gender, and ethnic identities. The influential work of Anderson (1983) proposed that print capitalism was essential in promoting the creation of national imagined communities. The widespread dissemination of newspapers and novels creates an awareness of the 'steady, anonymous, simultaneous experience' of communities of national readers. The notion of simultaneity in time and a clearly defined national space is crucial to the construction of national consciousness today. Newspapers connect dispersed citizens with the land, people, and discourses of a nation. The ritual of reading the newspaper or watching the national news on TV continues to be an essential element in the construction of a national community.

In addition, most countries treat broadcasting as a national public resource with a unique responsibility to represent and support the national culture. A classic example is the British Broadcasting Corporation (BBC), known for its balanced and high-quality programming that reflects a diversity of subject, equality in representation, and independence from outside governmental, religious, or commercial influence. However, the belief in a singular national identity that is itself based on a culture, religion, and way of life that we all belong to is changing. As the world becomes more multicultural it is very difficult to hold on to a single, essential, national identity. Today, we belong to a world that is a vast cultural market from which we can pick and choose our preferences for music, fashion, food, and so on. We belong to many subcultural groups and hence we have multiple identities.

The Mass Media and Cultural Change

That the reality presented by the media is a socially constructed one has two important implications: first, we can understand the media as a debating ground for our system of values and beliefs; second, we can think of media effects not as simple, direct effects but as a much wider part of the cultural fabric (Dodd, 1998). The mass media affect us not just at the individual level but also at the social level. The mass media influence cultural change through cultural learning.

The mass media and cultural learning

The media create awareness

The mass media serve an awareness function, creating interest in an event or idea by reporting its existence (Dodd, 1998). Such was the case with the Bali bombing in 2005, which brought instant world attention to the perceived terrorist threat to Australia. Similarly, the coverage of H1N1 flu drew attention to public hygiene and brought great changes to people's behaviour in all parts of the world.

The media set agendas

The mass media set an agenda by drawing the public's attention to certain events or issues (Dodd, 1998). Agenda-setting can be achieved by giving prominence to certain people, events, or places through media coverage. Agenda-setting inevitably occurs because the media must be selective in reporting news and other events. It is impossible to report on every newsworthy event. News outlets, as gate-keepers of information, make choices about what to report and how to report it. Thus what the public knows about current affairs at a time is largely a product of media gate-keeping. For example, the extensive coverage in the Australian media of the plight of struggling pensioners made this issue a public priority and policy makers had to address the ensuing public concern.

The media promote stereotypes

Most people rely on the mass media to form perceptions of others with whom they do not have regular interpersonal contact. Thus, the media play a major role in forming and maintaining stereotypes. The media can create and reinforce stereotypes regarding old age, sexuality, religion, war, parenthood, and myriad other aspects of human life. News programmes can help to erase misunderstandings on issues vulnerable to stereotyping. Conversely, entertainment in movies, theatres, and television may inadvertently reinforce negative stereotypes. In response, there have been conscious efforts from various parts of society to eradicate sexism and negative male and female stereotypes, particularly from television and books. The representation of ethnic minorities has also been the subject of considerable attention and research. For instance, studies have found that when ethnic minorities are present in news reports, they tend to be linked to violence, gambling, crime, or alcoholism. Consequently the image of African-Americans, Hispanics, Asians, Muslims, and other minority groups has been harmed by negative stereotypes in the media.

The media accelerate change

The mass media serve as accelerators for change, creating a climate in which change can more easily occur (Dodd, 1998). For example, what we regard as elements of a healthy lifestyle have changed considerably over the years, not least because of government-sponsored advertising campaigns against smoking and drink driving but promoting healthy eating. In the same way, the mass news coverage of issues like global warming, climate change, and the energy crisis has functioned as an accelerator for changes in people's behaviour, evident in the current concern for energy consumption and the preservation of natural resources.

The mass media and intercultural communication

By looking at examples of how the media and culture interrelate, we can understand the importance of the media in the intercultural communication context and be aware of the need to develop skills in understanding the media and culture.

- *Be conscious of ways in which the media may have affected your perceptions of a particular group.* The mass media can promote positive or negative stereotypes. We need to keep up to date about current events and understand the source of our personal feelings. This can assist you in your intercultural communication.
- *Use the media as a tool for understanding culture.* The mass media can open our eyes to what is considered important in a culture. We cannot personally experience some cultures fully, but we may have an opportunity to interact with people from those cultures. Learning the agenda of a culture can improve our understanding of that culture and hence assist us in interacting with its members.
- *Broaden our background knowledge.* We need a broad knowledge of cultures other than our own. A common criticism of recent mass communication or journalism graduates is that they lack the background knowledge to carry out anything more than a superficial interview. Your articles will be superficial or incorrect or even offensive if you do not have an understanding of the influence of the culture and context within which the reported events occurred.

Summary

This chapter focused on the impact of globalization and technology on the mass media and the role of the media in shaping communication, identities, and culture. It explained the impact of globalization and technology on mass media and how the mass media shape people's thinking, doing, identities, and communication. We live in a media-saturated society, where almost every aspect of our life is influenced by the mass media. Advances in communication technologies have enabled the internationalization of media products, reducing the geographic distance between countries, people, and cultures. However, we cannot automatically equate technology with the transformation and emancipation of society. Simply giving computers to marginalized people, for example, does not necessarily make their voices heard or their faces seen. The same mass media that inform us of events across the world can also distort our perception of social reality.

This chapter also illustrated the influence of the mass media on cultural change, and suggested skills to better understand the relationship between the mass media and culture. The media can promote social learning by giving prominence to certain issues, people, and places. On the other hand, the media can also promote stereotypes of disadvantaged groups, including women and ethnic minorities. To promote an intercultural understanding, we must appreciate the impact of the mass media in shaping our perception, thinking, and behaviour, and make conscious efforts to use the media as a tool for understanding other cultures.

Case Study:
OhMyNews in South Korea

The online newspaper *OhMyNews* was set up by journalist Oh Yeon-Ho in February 2000 and has since been very successful. It has been included in 'hybrid' types of media, meaning that it incorporates print and electronic forms. While South Korea today is a democracy, most middle-aged Koreans have lived through dictatorships and years of political unrest. Rapid industrialization has changed South Korea into one of the world's fastest-growing economies; the embrace of new technologies, particularly the internet, has been phenomenal. South Korea is the most connected society in the world today, with broadband connections in 83 per cent of households. Hence, the success of *OhMyNews* is in its high level of connectivity. But there are other reasons for its success, both social and political.

The politics and media of South Korea are known for their relative conservativeness. For many years alternative news, opinions, and dissenting views were not tolerated, and dissenting journalists were imprisoned. While South Korean university students played a key role in opposing successive dictatorships, these regimes were supported with the aid of South Korea's key ally, the USA (which continues to maintain a large military base there), thus providing a formidable task for those who wanted political change. In 2002, two years after the establishment of *OhMyNews*, two schoolgirls were run over by a US armoured carrier. While the mainstream media ignored the story, *OhMyNews* picked it up and called for a popular protest. The anti-US protest became the largest in Korean history and, more importantly, the mainstream media were forced to pay attention to what had then become the key story in South Korea. Similarly, in December of that same year, presidential elections were held in the country. While the mainstream media favoured the more conservative candidates, the more left-wing Millennium party candidate Roh Moo-Hyun was given less space, even though he came from the governing party at the time. *OhMyNews* strongly supported his candidature, providing online space for discussions of the merits of South Korean politics, corruption, the role of industrial and media monopolies, and the need for social change in Korea. The platform that this online newspaper gave to Roh Moo-Hyun invariably contributed to his victory; he was strongly supported by younger voters, who are among the main consumers of *OhMyNews*. The first interview that he gave after his win was to *OhMyNews*.

Some of the achievements of *OhMyNews* are the following:

1 It has provided a platform for democratic dissent in a context in which dissent is frowned upon. The 'Net' has been turned into a public space, available to all for discussion, debate, and popular action. It gives opportunities for ordinary people to write their version of the news, thus liberating and empowering those people. More than 33,000 'netizens' contribute to *OhMyNews*. This type of participation enables people not only to contribute to news production but also to play a role in deciding which news is important. *OhMyNews* stories include sports and politics, but also stories told by its reader/producers about their lives.

2 This empowerment has resulted in the beginning of a potent social movement under 'anyone can be a journalist'. This is the recognition that new technologies, in particular the internet, have the potential to break down the barriers between professional journalists – who have been the opinion makers, gate-keepers, and keepers of journalistic norms – and ordinary people, who were previously just consumers of news. Just as the Middle Eastern satellite broadcaster Al Jazeera has provided alternatives to both Western and Middle-East-based media, *OhMyNews* has given the internet generation in South Korea a new media choice. 'Our main concept is the citizen reporter,' says Oh. 'Our second concept is: Please communicate in your style; if it is convenient for you, that's fine. Don't just follow the professional reporters.'

3 The existence of *OhMyNews* and other alternative news sources is a threat to controlled media monopolies and their power to censor those who are outside the political establishment. Today *OhMyNews* is among the six most influential media outlets in Korea. It has helped its readers to recognize that they have the power to make their elected representatives, public servants, and industrial houses accountable. It has contributed to making South Korean politics transparent, with thousands of netizens now having the opportunity to discuss the latest corruption scandal or government action.

4 It has added to the credibility of news and helped it to strike a chord with the younger generation who have been, to some extent, ignored by the mainstream media. Young people in South Korea often resent established media structures and practices. They appreciate the freedom that *OhMyNews* gives them and use it to their own advantage.

5 *OhMyNews* is an example of new media blazing a new trail. It is an alternative to old media, and some would say that it has helped to replace print media (e.g. newspapers) whose circulation the world over is in decline. In this sense, *OhMyNews* is the future.

References for case study

OhMyNews International [online]. Accessed 25 May 2008 at http://english. ohmynews.com

Personal communication with Pradip Thomas in the School of Journalism and Communication at the University of Queensland, Australia. Used with permission.

Questions for discussion

1 Do you believe that you must be in mainstream journalism in order to speak to the public, or do you think one needs to join alternative types of media to successfully reach your audience?
2 Do you think *OhMyNews* is a type of hybrid media?
3 Do new technologies bring with them only positive change? What are their costs and benefits?
4 Do you believe that a project like *OhMyNews* could be successful in your society? Why or why not?
5 How do you define blogging? Do you regularly read any blogs or alternative media sources, such as *OhMyNews*? How would you evaluate the credibility of such media outlets?

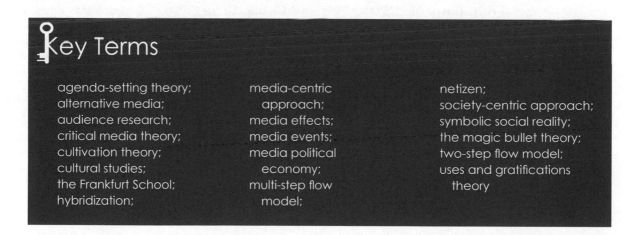

Key Terms

agenda-setting theory;
alternative media;
audience research;
critical media theory;
cultivation theory;
cultural studies;
the Frankfurt School;
hybridization;

media-centric approach;
media effects;
media events;
media political economy;
multi-step flow model;

netizen;
society-centric approach;
symbolic social reality;
the magic bullet theory;
two-step flow model;
uses and gratifications theory

Further Reading

Cultural studies

Ang, Ien (1998) 'Doing cultural studies at the crossroads: local/global negotiations', *European Journal of Cultural Studies*, 1 (1): 13–31.

Turner, Graeme (2005) 'Cultural identity, soap narrative, and reality TV', *Television & New Media*, 6 (4): 415–422.

Volčič, Zala and Erjavec, Karmen (2008) 'Technological developments in Central-Eastern Europe: a case-study of a computer literacy project in Slovenia', *Information Communication & Society*, 11 (3): 326–347.

Globalization, homogenization, and hybridization

Featherstone, Mike (1990) 'Global culture: an introduction', *Theory, Culture and Society*, 7 (1): 1–15.
Kellner, Douglas (1989) *Critical Theory, Marxism, and Modernity*. Cambridge and Baltimore: Polity and Johns Hopkins University Press.
Kraidy, Marwan M. (2002) 'Hybridity in cultural globalization', *Communication Theory*, 12 (3): 316–339.

Media representation and media effects

Becker, An (2004) 'Television, disordered eating and young women in Fiji: negotiating body image and identity during rapid social change', *Culture, Medicine and Psychiatry*, 28: 533–559.
Cho, Hiromi and Lacy, Stephen (2000) 'International conflict coverage in Japanese local daily newspapers', *Journalism and Mass Communication Quarterly*, 77 (4): 830–845.
Frith, Katherine; Shaw, Ping and Cheng, Hong (2005) 'The construction of beauty: a cross-cultural analysis of women's magazine advertising', *Journal of Communication*, 55 (1): 56–70.
Peck, Janice (1993) 'Selling goods and selling God: advertising, televangelism and the commodity form', *Journal of Communication Inquiry*, 17 (1): 5–24.
Skeggs, Bev; Thumim, Nancy and Wood, Helen (2008) '"Oh goodness, I am watching reality TV": how methods make class in audience research', *European Journal of Cultural Studies*, 11 (1): 5–24.

12

Immigration and Acculturation

We may have different religions, different languages, different colored skin, but we all belong to one human race.

Kofi Annan, Ghanian diplomat, 7th UN Secretary-General, 1938–

Learning Objectives

At the end of this chapter, you should be able to:

- Understand immigration as a major contributor to cultural diversity.
- Define diaspora, migrancy, and transnationalism.
- Describe the stages of culture shock and acculturation orientations.
- Identify the factors that influence cross-cultural adaptation.
- Develop communication strategies to facilitate cross-cultural adaptation.

Immigration and Cultural Diversity

Our society is becoming more culturally and ethnically diverse. An important contributor to cultural diversity is immigration. Advances in technology, modern transportation facilities, telecommunication, and international business transactions have made it much easier for people to travel and live in other countries. Globalization not only redefines the movements and mobility of people in contemporary societies but also delineates new parameters for interpreting immigration. Historically, immigration was conceptualized as the restricted cross-border movements of people, emphasizing the permanent relocation and settlement of usually unskilled, often indentured or contracted labour or people who were displaced by political turmoil and thus had little option other than resettlement in a new country. Today, growing affluence and the emergence of a new group of skilled or educated people have fuelled a new global movement of migrants who are in search of better economic opportunities, an enhanced quality of life, greater freedom, and higher expectations. These people form an integral part of the immigrant population today – skilled migrants. Relocated into the legal and political institutions of the host culture, migrants aspire to a higher quality of life, a good education for themselves or their children, the freedom to be their own boss, autonomy in their choice of work, and prosperity.

Although the reasons for migrating vary, all immigrants face the same task of moving between their ethnic group and the mainstream cultural group of their new country. Acculturation, a process whereby immigrants are integrated into the host cultural environment, is essential to being able to move between two cultures effectively as the circumstances and situations demand. This capability not only involves a mental reconciliation of sometimes incompatible pressures for both assimilation into the mainstream and differentiation from it, but also is important for immigrants' economic survival in a host country. Ien Ang (2001: 34), a cultural studies scholar, states that while migrants derive a sense of belonging from their identification with their homeland, they are also fully aware that 'this very identification with an imaged "where you're from" is also a sign of, and surrender to, a condition of actual marginalization in the place "where you're at".' Immigrants' ability to achieve a sense of place in the host country, where they feel somewhat 'out of place' at least upon arrival, is crucial to their psychological and social well-being.

Living in a multicultural society is a long educational process, in which tensions between host and home cultures are constantly evident. In order to maximize the benefits of cultural diversity, a country that embraces a multicultural policy must still be aware of the potential threats such a policy poses to cultural uniqueness. Around the world, host nationals express concerns about the threat that incoming ethnic cultures pose to mainstream cultural values, the existing political and economic power structure, and the distribution of employment opportunities. Migrants everywhere, on the other hand, form associations to maintain their ethnic and cultural heritages and promote the survival of their languages within mainstream institutions. For example, in both Germany and France, there is growing anxiety about the withdrawal of immigrant groups into their home cultures and their increasing unwillingness to integrate into the host culture. Situations like this raise questions for all multicultural nations. Does multiculturalism pose a threat to cultural identity? Do host nationals and immigrants view multiculturalism as equally beneficial? What do immigrants believe that they should do to acculturate into a host country? Is this understanding shared by host nationals? Our understanding of what multiculturalism means influences our acculturation strategies.

This chapter concentrates on immigration and acculturation. We first define and explain the terms 'diaspora', 'migrancy', and 'transnationalism'. Current practices in relation to transnationalism, migrancy, immigration, and identity are reviewed so as to explore the concepts and analyse their strengths and weaknesses. Next, we discuss the concept of multiculturalism and its differentiated benefits for host nationals and immigrants. The term 'acculturation' is defined and the stages of culture shock explained. This chapter also identifies the personal, social, and political factors that predict acculturation outcomes. Finally, it concludes with a discussion on communication strategies for facilitating cross-cultural adaptation.

Migration and Globalization

Human migration is more than one million years old and continues in response to complex human cultural and existential circumstances. The concept of migration contains emigration and immigration, which both involve spatial and social transformations. In modern times, profound changes in the world's political and economic order have generated large movements of people in almost every region. Viewed in a global context, the total world population of immigrants – that is, people living outside their country of birth or citizenship – is huge. Massey and Taylor (2004: 1) wrote that if these people, estimated at some 160 million, were united in a single country they would 'create a nation of immigrants'.

Trends of migration: past, present, and future

Geographical mobility has consistently characterized the lives of populations in all historical eras. For example, following the lifting of restrictions on race-based immigration in the 1950s and 1960s, Asians and Africans began to migrate in large numbers to North America, Australasia, and Europe. There has also been substantial migration from Latin America into the United States and significant labour migration into newly industrialized nations such as South Korea, Malaysia, and Singapore during the 1970s and 1980s (Brubaker, 2001). In Europe, the countries with the highest emigration rates until 1960 were Italy, Spain, Portugal, the former Yugoslavia, and Greece (Vukeljic, 2008).

There is a widespread consensus among migration scholars that it was not until the 1980s that migration came to be one of the most important factors of global change (Castles, 2000). According to a report from the International Organization for Migration (2006), the number of international migrants was thought to have reached between 185 and 192 million in 2005, an upward trend that is likely to continue. Most countries are affected by a range of migratory phenomena, such as labour migration, refugees, and permanent settlement. A salient feature of the Asia–Pacific system in recent years is the increasing scale and significance of female migration (Ehrenreich and Russell-Hochschild, 2002). For example, a growing number of immigrant domestic workers are from the Philippines, Indonesia, and Sri Lanka (International Organization for Migration, 2006). Migration impacts not only the migrants themselves, but also the receiving societies.

Diaspora, migrancy, and transnationalism

The term 'diaspora' is based on the Greek terms *speiro*, meaning 'to sow', and the preposition *dia,* meaning 'over'. The Greeks used diaspora to mean migration and colonization. In Hebrew, the term initially referred to the settling of scattered colonies of Jews outside Palestine after the Babylonian exile, and then came to have a more general connotation of people settled away from their ancestral homeland. The meaning of diaspora has shifted over time and now refers not only to traditional migrant groups, such as Jews, but also to much wider communities comprised of voluntary migrants living in more than one culture. For example, in 2000 there were an estimated five million Philippine citizens living in over 160 countries (Ehrenreich and Russell-Hochschild, 2002). Diasporas are not temporary; they are lasting communities. They differentiate themselves from their new environment, identify themselves with other members of diasporas through a network of symbols and meanings, and form an 'imagined community' (Anderson, 1983). Such a community maintains the identification of members outside the national borders of space and time in order to live within the new environment (Clifford, 1997).

The concepts of migrancy and transnationalism are intertwined. *Migrancy* highlights movement, so that greater attention is paid to movement in both space and time in transnational practices. Basch et al. (1994) defined *transnationalism* as the process by which migrants forge and sustain multi-stranded social relations that link together their societies of origin and settlement. Many immigrants today build social networks that cross geographic, cultural, and political borders. For example, ethnic business entrepreneurs in Australia maintain close ties with their ethnic group, because bonds of solidarity within the ethnic community provide resources for business operations as they establish and develop these businesses (Dyer and Ross, 2000). In addition, ethnic communities may be a source of intangible assets such as values, knowledge, and networks upon which ethnic business people may draw (Greene, 1997). However, clientele from the ethnic community alone are insufficient to sustain ethnic businesses. To survive in a competitive market in a host country, ethnic businesses have to expand their target customers to include the mainstream group. Those who present themselves well in both cultural contexts can reap the financial reward from drawing upon a wider clientele. Immigrants who develop and maintain multiple relationships – familial, economic, social, organizational, religious, and political – that span borders are referred to as *transmigrants*.

Sociologists generally focus on the receiving end of immigration, while anthropologists tend to work at both ends of the immigration process, beginning in the country of birth and asking what prompts individuals to leave particular communities, what happens to them in their place of origin, and how they remain connected to their former homeland. While sociological and anthropological approaches appear to differ in their methodologies, they do not differ in their outcomes; both fields have developed 'push-and-pull theories' in an attempt to explain the reasons, selectivity, flow, and scope of migration (Kearney, 1995). For example, predominant push factors include economic stagnation, declining living standards, a reduction in national resources, a low personal income, unemployment, political and other discrimination, political persecution, alienation, and natural disasters. On the other hand, the principal pull factors are economic prosperity, education, appropriate employment, and a higher income.

As Østergaard-Nielsen (2003) observed, immigration is no longer considered a one-way or two-way journey. Instead, immigrants bridge here and there by continuously coming or going, or by engaging economically, socially, or politically in their home country while residing abroad. In essence, sociological and anthropological approaches appear to agree that immigrants do not make a sharp break with their homeland; for example, they continue to observe ethnic festivals or religious practices while living in the host culture.

Photo 12.1
On the first of Syawal in the Muslim calendar, the Muslim community in Brisbane gather for prayer after fasting for a whole month during Ramadhan.
Copyright © Abdul Lattif Ahmed. Used with permission.

Identity reconstruction for immigrants

Migrancy and transnationalism necessitate the reconsideration and reconstruction of identity. The difficulty that confronts immigrants in terms of how they reconstruct their identity in order to fit in with the new society has been extensively researched and commented on in the scholarly literature. For example, the *melting-pot* ideal used to be the dominating discourse of immigrant identity in Australia and the United States. People with this ideal take the view that national identity should be an amalgam of cultures – a melting pot – so that differences between 'us' and 'them' are reduced, in the hope that 'we' become more like 'them' and 'they' see us as less alien and more like 'them' (Zubrzycki, 1997). Over time has come the realization that a multitude of ethnic cultures can coexist in a given environment, retaining their original heritage while functioning in the mainstream culture. This has led to a change of perspective from the melting pot to the *salad bowl* to depict contemporary American society (Ogden et al., 2004). Similarly, Canada has been described as a mosaic of cultural groups, to reflect the distinguishable constituent parts of the multiple cultures there.

The survival of ethnicity has directed scholars' attention towards understanding how immigrants integrate or switch between cultures. When immigrants interact with people from host cultures, they switch not only between languages but also between cultures. Central to this culture-switching process is the presentation of the self in terms of their relationships to the ingroup (their ethnic group) and outgroup (the mainstream culture group).

Connectedness to either their own ethnic group or the larger cultural group is not merely an affiliation between the self and others, but entails fundamental differences in the way the self is construed under different circumstances (Triandis, 1989). As Waters (1995: 3) stated, migrancy and transnationalism are the 'social process in which the constraints of geography and social and cultural arrangements recede and in which people become increasingly aware that they are receding'. In this process, the boundaries that used to define one's identities also recede.

Diversity and Multiculturalism

The increase in cultural diversity has led to the promotion of multiculturalism, which 'aims to achieve social cohesion through an environment where diverse cultures are recognized and valued' (Department of Premier and Cabinet, 2000: 4). The concepts of multiculturalism and diversity have captured the imagination of the public and scholars alike, suggesting reconfiguring economic arrangements, adjusting political systems, and a recasting of cultural identities.

Attitudes toward diversity and multiculturalism

Multiculturalism stresses the importance of recognizing cultural diversity within a given social and political environment. On the one hand, it promotes a multiethnic or multicultural coexistence; on the other, it can lead to group distinctions (Brewer, 1997) and threaten social cohesion (Berry, 2001). Berry and Kalin (1995) argue that groups were more in favour of multiculturalism when they see the advantages for themselves. The *ideological asymmetry hypothesis* (Sidanius and Pratto, 1999) suggests that hierarchy-attenuating ideologies such as multiculturalism appeal more to low-status groups than to high-status groups, because the existing status hierarchy tends to be more beneficial for members of high- rather than low-status groups. For minority and lower-status groups, multiculturalism offers the possibility of maintaining their own culture and at the same time obtaining a higher social status in society. Majority group members, on the other hand, may see ethnic minorities and their desire to maintain their own culture as a threat to mainstream cultural identity and their higher-status position. Thus, multiculturalism has more to offer to the less powerful than to the more powerful group.

Multiculturalism holds that a multitude of ethnic cultures can coexist in the mainstream or host culture and retain their original ethnic cultural heritage (Tadmor and Tetlock, 2006). But the question still remains – to what extent can immigrants maintain their access to ethnic language, religion, customs and traditions, and ethnic organizations without posing a threat to the overall political unity of the host society? Studies conducted with Asian immigrants in Australia showed that Asian immigrants tended to view multiculturalism as a greater benefit than did Anglo-Australians, who saw it as more of a threat (Liu, 2007). The perceived threat to one's own culture from another culture is one of the greatest stumbling blocks in intercultural relations (Stephan et al., 1999). Such fears interfere with diplomatic relations, business cooperation, and interpersonal relations between members of different cultures and can even lead to wars between nations. Such fears may also lead to prejudice by people in one culture against another. According to the *multicultural hypothesis*, confidence in one's cultural identity involves a sense of security, which is a psychological precondition for the acceptance of those who are culturally different (Berry et al., 1977). When people feel their cultural identity is threatened, they reject others. The extent to which members of the majority tolerate ethnic culture maintenance plays an important role in the construction of a truly multicultural society.

Theory Corner

Integrated threat theory

A significant amount of research indicates that perception of threat plays an important role in prejudice toward outgroups in general and immigrants in particular. Integrated threat theory, advanced by Walter G. Stephan and his associates (1999), identifies four domains of threat: realistic, symbolic, negative stereotypes, and intergroup anxiety. *Realistic threat* concerns a threat to the political and economic power and the well-being of the ingroup. Immigrants are likely to evoke such threat, as they need jobs and may also require additional resources from the host society. *Symbolic threat* concerns group differences in values, beliefs, morals, and attitudes, which may lead to prejudice against members of outgroups. *Negative stereotypes* serve as a basis for negative expectations concerning the behaviour of members of the stereotyped group. For example, when migrant group members are perceived to be untrustworthy, mainstream group members may feel threatened when interacting with them. The fourth type of threat, *intergroup anxiety*, refers to people's feeling of being personally threatened in intergroup interactions because they are concerned about negative outcomes for themselves, such as being embarrassed, rejected, or ridiculed. Interacting with immigrants is often difficult for people from the host culture because of differences in language and cultural values, and this adds to intergroup anxiety in interaction.

Reference

Stephan, Walter G.; Ybarra, Oscar and Bachman, Guy (1999) 'Prejudice toward immigrants', *Journal of Applied Social Psychology*, 29 (11): 2221–2237.

(Continued)

Further reading on integrated threat theory

Rohmann, Anette; Florack, Arnd and Piontkowski, Ursula (2006) 'The role of discordant acculturation attitudes in perceived threat: an analysis of host and immigrant attitudes in Germany', *International Journal of Intercultural Relations*, 30: 683–702.

Challenges faced by host nationals and immigrants

The arrival of immigrants as new settlers brings changes to the host cultural environment. As pointed out by Sayegh and Lasry (1993: 99), it is difficult 'to imagine a host society which would not be transformed after immigrants have been accepted as full participants into the social and institutional networks of that society'. Thus both the immigrant group and host nationals undergo psychological and sociological adjustment as a result of the presence of culturally distinctive others (Ward and Kennedy, 2001). Under some circumstances, a psychological adjustment for members of the majority may be even more difficult than that experienced by immigrants. The reason for this is that immigrants, in many cases, are aware of the need to adjust to their host cultural environment as soon as, if not well before, they set foot in that host country. The majority, however, are not likely to be so well-prepared to accept or adjust to the changes in their lives brought about by the immigrant population. Hence, in discussing multiculturalism it is important to take into consideration both the ethnic minority and the majority group because the lack of accommodating attitudes in either group may hamper the realization of a positively diverse and equal society.

Significant debate has surrounded the question of how immigrants should live in their host societies. In some countries, immigrants are increasingly seen as a source of social disturbance and economic burden, and opinion polls show unease with the growing visibility

Photo 12.2
Names of visitors from different parts of the world were painted in one street of Ubud in Indonesia – a symbol of multiculturalism. Copyright © Joan Burnett. Used with permission.

of foreign cultures. There seems to be no consistent framework for immigrant ethnic minorities to participate in the political and social life of European countries. Some European countries like Germany see immigrants mainly as temporary labour, whereas the traditional immigration countries including the United States and Canada see immigrants as permanent settlers (Hargreaves, 1995). Governments also differ in the degree of cultural diversity they are ready to accept. The 2004 French law banning the wearing of religious insignia in schools, for instance, is now in place, and there have been many heated public debates about the issue of the role of religion in the public sphere. In Western European countries such as the Netherlands and France, young Muslim women wearing the *hijab*, a headscarf that fully covers the hair and neck of Muslim women, have become the symbols of controversies (Vivian, 1999). Thus, the presence of visible multicultural symbols, such as ethnic shops and clothing, is not an indicator of a truly multicultural society unless there is both mutual acceptance and an equal societal participation by all groups.

Acculturation and Culture Shock

When immigrants come to live in a new culture, they have to learn to adapt to the new cultural environment. *Acculturation* refers to the changes that cultural groups undergo after being in contact over a period of time (Berry, 1986). Acculturation is often marked by physical and psychological changes that occur as a result of the adaptation required to function in a new and different cultural context.

Acculturation orientations

The most widely applied model of acculturation was developed by John Berry (1980, 1990). According to his model, immigrants are confronted with two basic issues: maintenance of their heritage culture and maintenance of relationships with the host society. On this continuum, acculturation orientations range from a positive value being placed on both the heritage and the new culture (integration); a negative value on the old and positive on the new (assimilation); a positive on the old and a negative on the new (separation); and a negative on both cultures (marginalization). For example, individuals who wish to maintain their ethnic traditions and at the same time become an integral part of the host society are *integrationists*. *Marginalization* refers to individuals devaluing their cultural heritage but not having significant psychological contact with the host society either. Marginalized people may feel as though they do not belong anywhere, or in a variant of this orientation they may reject an ethnic identity altogether as a valid source of self-esteem (Bourhis et al., 2007, refer to such people as *individualists*). *Assimilation* and *separation* both refer to rejecting one culture and living exclusively in the other. Many immigrants move between these orientations and over time will gravitate towards one, most commonly integration or assimilation. People adapting to new cultures face changes in their diet, climate, housing, communication, roles, social networks, norms, and values. The stress associated with such changes is called *acculturation stress*.

A shortcoming of Berry's original model is that it places the emphasis in acculturation on minority or immigrant groups, on the assumption that immigrants have the freedom to pursue the acculturation strategy they prefer in the host society. In reality, host-culture attitudes can exert a strong influence on how immigrants experience the acculturation process (Kosic et al., 2005). Like immigrants, members of a host society also develop acculturation attitudes (Rohmann et al., 2006). For them, acculturation centres on whether they want immigrants to maintain their heritage culture and whether they value intergroup contact. Their acculturation attitudes – in a model analogous to Berry's but referring to the host culture – are referred to as integration, assimilation, segregation, and individualism (Bourhis et al., 1997).

Discordance between majority and minority acculturation attitudes leads to stereotyping, prejudice, and discrimination (Zagefka and Brown, 2002). To overcome the limitations of the original model, Berry (2005) proposed a three-dimensional model including cultural maintenance, contact, and participation and the power to decide on how to acculturate. With the promotion of cultural diversity and multiculturalism, immigrants are more welcome to integrate into a host culture while maintaining ties with their own ethnic heritage. Integration has been found to be the most common acculturation strategy, while marginalization is usually the least preferred (Liu, 2006).

Integration offers immigrants the opportunity to keep their ethnic cultural practice while maintaining a positive relationship with a host society. Integration probably benefits immigrants most, as among other advantages it provides them with an opportunity to raise their lower social status. An important assumption of social identity theory is that membership in a high-status group is desirable because it contributes to a positive social identity (Hogg and Abrams, 1988). To maintain a positive self-concept derived from a satisfying social identity, individuals who belong to a group of subordinate status may either strive for a higher status by leaving their low-status group or try to upgrade the status position of their group as a whole (Tajfel, 1978). In the case of immigrants it is difficult, if not impossible, for them to upgrade the status position of their whole ethnic group. Efforts to achieve a positive social identity therefore are often focused on integrating into the host group rather than remaining as a member of the foreign outgroup. Evidence from previous research also indicates that the integration strategy is linked to good psychological adjustment, a sense of belonging, and a feeling of acceptance.

Culture shock

Culture shock refers to the feelings of disorientation and anxiety that a sojourner experiences when entering a new culture. It occurs in social interactions between sojourners and host nationals when familiar cultural norms and values governing behaviours are questioned in the new cultural environment (Furnham and Bochner, 1982). Culture shock is a psychological and social process that progresses in stages. For some people it may take several weeks to overcome psychological stress; for others the frustration of culture shock may last as long as a year. Symptoms of culture shock include depression, helplessness, anxiety, homesickness, confusion, irritability, isolation, intolerance, defensiveness, and withdrawal – all indicators of psychological stress.

Adler (1975) noted that culture shock progresses through several developmental stages. The most widely known model is the *U-curved model*. The initial stage of culture shock, usually called the *honeymoon stage*, is characterized by intense excitement associated with being somewhere different and unusual. The new arrival may feel euphoric and excited with all the new things encountered. The second stage is called *disintegration*, when frustration and stress begin to set in owing to the differences experienced in the new culture. The new environment requires a great deal of conscious energy that is not required in the old environment, which leads to cognitive overload and fatigue. Communication difficulties may occur. In this stage, there may be feelings of discontent, impatience, anger, sadness, and feelings of incompetence. The third stage of culture shock is called the *reorientation* or adjustment phase, which involves the reintegration of new cues and an increased ability to function in the new culture. Immigrants start to seek solutions to their problems. A sense of psychological balance may be experienced, which initiates an evaluation of the old ways versus the new. The fourth stage of culture shock is labelled the *adaptation* stage. In this stage, people become more comfortable in the new culture as it becomes more predictable; they actively engage in the culture with their new problem-solving and conflict resolution tools, with some success. The final stage is described as *biculturalism*, where people are able to cope comfortably in both the home and the new cultures. This stage is accompanied by a more solid feeling of belonging, as people have recovered from the symptoms of culture shock.

Culture shock can also be experienced by people who return to their native home country after an extended stay in a foreign culture. Such an experience is referred to as *reverse culture shock*. This type of culture shock may cause greater distress and confusion than the original shock experienced in the new culture. In reverse culture shock, the home culture is compared adversely to the admired aspects of the new culture. Research indicates that no one wants to admit that he or she is having difficulty readjusting to the home culture, so the re-entry process often involves suffering in silence. Upon first returning home, there is a sense of relief and excitement about being back in familiar surroundings, seeing old friends and family, and eating familiar food. However, to the surprise of everyone, especially the returning expatriate, a sense of depression and a negative outlook can follow the initial re-entry cycle. Several factors contribute to the downturn phase. First, upon re-entry to the home culture, there is feeling of need to search for an identity. Second, the home culture may look so negative at times that the re-entering person longs for the 'good old days' in the host country where he or she lived for the previous period. Third, the old values, beliefs, and ways of thinking and living, with which the person was once familiar, may have changed, resulting in a sense of loss or ambiguity. Finally, people too may have changed over the intervening years; thus resuming deep friendships with old friends may not be automatic or easy.

Cross-Cultural Adaptation

Regardless of their reasons for calling the new country home, all sojourners have to adapt to an unfamiliar cultural terrain. *Cross-cultural adaptation* refers to the process of increasing one's level of fitness in a new cultural environment (Kim, 1988). A number of factors can influence the level of anxiety, distress, and frustration experienced by sojourners or new immigrants, hence influencing cross-cultural adaptation outcomes.

Factors influencing cross-cultural adaptation process

Successful cross-cultural adaptation increases one's ability to function in the host culture and fosters a sense of belonging for immigrants or sojourners. Kim (1986, 1988) notes that one's background characteristics can influence acculturation. The following section extends Kim's (2001) work (see the Theory Corner below) by identifying additional factors that predict the outcomes of cross-cultural adaptation.

Theory Corner

The stress-adaptation-growth model

Communication scholar Young Y. Kim (2001) explains the intercultural adaptation process in a new culture in her stress-adaptation-growth model. According to this model, adaptation is a progressive series of positive and negative experiences, rather than a smooth, continuous process. This process can be pictured as a coiled spring, which stretches and grows but is pulled back by its own tension. Kim argues that acculturation is an interaction between the stranger and the host culture. Personal and social communication, the host environment, and individual predisposing factors are the central features of the acculturation process.

Personal communication refers to the individual's ability to use verbal and nonverbal codes to communicate in the host environment. *Social communication* refers to the interaction between the newcomer and host nationals. The *environment* includes the degree to which the host culture is receptive to strangers, the extent to which host nationals exert pressure on newcomers to conform to their culture's values, beliefs, and practices, and ethnic group strength. *Predisposing factors* include how much people know about their new culture, their ability to speak the language, the probability of employment, their understanding of the cultural institutions, and the characteristics that newcomers have regarding orientation change and personal resistance.

Reference

Kim, Young Y. (2001) *Becoming Intercultural: An Integrative Theory of Communication and Cross-Cultural Adaptation*. Thousand Oaks, CA: SAGE.

Further reading on cross-cultural adaptation

Arnold, Anne-Katrin and Schneider, Beate (2007) 'Communicating separation? Ethnic media and ethnic journalists as institutions of integration in Germany', *Journalism*, 8 (2): 115–136.

Miglietta, Anna and Tartaglia, Stefano (2009) 'The influence of length of stay, linguistic competence, and media exposure in immigrants' adaptation', *Cross-Cultural Research*, 43 (1): 46–61.

Similarity between the host and home cultures

The degree of similarity between the host and the home cultures of immigrants can predict the acculturation stress experienced by immigrants adapting to new cultures. For example, Sudanese immigrants in Australia exhibit significantly larger psychological and cultural distance as compared to those from New Zealand. In addition to physical appearance and language, cultural traits such as beliefs and values may also be used to set one group of immigrants apart from others. The early Chinese settlers in Australia in the 1840s, for example, were resented because they were efficient, hardworking, and economically competitive and were therefore viewed as a threat to the livelihoods of the European migrants (Ang, 2000). Increasing cultural distance encourages immigrants to remain psychologically located within their ethnic groups. This creates a challenge, particularly for ethnic business people who need to be accepted by both the co-ethnic and the mainstream groups in sustaining businesses and clientele.

Ethnic social support

Immigrants can extend their connection to their home culture through various types of ethnic associations, including religious groups. Ethnic community networks provide valuable support for immigrants in adjusting to a new culture. For example, previous research has identified social networks as a critical part of the entrepreneurial activities of immigrants in many countries

(Light and Gold, 2000). When immigrants relocate from a home country, they bring with them significant attachments to their home culture. They also extend this attachment in the host country by connecting to ethnic social networks which can provide an initial cushion for negotiating a sense of place, as evidenced by an ethnic residential concentration in certain areas. Ethnic social support can therefore create a space where immigrants can bridge cultural distance and gradually build connections with the mainstream culture.

Photo 12.3
Translation services provided by the Chinese community in Brisbane aim to support Chinese migrants in settling in the host country.
Copyright © Shuang Liu. Used with permission.

Personal characteristics and background

Demographic factors such as age, native language, and education; personal experience such as previous exposure to other cultures; and personality characteristics such as extraversion may all influence cross-cultural adaptation outcomes. Younger migrants generally adapt more easily than older ones, particularly when they are also well-educated. The ability to speak the language of the host culture certainly facilitates one's ability to adapt and function in the new culture and therefore reduces acculturation stress. Previous exposure to other cultures also better prepares a person psychologically to deal with the stress and frustration associated with settling into a new culture. For example, international students cope with the settling-in process better if they have travelled to other countries where they cannot use their native language to communicate.

Effects of mainstream media

As an institution of culture and an influential shaper of cultural thought, the mass media influence the consciousness of the public through the symbolic environment they create and sustain (McLuhan and Fiore, 1967; see also Chapter 11). This symbolic environment is commonly referred to as symbolic social reality (Adoni and Mane, 1984). When an ethnic group is portrayed in the mass media, that particular symbolic social reality becomes a common category utilized by others to identify members of that ethnic group (Potter and Reicher, 1987). Because of this naturalizing effect on the materials they present, the mass media can serve as a contributor to perpetuating or diminishing racial stereotypes (Mastro and Greenberg, 2000). This role of the mass media in activating and perpetuating racial stereotypes is particularly significant when the audience either has little direct experience of the group or lacks other sources of verification (Khan et al., 1999). For example, Lee and Wu (2004) found that exposure to negative images associated with Asian-Americans created doubts and ambivalence about them among other racial groups. When negative stereotypes are perceived to be real, prejudice is a likely outcome. The symbolic social reality of ethnic minorities constructed by the mainstream mass media not only shapes the ethnic majority's knowledge and beliefs about them, but also serves as an input for the construction of the subjective world of ethnic minorities (Pfau et al., 1995). An ethnic group's perception of how they are portrayed in the mass media will affect their attitudes to the host culture and, subsequently, their desire to integrate into the host society.

Effects of ethnic media

In addition to exposure to mainstream media, ethnic minorities or immigrants also have access to ethnic media such as newspapers printed in their native language published in their host countries. Ethnic media have both intragroup and intergroup functions. As an intragroup function, ethnic media promote ethnic group cohesion not only through their news stories but also via the ethnic language they use (Ward and Hewstone, 1985). For example, Chinese ethnic groups in Australia, like other groups, value their own language as a tool in maintaining their cultural identity (Luo and Wiseman, 2000). Ethnic media also serve to help immigrants to broaden and deepen their knowledge about the unfamiliar host culture via their familiar language. Past studies have found that ethnic minorities, especially during the early stages in the new culture, may avoid interpersonal encounters when they can instead use less personal mass media, such as newspapers printed in their native language, as alternative and less stressful sources of learning about the host environment (Adoni and Mane, 1984). Ethnic media, therefore, play a positive role in affecting immigrants' cross-cultural adaptation.

Intergroup contact

The amount of interpersonal contact between immigrants and host nationals can influence the process of cross-cultural adaptation. Contact between groups has long been considered an important strategy for improving intergroup relations. Pettigrew (1997) examined the responses of over 3,800 majority group members from France, Great Britain, the Netherlands, and Germany and found that intergroup contact played a critical role in reducing bias. Appropriate and friendly intergroup contact may translate into more positive perceptions and may also strengthen ingroup identification by creating positive feelings about it. Potentially negative stereotypes created by the mass media may also be reduced by more frequent contact. For example, Hartmann and Husband (1972) demonstrated that among adolescents living in low-immigration areas, the tendency to define race relations in terms used by the mass media was greater than among those living in high-immigration areas. Intergroup contact or intercultural friendships can facilitate immigrants' cross-cultural adaptation.

Political and social environment

The host culture's political and social environment has a major impact on adjustment to new cultural surroundings. Specific outgroups are more (or less) welcome in a culture. For example, the September 11 attack in New York in 2001 triggered a worldwide fear of terrorism. As a result, immigrants from the Middle East are now less welcome in some countries. The Cronulla riots in Australia (see Chapter 1) illustrate the post 9/11 prejudice against people of, in that case, Lebanese origin. Factors affecting the degree of tolerance of particular outgroups include the social or political policies of the mainstream culture, such as political representation, citizenship criteria, language requirements, and employment opportunities. During the White Australia policy era, immigrants in Australia were expected to assimilate to the host culture, regardless of their heritage culture. Since the 1970s, in line with the promotion of multicultural policy, integration rather than assimilation has been encouraged. Thus, the host culture's attitudes towards immigrants, along with immigration policies, can influence the acculturation of immigrants or sojourners.

Developing strategies for cross-cultural adaptation

Immigration invariably means having to live in both the home culture and the host culture. Consequently, migrants must engage in communication with three types of audience: members of the mainstream culture, people from the home country, and their children who have grown up in the new culture. First, migrants have to learn how to communicate with members of the dominant culture in the host country. This involves learning about a new culture and its practices and discourses. They face a choice of how to respond to the new culture they encounter – allowing themselves to be assimilated into the new culture (assimilation), opting to minimize their engagement with the new culture by withdrawing into an ethnic enclave (separation), developing the skills of functioning simultaneously in two different cultures and of effectively moving between cultures (integration), or withdrawing from both the host and home cultures (marginalization). Second, immigrants must relearn how to communicate with people from the home country. Engaging with the home culture can take the form of remaining as a part of it by keeping in regular contact with people from the home country. Some immigrants, for example Vietnamese refugees who arrived in Australia in the 1970s, may lose touch with the old country owing to the prevailing conditions there. If this happens they will eventually only have a historical understanding of the 'home' country and they will lose the ability to move between the two cultures. Third, immigrants have to learn to 'translate' between their old culture and their children's hybridized culture (Liu and Louw, 2009). Learning to cope with their children's hybrid culture is part of daily life for older generations of immigrants, as dealing with their parents' and grandparents' different culture is a part of the everyday routine for second or third generation immigrants.

This myriad of relationships requires immigrants to adopt strategies to integrate into the host country. Learning as much as possible about the new culture is the first step of acculturation. Successful cross-cultural adaptation is related not only to the psychological and social well-being of the immigrants but also to their economic survival. Part of the process of acculturation is learning survival skills, including how to use banking services, where to go shopping, when to eat, how to work and rest, and how to use public transport among other things essential to daily life. Building intercultural friendships can be helpful as it not only gives immigrants local guidance but also increases the opportunity for intergroup contact, hence promoting mutual understanding. It is not uncommon to find many immigrants remaining within a network of their own ethnic group, not being aware that the best way to get acquainted with another culture is to establish relationships with members of that culture. Further, cross-cultural adaptation also requires immigrants to learn to accept differences.

As intercultural communicators, we should try to understand and interpret the things we experience as they are within a particular cultural context, rather than using our own cultural norms as the only judgment criteria. Regardless of how well we have prepared ourselves before entering a new culture, there will always be moments when we experience culture shock, encounter difficulties, or feel frustrated at our own incapability to accomplish our goals. Therefore, a positive attitude toward a new culture is something we should carry with us throughout the cross-cultural adaptation process.

Summary

This chapter explained the reasons for immigration becoming a larger contributor to cultural diversity today than in the past. The terms 'diaspora', 'migrancy', and 'transnationalism' were defined. The meaning of diaspora has shifted over time and now refers not just to involuntary immigrant groups such as Jews, but also to wider communities of voluntary migrants living in more than one culture. The concepts of migrancy and transnationalism are intertwined. The transnational movement associated with migrancy is no longer a one-way journey. Many immigrants today build social networks across geographic, cultural, and political borders, hence engaging in the process of transnationalism. This chapter described the characteristics of culture shock. It also introduced Berry's acculturation model and identified the personal, social, and environmental factors influencing the acculturation process. The chapter concluded with a discussion on communication strategies to facilitate cross-cultural adaptation.

Immigrants bring to a host country their home cultural traditions and customs. At the same time, they need to integrate into the host cultural environment by adapting to its values, attitudes, and practices. The cultural diversity immigrants bring to the host country also means changes for mainstream cultural beliefs, values, and identities. Thus diversity creates challenges for both sides. It is not only the immigrant group but also the host nationals who must undergo a psychological and sociological adjustment as a result of the presence of culturally distinctive others. Evidence from previous research has suggested that the integration orientation is associated with the most positive acculturation outcomes. The extent to which each host society has provided immigrants with an environment in which they feel welcome to integrate needs further scholarly research.

Case Study:
Migration and diversity in Australia

Australia has become one of the most culturally diverse countries in the world. One can hardly walk along a major city street without passing a Chinese restaurant, a Vietnamese grocery store, an Italian deli, or a Japanese sushi bar. The most significant contributor to this multicultural environment is the ever-increasing levels of immigration. As Castles (1992: 549) pointed out, nowhere is this more apparent than in a country like Australia where 'immigration has always been a central part of nation building'. Since 1945, around 6.8 million people have come to Australia as new settlers. Their contribution to Australian society, culture, and prosperity is an important factor in shaping the nation.

Australia has now had more than sixty years of post-war migration. Transported criminals were the basis of the first migration from Europe. Starting in 1788, some 160,000 convicts were shipped to the Australian colonies. From that time, free immigrants also began coming to Australia. The rapid growth of the wool industry in the 1820s created an enormous demand for labour and sparked an increase in the migration of free people from the United Kingdom. The social upheavals of industrialization in Britain also resulted in many people emigrating to escape widespread poverty and unemployment. The myth of *terra nullius*, or an empty land, encouraged immigration, and many people in the indigenous population were pushed from their traditional territory to share the land, willing or not, with the newcomers. This pressure, along with the conflict and serious discrimination against them, began to tell on the indigenous population, whose numbers, influence, and visibility steadily decreased.

A major impetus for Australian immigration following its initial post-convict settlement was the discovery of vast alluvial goldfields that attracted a mass influx of immigrants in the 1850s, coupled with the extension of parliamentary democracy and the establishment of inland towns. These early unrestricted population movements, which firmly established Australia as a colony of settlement, saw the number of settlers grow to over one million by 1861. At the same time, during the Gold Rush era of 1851 to 1860, early migration peaked at arrivals of around 50,000 people a year; Chinese immigrants were the largest non-British group. More restricted immigration had begun by the 1880s, at the start of the movement known as 'White Australia' when Victoria introduced legislation to discourage immigration by taxing Chinese migrants. The 'White Australia policy' reflected Australians' fear of the 'Yellow Hordes', as they perceived Asian immigrants. This policy was strongly assimilationist and also reflected the belief, current at that time, that a population had to be culturally homogeneous to be truly egalitarian and democratic. Pressure to assimilate was applied both to immigrants and to the indigenous population, so that the dominant Anglo-Celtic group came to be seen as 'native' Australians.

In the mid-twentieth century, Australia's outlook on the world was significantly changed because of the Second World War. Australia then had a population of only seven million people, and the devastating effects of the Depression and the war led to a policy of 'Populate or Perish'. Australia opened the floodgates to mainly British and European migrants, many of whom had been displaced by the war and the Nazi Holocaust. Immigration policies aimed to attract migrants to the industrial workforce. A more ambitious part of Australia's migration programme followed after the end of the Second World War. The re-settling of ex-servicemen, refugees, and young people was a significant chapter in Australian immigration history. Australia negotiated agreements with other governments and international organizations to help achieve high migration targets. For example, a system of free passage for United Kingdom residents (the 'ten-pound migrants'), and an assisted passage scheme for British Empire and United States ex-servicemen, vastly increased immigration. Australian immigration drew heavily on its traditional connections with the British who, until the 1960s, continued to get virtually free passage for themselves and their families. At various times in the 1950s and 1960s, the Netherlands, Germany, Italy, Greece, Turkey, and Yugoslavia were also important sources of immigrants.

The 'White Australia policy' was removed in 1973 by the then Whitlam Labour Government. Furthermore, in 1967, indigenous people had been recognized as full Australian citizens through a national referendum. When the legislation removed race as a factor in Australia's immigration policies the assimilation policy was still in force, reflecting both the perceived national need for homogeneity and an opportunistic political aim of nation building through imported population growth. The impetus to change social and political thinking on Australian immigration came with the creation of a commission by the Fraser Liberal–National government in 1977. The Ethnic Affairs Commission's aim was to review migrant post-arrival programmes and services, to make recommendations for their improvement, and to devise means for their implementation. The Commission's findings – 'The Galbally Report', named after the eminent lawyer Frank Galbally – were presented to the Fraser government in 1978 and outlined recommendations for changes in the pattern of migration, attitudes toward immigration, responsibilities for international refugees, and the needs of a growing number of ethnic groups in Australia's community. The report claimed that it marked 'changed thinking' on Australian immigration to embrace a new ideology of settlement and multiculturalism. In the 1980s the nation implemented this policy of multiculturalism, adopting an institutionalized diversity. The evolution of Australia's immigration policies at several phases over time was reflected in the Australian Department of Immigration and Multicultural Affairs Fact Sheets (2009).

The policy of multiculturalism enhanced immigrants' situation in Australia for twenty years. Unfortunately, prejudice and discrimination against the non-immigrant indigenous population were little affected by this policy. In addition, a change of government in 1996 allowed the policy to be eroded to some extent, as immigration was increasingly restricted. The situation for immigrants today is thus more fragile than in the recent past, as various conflicts illustrate.

Immigration has been a key contributor to population growth in Australia. In the immediate post-war period, only 10 per cent of Australia's population had been born overseas. Today, nearly one in four of Australia's more than 21 million people were born overseas and approximately 200 languages, including indigenous languages, are spoken in the country. New Zealand and the United Kingdom are still the largest source countries for migrants, but other regions, notably Asia, have also become more significant contributors. The number of settlers arriving in Australia between July 2007 and June 2008 totalled 149,400, and they came from nearly 200 countries. The major source countries are New Zealand, the United Kingdom, India, mainland China, the Philippines, South Africa, Sri Lanka, Malaysia, Vietnam, and Korea.

References for case study

Castles, Stephen (1992) 'The Australian model of immigration and multiculturalism: is it applicable to Europe?', *International Immigration Review*, 26 (2): 549–567.

Department of Immigration and Multicultural Affairs (2009) 'Fact sheets: more than 60 years of postwar migration' [online]. Accessed 19 July 2009 at http://www.immi.gov.au/media/fact-sheets/04fifty.htm

Questions for discussion

1   What factors can influence immigration flow?
2   What factors can influence immigration policy change?
3   When immigrants enter a new country, they often feel 'out of place'. What roles does the host cultural environment play in influencing their sense of place?
4   Does multiculturalism pose a threat to our cultural uniqueness? Why or why not?
5   Do you think host nationals and immigrants view multiculturalism as beneficial? Why or why not?

Key Terms

acculturation;
assimilation;
cross-cultural adaptation;
culture shock;
diaspora;
ideological asymmetry

hypothesis;
integrated threat theory;
integration;
marginalization;
migrancy;
multicultural hypothesis;

multiculturalism;
reverse culture shock;
stress–adaptation–growth
   model;
transmigrants;
transnationalism

Further Reading

Acculturation orientations and strategies

Arnold, Anne-Katrin and Schneider, Beate (2007) 'Communicating separation? Ethnic media and ethnic journalists as institutions of integration in Germany', *Journalism*, 8 (2): 115–136.

Cabassa, Leopoldo J. (2003) 'Measuring acculturation: where we are and where we need to go', *Hispanic Journal of Behavioral Sciences*, 25 (2): 127–146.

Moon, Seung-jun and Park, Cheong Yi (2007) 'Media effects on acculturation and biculturalism: a case study of Korean immigrants in Los Angeles' Koreatown', *Mass Communication & Society*, 10 (3): 319–343.

Rohmann, Anette; Florack, Arnd and Piontkowski, Ursula (2006) 'The role of discordant acculturation attitudes in perceived threat: an analysis of host and immigrant attitudes in Germany', *International Journal of Intercultural Relations*, 30: 683–702.

Shi, Yan (2008) 'Chinese immigrant women workers' mediated negotiations with constraints on their cultural identities', *Feminist Media Studies*, 8 (2): 143–161.

Culture shock

Pyvis, David and Chapman, Anne (2005) 'Culture shock and the international student "offshore"', *Journal of Research in International Education*, 4 (2): 23–42.

Factors influencing cross-cultural adaptation

Clement, Richard; Baker, Susan C. and Josephson, Gordon (2005) 'Media effects on ethnic identity among linguistic majorities and minorities: a longitudinal study of a bilingual setting', *Human Communication Research*, 31 (3): 399–422.

Deuze, Mark (2006) 'Ethnic media, community media and participatory culture', *Journalism*, 7 (3): 262–280.

Miglietta, Anna and Tartaglia, Stefano (2009) 'The influence of length of stay, linguistic competence, and media exposure in immigrants' adaptation', *Cross-Cultural Research*, 43 (1): 46–61.

Multiculturalism

Goodin, Robert (2006) 'Liberal multiculturalism: protective and polyglot', *Political Theory*, 34 (2): 289–303.

Transnationalism

Elsrud, Torun (2008) 'Othering through genderization in the regional press: constructing brutal others out of immigrants in rural Sweden', *European Journal of Cultural Studies*, 11 (4): 423–446.

Green, Alison and Power, Mary (2006) 'Defining transnationalism boundaries: New Zealand migrants in Australia', *Australian Journal of Communication*, 33 (1): 35–52.

Tynes, Robert (2007) 'Nation-building and the diaspora on Leonenet: a case of Sierra Leone in cyberspace', *New Media & Society*, 9 (3): 497–518.

13

Becoming an Effective Intercultural Communicator

We ought to think that we are one of the leaves of
a tree, and the tree is all humanity. We cannot live
without the others, without the tree.

Pablo Casals, Spanish cellist and musician, 1876–1973

Learning Objectives

At the end of this chapter, you should be able to:

- Identify the global and local dimensions of culture.
- Explain the dialectic of homogenization and fragmentation of cultures.
- Describe the contributors of cultural diffusion, convergence, and hybridity.
- Suggest strategies to develop intercultural competence.

Global and Local Dimensions of Culture

One of the challenges facing intercultural scholars is a shifting understanding of cultural boundaries in societies characterized by emerging forms of economic and cultural globalization. The 'global village' described by McLuhan in the 1960s represents only a partial social reality of the world we inhabit today. As Adams and Carfagna (2006: 23) write, 'Globalization is making the world truly round because it is bringing all of humanity into a single eco-system of embedded, overlapping networks. Borders, boundaries, delineations, and walls of any kind are slowly giving way to the compelling force of integration and interdependence.' Indeed, our global village is becoming increasingly interconnected at political, economic, cultural, social, and even personal levels.

Yet, as Skalli (2006) points out, all these interconnections are embedded in a system of inherent differences. At one end of the economic scale, cosmopolitan elites work and study in several different countries, mastering multiple languages and moving seamlessly between cultural contexts. At the other end, ethnic minorities are trying to find ways to preserve elements of their own cultural practice while adjusting to the cultures of their host countries. In the internet era, media content – once subject to limits imposed by both legal regimes and transportation technology – now circulates around the globe at the speed of light. Mass cultural products, such as Latin American *telenovelas*, Egyptian melodramas, Arab reality TV, and televised Hindu epics, have generated passionate global debates about politics, international wars, women's emancipation, global understanding, and the possibilities for cultural hybridity. Global trends of homogenization and local processes of fragmentation suggest multiple ways in which the global and local cultural realms are connected.

Global employment of media technologies has enormous potential to facilitate cultural, social, and political communication and understanding. For example, transnational media corporations create programming templates that can be customized to individual countries. The internationally successful TV show 'franchises', such as *Biggest Loser* or *Who Wants to Be a Millionaire?*, add local interest to standard formats by recruiting cast members from the countries in which they are broadcast. As an example of this type of 'glocalization', the TV show *Temptation Island* was filmed on the same island in shifts – each shift was devoted to a different country and its associated cast members. These changes do not mean that cultural differences are being eradicated and that the whole world is being subsumed into one global culture. They do, however, mean that cultures are circulating in new and different ways and that people are likely to reflect more and more about their similarities to and differences from one another. This is a time in which *cultural hybridization*, a new cultural form that combines elements of other cultures, is proliferating. It is also a time when an understanding of intercultural communication is even more important, but is becoming increasingly complicated.

This chapter addresses the various challenges we face in an increasingly globalized society. We first explain the dialectic of homogenization and fragmentation of cultures and the human effects of these processes. The chapter then presents arguments about how to understand the global through local context and how local cultures challenge, negotiate, and adjust to globalization. A description of factors that influence cultural convergence and hybridization is provided. Finally, components of intercultural competence are identified and strategies to improve intercultural communication suggested. Along with the rest of the book this chapter aims to equip you with the knowledge and skills to become an effective intercultural communicator.

Homogenization and Fragmentation

There are two countervailing tendencies associated with globalization: the overcoming of cultural or economic differences, known as *homogenization*, and new forms of cultural *fragmentation* and innovation. The dialectic between them is reflected by the cultures themselves as well as by people living in culturally diverse societies.

Homogenization and fragmentation of cultures

Globalization generally refers to an accelerated interconnectivity in the economic, social, political, cultural, and even personal aspects of life. Today, almost everywhere we can see the familiar signs of an interdependent economy (Lustig and Koester, 2010). It is hard to avoid products from international locations: food from Thailand, clothes from China, electronics from Vietnam, or movies from North America. However, the suggestion that the spread of Western globalization means that we need to be less attuned to cultural differences is misguided. On the one hand, the forms of isolation and insulation that once nurtured cultural uniqueness are being eroded, thanks to increasing economic and political interdependence and the spread of transport and communication technologies that shrink space and transmit culture. On the other hand, these same tendencies generate unique and culturally distinctive responses and enhanced opportunities for the expression and circulation of culture-specific products. Satellite television, for example, enables people around the world to remain in instantaneous contact, so that viewers in one hemisphere can watch real-time events unfolding in the other parts of the world. At the same time, new information and communication technologies (ICTs) are making it possible for indigenous cultures to create their own media outlets and products, to circulate them widely, and to create connections with other indigenous peoples who may share the same political and social concerns. These same ICTs also make it possible for diasporic communities to maintain close ties with their countries of origin, even if they are living at the heart of their new cultures.

The dialectic of homogenization and fragmentation can be described as engagement versus isolationism, or globalism versus nationalism (Lustig and Koestger, 2010). Economic interdependence sustains engagement and globalism. For example, in almost every country, we can find signs of McDonald's, KFC, Pizza Hut, Toyota, Sony, Nestlé, and Coca-Cola, all contributing to globalism and the homogenization of cultures. Nevertheless, the desire to preserve cultural uniqueness promotes isolationism and nationalism. Nations may take measures to protect their local economies from foreign products. For example, when a cyclone destroyed many banana plantations in Australia in 2007, the price of bananas increased greatly owing to this local shortage of the banana supply. Then, to safeguard the local economy, regulations were issued to prohibit the importation of cheap bananas from overseas.

Nations may also protect their people from the perceived effects of the beliefs, values, norms, and social practices coming from an exposure to 'outside' cultural products. This type of isolationism is illustrated by the censorship of imported movies in many countries. For example, the film *A Clockwork Orange* by the American film director Stanley Kubrick was banned in the UK in 1972 because the film was claimed to incite copycat violence. The film takes place in a future England and follows a teenage gang leader who enjoys rape and violence. He volunteers for a rehabilitation programme which removes his desire for violence, but the programme leaves him suicidal. It was only in 1999 that the film was permitted to be shown in Britain.

Different countries may add their own innovations to mass cultural products as a way of preserving their national characteristics. For example, music is readily marketed as a commercial product across cultural borders, but it is adapted, modulated, and transformed as it travels around the world. Rap music, which started in African-American neighbourhoods in the United States, has been taken up in a variety of countries such as Japan, Germany, and South Africa, with each culture adding its own innovations to the original style. Globalization then works *dialectically*: on the one hand, there is a growing interconnectedness; on the other hand, there is a rise in deep-seated xenophobia and nationalistic sentiments.

Homogenization and fragmentation of social and ethnic groups

We find ourselves living in a world of increasing cultural mobility. Modern means of transportation and technology make travel faster and easier. As Edwards and Usher (2008: 16) note, 'What in the past would have taken months to move around the globe now takes hours or even seconds.' Moreover, thanks to the internet, people find themselves moving among different cultures without leaving home, or staying immersed in their home cultures even after they have geographically located elsewhere. At the same time, the uneven diffusion of technology and the uneven characteristics of Western globalization may create new forms of social and cultural stratification between those who participate in an increasingly transnational economy and those who still live and work under more traditional conditions. A mutual cultural exposure does not necessarily imply mutual benefits, acceptance, or harmony. Recent conflicts suggest that this cultural exposusre can highlight and exacerbate cultural differences between groups or nations. Just as those living in traditional communities may feel shocked and threatened by the products of contemporary consumer culture, those living in the capitals of consumerism may find their own values and practices challenged by more traditional cultures. These issues make the dynamics of the global and local nexus more complex.

Scholarly discussions about global versus local, or about the homogenization and fragmentation of cultures, are gradually shifting away from a black-and-white view as people recognize that 'cultural experience is both unified

Photo 13.1
Advertisement at Singapore Changi International Airport cleverly used Asian warrior characters to promote Australian Qantas Airways. Copyright © Joan Burnett. Used with permission.

beyond localities and fragmented within them' (Skalli, 2006: 20). Despite the presence of a global economy and mass cultural products, people still interpret what they see or have by drawing upon their local beliefs, values, and norms. Thus, at the same time as we recognize the far-reaching effects of technological, societal, and economic forces, we also need to recognize that all the messages that we experience are interpreted through the meaning systems of culture (Lustig and Koester, 2010). In focusing on the cultural dimensions of the integration/fragmentation dialectic, we do not dissociate the economic and political aspects from the rest of the cultural realm. Rather, we view them through the lenses of culture and maintain their importance in the cultural prism.

Theory Corner

Coordinated management of meaning

Coordinated management of meaning (CMM) began as an interpretive theory focusing on interpersonal communication, but has now become a practical theory to improve patterns of communication. The term *coordination* highlights the fact that whatever we do always intermeshes with the interpretations and actions of other people. CMM theorists (Pearce, 2005) believe that communication is, at the same time, idiosyncratic and social, and that it is necessary to describe the cultural context if we are going to understand communication within and/or across cultures. It is also necessary to understand individuals' interpretations of their communication.

CMM theorists have identified three goals of the theory: 1) to understand who we are, what it means to live a life, and how that is related to particular instances of communication; 2) to render cultures comparable while acknowledging their incommensurability; and 3) to generate an illuminating critique of cultural practices. Given that we have to engage in interaction with people who are not like us, the challenge is to find ways of acting together in order to create a social world where culture wars are minimized and people can find comfort and stability in their cultural traditions.

Reference

Pearce, Barnett W. (2005) 'The coordinated management of meaning (CMM)', in W.B. Gudykunst (ed.), *Theorizing about Intercultural Communication*. Thousand Oaks, CA: SAGE. pp. 35–54.

Further reading on cultural hybridity and communication

Jacobson, Thomas (2000) 'Cultural hybridity and the public sphere', in K.G. Wilkins (ed.), *Redeveloping Communication for Social Change: Theory, Practice, and Power*. Lanham, MD: Rowman and Littlefield. pp. 55–69.

From Local to Global

In the twentieth century, Jimmy Carter, the thirty-ninth President of the United States, commented that 'We become not a melting pot but a beautiful mosaic. Different people, different beliefs, different yearnings, different hopes, different dreams.' In the twenty-first century, however, the world can no longer be viewed as a mosaic with distinct parts (Cooper et al., 2007). With each contact between cultures, we leave some traces of our 'village' culture behind and add some new traits to it from other cultures. Albeit at a slow pace, cultures are changing, merging into one another. It is crucial to understand the dynamic interplay between localities and globalities around the world.

Cultural diffusion and convergence

Through an interaction between cultures, one culture may learn and adopt certain practices from the other. *Cultural diffusion* happens when a culture learns or adopts a new idea or practice from another culture or cultures. Products can carry cultural values; many products represent a particular national identity and hence become cultural icons. An *icon* is a symbol that is idolized in a culture or is employed to represent it. For example, McDonald's represents the value placed on standardization, efficiency, and control in American culture; Japanese gardens reflect the value of harmony in Japanese culture; koalas and kangaroos represent Australia to many as a friendly, carefree, and relaxed country. It is believed that the receiving culture can unconsciously or uncritically absorb the values being transmitted via iconic products. For example, fast food has become an integral part of life in China since it opened up to the world in the 1980s. Signs of McDonald's, KFC, and Pizza Hut can be seen in almost every city or town, as they can in the rest of the world. The concepts of efficiency, standardization, and quantification which are valued in Western cultures are infusing into the Chinese food culture, where harmony, balance, and perfection used to be valued in traditional Chinese cooking.

The increased sharing of information and agreement on mixing West with East leads to *cultural convergence*. While the diffusion model focuses on what one culture does to another, the convergence model focuses on the relationship between individuals or groups of people who share information and converge over time toward a greater degree of mutual agreement (Jandt, 2007). In Russia, where more than 75 McDonald's outlets have been opened in the last ten years, the company has had to respond to local practices and cultivate local interests. In addition to positioning itself by emphasizing its novelty and efficiency, McDonald's cultivates an image of ordinariness, a place where ordinary people work and dine. Collective responsibility is very important in Russian culture, and so McDonald's is also situating itself as a responsible member of local communities by sponsoring sports events and making donations to children's programmes. Consumption practices in Russia, not just of food, are being transformed. Hence a globalization of products encourages the local to become global, which leads to cultural convergence.

Cultural hegemony and colonialism

Some nations perceive the increasing popularity of culturally iconic products, particularly those from the West, as a form of *cultural hegemony*, or the structurally enabled predominant influence of one culture over another. Cultural hegemony is faced not only by developing countries. For example, the French resistance to any of the linguistic influences of English is well-documented in the literature, as are Japan's resistance to American movies and India's resistance to Coca-Cola. When products travel from one culture to another, they transmit cultural values to the receiving culture and change people's lives. For example, Coca-Cola is seen as a symbol of modernity and Westernization in China, particularly among young people. Many people order Coca-Cola in restaurants. They do not necessarily like the taste; rather, they drink it to symbolize their 'Western-ness'. Similarly, private ownership of cars was not popular in China in the 1980s. However, since the 1990s, a car has become more and more of a 'necessity' for business people, government officials, and families – but as a status symbol rather than as a means of transportation. The ownership of foreign cars, in particular, shows the status of the owner: Toyota, Audi, Ford, and Hyundai are among the popular foreign models. In addition, imported televisions, cameras, mobile phones, refrigerators, washing machines, and cosmetic products, among others, all play a role in Westernizing the traditional Chinese ways of thinking and living.

Photo 13.2
Kola Turka – the Turkish version of Coca-Cola – standing in a public square in Istanbul.
Copyright © Zala Volčič. Used with permission.

Contact between cultures may also lead to cultural colonialism. At the core of *cultural colonialism* is the concept of 'othering', predominantly used to refer to stereotypical images of non-white populations (Jandt, 2007). Cultural colonialism has a long history. For example, when European seafarers discovered and colonized the Hawaiian Islands, they labelled the Hawaiian population as 'the other' on the basis of their not being civilized by European standards. Similarly, in Australia, the Aborigines were labelled by Anglo-Saxon Australians as not evolved or civilized. Khan et al. (1999) argue that colonialism continues in many ways, including domination via the mass media. The mass media are not value-free, but carry important cultural values. They shape our perceptions of events and groups of people by providing a staple diet of news and entertainment to people in dispersed locations. The negative portrayal of the Muslim community in newspapers, for example, plays an important role in shaping our perception of that ethnic group, reinforcing stereotypes and sharpening the lines between 'us' and 'them'.

From Global to Local

Globalization brings changes to every aspect of our life. However, local customs and traditions do not just fade away when global cultural products flow across borders. Central to the cultural diffusion and convergence process is how global cultural products and meanings are adapted by local cultures.

Cultural hybridization

The transmission of cultural values and transformation of the lives of people via cultural products depend on how well these products are received by local cultures. *Cultural hybridization* refers to a new cultural form that combines elements of other cultures. For years, business people and corporations have devoted huge amounts of resources to adapting global products to local needs. For example, the McDonald's menu in New Delhi does not contain beef patties as 80 per cent of the population are Hindu, a religion whose followers do not consume beef. In Japan, McDonald's serves soup and fried rice to cater to Japanese eating habits. KFC is positioned as part of the fabric of life in China since its entry to Beijing in the 1980s as the first fast food chain, and has now spread to almost every city in China, with more than 100 KFC restaurants in both Beijing and Shanghai. One contributor to its huge success is that KFC has tailored its menu specifically to Chinese tastes. For example, the 'old Peking flavour' twister sandwich is styled following the way Peking duck is served, but with KFC's own brand of fried chicken and cucumber shreds. Instead of coleslaw, which is not part of traditional Chinese cuisine and does not appeal to Chinese tastes, customers can order seasonal vegetables, such as bamboo shoots in spring, lotus roots in summer, and rice porridge in the cold winter months. This localization of global products, therefore, plays an important role in their acceptance and sustainability in receiving cultures.

Cultural branding

An important aspect of the global/local process is a phenomenon called 'branding', whereby business entities and nations position themselves and their products as globally recognizable. A brand is usually understood as the association of a product or service with a symbolic image that confers recognition, as well as additional value (or *added value*) to a product (Volčič, 2008). International brands competing in a global marketplace, such as Nestlé, have to differentiate themselves from one another. Brand is something in the mind of consumers that motivates them to choose one product over another or to pay more for a product than they otherwise would. Brands are also capable of evoking beliefs and emotions and prompting behaviours. For example, in 1998, the British 'Cool Britannia' campaign attempted to move Great Britain away from its traditional image of the Queen, rain, aloofness, and snobbery towards a 'cool' image. Other examples of cultural branding include attempts to globally brand a national image and transform it into commodities. Colombia is branded as *Café de Colombia*; Switzerland is powerfully represented by its delicious chocolates and cheese; Brazil is promoted by samba dancing, carnivals, magic, sports, adventure, and music; Singapore is known as a country *So Easy to Enjoy*; Poland has *The Natural Choice*; Turkey has *Welcome to Friends*. Such cultural branding encourages the employment of a marketable representation of difference, which emphasizes its local distinctiveness and oven exoticism.

Cultural knowledge

The interconnectivity brought about by globalization means that we must be equipped with global knowledge, situating world events in our local geographic, political, historic, environmental, and cultural context. The instantaneous media coverage of events across the globe has reinforced the important role that the mass media play in international politics. Terms such as 'the CNN effect' have become useful to explain how technologies can deprive international politicians of time for careful deliberation. Nevertheless, as the self-proclaimed world news leader, CNN has its local imitators as well. Al Jazeera is a pan-Arab news station *par excellence*, established in Qatar in 1996. Al Jazeera has swept through the Middle East and become the first station to air live footage from an Arab perspective. Because it aired interviews with Osama Bin Laden and was first on the scene during the war in Afghanistan and later in Iraq, Al Jazeera has achieved global fame. With teams of reporters throughout the Middle East, it is able to provide firsthand news that few Western media outlets can compete with. The channel has now gained sufficient recognition to open an English-language world news channel, drawing news from its reporters around the world. Global issues including climate change, energy emission, international trade, poverty, sustainable development, peace, migration, and health are interpreted differently by people in different local contexts. Our understanding of the localization of those global issues will facilitate our intercultural communication.

Along with the changes brought about by globalization and ICTs is the need for us to redefine personal and cultural identities. At the same time people see themselves as 'global citizens', they identify themselves by a nation or a local community. The conceptualization of identity as multiple and fluid and changing according to situational characteristics, rather than a fixed product, gives people more freedom to define themselves along narrower categories. Similarly, while global cultural icons invoke a Western cultural homogenization, these symbols at the same time may trigger a stronger desire for local cultures to form into distinctive communities and maintain their local traditions. In this sense the more global our society becomes, the more provincial our attitudes may become. The balance between global and local, when we view it through a cultural prism, occurs along a continuum rather than as an all-or-none phenomenon. Therefore, we cannot escape building up our cultural knowledge repertoire if we are to function effectively in both global and local contexts.

Theory Corner

Cultural schema theory

Cultural schema theory has been applied to study intercultural communication and cross-cultural adaptation (Nishida, 2005). Schemas are defined as a generalized knowledge of past experiences organized into related categories and used to guide our behaviours in familiar situations. When entering into communication with others, each of us brings a stock of knowledge about appropriate behaviours in our own culture. This pre-acquainted knowledge is referred to as *cultural schemas*. When a person interacts with members of the same culture over time, cultural schemas are generated in the mind. As the person encounters more of these similar situations, the cultural schemas become more organized, abstract, compact, and useable. Our communication becomes much easier through the application of cultural schemas.

However, when sojourners enter into a new culture, they experience cognitive uncertainty and anxiety because of their lack of cultural schemas for the new situation. They usually go through two processes to adapt to the host culture: self-regulation and self-direction. In the *self-regulation stage*, sojourners try to resolve ambiguities and establish an integration of information by drawing upon their home culture schemas. In the *self-direction stage*, they try to re-organize their home culture schemas or generate host culture schemas to adapt to the new environment.

Reference

Nishida, Hiroko (2005) 'Cultural schema theory', in W.B. Gudykunst (ed.), *Theorizing about Intercultural Communication*. Thousand Oaks, CA: SAGE. pp. 401–418.

Further reading on communication across cultures

Martin, Judith N.; Hammer, Mitchell R. and Braddord, Lisa (1994) 'The influence of cultural and situational contexts on Hispanic and non-Hispanic communication competence behaviors', *Communication Quarterly*, 42 (2): 160–179.

Developing Intercultural Competence

The study of communication competence dates back to the time of Aristotle, as shown in his book *Rhetoric*, where the art of persuasion in public speaking is explored. The term 'communication competence' has been defined in various ways by scholars. This chapter adopts John M. Wiemann's (1977: 198) definition that conceptualizes *communicative competence* as 'the ability of an interactant to choose among available communicative behaviors in order that he [sic] may successfully accomplish his own interpersonal goals during an encounter while maintaining the face and line of his fellow interactants within the constraints of the situation'. This definition simultaneously highlights the importance of the ability of interactants in accomplishing their goals and in showing concern to others in the interaction. As intercultural communication involves people who are culturally different, this definition applies well to the study of intercultural communication competence.

Photo 13.3
This artwork at the international airport in Beijing symbolizes the history and cultural tradition of Ancient China.
Copyright © Shuang Liu. Used with permission.

Components of intercultural competence

Building on Brian Spitzberg and William Cupach's (1984) model, which emphasizes communication competence as a context-specific behaviour, we describe four domains of intercultural communication competence: the knowledge component, the affective component, the psychomotor component, and the situational component.

The knowledge component

The knowledge component refers to the level of cultural knowledge a person has about another person with whom he or she is interacting. For example, touching the head of a child or showing the soles of one's shoes to other people is considered culturally inappropriate in Thailand, but these behaviours are considered as normal and acceptable in Australia. If an Australian and a Thai are in conversation, knowledge of each other's cultural taboos should prevent the occurrence of offence owing to behaviour that is perceived as inappropriate. Hence, the more knowledge people have about other cultures, the more likely they are to be perceived as interculturally competent.

The affective component

The affective component involves the emotional aspects of an individual in a communication situation, such as fear, like or dislike, anger, or stress. Emotions affect our motivation to interact with others from different cultures. For example, some people are more motivated to approach others and engage in an intercultural conversation, whereas others tend to be more apprehensive about communicating with 'foreigners'. Communicating with culturally different others suggests experiencing uncertainty and ambiguity when familiar cultural cues may not be adequate enough to interpret messages. Thus, an effective intercultural communicator needs to tolerate ambiguity and uncertainty.

The psychomotor component

The psychomotor component is the actual enactment of the knowledge and affective components. It involves the ability to use verbal and nonverbal codes to communicate messages in an interaction, and the degree to which one can communicate those messages in a culturally appropriate way. When we enter into communication with others, we assume certain roles. A role defines one's relative position in the communication event, together with an expected set of verbal and nonverbal behaviours. Roles vary significantly across cultures; the role expectations for a university student in North America differ from those in South Korea. A difference of role expectations may result in a misunderstanding. Thus, both what we communicate and how we communicate it determine communication outcomes.

The situational component

The situational component refers to the actual context in which intercultural communication occurs, including the environmental context, any previous contact between the communicators, and the status differential. For example, the degree of formality in word choice varies depending on the status in a hierarchy and the relationship between interactants. In a traditional Confucian family in China, children are taught to respect their elders and to obey their parents' decisions. They are not expected to 'talk back' to their parents. Similar principles apply to their communication with teachers at school. It is not surprising to see first generation Asian immigrants in the West finding it difficult to accept younger generations brought up in the new environment debating with their parents about decisions on their career paths.

The four components of intercultural communication competence are interrelated. Generally, as knowledge increases, one's attitudes to intercultural communication become more positive and the motivation to engage in it increases. As motivation increases, one is more likely to translate it into behaviours – that is, to participate in intercultural communication. If the outcomes from intercultural encounters are successful, this positive experience functions as feedback and encourages the person to participate in future interactions.

Greater opportunities for intercultural encounters can enable the person to build a richer intercultural knowledge stock, which in turn can facilitate subsequent communication.

Strategies to develop intercultural communication competence

Increased intercultural contact provides opportunities for understanding between people as well as the potential for misunderstanding. How do we develop sufficient intercultural communication competence to ensure more successes than failures when communicating with culturally different others?

Seek commonalities

In an intercultural encounter, the first thing we tend to perceive is differences: differences in appearance, dress, language, diet, religion, customs, and even political orientations. If we adopt a self-focused conversation or use only our own cultural norms to guide us, our intercultural communication is unlikely to be successful. To overcome the barrier of difference, we need to build a mutual understanding with the other interactant. One way to achieve this is to focus on similarities rather than differences. As we gain more knowledge about each other, we may find that, despite the visible differences we share similarities in a number of ways. As Morris (1994: 6) described, 'We may wear different hats but we all show the same smile; we may speak different languages but they are all rooted in the same basic grammar; we may have different marriage customs but we all fall in love.' Perceived similarities reduce uncertainty and hence facilitate intercultural communication.

Overcome stereotyping and prejudice

One of the most important barriers to intercultural competence is ethnocentrism: the degree to which other cultures are judged as inferior to one's own. Ethnocentrism is usually based on stereotyping and prejudice about outgroup members compared to the ingroup. Stereotyping and prejudice tend to inhibit us from seeing evidence that does not confirm our presumptions. In order for people to become more competent intercultural communicators, it is important to decrease ethnocentrism and avoid prejudiced attitudes. One way to achieve this goal is to practise cultural relativism, which encourages us to understand the behaviour of others from their own cultural perspectives. However, we acknowledge that cultural relativism has its own limitations.

Develop flexibility and openness

Universally, communication is rule-governed behaviour, but rules vary from culture to culture. In every culture people organize their activities around time. Some cultures require people to be punctual when attending meetings, and being late for one is considered bad manners; in other cultures a meeting will not start until everyone has arrived and being half an hour late is considered acceptable. Cultural rules also govern the distance that is perceived as appropriate between speakers, the loudness at which a person should speak during an interaction, the appropriate amount of gestures, and the appropriate information to be shared between speakers based on their relationship. When we enter an intercultural interaction, we may not know all the rules governing appropriate behaviours in the other culture. We must keep an open mind and be aware that what we practise in our culture may neither be the only correct way nor the best way of doing things, and we must be flexible in adapting our communication as the situation requires.

Summary

This concluding chapter has focused on the various issues and challenges we face living in an increasingly globalized society. We presented arguments on how to understand the global through the local context, and how local cultures can challenge, negotiate, and adjust to globalization. On the one hand, increasing economic and political interdependence and the spread of transport and communication technologies homogenize cultures. On the other hand, these same tendencies generate unique and culturally distinctive responses and opportunities for the expression and circulation of culturally specific products. However, scholarly discussions about the homogenization and fragmentation of cultures are gradually shifting away from a black-and-white view of this dialectic. It is now recognized that 'cultural experience is both unified beyond localities and fragmented within them' (Skalli, 2006: 20). In focusing on the integration/fragmentation dialectic, we do not disconnect economic and political aspects from the cultural realm. This chapter concluded by suggesting strategies to become effective intercultural communicators.

Globalization and information technologies are now affecting every aspect of our life. Advances in telecommunication and transportation facilities bring people from different parts of the world into contact at school, at work, in our neighbourhood, and in cyberspace. Living in a global village is no longer a dream but a reality we have to face, regardless of our culture of origin. It is often said that globalization has fundamentally reshaped the world known to our ancestors. The flow of many global cultural products, including movies, television programmes, music, cars, electric appliances, and even food, has not only transmitted cultural values from one country to another but also transformed people's way of living. Multiculturalism recognizes that different cultures can coexist in the same environment and benefit each other. Cultural differences can provide a rich resource for creative learning about the world if culturally unlike individuals communicate effectively. Hence, becoming more intercultural is an important challenge for everyone, and intercultural communication competence is an important skill that all of us need to develop.

Case Study:
Doctors without Borders

Médecins Sans Frontières (MSF), or Doctors without Borders, is a global humanitarian and non-governmental organization that is best known for its projects in war-torn regions. The organization was created in 1971 by a small group of French doctors and medical journalists who were concerned with the plight of populations in emergency situations and who believed that everyone has the right to medical care, regardless of their race, religion, creed, or political affiliation. Often in crisis situations people's lives shrink to the immediacy of survival. MSF believes that people's needs supersede national borders; it aims to avoid national bureaucracies and short-term goal-oriented international politics by providing rapid medical intervention in the face of crisis. Hence, Doctors without Borders started as a conscious, collective, and organized attempt to bring about large-scale change to needy regions by non-institutionalized means. Their mission statement, 'Doctors Yes, Borders No', reflects their motivation to go beyond national politics to provide real medical help to people.

MSF's borderless philosophy reflects one aspect of globalization – the recognition of increasing forms of interdependence as well as a commitment to human rights that transcends national or regional boundaries. MSF provides aid to those who are, in many cases, the victims of international, economic, and political struggles associated with shifting balances of power, migration, and economic relations. Today, MSF is the world's leading independent international medical relief organization. Doctors from MSF work in over 60 countries affected by natural and social disasters, armed conflicts, and epidemics. The organization's funding comes mostly from private donors (approximately 80 per cent), while governmental and corporate donations make up the remaining 20 per cent, giving MSF an annual budget of approximately US$400 million. In addition to medical treatment, the organization also provides healthcare and medical training. MSF remains independent of any political, religious, or economic interests.

MSF received the 1999 Nobel Peace Prize in recognition of its members' continuing efforts to provide medical care in acute crises, as well as raising international awareness of potential humanitarian disasters. Dr James Orbinski, president of the organization at the time, accepted the prize on behalf of MSF with the words: 'Humanitarian action is more than simple generosity, simple charity. It aims to build spaces of normalcy in the midst of what is profoundly abnormal. More than offering material assistance, we aim to enable individuals to regain their rights and dignity as human beings.' In 2007 over 26,000 doctors, nurses, other medical professionals, logistical experts, water and sanitation engineers, and administrators provided medical aid all around the world. Over the past two decades, MSF has developed a great technical capacity, lending credibility to its claim of being able to commence field operations almost anywhere in the world within 48 hours.

The organization mobilizes people around the idea that we need to deliver humanitarian and emergency care. MSF provides medical care to people who are caught in war zones and who may be injured by gunshot, knife or machete wounds, bombings, or sexual violence. For example, MSF played a significant role in providing medical care in the former Yugoslav wars of the 1990s — conflicts that resulted, at least in part, from the shifting balance of power in the post-Cold War era and tensions over the control of land and resources. The organization delivers surgical care in 25 countries, including the Democratic Republic of Congo, Haiti, Nigeria, and Chechnya, and in northern Iraq, Iran, and Jordan for Iraqi civilians. MSF also provides medical care for refugees and internally displaced people who have fled to camps and other temporary shelters. Today in places like Chad, Colombia, Somalia, and Sudan, MSF is running vaccination campaigns and water-and-sanitation projects, giving basic medical care through established and mobile clinics, building or rehabilitating hospitals, treating malnutrition and infectious diseases, and offering mental health support. Field teams also provide shelter and basic supplies such as blankets, plastic sheeting, or cooking pots when people have been uprooted from their homes and have nothing to help them survive.

MSF has a long history of responding to epidemic outbreaks of cholera, meningitis, measles, malaria, and other infectious diseases that can spread rapidly and be fatal if not treated. Over the past decade, MSF has been involved in the treatment of the pandemics of HIV/AIDS and tuberculosis. Through the Campaign for Access to Essential Medicines, MSF pushes for improved treatments for diseases that disproportionately affect the poor across the world. MSF has also called attention to the need for appropriate paediatric formulations for children with HIV/AIDS. In 1999, MSF co-founded the Drugs for Neglected Diseases initiative that brought together researchers, medical practitioners, and pharmaceutical companies to explore alternative ways of developing medicines. This project highlights the importance of basing research and development priorities on need rather than profit.

MSF remains an inspiring source for global activists. Its medical teams often witness violence, atrocities, and neglect in the course of their work, largely in regions that receive scant international attention. At times, MSF speaks out publicly in an effort to bring a forgotten crisis to global attention, to alert the public to abuses occurring beyond the headlines, to criticize the inadequacies of the aid system, and to challenge the diversion of humanitarian aid for political interests. For example, in 1985 MSF spoke out against the Ethiopian government's forced displacement of hundreds of thousands of its people. The organization took the unprecedented step of calling for an international military response to the 1994 Rwandan genocide and condemned the Serbian massacre of civilians at Srebrenica in 1995. In thinking about cross-cultural connections, MSF is important because it adopts a borderless sense of space and an ethos of direct intervention and media involvement. Alongside Doctors without Borders, we now have reporters, pharmacists, engineers, sociologists, and even Clowns *sans Frontières*. MSF has been recognized as an international organization embodying the insistence on a human right to health and the dignity of life that goes with it.

Reference for case study

Médecins Sans Frontières [online]. Accessed 26 July 2009 at http://www.msf.org

Questions for discussion

1 What type of organization is Doctors without Borders and how did it come into existence?
2 What intercultural philosophy is the organization based on?
3 How do you think this organization helps to facilitate a better intercultural understanding between people?
4 Why do you think it is important that MSF also speaks out about matters that call for public education?
5 What kind of challenges or difficulties do you think MSF doctors encounter working in crises or war regions?

Key Terms

branding;
communicative competence;
coordinated management of meaning;
cultural colonialism;
cultural hegemony;
cultural hybridization;
cultural schema theory;
diffusion;
divergence;
fragmentation;
homogenization;
icon;
intercultural competence

Further Reading

Globalization and localization

Chan, Joseph M. (2005) 'Global media and the dialectics of the global', *Global Media and Communication*, 1 (1): 24–28.

Ertep, Hakan (2009) 'Chaos or homogenization? The role of shop signs in transforming urban fabric in Beyoglu, Istanbul', *Visual Communication*, 8 (3): 263–272.

Jacobson, Thomas (2000) 'Cultural hybridity and the public sphere', in K.G. Wilkins (ed.), *Redeveloping Communication for Social Change: Theory, Practice, and Power*. Lanham, MD: Rowman and Littlefield. pp. 55–69.

Juluri, Vamsee (2002) 'Music television and the invention of youth culture in India', *Television & New Media*, 3 (4): 367–386.

Wang, Georgette and Yueh-yu Yeh, Emilie (2005) 'Globalization and hybridization in cultural products: the cases of *Mulan* and *Crouching Tiger, Hidden Dragon*', *International Journal of Cultural Studies*, 8 (3):175–193.

Winseck, Dwayne R. and Pike, Robert M. (2008) 'Communication and empire: media markets, power and globalization, 1860–1910', *Global Media and Communication*, 4 (1): 7–36.

Identity construction

Aronczyk, Melissa (2008) '"Living the brand": nationality, globality, and the identity strategies of nation branding consultants', *International Journal of Communication*, 2: 41–65.
Lee, Pei-Wen (2006) 'Bridging cultures: understanding the construction of relational identity in intercultural friendship', *Journal of Intercultural Communication Research*, 35 (1): 3–22.

Intercultural competence

Arasaratnam, Lily (2007) 'Research in intercultural communication competence: past perspectives and future directions', *Intercultural Communication*, 13 (2): 66–74.
Beamer, Linda (1992) 'Learning intercultural communication competence', *Journal of Business Communication*, 29 (1): 285–303.
Martin, Judith N.; Hammer, Mitchell R. and Braddord, Lisa (1994) 'The influence of cultural and situational contexts on Hispanic and non-Hispanic communication competence behaviors', *Communication Quarterly*, 42 (2): 160–179.
Paramasivam, Shamala (2007) 'Managing disagreement while managing not to disagree: polite disagreement in negotiation discourse', *Journal of Intercultural Communication Research*, 36 (2): 91–116.

Glossary

Accommodating
One of the five conflict management styles, it refers to behaviours that conceal or play down differences by emphasizing common interests.

Acculturation
A process of various physical and psychological changes that occur as a result of the adaptation required to function in a new and different cultural context.

Affection
One of the three basic needs identified by William Schutz, it refers to showing love to and being loved by others.

Affective conflict
Conflict arising from interpersonal tensions and largely emotional in nature.

Affective content
The non-verbally conveyed feeling that accompanies a verbal message.

Agenda-setting theory
This theory proposes that the mass media focus our attention on certain topics and issues and set the agenda for what we consider to be newsworthy, interesting, and relevant.

Alternative media
A product of internet technology that is not controlled by traditional commercial media imperatives, and allows members of society to participate in news production and dissemination.

Anti-Semitism
A prejudiced perception of Jews, which may be expressed in the form of hatred toward them.

Anxiety/uncertainty management theory
Developed by William B. Gudykunst and based on the uncertainty reduction theory proposed by Berger and Calabrese in 1975, the theory claims that effective interpersonal and intercultural communication is a function of how individuals manage the anxiety and uncertainty they experience in communication.

Assimilation
Immigrants' cross-cultural adaptation strategy. It is characterized by an attachment of low significance to one's ethnic cultural heritage while viewing oneself as a member of the host society.

Attribution theory
This theory assumes that a person seeking to understand why another person acts in a certain way may attribute one or more causes to the behaviour in question.

Audience research
Research on audience tastes, preferences, habits, and demographics, which is often linked to broader questions of media effects.

Avoiding
One of the five conflict management styles, it refers to a physical withdrawal or a refusal to discuss the conflict.

Belief
Individuals' understanding of reality as viewed and interpreted through their culture window.

Branding
The efforts of business entities and nation-states alike in positioning themselves and their products as globally recognizable.

Categorization
The process of ordering the environment by grouping persons, objects, and events on the basis of their being perceived as sharing similar features or characteristics.

Channel
The means by which a message moves from one person to another. The channel can be sound, words, letters, telephone, the internet, fax, and so on.

Chronemics
The use of time. Cultures can be referred to as either polychronic or monochronic in the way in which its members view time.

Classical rhetorical theory
This theory views communication as a practical art of discourse and humans as rational beings who can be persuaded by compelling and carefully constructed arguments.

Cognitive conflict
Conflict arising from the perception of disagreements about the differences in viewpoints, ideas, and opinions.

Cognitive content
The literal content of a message expressed through the verbal code.

Collaborating
One of the five conflict management styles, it refers to facing a conflict directly and examining possible solutions.

Collective identity
Identity based on group membership and an identification with and perceived acceptance into a group that has united systems of symbols, values, norms, and rules.

Collectivism
Cultures characterized by extended primary groups in which people see themselves as interdependent with others, and individual goals are secondary to those of the group.

Communication
The process by which people use shared verbal or nonverbal code systems and media to exchange information in a particular context.

Communication accommodation theory
The theory is based on three assumptions: 1) communication is embedded in a socio-historical context; 2) communication is both about exchanges of referential meaning and the negotiation of personal and social identities; 3) interactants achieve the informational and relational functions of communication by accommodating their communicative behaviour through linguistic and non-linguistic moves.

Communication style
How language is used to communicate meaning.

Communicative competence
The ability of a communicator to select the most appropriate and effective codes for each specific exchange and for the needs and goals of the interactants involved.

Communicative ethical approach
This approach recognizes that humans are socialized into a particular set of cultural norms and yet are capable of critically reflecting upon and changing them.

Competing
One of the five conflict management styles, it refers to the use of power in satisfying one's position even though this means ignoring the needs of an opponent.

Compromising
One of the five conflict management styles, it refers to behaviours that aim at finding a midpoint between the opposing viewpoints.

Conflict
The interaction of interdependent people who perceive an opposition of goals, aims, and values and also see the other party as potentially interfering with the realization of these goals.

Confucian work dynamism
Also known as long-term orientation, it is a cultural dimension which refers to the work practices and outcomes of dedicated, motivated, responsible, and educated individuals with a sense of commitment and an organizational identity and loyalty.

Connotation
The cultural meanings that become attached to a word or an object.

Constructivist
Constructivists argue that language acquisition involves unveiling the patterns of language and requires interaction with a structured environment.

Control
One of the three basic needs identified by William Schutz, it refers to our ability to influence others, our environment, and ourselves.

Coordinated management of meaning
CMM theorists believe that communication is idiosyncratic and social, and that it is necessary to understand our own and others' interpretations of the communication context.

Creole
A new language developed from the prolonged contact of two or more languages, such as Louisiana Creole French.

Critical media theory
This provides a Marxist-inspired analysis of the media and communication both by questioning who benefits and who is disadvantaged by the existing capitalist media system and by critiquing its ideological foundations.

Cross-cultural adaptation
The process of increasing one's level of fitness into a new cultural environment.

Cultivation theory
Postulated by George Gerbner, it suggests that there exists a relationship between heavy television viewing and the nature of people's worldviews.

Cultural adaptation
The process of adjusting to a new culture, incorporating and accepting different cultural practices and values.

Cultural colonialism
The ideological domination of one culture over another, in which the subordinate group is often displaced from the mainstream ideology to assume the role of 'other'.

Cultural convergence
The outcome of an increased sharing of information and agreement on mixing West with East.

Cultural hegemony
The predominant influence of one culture over another, generally in reference to the predominance of Western cultural products and values in other non-Western cultures.

Cultural hybridization
The new cultural forms that emerge when elements of multiple cultures are combined.

Cultural identity
Our social identities based on our cultural membership, they are our identification with and perceived acceptance into a larger culture group into which we are socialized and with which we share a system of symbols, values, norms, and traditions.

Cultural relativism
The degree to which an individual judges another culture by its context.

Cultural schema theory
This theory suggests that a generalized knowledge of past experiences is organized into related categories, known as cultural schemas, which are used to guide our behaviours in familiar situations within our cultural context.

Cultural studies
Cultural-studies scholars are interested in the role that culture plays in both preserving and transforming social relations.

Culture
The particular way of life of a group of people, comprising the deposit of knowledge, experience, beliefs, values, traditions, religion, notions of time, roles, spatial relations, worldviews, material objects, and geographic territory.

Culture shock
The feelings of disorientation and anxiety that a sojourner experiences when familiar cultural norms and values governing behaviours are questioned in a new cultural environment.

Decoding
The process by which a receiver converts a message encoded in verbal or nonverbal codes back into its meaning.

Denotation
The descriptive, literal meaning of a word or an object.

Diaspora
Communities of voluntary migrants living in more than one culture.

Diffusion
Diffusion occurs when a culture learns or adopts a new idea or practice from another culture or cultures.

Direct/indirect style
One of Gudykunst and Ting-Toomey's four verbal communication styles, it refers to the level of directness with which the speaker's intentions, wants, and desires are communicated in the interaction.

Display rules
The rules which govern when, how much, and in what context various nonverbal expressions are required, permitted, preferred, or prohibited.

Diversity
The existence of different cultures within a larger society.

Elaborate/succinct style
One of Gudykunst and Ting-Toomey's four verbal communication styles, it refers to the quantity of talk a culture values.

Encoding
The internal process by which thoughts, feelings, and concepts are converted into a message by using shared verbal or nonverbal codes.

Ethical relativism
This denies the existence of a single universal set of values and norms and instead conceives of them as relative to particular individuals or groups.

Ethical universalism
The proposed existence of a universal ethical principle that guides behaviour across all societies at any time – what is wrong in one place will be wrong elsewhere.

Ethics
This is concerned with what is understood as right or wrong, good or bad: the standards and rules that guide the behaviour of members of a society.

Ethnic identity
A sense of belonging to or an identification with an ethnic group; ethnicity can be based on national origin, race, or religion.

Ethnocentrism
Seeing one's own culture as the centre of the universe and other cultures as insignificant or even inferior.

Ethnography
A method used mainly by anthropologists to study culture in its natural setting.

Ethnolinguistic vitality
The degree of prestige, acceptability, and importance attached to a group's language.

Expectancy violation theory
Developed by Judee Burgoon, this assumes that humans can anticipate certain behaviour from those with whom they interact. When expectations are violated, the violation can exert a significant impact on the communicators' interaction patterns, their impressions of one another, and the outcomes of their interactions.

Face-negotiation theory
Developed by Stella Ting-Toomey, this uses self-face concern and other-face concern to explain conflict management strategies.

Feedback
Information generated by the receiver and made available to the source, which allows the source to make qualitative judgments about the communication event.

Femininity
An aspect of Hofstede's masculinity-femininity cultural dimension. Dominant values of feminist cultures permit more overlapping social roles for the sexes and place a high value on feminine traits such as quality of life, interpersonal relationships, and concern for the weak.

Folk culture
This consists of the taken-for-granted and repetitive nature of the everyday culture of which individuals have mastery.

Formal versus informal relationships
One of Yum's model of five relationship types, this indicates the extent to which a society is dependent on the level of hierarchical structure in developing relationships.

Fragmentation
The increasing separation and differentiation between cultures and groups as a consequence of globalization processes.

Frankfurt School
A multi-disciplinary group of German-American theorists, who sought to provide a critical analysis and explanation of the changes in capitalist societies.

Gender constancy
The understanding that, from birth, a person will adopt and inhabit the gender role assigned to his or her sex.

Gender identity
A part of a personal identity that entails the social roles, assumptions, and expectations established for each sex.

Global transformation
The worldwide economic and technological changes that influence how people relate to one another.

Global village
Marshall McLuhan's description of a world in which communication technology brings news and information to the most remote parts of the world.

Globalist
Viewing globalization as an inevitable development which cannot be significantly influenced by human intervention through traditional political institutions, such as nation-states.

Globalization
The process of increasing interconnectedness between societies such that events in one place of the world are having more and deeper effects on people and societies far away.

Goal conflict
This occurs when people disagree about preferred goals and ends, such as if an externally imposed goal is at odds with one's personal goals.

Group communication
Communication that occurs in limited-size groups in which decision making or problem solving occurs.

Halo effect
The tendency to presume that someone who has one good trait is likely to have other good traits.

Haptics
The use of touch to send messages within certain contexts.

High-intensity conflict
This involves a series of intense, complex battles between conventional military forces.

High-contact cultures
Cultures in which people tend to show affection more openly by touching frequently, standing closer to each other during conversation, and using more emotional expressions.

High-context culture
One of Edward Hall's cultural dimensions. Members of high-context cultures gather information from the physical, social, and psychological context and employ a restricted code system.

Homogenization
Increasing cultural uniformity and the diminishing of cultural and economic differences.

Human relationships
An interactional process of connecting ourselves with others in the network of social needs.

Hybridization
The process and impact of media convergence in which new cultural forms are created, generally understood to be a consequence of globalization.

Icon
A symbol that tends to be idolized in a culture and which often represents certain values, beliefs, or practices.

Identity
Each individual's particular way of identifying him- or herself within specific cultural contexts. Identities can be defined by religion, gender, class, race, ethnicity, political orientation, social group, occupation, and geographic region.

Ideological asymmetry hypothesis
This suggests that hierarchy-attenuating ideologies, such as multiculturalism, appeal more to low-status groups than to high-status groups, as the former potentially benefit more from the arrangement than the latter.

Immigrants
People who leave their home country to live in another country on a permanent status.

Implicit personality theory
This suggests that we organize our individual perceptions into clusters. Individual personality traits are related to other traits, and when we identify an individual trait in someone, we assume he or she also possess, other traits in the cluster.

Inclusion
One of the three basic needs identified by William Schutz, this refers to a sense of belonging or of being involved with others.

Individual identity
Categorizing an individual as different from others and the specific relationships each individual has with other individuals.

Individualism
An aspect of Hofstede's individualism–collectivism cultural dimension, individualism emphasizes individuals' goals over group goals.

Ingroup
A special class of membership group characterized by internal cohesiveness among its members.

Ingroup versus outgroup relationships
One of Yum's five relationship types, this is concerned with the extent to which the boundary between ingroups and outgroups is sharpened or blurred within a culture.

Instrumental/affective style
One of Gudykunst and Ting-Toomey's verbal communication styles. Instrumental style is goal-oriented, sender-focused, and the speaker uses communication to achieve an outcome, whereas affective style is receiver-focused, process-oriented, and is less concerned with the outcome.

Integrated threat theory
This identifies four domains of threat: realistic threat, symbolic threat, negative stereotypes, and intergroup anxiety.

Integration
Immigrants' cross-cultural adaptation strategy. People who adopt inte-gration strategy try to maintain their heritage, cultural traditions, and practices while attempting to gain acceptance into the host culture.

Interactive model
Viewing communication as a process of creating and sharing meaning upon which context, experience, and perception exert influence.

Intercultural communication
Communication between individuals from different cultural or ethnic backgrounds, or between people from subculture groups.

Intercultural conflict
Perceived or actual incompatibility of goals, interests, resources, values, expectations, processes, or outcomes between two or more interdependent parties from different cultures.

Intergroup conflict
This occurs when two cultural or social groups perceive disagreements over resources, stereotypes, territory, policies, religion, and identities.

International conflict
This refers to disputes and disagreements between two or more nations.

Interorganizational conflict
This arises from disputes and disagreements between two or more organizations.

Interpersonal communication
The processing and sharing of meaning between two or more people when relatively mutual opportunities for speaking and listening occur.

Interpersonal conflict
This occurs at the level of individuals when they are competing for scarce resources or having disagreements.

Interpretation
With regard to perception process, interpretation refers to attaching meaning to information obtained through the sensory organs.

Intrapersonal communication
The processing and sharing of meaning within the self.

Islamophobia
Expressions against Islam or anything Muslim.

Kinesics
The communicative qualities of body language, including gestures, hand and arm movements, facial expressions, eye contact, and posture.

Long-term versus short-term relationships
One of Yum's five relationship types, this is concerned with the level of reciprocity and flexibility in relationships within a particular culture.

Low-contact cultures
Cultures that display a low degree of affiliation, where individuals often have greater personal space requirements and there is less touching in interactions.

Low-context culture
One of Edward Hall's cultural dimensions. Members of low-context cultures gather information predominantly from verbal codes.

Low-intensity conflict
This involves the use of military armed forces by at least one of the parties involved.

Marginalization
One acculturation orientation, this refers to an individual's loss of ethnic cultural heritage and his or her absence of contact with the host society.

Masculinity
An aspect of Hofstede's masculinity–femininity cultural dimension, masculine cultures strive for a maximal distinction between male and female roles and the attributes ascribed to them.

Mass communication
The process of understanding and sharing meaning through messages constructed specifically for and broadcast to a mass audience.

Media effects
A field of research that is concerned with examining impacts of the media on audiences, their nature, and consequences.

Media events
Grand-scale interruptions of everyday life when all the media attend to one event, such as coverage of the Olympic Games. These events are mediated, filtered, hyped, and broadcast en masse so that we perceive them as significant and out of the ordinary.

Media political economy
This is associated with questions about both the domination of a state or economic power in media spheres and the processes of privatization, concentration, commercialization, and deregulation.

Media-centric approach
One of the two descriptors used by McQuail to categorize approaches to understanding the media, it attributes much more autonomy and influence to the media and concentrates on the media's own sphere of activity.

Migrancy
The movement of individuals from one location to another across national or cultural borders.

Monochronic time orientation
One of Edward Hall's two categories of time orientation. Cultures with monochronic time orientations view time as linear, progressive, and being able to be compartmentalized. People tend to do one thing at a time.

Morphology
The combination of basic units of meaning, morphemes, to create words.

Multicultural hypothesis
This claims that confidence in one's cultural identity involves a sense of security, which is a psychological precondition for the acceptance of those who are culturally different.

Multiculturalism
At a descriptive level, multiculturalism can be used to characterize a society with diverse cultures; as an attitude, it can refer to a society's tolerance toward diversity and acceptance of equal societal participation.

Multi-step flow model
A model of media effects which argues that information flow in a culture or group is filtered through a series of opinion leaders before reaching all other segments of the society.

National identity
A type of identity that is characterized by one's individual perception of him- or herself as a member of a nation.

Netizen
An internet user who participates in alternative media, actively performing the functions of a community member or citizen online, such as information dissemination, comment, and an engagement with other members.

Noise
Psychological, semantic, or physical elements that interfere with the transfer of a message.

Nominalist
Nominalists argue that our perception of the external reality is not shaped by language but by material reality, and that any thought can be expressed in any language and can convey the same meaning.

Nonverbal communication
The use of non-spoken symbols to communicate a message.

Olfactics
Humans' perception and use of smell, scent, and odour.

Organizational communication
Communication that takes place in an organizational setting and which involves people working together to achieve individual or collective goals.

Orientalism
Developed by Edward Said as a discourse for understanding the relationship between East and West, based on the European cultural power and domination of political and economic interests.

Outgroup
A non-membership group whose attributes are dissimilar from those of the ingroup, or who opposes the accomplishment of the ingroup's goals.

Outgroup homogeneity effect
The tendency to see members of outgroups as 'all alike', without recognizing the individual differences we appreciate in ingroup members.

Paralanguage
The vocal qualities that accompany speech, this can be divided into voice qualities and vocalizations.

Perception
An active process in which humans use sensory organs to identify the existence of all kinds of stimuli and then subject them to evaluation and interpretation.

Personal/contextual style
One of Gudykunst and Ting-Toomey's four verbal communication styles, this is concerned with the extent to which a speaker emphasizes the self, as opposed to his or her role.

Personal identity
This defines an individual in terms of his or her difference to others. Aspects of personal identity include age, gender, nationality, and religion.

Personal versus public relationships
One of Yum's five relationship types, this is concerned with the extent to which public and private relationships are either kept separated or permitted to overlap.

Phonology
Rules of a language that determine how sounds are combined to form words.

Pidgin
Formed and used when two communities that do not share a common language come into contact and attempt to communicate. A pidgin has a reduced grammatical structure and a reduced lexicon, and its use is dependent on situational factors.

Polychronic time orientation
One of Edward Hall's two categories of time orientation. Cultures with polychronic time orientations conceive of time as cyclical and attempt to perform multiple tasks simultaneously.

Popular culture
Popular culture refers to artifacts and styles of human expression developed from ordinary people. It can include such cultural products as music, talk shows, soap operas, cooking, clothing, consumption, and the many facets of entertainment such as sports and literature.

Power distance
One of Hofstede's cultural dimensions, this refers to the extent to which a culture tolerates inequality in power distribution.

Pragmatics
The impact of language on human perception and behaviours and on how language is used in a social context.

Prejudice
A negative attitude toward individuals resulting from negative stereotypes.

Proxemics
The use of space, including personal space, fixed and semi-fixed space, and territoriality.

Racism
The belief that one racial group is superior and that other racial groups are necessarily inferior.

Receiver
The intended target of a message, who should share the same code as the source.

Relativists
Relativists believe that our language determines our ideas, thought patterns, and perceptions of reality.

Reverse culture shock
Experienced by people who return to their native home country after an extended stay in a foreign culture.

Selective attention
The act of allowing only immediately relevant information to filter through the sensory organs.

Selective exposure
We selectively expose ourselves to certain kinds of information from our environment, pay attention to one element of this, and retain the information that is most likely to be used in the future.

Selective retention
Selective retention occurs when people attempt to record in their memory what they perceive as important so that it might be recalled later.

Self-fulfilling prophecy
A statement that causes itself to become true by directly or indirectly altering actions.

Semantics
The study of the meaning of words and the relationship between words and their referents.

Separation
An acculturation orientation which is characterized by maintaining one's ethnic culture but not participating in the host culture.

Similarity attraction paradigm
Proposed by Byrne, this suggests that attraction between individuals is based on their perceived similarity in their respective views of the world, with each validating the other.

Social exchange theory
This posits that individuals establish and continue social relations on the basis of their expectations that such relations will be mutually beneficial.

Social identity
Those parts of an individual's self-concept which derive from his or her knowledge of membership in a social group together with the value and emotional significance attached to that membership.

Social identity theory
This claims that identity formation is a product of social categorization; individuals form identities based on the various social categories to which they belong, which then influence the norms and values they adopt.

Social penetration theory
This states that, as an interpersonal relationship evolves, the interpersonal exchange of information reflects one of four stages of relationship development – orientation, exploratory affective exchange, affective exchange, or stable exchange.

Society-centric approach
One of the two descriptors used by McQuail to categorize approaches to understanding the media, this views the media as a reflection of political and economic forces.

Source
The sender, or origin, of the message being sent. A source is someone who has a need to communicate.

Stereotype
Preconceived beliefs about the characteristics of a certain group based on physical attributes or a social status that may not be generalizable to all members of that group.

Stress–adaptation–growth model
This model claims that cultural adaptation is a progressive series of positive and negative experiences which are based on an interaction between a 'stranger' and a host culture.

Subculture
The smaller, coherent collective groups that exist within a larger dominant culture and which are often distinctive because of race, social class, gender, etc.

Subgroups
Groups that exist within the larger cultural environment.

Symbolic social reality
This suggests that there is a distinction between objective reality and social reality that is a product of mediation.

Syntax
The study of grammatical and structural rules of language which we use to combine words into sentences to communicate meaning.

The magic bullet theory
Concerned with media effects, the magic bullet theory argues that the mass media have a direct, immediate, and powerful effect on a passive mass audience.

Third culture
This refers to creating 'cultural synergy' or a common ground where people from different cultures can converge and negotiate their cultural differences.

Third gender
This is culturally defined by roles instead of by sex. Typically, third-gender members adopt the gender roles traditionally ascribed to the opposite sex.

Traditionalist
Traditionalists believe that most economic and social activities are regional rather than global, and they see a significant role for nation-states.

Transformationalist
Transformationalists believe that globalization represents a significant shift, but they question the inevitability of its impacts. They argue that there is still significant scope for national, local, and other agencies.

Translation
The process of converting a source text, either spoken or written, into a different language.

Transmigrants
Immigrants who develop and maintain multiple relationship networks – familial, economic, social, organizational, religious, and political – that span borders.

Transmission model
Based on Claude Shannon and Warren Weaver's abstract representation of communication as a linear process whereby information 'packages' are transmitted from source to receiver, as if along a pipeline.

Transnationalism
The multiple networks immigrants create across geographic, cultural, and political borders.

Two-step flow model
A model of media effects in which the first stage is the direct transmission of information to a small group of well-informed opinion leaders who then, in the second stage, interpret and disseminate the message to less directly involved members of society.

Uncertainty avoidance
One of Hofstede's cultural dimensions, this refers to a culture's tolerance of ambiguity and acceptance of risk and uncertainty.

Universalistic versus particularistic relationships
One of Yum's five relationship types, this refers to the extent to which differences between people based on a social hierarchy are highlighted or are minimized in particular cultures.

Uses and gratifications theory
Used to investigate and analyse what people do with the media and how they use it.

Value
Concepts of ultimate significance and of long-term importance, values inform the cultural group members of how to judge good or bad, right or wrong, true or false, etc.

Value orientation theory
This theory claims that cultures develop unique positions in five value orientations: man–nature orientation, activity orientation, time orientation, human nature orientation, and relational orientation.

Verbal code
In spoken or written language, this comprises a set of rules governing the use of words in creating a message.

Worldview
The philosophical outlook a culture has about the nature of the universe, the nature of humankind, and the relationship between humanity and the universe.

References

ABS (Australian Bureau of Statistics) (2005) *Year Book Australia 2005* [online]. Accessed 2 October 2006 at http//www.abs.gov.au/AUSSTATS/abs@nsf/Lookup/0A5AABD7621230ADCA256F7200832F77

Adams, J. Michael and Carfagna, Angelo (2006) *Coming of Age in a Globalized World: The Next Generation*. Bloomfield, CT: Kumarian.

Adler, Peter S. (1975) 'The transitional experience: an alternative view of culture shock', *Journal of Humanistic Psychology*, 15: 13–23.

Adoni, Hanna and Mane, Sherrill (1984) 'Media and the social construction of reality: toward an integration of theory and research', *Communication Research*, 11 (3): 323–340.

Adorno, Theodor W. (2001) *The Culture Industry: Selected Essays on Mass Culture* (2nd edn). London/New York: Routledge.

Alba, Richard D. (1990) *Ethnic Identity: The Transformation of White America*. New Haven, CT: Yale University Press.

Allport, Gordon (1954) *The Nature of Prejudice*. New York: Macmillan.

Althusser, Louis (1971) 'Ideology and ideological state apparatuses', *Lenin and Philosophy and Other Essays*. New York: Monthly Review.

Altman, Irwin and Taylor, Dalmas (1973) *Social Penetration: The Development of Interpersonal Relationship*. New York: Holt, Rinehart and Winston.

Amason, Anne C. (1996) 'Distinguishing the effects of functional and dysfunctional conflict on strategic decision-making: resolving a paradox for top management teams', *Academy of Management Journal*, 39: 123–148.

Anderson, Benedict (1983) *Imagined Communities: Reflections on the Origin and Spread of Nationalism*. London: Verso.

Anderson, Jennifer (1987) 'Japanese tea ritual: religion in practice', *Man: Journal of the Royal Anthropological Society of Great Britain and Ireland*, 22 (3): 475–498.

Ang, Ien (2000) 'Transforming Chinese identities in Australia: between assimilation, multiculturalism, and diaspora', in T.A. See (ed.), *Intercultural Relations, Cultural Transformation, and Identity*. Manila: Kaisa Para Sa Kaunlaran. pp. 248–258.

Ang, Ien (2001) *On Not Speaking Chinese: Living between Asia and the West*. London: Routledge.

Anti-Semitism Worldwide Report (2007) *Report 2007* [online]. Accessed 18 September 2008 at http://www.tau.ac.il/Anti-Semitism/asw2007/gen-analysis-07.pdf

Ardizzoni, Michela (2007) *North/South, East/West: Mapping Italianness on Television*. Boulder, CO: Lexington Books.

Arendt, Hannah (1958) *The Human Condition*. Chicago: University of Chicago Press.

Argent, Hedi (2003) *Models of Adoption Support: What Works and What Doesn't*. London: British Association of Adoption and Fostering.

ASAPS (American Society for Aesthetic Plastic Surgery) (2006) '11.5 Million Cosmetic Procedures in 2005' [online]. Accessed 2 March 2009 at http://www.surgery.org/public/news-release

Augsburger, David (1992) *Conflict Mediation across Cultures*. Louisville, KY: Westminster/John Knox.

Ayoko, Oluremi B. (2007) 'Communication openness, conflict events and reactions to conflict in culturally diverse workgroups', *Cross-Cultural Management*, 14 (2): 105–123.

Banks, Ingrid (2000) *Hair Matters: Beauty, Power and Black Women's Consciousness*. New York: New York University Press.

Barbour, Stephen (2002) 'Nationalism, language, Europe', in S. Barbour and C. Carmichael (eds), *Language and Nationalism in Europe*. Oxford: Oxford University Press. pp. 1–17.

Barker, Valerie; Giles, Howard; Noels, Kimberly; Duck, July; Hecht, Michael and Clement, Richarde (2001) 'The English-only movement: a communication analysis of changing perceptions of language vitality', *Journal of Communication*, 51 (1): 3–37.

Basch, Linda; Schiller, Nina G. and Blanc, Cristina S. (1994) *Nations Unbound: Transnational Projects, Postcolonial Predicaments, and Deterritorialized Nation-States*. Langhorne, PA: Gordon and Breach.

Baxter, Leslie (1988) 'A dialectical perspective on communication strategies in relationship development', in S.W. Duck (ed.), *Handbook of Personal Relationships: Theory, Research, and Interventions*. New York: Wiley. pp. 257–273.

Baylis, John and Smith, Steve (eds) (2001) *The Globalization of World Politics: An Introduction to International Relations*. Oxford: Oxford University Press.

Beamer, Linda and Varner, Iris (2008) *Intercultural Communication in the Global Workplace* (4th edn). Boston, MA: McGraw-Hill/Irwin.

Becker, An (2004) 'Television, disordered eating and young women in Fiji: negotiating body image and identity during rapid social change', *Culture, Medicine and Psychiatry,* 28: 533–559.

Bennett, Milton J. (1986) 'A developmental approach to training for intercultural sensitivity', *International Journal of Intercultural Relations*, 10 (2): 179–195.

Bennett, Milton J. (1993) 'Towards ethnorelativism: a developmental model of intercultural sensitivity', in M. Paige (ed.), *Education for the Intercultural Experience*. Yarmouth, ME: Intercultural Press. pp. 343–354.

Berger, Charles R. and Calabrese, Richard J. (1975) 'Some explorations in initial interaction and beyond: toward a developmental theory of interpersonal communication', *Human Communication Theory*, 1: 99–112.

Berlo, David (1960) *The Process of Communication*. New York: Holt, Rinehart and Winston.

Berry, John W. (1980) 'Acculturation as varieties of adaptation', in A.M. Padilla (ed.), *Acculturation: Theory, Models and Some New Findings*. Washington, DC: Westview. pp. 9–25.

Berry, John W. (1986) 'Multiculturalism and psychology in plural societies', in L. Ekstrand (ed.), *Ethnic Minorities and Immigrants in a Cross-Cultural Perspective*. Lisse: Swets & Zeitlinger. pp. 35–51.

Berry, John W. (1990) 'Psychology of acculturation: understanding individuals moving between cultures', in R. Brislin (ed.), *Applied Cross-cultural Psychology*. Newbury Park, CA: SAGE. pp. 232–253.

Berry, John W. (2001) 'A psychology of immigration', *Journal of Social Issues*, 57: 615–631.

Berry, John W. (2005) 'Acculturation: living successfully in two cultures', *International Journal of Intercultural Relations*, 29: 697–712.

Berry, John W. and Kalin, Rudolf (1995) 'Multicultural and ethnic attitudes in Canada: overview of the 1991 survey', *Canadian Journal of Behavioural Science*, 27: 301–320.

Berry, John W., Kalin, Rudolf and Taylor, Donald M. (1977) *Multiculturalism and Ethnic Attitudes in Canada*. Ottawa: Ministry of Supply and Services.

Birdwhistell, Ray (1970) *Kinesics and Context: Essays on Body Motion Communication*. Philadelphia: University of Pennsylvania Press.

Bitzer, Lloyad F. (1968) 'The rhetorical situation', *Philosophy and Rhetoric*, 1: 1–14.

Blake, Robert R. and Mouton, Jane S. (1964) *The Managerial Grid*. Houston, MA: Gulf.

Blank, Thomas; Schmidt, Peter and Westle, Bettina (2001) 'Patriotism – a contradiction, a possibility, or an empirical reality?' Paper presented at the ECPR Workshop 26, National Identity in Europe, Grenoble, France.

Bogardus, Emory S. (1933) 'A social distance scale', *Sociology and Social Research*, 17: 265–271.

Bonvillain, Nancy (2008) *Language, Culture and Communication: The Meaning of Messages* (5th edn). Upper Saddle River, NJ: Pearson/Prentice Hall.

Boulding, Kenneth (1956) *The Image*. Ann Arbor, MI: University of Michigan Press.

Bourdieu, Pierre (1977) *Outline of a Theory and Practice*. Cambridge: Cambridge University Press.

Bourhis, Richard Y., El-Geledi, Shaha and Sachdev, Itesh (2007) 'Language, ethnicity, and intergroup relations', in A. Weatherall, C. Gallois and B.M. Watson (eds), *Language, Discourse, and Social Psychology*. Basingstoke, England: Palgrave Macmillan. pp. 15–50.

Bourhis, Richard Y.; Moïse, Lena C.; Perreault, Stephane and Senécal, Sacha (1997) 'Towards an interactive acculturation model: a social psychological approach', *International Journal of Psychology*, 32 (6): 369–386.

Boussouar, Brice and Mailliet, Anne (2008) German Nudists versus Polish Puritans [online]. Accessed 10 November 2008 at http://www.france24.com/en/20080803-usedom-island-baltic-sea-border-germany-nudists-poland-puritans

Brewer, Marilynn B. (1997) 'The social psychology of intergroup relations: can research inform practice?', *Journal of Social Issues*, 53: 197–211.

Brislin, Richard W. (1981) *Cross-cultural Encounters*. Elmsford, NY: Pergamon.

Brislin, Richard W. (1988) 'Increasing awareness of class, ethnicity, culture and race by expanding on students' own experiences', in I. Cohen (ed.), *The G. Stanley Lecture Hall Series*, Vol. 8. Washington, DC: American Psychological Association. pp. 137–180.

Brubaker, Roger (2001) 'The return of assimilation? Changing perspectives on immigration and its sequels in France, Germany, and the United States', *Ethnic and Racial Studies*, 24 (4): 531–548.

Burgoon, Judee (1978) 'A communication model of personal space violation: expectation and an initial test', *Human Communication Research*, 4: 129–142.

Buruma, Ian (2007) *Murder in Amsterdam: Liberal Europe, Islam, and the Limits of Tolerance*. London: Powell.

Byrne, Donn (1971) *The Attraction Paradigm*. New York: Academic.

Carbaugh, Donal; Berry, Michael and Nurmikari-Berry, Marjatta (2006) 'Coding personhood through cultural terms and practices: silence and quietude as a Finnish "natural way of being"', *Journal of Language and Social Psychology*, 25: 203–220.

Caspie, Avner and Gorsky, Paul (2006) 'Online deception: prevalence, motivation, and emotion', *CyberPsychology & Behavior*, 9 (1): 54–59.

Castells, Manuel (1997) *The Power of Identity*. Oxford: Blackwell.

Castles, Stephen (1992) 'The Australian model of immigration and multiculturalism: is it applicable to Europe?', *International Immigration Review*, 26 (2): 549–567.

Castles, Stephen (2000) *Ethnicity and Globalisation*. London: SAGE.

Chan, Ricky Y.K., Cheng, Louis T.W. and Szeto, Ricky W.F. (2002) 'The dynamics of Guanxi and ethics for Chinese executives', *Journal of Business Ethics*, 41: 327–336.

Charon, Joel M. (2007) *Ten Questions: A Sociological Perspective* (6th edn). Belmont, CA: Wadsworth.

Chen, Guo-ming and Starosta, William J. (2005) *Foundations of Intercultural Communication*. Lanham, ML: American University Press.

Chomsky, Noam (1968) *Language and Mind*. New York: Harcourt, Brace & World.

Chomsky, Noam (1975) *Reflections on Language*. New York: Pantheon.

Chomsky, Noam (1980) *Rules and Representations*. Oxford: Blackwell.

Clark, Anna E. and Kashima, Yoshihisa (2007) 'Stereotypes help people connect with others in the community: a situated functional analysis of the stereotype consistency bias in communication', *Journal of Personality and Social Psychology*, 93 (6): 1028–1039.

Clark, Virginia; Eschholz, Paul and Rosa, Alfred (1998) *Language: Readings in Language and Culture*. New York: St. Martin's.

Clifford, James (1997) 'Diasporas', in M. Guibenau and J. Rex (eds), *The Ethnicity Reader: Nationalism, Multiculturalism and Migration*. Cambridge: Polity. pp. 283–290.

Coleman, Peter T. (2000) 'Power and conflict', in M. Deutsch and P.T. Coleman (eds), *The Handbook of Conflict Resolution*. New York: New York Press. pp. 115–123.

Colovic, Ivan (2002) *Politics of Identity in Serbia*. New York: New York University Press.

Condon, John C. (1977) *Interpersonal Communication*. New York: Macmillan.

Condon, John C. (1985) *Good Neighbors: Communicating with the Mexicans*. Yarmouth, ME: Intercultural Press.

Condon, John C. and Yousef, Fathi S. (1975) *An Introduction to Intercultural Communication*. Indianapolis, IN: Bobbs-Merrill.

Cooper, Pamela J.; Calloway-Thomas, Carolyn and Simonds, Cheri J. (2007) *Intercultural Communication: A Text with Readings*. Boston, MA: Pearson.

Couldry, Nick (2000) *The Place of Media Power*. London: Routledge.

Cox, Taylor H.; Lobel, Sharon A. and McLeod, Poppy L. (1991) 'Effects of ethnic group cultural differences on cooperative and competitive behavior on a group task', *Academy of Management Journal*, 34 (4): 827–847.

Craig, Robert T. (1999) 'Communication theory as a field', *Communication Theory*, 9 (2): 119–161.

Dance, Frank E.X. (1970) 'The "concept" of communication', *Journal of Communication*, 20: 201–210.

Daniel, Jack (1976) 'The poor: aliens in an affluent society', in L. Samovar and R. Porter (eds), *Intercultural Communication: A Reader* (2nd edn). Belmont, CA: Wadsworth.

Daniels, Harvey (1985) 'Famous last words', in V. Clark, E. Paul and R. Alfred (eds), *Language: Introductory Reading*. New York: St. Martin's. pp. 18–36.

Davis, Kathy (1995) *Reshaping the Female Body: The Dilemma of Cosmetic Surgery*. New York: Routledge.

Dayan, Daniel and Katz, Elihu (1992) *Media Events*. Cambridge, MA: Harvard University Press.

Deetz, Stanley A. (1994) 'Future of the discipline: the challenges, the research and the social contribution', in S.A. Deetz (ed.), *Communication Yearbook 17*. Thousand Oaks, CA: SAGE. pp. 565–600.

Denzin, Norman K. and Lincoln, Yvonna S. (eds) (1998) *The Landscape of Qualitative Research*. London: SAGE.

Department of Economics and Social Affairs: Population Division (DESA) (2006) 'Trends in total migrant stock: the 2005 revision' [CD-ROM documentation]. New York: United Nations.

Department of Premier and Cabinet (2000) *Implementation of the Multicultural Queensland Policy 1999–2000*. Brisbane: Multicultural Affairs Queensland.

Dines, Gail and Humez, Jean M. (1995) *Gender, Race and Class in Media*. Thousand Oaks, CA: SAGE.

Dodd, Carley H. (1998) *Dynamics of Intercultural Communication* (5th edn). Boston, MA: McGraw-Hill.

Dyer, Linda M. and Ross, Christopher A. (2000) 'Ethnic enterprises and their clientele', *Journal of Small Business Management*, 38 (2): 48–66.

Edwards, John R. (ed.) (1998) *Language in Canada*. Cambridge, UK: Cambridge University Press.

Edwards, Richard and Usher, Robin (2008) *Globalisation and Pedagogy: Space, Place and Identity* (2nd edn). Abingdon, Oxon/New York: Routledge.

Ehrenreich, Barbara and Russell-Hochschild, Arlie (eds) (2002) *Global Women; Nannies, Maids and Sex Workers in the New Economy*. New York: Henry Holt.

Ekman, Paul and Friesen, Wallace V. (1969) 'The repertoire of nonverbal behavior: categories, origins, usage, and coding', *Semiotica*, 1: 49–98.

Ekman, Paul and Friesen, Wallace V. (1971) 'Constants across cultures in the face and emotion', *Journal of Personality and Social Psychology*, 17: 124–129.

Elliott, Deni (1997) 'The Great Hanshim earthquake and the ethics of intervention', in F.L. Casmir (ed.), *Ethics in Intercultural and International Communication*. Mahwah, NJ: Lawrence Erlbaum. pp. 43–58.

Erikson, Erik (1968) 'Identity, psychological', *International Encyclopaedia of the Social Sciences*, vol. 7. New York: Macmillan. pp. 46–48.

Erjavec, Karmen and Volčič, Zala (2007) 'The Kosovo battle: media's recontextualization of the Serbian nationalistic discourses', *Harvard Journal of Press and Politics*, 12: 67–86.

Evanoff, Richard (2004) 'Universalist, relativist, and constructivist approaches to intercultural ethics', *International Journal of Intercultural Relations*, 28: 439–458.

Everett, Daniel (2008) *Don't Sleep, There are Snakes: Life and Language in the Amazonian Jungle*. New York: Pantheon.

Fair, Jo E. (2003) '*Francophonie* and the national airwaves: a history of television in Senegal', in L. Parks and S. Kumar (eds), *Planet TV: A Global Television Reader*. New York: New York University Press. pp.189–210.

Fairclough, Norman (2001) *Language and Power*. Harlow, UK: Longman.

Fanon, Frantz (1990) *The Wretched of the Earth*. London: Penguin.

Fisher-Yoshida, Beth (2005) 'Reframing conflict: intercultural conflict as potential transformation', *Journal of Intercultural Communication*, 8: 1–16.

Fiske, John (1982) *Introduction to Communication Studies*. London: Methuen.

Foucault, Michel (2006) *History of Madness*. New York: Routledge.

Frith, Katherine; Shaw, Ping and Cheng, Hong (2005) 'The construction of beauty: a cross-cultural analysis of women's magazine advertising', *Journal of Communication*, 55 (1): 56–70.

Furnham, Adrian and Bochner, Stephen (1982) 'Social difficulty in a foreign culture: an empirical analysis of culture shock', in S. Bochner (ed.), *Culture in Contact: Studies in Cross-Cultural Interaction*. New York: Pergamon. pp. 161–198.

Gallois, Cindy; Ogay, Tania and Giles, Howard (2005) 'Communication accommodation theory: a look back and a look ahead', in W.B. Gudykunst (ed.), *Theorizing about Intercultural Communication*. Thousand Oaks, CA: SAGE. pp. 121–148.

Gauntlett, David (2002) *Media, Gender and Identity*. New York: Routledge.

Geertz, Clifford (1973) *The Interpretation of Cultures*. New York: Basic Books.

Gerbner, George (1956), 'Toward a general model of communication', *Audio-Visual Communication Review*, 4: 171–199.

Gilbert, Dennis (2003) *The American Class Structure in an Age of Growing Inequality*. Belmont, CA: Wadsworth.

Goonasekera, Anura (2001) 'Transnational communication: establishing effective linkages between North and South', in N. Chitty (ed.), *Mapping Globalization: International Media and a Crisis of Identity*. Southbank: Penang. pp. 270–281.

Gordon, Milton M. (1964) *Assimilation in American Life: The Role of Race, Religion and National Origins*. Oxford, UK: Oxford University Press.

Goss, Blaine (1995) *The Psychology of Human Communication* (2nd edn). Prospect Heights, IL: Waveland.

Gramsci, Antonio (2000) *The Antonio Gramsci Reader: Selected Writings: 1916–1935*. New York: New York University Press.

Grbich, Carol (2007) *Qualitative Data Analysis: An Introduction*. London: SAGE.

Greelis, Jim (2007) 'Pigeons in military history. World of Wings Center' [online]. Accessed 12 April 2009 at http://www.pigeonscenter.org/militarypigeons.html

Greene, Patricia G. (1997) 'A resource-based approach to ethnic business sponsorship: a consideration of Ismaili-Pakistani immigrants', *Journal of Small Business Management*, 35 (4): 58–71.

Griffin, Erin (2006) *A First Look at Communication Theory* (6th edn). Boston, MA: McGraw-Hill.

Gudykunst, William B. (1983) 'Toward a typology of stranger-host relationships', *International Journal of Intercultural Relations*, 7: 401–415.

Gudykunst, William B. (2004) *Bridging Differences: Effective Intergroup Communication* (4th edn). Thousand Oaks, CA: SAGE.

Gudykunst, William B. and Kim, Young Y. (1984) *Communicating with Strangers: An Approach to Intercultural Communication*. New York: McGraw-Hill.

Gudykunst, William B. and Ting-Toomey, Stella (1988) 'Verbal communication styles', in W.B. Gudykunst and S. Ting-Toomey (eds), *Culture and Interpersonal Communication*. Newbury Park, CA: SAGE. pp. 99–115.

Gupta, Nilanjana (1998) *Switching Channels: Ideologies of Television in India*. New Delhi: Oxford University Press.

Habermas, Jurgen (1989) *The Structural Transformation of the Public Sphere*. Cambridge, MA: MIT Press.

Hall, Bradford J. (2005) *Among Cultures: The Challenge of Communication* (2nd edn). Belmont, CA: Thomson Wadsworth.

Hall, Edward T. (1959) *The Silent Language*. New York: Doubleday.

Hall, Edward T. (1966) *The Hidden Dimension*. New York: Doubleday.

Hall, Edward T. (1976) *Beyond Culture*. New York: Doubleday.

Hall, Edward T. (1977) *Beyond Culture*. New York: Doubleday.

Hall, Edward T. and Hall, Mildred R. (1990) *Understanding Cultural Differences: Germans, French, and Americans*. Yarmouth, ME: Intercultural Press.

Hall, Stuart (1996) *Modernity: An Introduction to Modern Societies*. Cambridge: Blackwell.

Hall, Stuart (2001) 'Negotiating Caribbean identities', in B. Meeks and F. Lindahl (eds), *New Caribbean Thought: A Reader*. Jamaica, Barbados, and Trinidad and Tobago: University of the West Indies Press. pp. 122–145.

Hancock, Jeffrey and Toma, Catalina L. (2009) 'Putting your best face forward: the accuracy of online dating photographs', *Journal of Communication*, 59 (2): 367–386.

Hardiman, Rita (2001) 'Reflections on white identity development theory', in C.L. Wijeyesinghe and B.W. Jackson III (eds), *New Perspectives on Racial Identity Development: A Theoretical and Practical Anthology*. New York: New York University Press. pp. 12–34.

Hargreaves, Alec (1995) *Immigration, Race and Ethnicity in Contemporary France*. London: Routledge.

Harris, Philip R. and Morgan, Robert T. (1987) *Managing Cultural Differences*. Houston, TX: Gulf.

Hartmann, Paul and Husband, Charles (1972) 'The mass media and racial conflict', in D. McQuail (ed.), *Sociology of Mass Communications*. Harmondsworth: Penguin. pp. 435–455.

Harvey, David (2001) *Spaces of Capital: Towards a Critical Geography*. New York: Routledge.

Heidelberg Institute for International Conflict Research (HIICR) (2007) *A 2007 Report* [online]. Accessed 18 October 2008 at http://www.hiik.de/en/konfliktbarometer/pdf/ConflictBarometer_2007.pdf

Heider, Fritz (1958) *The Psychology of Interpersonal Relations*. New York: Wiley.

Held, David and McGrew, Anthony (eds) (2007) *Globalization Theory: Approaches and Controversies*. Cambridge: Polity.

Herdt, Gilbert (ed.) (1996) *Third Sex, Third Gender: Beyond Sexual Dimorphism in Culture and History*. New York: Zone.

Hestroni, Amir (2000) 'Relationship between values and appeals in Israeli advertising: a smallest space analysis', *Journal of Advertising*, 29 (3): 55–68.

Hilton, James L. and von Hippel, William (1996) 'Stereotypes', *Annual Review of Psychology*, 47: 237–271.

Hobsbawm, Eric (1983) *Nations and Nationalisms since 1780: Program, Myth, Reality*. Cambridge: Cambridge University Press.

Hoff, Erika (2001) *Language Development* (2nd edn). New York: Brooks/Cole.

Hofstede, Geert (1980) *Culture's Consequences: International Differences in Work Related Values*. Beverly Hills, CA: SAGE.

Hofstede, Geert (1983) 'National culture in four dimensions', *International Studies of Management and Organization*, 13: 46–74.

Hofstede, Geert (1991) *Cultures and Organizations: Software of the Mind*. New York: McGraw-Hill.

Hofstede, Geert (2001) *Culture's Consequences: Comparing Values, Behaviors, Institutions and Organizations across Nations* (2nd edn). Thousand Oaks, CA: SAGE.

Hofstede, Geert and Bond, Michael H. (1988) 'The Confucius connection: from cultural roots to economic growth', *Organizational Dynamics*, 16: 5–21.

Hogg, Michael A. and Abrams, Dominic (1988) *Social Identifications: A Social Psychology of Intergroup Relations and Group Processes*. London: Routledge.

Hogg, Michael A. and Mullin, Ben (1999) 'Joining groups to reduce uncertainty: subjective uncertainty reduction and group identification', in D. Abrams and M.A. Hogg (eds), *Social Identity and Social Cognition*. Oxford: Blackwell. pp. 34–45.

House, Robert J.; Hanges, Paul J.; Javidan, Mansour J.; Dorfman, Peter W. and Gupta, Vipin (eds) (2004) *Culture, Leadership and Organizations: The GLOBE Study of 62 Societies*. Thousand Oaks, CA: SAGE.

Hui, C. Harry and Triandis, Harry C. (1986) 'Individualism-collectivism: a study of cross-cultural researchers', *Journal of Cross-Cultural Psychology*, 17 (2): 225–248.

Hutchinson, John (1987) *The Dynamics of Cultural Nationalism: The Gaelic Revival and the Creation of the Irish Nation State*. London: Allen and Unwin.

Hutchinson, John and Smith, Anthony D. (1996) *Ethnicity*. Oxford: Oxford University Press.

IDP Education (2008) 'Education replaces tourism as Australia's No. 1 services export' [online]. Accessed 26 June 2008 at http:www.idp.com/about_idp/media/2008/February/tourism_no_services_export

Institute of International Education (IIE) (2006) 'New enrolment of foreign students in the US climbs in 2005/06' [online]. Accessed 26 June 2008 at http://opendoors.iienetwork.org/?p=89251

International Organization for Migration (2006) *World Migration* [online]. Accessed 24 July 2009 at http://www.iom.int/iomwebsite/Publication/Servlet SearchPublication?event=detail&id=4171

Jandt, Fred E. (2007) *An Introduction to Intercultural Communication: Identities in a Global Community* (5th edn). Thousand Oaks, CA: SAGE.

Jarvenpaa, Sirkka L. and Tractinsky, Noam (1999) 'Consumer trust in an internet store: a cross-cultural validation', *Journal of Commuter-Mediated Communication*, 5 (1): 1–36.

Jaspars, Jos and Hewstone, Miles (1982) 'Cross-cultural interaction, social attribution, and intergroup relations', in S. Bochner (ed.), *Cultures in Contact*. Elmsord, NY: Pergamon. pp. 127–156.

Jenkins, Richard (1996) *Social Identity*. London: Routledge.

Jitpiromsri, Srisompob (2006) 'Unpacking Thailand's southern conflict: the poverty of structural explanation', *Critical Asian Studies*, 38 (1): 95–117.

Jitpiromsri, Srisompob (2008) '4.5 Years of the southern fire: the failure of policy in Red Zone', *DWS's Research Database* [online]. Accessed 18 September 2008 at http://www.deepsouthwatch.org /index.php?l=content&id=265

Kearney, Michael (1995) 'The local and the global: the anthropology of globalization and transnationalism', *Annual Review of Anthropology*, 24 (2): 547–565.

Kelley, Harold H. and Thibaut, John W. (1978) *Interpersonal Relations: A Theory of Interdependence*. New York: Wiley.

Kim, Young Y. (1986) *Interethnic Communication: Current Research*. Newbury Park, CA: SAGE.

Kim, Young Y. (1988) *Cross-Cultural Adaptation: Current Approaches*. Newbury Park, CA: SAGE.

Kim, Young Y. (2001) *Becoming Intercultural: An Integrative Theory of Communication and Cross-Cultural Adaptation*. Thousand Oaks, CA: SAGE.

Khan, Fazal R.; Abbasi, Abdus S.; Mahsud, Mohammad N.; Zafar, Hashmat A. and Kaltikhel, Asmat U. (1999) 'The press and Sindhi-Mohajir ethnic relations in Hyderland: do the newspapers cultivate ethnicity?', in A. Goonasekera and Y. Ito (eds), *Mass Media and Cultural Identity*. London: Pluto. pp. 129–191.

Klopf, Donald W. (1995) *Intercultural Encounters: The Fundamentals of Intercultural Communication*. Englewood, CO: Morton.

Kluckhohn, Clyde (1951) 'Values and value orientation in the theory of action', in T. Parsons and E. Shils (eds), *Toward a General Theory of Action*. Cambridge, MA: Harvard University Press. pp. 388–433.

Kluckhohn, Florence and Strodtbeck, Frederick (1961) *Variations in Value Orientations*. Evanston, IL: Row, Peterson and Co.

Knapp, Mark L. and Hall, Judith A. (1997) *Nonverbal Communication in Human Interaction* (4th edn). Philadelphia, PA: Harcourt, Brace, Jovanovich.

Kolar-Panov, Dona (1997) *Video, War and the Diasporic Imagination*. New York: Routledge.

Kosic, Ankica; Mannetti, Lucia and Sam, David L. (2005) 'The role of majority attitudes towards out-group in the perception of the acculturation strategies of immigrants', *International Journal of Intercultural Relations*, 29: 273–288.

Kraidy, Marwan (2005) *Hybridity, or the Cultural Logic of Globalization*. Philadelphia, PA: Temple University Press.

Lakoff, Robin (1975) *Language and Woman's Place*. New York: Harper & Row.

Lasswell, Harold (1948) 'The structure and function of communication in society', in L. Boyson (ed.), *The Communication of Ideas*. New York: Harper. pp. 32–51.

Lee, Chol and Green, Robert T. (1991) 'Cross-cultural examination of the Fishbein behavioral intentions model', *Journal of International Business Studies*, 21 (2): 289–305.

Lee, Kang (2000) *Childhood Cognitive Development: The Essential Readings*. Oxford: Blackwell.

Lee, Tien-Tsung and Wu, Danis H. (2004, May) 'Media use and attitudes toward Asian Americans'. Paper presented at 54th Convention of International Communication Association, New Orleans.

Lesko, Alexandra C. and Corpus, Jennifer H. (2006) 'Discounting the difficult: how high-match-identified women respond to stereotype threat', *Sex Roles*, 54: 113–125.

Levi-Strauss, Claude (1962) *The Savage Mind*. Chicago: University of Chicago Press.

Lewicki, Roy J.; Saunders, David M.; Barry, Bruce and Minton, John (2003) *Essentials of Negotiation* (3rd edn). Boston, MA: McGraw-Hill/Irwin.

Liang, Ting-Peng and Huang, Jin-Shiang (1998) 'An empirical study on consumer acceptance of products in electronic markets: a transaction cost model', *Decision Support Systems*, 24: 29–43.

Light, Ivan H. and Gold, Steven J. (2000) *Ethnic Economies*. San Diego, CA: Academic Press.

Lippmann, Walter (1922) *Public Opinion*. New York: Macmillan.

Littlejohn, Stephen W. (1982) 'An overview of contributions to human communication theory from other disciplines', in Frank E.S. Dance (ed.), *Human Communication Theory: Comparative Essays*. New York: Harper & Row. pp. 243–285.

Littlejohn, Stephen W. (1996a) 'Communication theory', in E. Enos (ed.), *Encyclopedia of Rhetoric and Composition: Communication from Ancient Times to the Information Age*. New York: Garland. pp. 117–121.

Littlejohn, Stephen W. (1996b) *Theories of Human Communication* (5th edn). Belmont, CA: Wadsworth.

Liu, Shuang (2006) 'An examination of the effects of print media exposure and contact on the subjective social reality and acculturation attitudes', *International Journal of Intercultural Relations*, 30: 365–382.

Liu, Shuang (2007) 'Living with others: mapping the routes to acculturation in a multicultural society', *International Journal of Intercultural Relations*, 31 (6): 761–778.

Liu, Shuang and Chen, Guo-ming (1999) 'Assessing Chinese conflict management styles in joint ventures', *Intercultural Communication Studies*, IX-2: 71–88.

Liu, Shuang and Chen, Guo-ming (2002) 'Collaboration over avoidance: conflict management styles in state-owned enterprises in China', in G. Chen and R. Ma (eds), *Chinese Conflict Management and Resolution*. Westport, CT: Ablex. pp. 163–182.

Liu, Shuang and Louw, Eric (2009) 'Cultural translation and identity performance of Chinese business people in Australia', *China Media Research*, 9 (1): 1–9.

Louw, Eric (2004a) 'Political power, national identity, and language: the case of Afrikaans', *International Journal of the Sociology of Language*, 170 (1): 43–58.

Louw, Eric (2004b) *The Rise, Fall, and Legacy of Apartheid*. Westport, CT: Praege.

Lowenstein, Ralph L. and Merrill, John C. (1990) *Macromedia: Mission, Message, and Morality*. New York: Longman.

Lull, James (2000) *Media, Communication, Culture: A Global Perspective* (2nd edn). New York: Columbia University Press.

Luo, Shiow-Huey and Wiseman, Richard L. (2000) 'Ethnic language maintenance among Chinese immigrant children in the United States', *International Journal of Intercultural Relations*, 24 (3): 307–324.

Lustig, Myron and Koester, Jolene (2010) *Intercultural Competence: Interpersonal Communication across Cultures* (6th edn). Boston, MA: Pearson/Allyn & Bacon.

Mader, Thomas F. and Mader, Diane C. (1990) *Understanding One Another: Communicating Interpersonally*. Dubuque, IA: Brown.

Malotki, Ekkehart (1983) *Hopi Time: A Linguistic Analysis of the Temporal Concepts in the Hopi Language*. New York: Mouton De Gruyter.

Marden, Peter and Mercer, David (1998) 'Locating strangers: multiculturalism, citizenship and nationhood in Australia', *Political Geography*, 17 (8): 939–958.

Markus, Hazel R. and Kitayama, Shinobu (1991) 'Culture and the self: implications for cognition, emotion, and motivation', *Psychological Review*, 98: 224–253.

Martin, Judith and Nakayama, Thomas (2000) *Intercultural Communication in Contexts*. Mountain View, CA: Mayfield.

Martin, Judith and Nakayama, Thomas (2001) *Experiencing Intercultural Communication: An Introduction*. Mountain View, CA: Mayfield.

Massey, Douglas and Taylor, Edward J. (eds) (2004) *International Migration: Prospects and Policies*. Oxford: Oxford University Press.

Mastro, Dana E. and Greenberg, Bradley S. (2000) 'The portrayal of racial minorities on prime time television', *Journal of Broadcasting and Electronic Media*, 44 (4): 690–703.

McCombs, Maxwell and Shaw, Donald (1972) 'The agenda-setting function of the mass media', *Public Opinion Quarterly*, 36: 176–187.

McCowan, Clint (2003) 'Imagining the Zapatistas: rebellion, representation and popular culture', *International Third World Studies Journal and Review,* XIV: 29–34.

McLuhan, Marshall (1964) *Understanding Media: The Extension of Man.* New York: McGraw-Hill.

McLuhan, Marshall and Fiore, Quentin (1967) *The Medium is the Message.* New York: Random House.

McQuail, Denis (2005) *McQuail's Mass Communication Theory* (5th edn). London: SAGE.

McSweeney, Brendan (2002) 'Hofstede's model of national cultural differences and their consequences: a triumph of faith – a failure of analysis', *Human Relations*, 55: 89–118.

McWhorter, John (2002) *The Power of Babel: The Natural History of Language.* New York: Random House.

Mehrabian, Albert (1982) *Silent Messages: Implicit Communication of Emotion and Attitudes* (2nd edn). Belmont, CA: Wadsworth.

Merry, Sally E. (1989) 'Mediation in cross-cultural perspective', in K. Kressell and D. Pruitt (eds), *The Mediation of Disputes: Empirical Studies in the Resolution of Social Conflict.* San Francisco, CA: Jossey-Bass. pp. 75–103.

Merton, Robert K. (1968) *Social Theory and Social Structure.* New York: Free.

Miller, Katherine (1995) *Organizational Communication: Approaches and Processes.* Belmont, CA: Wadsworth.

Mohanty, Chandra Talpade (2003) *Feminism without Borders: Decolonizing Theory, Practicing Solidarity.* Durham, NC: Duke University Press.

Morley, David (1980) *The Nationwide Audience.* London: BFI.

Morley, David (2000) *Home Territories: Media, Mobility and Identity.* London and New York: Routledge.

Morley, David and Robins, Kevin (1995) *Spaces of Identity: Global Media, Electronic Landscapes and Cultural Boundaries.* London: Routledge.

Morris, Desmond (1994) *The Human Animal: A Personal View of the Human Species.* New York: Crown.

Morris, Merrill and Ogan, Christine (1996) 'The internet as mass medium', *Journal of Communication*, 56 (1): 39–50.

Mortensen, C. David (1972) *Communication: The Study of Human Interaction.* New York: McGraw-Hill.

Motley, Michael T. (1990) 'On whether one can(not) not communicate: an examination via traditional communication postulates', *Western Journal of Speech Communication*, 54: 1–20.

Mulder, Niels (1996) *Inside Thai Society: Interpretations of Everyday Life.* Amsterdam: Pepin.

Mullen, Brian and Hu, Li-Tze (1989) 'Perceptions of ingroup and outgroup variability: a meta-analytic integration', *Basic and Applied Social Psychology*, 10: 233–252.

Naficy, Hamid (1993) *The Making of Exile Cultures: Iranian Television in Los Angeles*. Minneapolis: University of Minnesota Press.

Neuliep, James (2006) *Intercultural Communication: A Contextual Approach* (3rd edn). Thousand Oaks, CA: SAGE.

Newbold, Chris (1995) 'The media effects tradition', in O. Boyd-Barrett and C. Newbold (eds), *Approaches to Media: A Reader*. London: Hodder Arnold. pp. 118–123.

Niehoff, Arthur (1964) 'Theravada Buddhism: a vehicle for technical change', *Human Organization*, 23: 108–112.

Nisbett, Richard E. and Miyamoto, Yuri (2005) 'The influence of culture: holistic versus analytic perception', *Trends in Cognitive Sciences*, 9 (10): 467–473.

Nishida, Hiroko (2005) 'Cultural schema theory', in W.B. Gudykunst (ed.), *Theorizing about Intercultural Communication*. Thousand Oaks, CA: SAGE. pp. 401–410.

Nua Internet Survey (2006) 'How many online?' [online]. Accessed 18 April 2008 at http://www.nua.ie.surveys/how_many_online/index.html

ODIHR report (2008) 'Report' [online]. Accessed 18 April 2008 at http://www1. yadvashem.org/about_holocaust/holocaust_antisemitism/media_holocaust. html#FAQS

Oetzel, John G. (2002) 'The effects of culture and cultural diversity on communication in work groups: synthesizing vertical and cultural differences with a face-negotiation perspective', in L.R. Frey (ed.), *New Directions in Group Communication*. Thousand Oaks, CA: SAGE. pp. 121–137.

Ogden, Denise T.; Ogden, James R. and Schau, Hope J. (2004) 'Exploring the impact of culture and acculturation on consumer purchase decisions: toward a microcultural perspective', *Academy of Marketing Science Review*, 3 [online]. Available at http://www.amsreview.org/articles/ogden03_2004.pdf

Okabe, Roichi (1983) 'Cultural assumptions of East and West', in W.B. Gudykunst (ed.), *Intercultural Communication Theory*. Beverly Hills, CA: SAGE. pp. 21–44.

Østergaard-Nielsen, Eva (ed.) (2003) *International Migration and Sending Countries: Perceptions, Policies and Transnational Relations*. New York: Palgrave Macmillan.

Pacanowsky, Mochael E. and O'Donnell-Trujillo, Nick (1983) 'Organizational communication as cultural performance', *Communication Monographs*, 50: 126–47.

Park, Robert, E. (1924) 'The concept of social distance', *Journal of Applied Sociology*, 33 (6): 881–893.

Pearce, Barnett W. (1989) *Communication and the Human Condition* Carbondale, IL: Southern Illinois University Press.

Pearce, Barnett W. (2005) 'The coordinated management of meaning (CMM)', in W. B. Gudykunst (ed.), *Theorizing about Intercultural Communication*. Thousand Oaks, CA: SAGE. pp. 35–54.

Pearson, Judy C. and Nelson, Paul E. (1997) *An Introduction to Human Communication: Understanding & Sharing* (2nd edn). Boston, MA: McGraw-Hill.

Pedersen, Paul B. and Jandt, Fred E. (1996) 'Culturally contextual models for creative conflict management', in F.E. Jandt and P.B. Pedersen (eds), *Constructive Conflict Management: Asia Pacific Cases*. Thousand Oaks, CA: SAGE. pp. 3–26.

Pettigrew, Thomas F. (1997) 'Generalized intergroup contact effects on prejudice', *Personality and Social Psychology Bulletin*, 23: 173–185.

Pew Research Report (2008) *Report* [online]. Accessed 2 December 2009 at http://pewresearch.org/pubs/743/united-states-religion

Pfau, Michael; Mullen, Lawrence; Derdrich, Tracy and Garrow, Kirsten (1995) 'Television viewing and public perceptions of attorneys', *Human Communication Research*, 21 (3): 307–330.

Piaget, Jean (1977) *The Development of Thought: Equilibration and Cognitive Structures*. New York: Viking.

Pondy, Louis R. (1967) 'Organizational conflict: concepts and models', *Administrative Science Quarterly*, 12: 296–320.

Potter, Jonathan and Reicher, Stephen (1987) 'Discourses of community and conflict: the organization of social categories in accounts of a "riot" ', *British Journal of Social Psychology*, 26 (1): 25–40.

Potter, Jonathan and Wetherell, Margaret (1987) *Discourse and Social Psychology: Beyond Attitudes and Behaviour*. London: SAGE.

Putnam, Linda L. and Poole, Marshall S. (1987) 'Conflict and negotiation', in F. Jablin, L. Putnam, K. Roberts, and L. Porter (eds), *Handbook of Organizational Communication*. Newbury Park, CA: SAGE. pp. 549–599.

Ramsey, Sheila, J. (1979) 'Nonverbal behavior: an intercultural perspective', in M. Asante, E. Newmark and C. Blake (eds), *Handbook of Intercultural Communication*. Beverly Hills, CA: SAGE. pp. 105–143.

Ritzer, George (2004) *The Globalization of Nothing*. Thousand Oaks, CA: Pine Forge.

Robins, Kevin (1996) 'Interrupting identities: Turkey/Europe', in S. Hall and P. du Gay (eds), *Questions of Cultural Identity*. London: SAGE. pp. 61–86.

Robinson, Peter W. (1996) *Deceit, Delusion, and Detection*. Thousand Oaks, CA: SAGE.

Robinson, Piers (1999) 'The CNN effect: can the news media drive foreign policy?', *Review of International Studies*, 25: 301–309.

Rogers, Everett M. (1995) *Diffusion of Innovations* (4th edn). New York: Free Press.

Rogers, Everett M. (1999) 'Georg Simmel's concept of the stranger and intercultural communication research', *Communication Theory*, 9 (1): 1–25.

Rogers, Everett M. and Steinfatt, Thomas M. (1999) *Intercultural Communication*. Prospect Heights, IL: Waveland.

Rohmann, Anette; Florack, Arnd and Piontkowski, Ursula (2006) 'The role of discordant acculturation attitudes in perceived threat: an analysis of host and immigrant attitudes in Germany', *International Journal of Intercultural Relations,* 30: 683–702.

Rubin, Alan M. (1986) 'Uses, gratifications, and media effects research', in J. Bryant and D. Zillmann (eds), *Perspectives on Media Effects*. Hillsdale, NJ: Lawrence Erlbaum. pp. 281–301.

Rybacki, Karyn and Rybacki, Donald (1991) *Communication Criticism: Approaches and Genres*. Belmont, CA: Wadsworth.

Said, Edward (1994a) *Culture and Imperialism*. New York: Vintage.

Said, Edward (1994b) *Orientalism*. New York: Vintage.

Salacuse, Jeswald W. (1991) *Making Global Deals: Negotiating in the International Market Place*. Boston, MA: Houghton Mifflin.

Samovar, Larry A. and Porter, Richard E. (1995) *Communication between Cultures* (2nd edn). Belmont, CA: Wadsworth.

Saussure, Ferdinand de (1983) *Course in General Linguistics* (edited by C. Bally and A. Sechehaye, translated and annotated by Roy Harris). London: Duckworth.

Sayegh, Liliane and Lasry, Jean-Claude (1993) 'Immigrants' adaptation in Canada: assimilation, acculturation, and orthogonal cultural identification', *Canadian Psychology*, 34 (1): 98–109.

Schneider, David J. (1973) 'Implicit personality theory: a review', *Psychological Bulletin*, 79 (5): 294–309.

Schramm, Wilbur (1971) 'The nature of communication between humans', in W. Schramm and D.F. Roberts (eds), *The Process and Effects of Mass Communication: Revised Version*. Urbana, IL: University of Illinois Press. pp. 3–53.

Schutz, William (1966) *The Interpersonal Underworld*. Palo Alto, CA: Science and Behavior.

Segall, Marshall H. (1979) *Cross-Cultural Psychology: Human Behavior in a Global Perspective*. Monterey, CA: Brooks/Cole.

Seib, Philip (1997) *Headline Diplomacy: How News Coverage Affects Foreign Policy*. London: Praeger.

Seton-Watson, Harry (1977) *Nations and States: An Enquiry into the Origins of Nations and the Politics of Nationalism*. Boulder, CO: Westview.

Shannon, Claude and Weaver, Warren (1949) *The Mathematical Theory of Communication*. Urbana, IL: University of Illinois Press.

Shepherd, G.J. (1993) 'Building a discipline of communication', *Journal of Communication*, 43 (3): 83–91.

Sidanius, Jim and Pratto, Felicia (1999) *Social Dominance: An Intergroup Theory of Social Hierarchy and Oppression*. Cambridge: Cambridge University Press.

Simmel, Georg (1950) *The Sociology of Georg Simmel* (translated by Kurt H. Wolff). New York: Free.

Singer, Marshall (1987) *Intercultural Communication: A Perceptual Approach*. Englewood Cliffs, NJ: Prentice-Hall.

Sitaram, K.S. and Haapanen, Lawrence W. (1979) 'The role of values in intercultural communication', in M.K. Asante and C.A. Blake (eds), *The Handbook of Intercultural Communication*. Beverly Hills, CA: SAGE. pp. 147–160.

Skalli, Loubna H. (2006) *Through a Local Prism*. Lanham, MD: Lexington.

Slobin, Dan I. (2000) 'Verbalized events: a dynamic approach to linguistic relativity and determinism', in S. Niemeier and R. Dirven (eds), *Evidence for Linguistic Relativity*. Amsterdam/Philadelphia: John Benjamins. pp. 107–138.

Smith, Anthony D. (1995) *Nations and Nationalism in a Global Era*. Cambridge: Polity.

Smith, Anthony D. (2007a) *Myths and Memories of the Nation*. Oxford: Oxford University Press.

Smith, Anthony D. (2007b) 'Nations in decline? The erosion and persistence of modern national identities', in M. Young, E. Zuelow and A. Sturm (eds), *Nationalism in a Global Era*. London: Routledge. pp. 16–30.

Soysal, Yasemin N. (1994) *Limits of Citizenship: Migrants and Postnational Membership in Europe*. Chicago, IL: University of Chicago Press.

Spitzberg, Brian H. and Cupach, William R. (1984) *Interpersonal Communication Competence*. Beverly Hills, CA: SAGE.

Steele, Claude M. and Aronson, Joshua (1995) 'Stereotype threat and the intellectual test performance of African Americans', *Attitudes and Social Cognition*, 69: 797–811.

Steele, Claude M., Spencer, Steven and Aronson, Joshua (2002) 'Contending with group image: the psychology of stereotype and social identity threat', *Advances in Experimental Social Psychology*, 34: 379–440.

Stephan, Walter G.; Ybarra, Oscar and Bachman, Guy (1999) 'Prejudice toward immigrants', *Journal of Applied Social Psychology*, 29 (11): 2221–2237.

Stewart, Edward and Bennett, Milton J. (1991) *American Cultural Patterns: A Cross-Cultural Perspective*. Yarmouth, ME: Intercultural Press.

Synnott, Anthony (1996) 'Sociology of smell', *Canadian Review of Sociology and Anthropology*, 28 (4): 437–460.

Tadmor, Carmit T. and Tetlock, Philip E. (2006) 'Biculturalism: a model of the effects of second-culture exposure on acculturation and integrative complexity', *Journal of Cross-Cultural Psychology*, 37 (2): 173–290.

Tajfel, Henri (1978) 'Social categorisation, social identity and social comparison', in H. Tajfel (ed.), *Differentiation between Social Groups: Studies in the Social Psychology of Intergroup Relations*. London: Academic. pp. 61–76.

Tajfel, Henri (1982) *Social Identity and Intergroup Relations*. Cambridge: Cambridge University Press.

Tajfel, Henri and Forgas, Joseph P. (1981) 'Social categorisation: cognitions, values and groups', in J.P. Forgas (ed.), *Social Cognition: Perspectives on Everyday Understanding*. London: Academic. pp. 113–140.

Tannen, Deborah (1990) *You Just Don't Understand: Women and Men in Conversation*. New York: William Morrow/Ballantine.

Tannen, Deborah (1994) *Talking from 9 to 5: How Women's and Men's Conversational Styles Affect Who Gets Heard, Who Gets Credit, and What Gets Done at Work*. New York: Oxford University Press.

Ting-Toomey, Stella (1988) 'Intercultural conflict style: a face-negotiation theory', in Y.Y. Kim and W.B. Gudykunst (eds), *Theories in Intercultural Communication*. Newbury Park, CA: SAGE. pp. 213–235.

Ting-Toomey, Stella (1994) 'Managing intercultural conflicts effectively', in L. Samovar and R. Porter (eds), *Intercultural Communication: A Reader* (7th edn). Belmont, CA: Wadsworth. pp. 360–372.

Ting-Toomey, Stella (2005a) 'Identity negotiation theory: crossing cultural boundaries', in W.B. Gudykunst (ed.), *Theorizing about Intercultural Communication*. Thousand Oaks, CA: SAGE. pp. 211–233.

Ting-Toomey, Stella (2005b) 'The matrix of face: updated face-negotiation theory', in W.B. Gudykunst (ed.), *Theorizing about Intercultural Communication*. Thousand Oaks, CA: SAGE. pp. 71–92.

Ting-Toomey, Stella and Chung, Leeva C. (2005) *Understanding Intercultural Communication*. Los Angeles, CA: Roxbury.

Tomaselli, Keyan and Heuva, William (2004) 'Television in Africa', in J. Sinclair and G. Turner (eds), *Contemporary World Television*. London: British Film Institute. pp. 96–98.

Tomlinson, John (1999) *Globalization and Culture*. Oxford: Polity.

Training and Development (1999) 'Training & development annual trend reports', *Training and Development*, 53 (1) November: 22–43.

Triandis, Harry C. (1977) *Interpersonal Behavior*. Monterey, CA: Brooks/Cole.

Triandis, Harry C. (1984) 'A theoretical framework for the more efficient construction of culture assimilators', *International Journal of Intercultural Relations*, 8: 301–330.

Triandis, Harry C. (1989) 'The self and social behavior in differing cultural contexts', *Psychological Review*, 60: 649–655.

Triandis, Harry C. (1995) *Individualism and Collectivism*. Boulder, CO: Westview.

Triandis, Harry C. (2000) 'Culture and conflict', *International Journal of Psychology*, 35 (2): 145–152.

Triandis, Harry C., McCusker, Christopher and Hui, C. Harry (1990) 'Multimethod probes of individualism and collectivism', *Journal of Personality and Social Psychology*, 59 (5): 1006–1020.

Tuchman, Gaye (1978) *Making News: A Study in the Construction of Reality*. New York: Free Press.

Turner, Graeme (1994) *Understanding Celebrity*. London: SAGE.

Turner, Graeme (2003) *British Cultural Studies: An Introduction* (3rd edn). London: Routledge.

Vivian, Bradford (1999) 'The veil and the visible', *Western Journal of Communication*, 63 (2): 115–140.

Volčič, Zala (2005) 'The notion of "The West" in the Serbian national imaginary', *European Journal of Cultural Studies*, 8 (2): 155–175.

Volčič, Zala (2008) 'Former Yugoslavia on the world wide web: commercialization and branding of nation-states', *International Communication Gazette*, 70 (5): 395–413.

Vukeljic, Marijana (2008) *Vpliv medijev na oblikovanje identitete druge generacije Srbov v Sloveniji* [*The Effects of Media on Forming Identities of the Serbian Second Generation in Slovenia*]. Maribor: Univerza Maribor Press.

Ward, Colleen and Hewstone, Miles (1985) 'Ethnicity, language and intergroup relations in Malaysia and Singapore: a social psychological analysis', *Journal of Multilingual and Multicultural Development*, 6: 271–296.

Ward, Colleen and Kennedy, Anthony (2001) 'Coping with cross-cultural transition', *Journal of Cross-Cultural Psychology*, 32 (5): 636–642.

Wasko, Janet (2001) *Understanding Disney: The Manufacture of Fantasy*. Cambridge: Polity.

Waters, Malcolm (1995) *Globalization*. New York/London: Routledge.

Weber, Elke U. and Hsee, Christopher (1998) 'Cross-cultural differences in risk perception, but cross-cultural similarities in attitudes towards perceived risk', *Management Sciences*, 44: 1205–1217.

Weick, Karl (1979) *The Social Psychology of Organizing* (2nd edn). Reading, MA: Addison-Wesley.

Whorf, Benjamin L. (1956) *Language, Thought and Reality: Selected Writings* (ed. J.B. Carroll). Cambridge, MA: Technology Press of MIT.

Wiemann, John M. (1977) 'Explication and test of a model of communicative competence', *Human Communication Research*, 3 (3): 195–213.

Williams, Raymond (1989) *Resources of Hope: Culture, Democracy, Socialism*. London: Verso.

Woodrow, Lindy (2006) 'Anxiety and speaking English as a second language', *RELC Journal*, 37: 308–327.

Xi, Changsheng (1994) 'Individualism and collectivism in American and Chinese societies', in A. Gonzalez, M. Houston and V. Chen (eds), *Our Voices: Essays in Culture, Ethnicity, and Communication*. Los Angeles: Roxbury. pp. 125–167.

Yamaguchi, Susumu (1998) 'Biased risk perceptions among Japanese: illustration of interdependence among risk companions', *Asian Journal of Social Psychology*, 1: 117–131.

Yum, June O. (1988) 'The impact of Confucianism on interpersonal relationships and communication patterns in East Asia', *Communication Monographs*, 55: 374–388.

Zagefka, Hanna and Brown, Rupert (2002) 'The relationship between acculturation strategies, relative fit and intergroup relations: immigrant – majority relations in Germany', *European Journal of Social Psychology*, 32 (2): 171–188.

Zhou, Lianxi and Hui, Michael K. (2003) 'Symbolic value of foreign products in the People's Republic of China', *Journal of International Marketing*, 11: 36–43.

Zubrzycki, Jerzy (1997) 'Australian multiculturalism for a new century: towards inclusiveness', *Immigration Policies and Australia's Population*. Australian Ethnic Affairs Council.

Index